Taste in America

By the author

NONFICTION

CHARMERS AND CRANKS
Biographical sketches of twelve American women

AN AMERICAN FAMILY: THE TAFTS 1678–1964

CRUSADES AND CRINOLINES
A biography of Ellen Curtis Demorest and William Jennings Demorest

GRACE COOLIDGE AND HER ERA

SILHOUETTE IN DIAMONDS
A biography of Mrs. Potter Palmer

THE GENERAL'S WIFE
A biography of Mrs. Ulysses S. Grant

FIRST LADY OF THE SOUTH
A biography of Mrs. Jefferson Davis

ANGEL OF THE BATTLEFIELD
A biography of Clara Barton

REBEL ROSE
A biography of Rose O'Neal Greenhow

PROUD KATE
A biography of Kate Chase

JOURNEY INTO LIGHT
A history of the blind

CHILD OF DESTINY
A biography of Dr. Elizabeth Blackwell

LADIES OF THE PRESS
A history of American newspaperwomen

FICTION

ISLE OF ESCAPE

FIFTY YEARS A WOMAN

HIGHLAND TWILIGHT

MARRIAGE IN GOTHAM

PROMENADE DECK

An illustrated history of the
evolution of architecture,
furnishings, fashions, and customs
of the American people

TASTE IN

AMERICA

by Ishbel Ross

THOMAS Y. CROWELL COMPANY, NEW YORK   *Established 1834*

DESIGNED BY BETTY BINNS

Manufactured in the United States of America

L.C. Card 67–23677

1   2   3   4   5   6   7   8   9   10

CONTENTS

1. *A New Land*   3

2. *Civilizing Forces*   30

3. *World of Plenty*   54

4. *A Sporting Nation*   78

5. *Fashioning the Home*   98

6. *Plush and Pomp*   133

7. *Sky High*   144

8. *Eve's Daughters*   167

9. *The Added Touch*   203

10. *Male Plumage*   232

11. *The Social Image Changes*   245

12. *Americans on the Move*   266

13. *The Great Awakening*   279

SOURCES OF ILLUSTRATIONS   303
NOTES   306
BIBLIOGRAPHY   319
INDEX   335

Taste in America

1   *A New Land*

HE world of skyscrapers in which Americans live today bears small resemblance to the primitive scene of the early seventeenth century when the colonists emerged from the first dark period of huts and rude shelters to build villages—the villages that grew into towns, and the towns that eventually became cities. Within two hundred years their descendants, who built at first in the tradition of their homelands, had made architectural history with a fresh and dramatic style essentially their own—the skyscraper.

In 1630 Nieuw Amsterdam had three hundred persons living in Dutch houses with stepped gables facing the street. Sloops careened in the harbor. The farms, then known as boweries, ranged north from the palisade, or wall, that ultimately gave its name to the street of millionaires. By 1700 more brick and wood buildings, many with tiled roofs, gave color and variety to the small settlement. Weather vanes shaped like roosters, lions, fish, or horses swung slowly with the wind. In another half century a naval officer, sailing in to Nieuw Amsterdam, was impressed with what he saw: "The nobleness of the town surprised me more than the fertile appearance of the country. I had no idea of finding a place in America, consisting of near 2000 houses, elegantly built of brick, raised on an eminence and the streets paved and spacious,

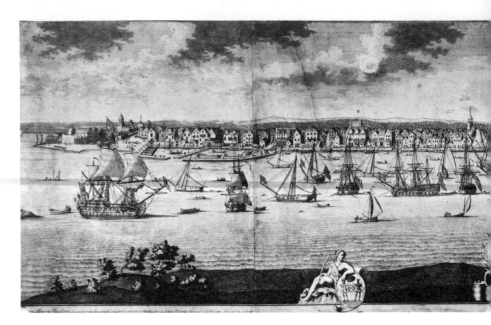

A view of Nieuw Amsterdam from what is now Brooklyn Heights, drawn by William Burgis of Boston in 1717. The spire of Trinity Church towers above the steep-roofed houses of the lower town. The harbor is filled with British ships.

The Hand-in-Hand Fire Company comes to the rescue in the 1750s. These busy gentlemen, carrying ladders and passing buckets of water from the well pump to their fire engine, are meeting one of the many fire hazards that beset Americans in the early days of settlement. In the background are the typical two-storied steep-roofed houses of early New York.

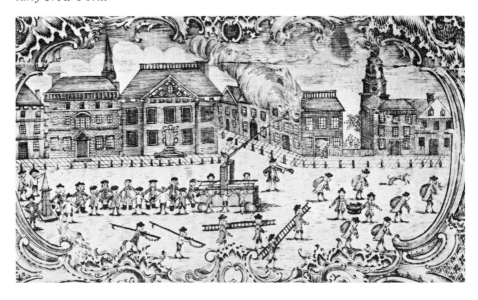

furnished with commodious keys and warehouses, and employing some hundreds of vessels in its foreign trade and fisheries—but such is this city that very few in England can rival it in its show."

The five early cities—New York, Boston, Philadelphia, Newport, and Charleston—all surprised visitors, who expected to land in a wilderness overrun by Indians and wild animals, a conception that lasted for several generations. True, the first arrivals had to pitch tents or seek shelter in caves and pits, which they lined with wood and roofed with ships' spars covered with brushwood or sod. They made their tents of sailcloth, and as they studied the bark houses and tepees of the Indians they fashioned their own wigwams, with poles held together by a thatched effect of brush and plaited rush or with deerskin stretched over frames. But the weather and the Indian assaults soon led them to erect simple frame houses, covered with clapboard and lined with a mud plaster bound with grass.

Although the first arrivals had been thankful for a roof over their heads and a pallet on which to rest, within fifty years houses with distinctive American characteristics and a variety of effects were being built. Thatched roofs gradually disappeared; dormer windows came into use; wooden chimneys were replaced by brick. Roofs became flatter; hand-hewn timbers and wooden pegs made for solid construction. The professional architect was still unknown in America, but skilled carpenters, working from plans and imported books, drew inspiration from James Gibbs's *Book of Architecture*, William Halfpenny's *Art of Sound Building*, and Isaac Ware's *A Complete Body of Architecture*. These were early-eighteenth-century writers whose subjects ranged from a complete discussion of Palladian effects to the details of paneling, window design, and chimney pieces, which the amateur builders adapted to climate and their resources.

The colonists were rich in materials for building, since a lavish supply of oak, pine, cherry, maple, redwood, and cypress surrounded them. They had granite, lime, and sandstone as well as dirt for adobe and grass for thatch. New England in general clung to wood structures, the tradition of its colonial houses today, although Boston and the other growing cities were forced to turn to brick houses because of fire hazards. Stone was used freely in Pennsylvania, but rarely in New England. Most roofs were shingled, although the Germans were disposed to use slate and the Dutch favored tiles.

The colonists had brought with them the East Anglican conception of the medieval house, with leaded casement windows, overhanging gable ends, and ornamental woodwork, and for an alternative the one-storied cottage with steeply pitched roof introduced into England by Flemish weavers in the fourteenth century. Parson Joseph Capen's house at Topsfield, Massachusetts, dating back to 1683, remains today the finest example of seventeenth-century American architecture. Each of its casement windows had thirty glass panes. Its vast chimney was pilastered, and the kitchen fireplace spanned half the width of a wall. Medieval in style, the Capen house, which preceded the simplified Cape Cod cottage as it is known today, represented the colonist's instinct to reproduce the world he knew.

In course of time Salem, Newburyport, New Bedford, and Shirley Center clearly reflected this derivative influence, and their clapboard houses with red brick chimneys and double-pitched roofs brought serenity and style to the New England of the mid-eighteenth century. But in general the early settlers built plain boxlike houses; only a few could afford the gables, pinnacles, and pendants that master builders introduced. Their doors usually were heavy planks studded with nails, unlike the Dutch doors that opened in two parts, and had leather hinges and knockers.

From 1740 until 1776 New York had the salty air of a seaport, and its warehouses, distilleries, and sugar houses created a modest skyline, accented here and there with a church spire or the cupola of a new edifice. Public buildings like King's College and the Federal-style City Hall already gave distinction to the growing city. John Singleton Copley, who was establishing himself as a portrait painter, observed that New York had more "grand buildings" than Boston and that its Dutch architecture gave it charm.

Boston, with ten thousand people in 1650, had character even from this early date. Its streets meandered, and the thatched roofs and simple cabins of the Plymouth and Bay colonies had changed to close-set rows of two-story houses with steep roofs. At first glance it had the look of old London, with one spire after another rising above the rooftops, and this essential quality did not change in the next two hundred years. Charles Dickens, visiting it in 1842 and taking notes with his customary sense of heightened perspective, thought that Boston looked like a toy town that could be taken up piecemeal and crammed into a little box. He found it a delightful sight: ". . . the air was clear, the houses were so bright and gay; the signboards were painted in such gaudy colors; the gilded letters were so very golden; the bricks were so very red, the stone was so very white, the blinds and area railings were so very green, the knobs and plates upon the street doors so marvellously bright and twinkling; and all so slight and unsubstantial in appearance that every thoroughfare in the city looked exactly like a scene in a pantomime."

Dickens found the private dwellings "large and elegant," the shops extremely good and the public buildings handsome. Houses were painted inside and out; rooms were wainscoted; garrets were plastered; and things looked trim and shipshape except for the noise and confusion in the streets, many of which were as narrow as lanes. Thomas Hamilton, a visitor from Scotland in 1832, noted that Boston "might in truth be easily mistaken for one of our more populous seaports."

But this was not true of Philadelphia, an orderly city laid out on William Penn's gridiron principle, which involved a network of parallelograms crisscrossing one another and in striking contrast to the haphazard lanes and streets that twisted and turned without a central plan. In 1760 Philadelphia, with a population of eighteen thousand, had veered away from the pattern of the British provincial town as a result of the regularity and stiffness imposed by the gridiron framework— clearly a design for the future. The first Philadelphians drove along paved streets and strolled on wide, flagged sidewalks long before the Liberty Bell proclaimed their independence. Many of their houses were of wood, three stories high and shingled. Their doors had shining brass knockers, and a graceful entry led from the street to the yard. John Adams, a connoisseur of interiors and always eager to let his wife Abigail know what he thought of other people's houses, found some of the mansions he visited "splendid, grand, spacious and elegant." A Swede named Peter Kalm, seeing Philadelphia for the first time in 1748, was impressed with its "grandeur and perfection." But Benjamin Franklin eventually found the "din of the Market" so troubling that he became one of America's earliest suburbanites.

As towns grew crowded, people moved farther out into the country. Fine houses were built all around Boston, with Josiah Quincy settling at Braintree in 1771. Other Bostonians, like the Faneuils, the Bromfields, and the Hancocks, surrounded their city houses with formal gardens. By degrees Cambridge became a unique suburb, harboring pedants, wits, and men of affairs. But the New England spirit did not permit the display practiced around New York, Philadelphia, and in the South. In these worldlier areas fortunes were early spent on country seats, with magnificent grounds and every luxury that could be imported, both for outdoors and inside.

These early settlers, seeking the good things of life as their fortunes mounted, laid out handsome gardens with fishponds, dug canals on their grounds, and imported exotic trees and plants to add to the native wealth already around them. A strong European influence was manifest, and some of the country seats long before 1776 were landscaped in the English, French, or Italian fashion, with statuary in the grounds and pergolas suggestive of the Petit Trianon. In New York fine houses were soon being built in the Georgian tradition, and country estates were laid out on Murray Hill and along the banks of the Hudson. Early hospitality was dispensed by Robert Murray on Murray Hill, by James Beekman on Mount Pleasant, by the Schermerhorns and the Rhinelanders along Turtle Bay, and by the Livingstons in New Jersey. Roger Morris and the Van Cortlandts were among the first New Yorkers to build country retreats along the Hudson. Other families whose names would make New York history settled on Long Island and Staten Island, while Peter Schuyler grew aloes and pomegranates on his estate near Passaic Falls in New Jersey, and had deer and elk roaming in a vast park.

But the utmost magnificence in country houses was found in the South. Although Jamestown began with two rows of timber houses, windowless garrets, some storehouses, and a corn loft, before long Virginia and Maryland had substantial brick houses built by the planters. Williamsburg became a model of English formalism, which the public can see today in its restored form. The Georgian tradition had been well established in America before the Revolution, and the affluent planters soon found that this type of architecture was equally adaptable to temperate or tropical climatic conditions. William Byrd's house, "Westover," built in the 1730s twenty-five miles from Williamsburg, was a notable example of the Georgian tradition. In course of time country mansions like "Brandon," the Virginian home of Benjamin Harrison on the James River, and "Mount Airy," the fantastic house built by John Tayloe II on the Rappahannock, also in Virginia, became the show places of the South, with their terraced courtyards and stone balustrades, bowling greens and conservatories, deer parks and race courses. It early became the fashion to encourage wildlife in enclosed parks.

The South moved faster than the North toward a luxurious pattern of life and strong architectural development. A number of the planters matched their growing wealth with stately architecture, although they experimented with other styles between 1750 and 1850.

The plantations were like many-acred settlements. Besides the main building there were cabins for the slaves and separate units, such as the stables and birdhouses, the brewhouse, cider mill and toolhouse, the milkroom and the kitchens. Inside the great house, beyond the portico, might be found high-ceilinged, spacious rooms hung with damask or Chinese wallpaper, and furnished with imported pieces. Rooms and halls were paneled, often in rosewood, and the pine or cedar fluted pillars and pilasters were the work of skilled carpenters of the colonial era. The ceilings were frescoed, and gilded settees, silken bellpulls, and quantities of bric-à-brac from France were characteristic of this type of home.

All this came to pass within the century that followed the landing of the Pilgrims in New England and the settlement of Virginia. The log-cabin tradition of the pioneers has less substance than is generally supposed. It was a later development on the frontier and was introduced by Swedish settlers along the Delaware. The early English colonists never saw log cabins, and it was not until 1750 that this style became a frontier tradition. German, Scottish, and Irish farmers carried the idea west with them from Delaware and soon found that the log cabin was well adapted to the frontier, with the forests being cleared and great logs to be found in abundance. At first the cabins were grimly cold and uncomfortable. Oiled paper or greased deerskin was stretched across the windows, and chinks in the walls were plastered with clay or mud. But when the technique of making them improved, and the logs were squared and dovetailed at the corners, they became warm and attractive.

The French explorers and trappers introduced their own particular style of log cabin, with the logs standing on end instead of being laid on their sides. The ceilings were beamed; the walls were plastered, and the floors were made of polished hardwood, when the stage of earth or sand had passed. The French added their imported furniture to the Indian skins and rugs they used, and they soon developed an interesting type of dwelling along the Mississippi that featured spacious piazzas. New Orleans, like Charleston, emerged as a city of pictorial interest. Its two-storied balconied houses ornamented with iron grillwork showed Creole influence and such Greek Revival details as pilasters. In time the new houses were built around courtyards, or had large paved areas between house and street. By the 1760s New Orleans had nearly five hundred houses, and many were already graced with the lacy balconies made by immigrant French artisans or by skillful Negro craftsmen who copied them.

Spain also gave its exotic touch to the early American landscape. The Indians of the Southwest had lived in pueblos long before the first Spanish colonists landed in 1598. The new settlers adopted the native

Indian style and blended it picturesquely with their own style of building, thus creating the distinctive architecture found today in the Southwest and in California. The Spaniards mixed adobe with straw and baked the combination into bricks. The ranch house, with tiled roof, thick stuccoed walls, and the combination of indoor and outdoor living that is popular again today, became a tradition. The early missions greatly influenced the architectural scene in California in later years, with a combination of Spanish Gothic and, ultimately, of Renaissance and baroque.

All these contributory factors from different civilizations left traces on the American scene. The early cities reflected these influences clearly and had distinctive characteristics. New Orleans became noted for its French and Spanish flavor; New York for its Dutch gables until rows of brownstone houses swept them away; Charleston for its spacious verandas; Savannah for its squares; Philadelphia and Baltimore for their rows and stoops; Boston for its English air; Bethlehem for the symmetry the Moravians had given to its streets.

The Federal, or as it was otherwise known, the Regency, style was dramatically introduced in the late eighteenth century and it left an ineradicable imprint on the nation's architecture. It was short-lived in its own right because of the speed with which it was superseded by the craze for Greek Revival architecture. The protagonists of one style moved easily into the other. The Federal houses could be distinguished from the early colonial types by their flat roofs, their boxlike shape, and the delicate carving and decorative detail inspired by the Adam brothers, English masters in the field of design.

The simplified versions of classic forms that characterized the Federal style had strong advocates in three gifted architects who came from Europe in the last decade of the eighteenth century—Benjamin Henry Latrobe from England, Pierre Charles L'Enfant from France, and James Hoban from Ireland. All had a hand in the creation of Washington. Latrobe was the major architect of the Capitol and Hoban of the White House. L'Enfant drew up the plan for Washington that gives it such incomparable vistas today.

Latrobe took over the design of the Capitol in 1803 and completed the work on the House of Representatives according to a plan worked out by Dr. William Thornton, who was responsible for the exterior walls. The Englishman had a free hand where the interior was concerned, and he changed the oval form to a semicircle. He developed the basic design for the rotunda connecting the two wings of the Capitol, although this work was not completed until Charles Bulfinch applied the finishing touches. Latrobe, instinctively an innovator, was refreshingly alive to the classical inheritance. When he designed the

The Joseph Capen house at Topsfield, Massachusetts, which dates back to 1683, is regarded as the finest example of seventeenth-century American architecture. Its steeply pitched roof has gable ends. The door is of studded planks with an iron lock and it has a huge pilastered chimney, all in the medieval tradition.

"Westover," William Byrd's Georgian mansion on the James River in Virginia, reflected the Palladian influence common to many of the plantation estates in the South. The brick mansion had a steep hipped roof and pedimented doorway. Its florid frescoed ceilings were in the French tradition.

Berry Hill in Halifax County, Virginia, built about 1830 by James Cole Bruce, is considered one of the finest examples of the so-called Southern Colonial style. Architects who worked in the Greek Revival tradition faithfully copied their classic models. Berry Hill is a re-created Parthenon with eight instead of six columns. (Lower right.)

The Elias Hasket Derby Summer House, now on the William C. Endicott Estate in Danvers, Massachusetts, was one of several houses designed by Samuel McIntire for the famous seafaring Derbys of Salem. Elias was a merchant prince who fostered the Adam influence as adapted by McIntire. He liked to see the sailing vessels that had enriched his family illustrated in the frescoes of his houses.

Octagon House was used as the Executive
Mansion by the Madisons after the White
House was burned by the British in 1814. It
had many historic moments; in one of its
rooms President Madison signed the
proclamation for the Treaty of Ghent, ending
the War of 1812. Designed by William
Thornton, it represents the octagonal style of
architecture popularized in the nineteenth
century by D. S. Fowler. In 1960 the
American Institute of Architects bought
Octagon House to use as their museum
headquarters.

Potter Palmer opened up the Gold Coast
along Lake Shore Drive with "The Castle," a
Chicago landmark noted for its curious
architecture as well as for the great parties
given there by his wife. For two decades world
celebrities paraded through Mrs. Potter Palmer's
art gallery, hung with the paintings of the French
Impressionists. The mansion was variously
described as being early English battlemented,
castellated Gothic, or Norman Gothic, but to
the public it was always "Mrs. Potter Palmer's
Castle."

The Hugo Reid Adobe built in 1839 was the
country house of Don Perfecto Hugo Reid and
his wife, Victoria, who brought her husband
Rancho Santa Anita as part of her dowry. The
walls are of whitewashed adobe blocks baked
in the sun, and the flat roof is made of
bulrushes bound with rawhide strips and
waterproofed by tar. Behind the high adobe
wall is the patio, an integral feature of the
Spanish-influenced California architecture.

Bank of Pennsylvania in 1798 he virtually introduced the Greek Revival style in America. His aim was simplicity. Reluctant to design a modern bank in the guise of a Greek temple, he used the Ionic columns outside, but the interior was a circular banking hall as practical as it was beautiful. He endowed the pumphouse for the Fairmount waterworks with charm as well as functional qualities, expressing the hope at the same time that Philadelphia might become the Athens of the Western world. Latrobe profoundly affected the aspect of William Penn's city, but his varied talents were put to use also in Virginia, Kentucky, New Orleans, and Washington. He was deeply versed in Stuart and Revett's *Antiquities of Athens*, an illustrated folio volume hungrily studied by builders as the Greek Revival movement swept the country. He disliked the monuments of the Roman Empire and insisted that Greece demonstrated the compatibility of art and democracy.

But Thomas Jefferson, with whom he worked, thought that the large and majestic effect of the Roman building suited the aspirations of an ambitious young country. A new nation was being born, and both Washington and Jefferson realized that the public buildings should express something affirmative, and not be a reconstruction of the England from which they had turned away. Jefferson disliked English baroque in the colonies and considered Williamsburg to be made up of "rude, misshapen piles." He gave his own touch to the Palladian influence as expressed by Wren. Monticello and the University of Virginia were his adaptations of this style.

Andrea Palladio's application of the principles of Roman architecture to his times and his revolt against ornamentation influenced Wren, and the Georgian style that eventually fused into straight colonial in America. Actually, traces of the Classic Revival that swept over England with the excavation of Pompeii and Herculaneum, and Robert Adam's adaptation of the Italian influence, showed in some of the houses built in Annapolis and Charleston before the Revolution. But with Greek Revival the whole country had become "architecturally free— and architecturally 'classic,' " in the opinion of Talbot Hamlin, author and professor.

The monumental Greek colonnades seemed best suited to state capitols, courthouses, and public buildings of one kind or another, and the time had come when many such structures were needed. The capitol at Richmond was the first to be designed in the style of the Greek temple, although Latrobe had preceded it with the pumphouse in Philadelphia that gleamed white through poplar trees and charmed visitors. Americans welcomed the Greek colonnades with enthusiasm as architects designed imposing country houses in the classical tradition. They were well suited to the large-scale entertaining of the cotton planters, and between 1830 and 1855 one after another of these mansions was built in Georgia, Alabama, Virginia, and Mississippi, or owners of existing houses added ballrooms and wings. Ionic columns, twin-curved staircases, and vast rooms distinguished many of them, and their chandeliers and elaborate furnishings were the background for countless parties before the Civil War dimmed the picture of the elegant and stately South.

In spite of the exotic infusion of styles in New Orleans, the Greek Revival took root in the Vieux Carré, too, and spread up the Mississippi, leaving some of its most durable traces in Natchez. The Doric touch soon invaded Saratoga Springs, Detroit, Chicago, Columbus, and Louisville. Families heading west could choose Georgian, Greek, or Egyptian styles, but the feeling spread that young America and ancient Greece had ideals in common, a belief fostered by the Greek war for independence. Newborn American towns were given such evocative names as Athens, Troy, Ithaca, and Ypsilanti. Women wore flowing Greek gowns and did their hair in tight curls bound by ribbon, in the classical fashion. The Grecian urn became a decorative object in the home, and a favorite motif in carving. By the late 1820s the Greek Revival phase of the more general Classic Revival had become universal. The classical influence spread rapidly in the cities, with churches, theaters, hotels, and schools showing varying degrees of the new architecture.

New York was slow to take it up, but in the end did more with it than any other city. The Great Fire of 1825 that wiped out a third of its buildings opened the way for monumental effects on Wall Street. Greek Revival temples added a stately touch to the mélange of warehouses, factories, offices, and banks close to Bowling Green. The Bowery Theater, opened in 1825, had a Doric portico, and Isaiah Rogers' Astor Hotel was in the Greek Revival tradition. The Canal Street Greek Doric Church and St. Mark's-in-the-Bouwerie were as much discussed as Henry Brevoort's Ionic portico on Fifth Avenue and the Edwin Forrest home. Greek columns took the place of pilasters on fashionable La Fayette Terrace and on London Terrace. During this period New Yorkers paid close attention to the fluted radiating fan and ellipsis over their doors. More marble was introduced to feed the classical hunger.

The approach to Greek Revival in New England was more restrained, and the architects who had come into view—twenty were practicing in 1846 in Boston—relied to some extent on their early colonial principles, as well as on the English handbooks they were constantly studying. Many had leaned heavily on Asher Benjamin's handbooks for carpenters and *Pain's British Palladio* by William Pain. Even the first important architect in the United States—Peter Harrison (1716–1775)—freely admitted his indebtedness to James Gibbs's *Rules for*

Drawing. Harrison was a diffident young Englishman who moved impressively into a field that had been usurped largely by carpenter-architects. The colonial and Georgian architecture that he found in America had no appeal for him, and he proceeded to introduce the Palladian style along the eastern seaboard. He used it with distinction in his Touro Synagogue and Redwood Library in Newport, where he lived. The library, still considered a gem of its kind, was copied from the design Palladio used in the Church of Santo Giorgio in Venice. Harrison's King's Chapel in Boston and Christ Church in Cambridge were equally admired.

The Greek Revival era brought a number of native architects into the building field. Charles Bulfinch of Boston, the most distinguished member of the group, leaned to the French elliptical salon, and the delicate classicism of the pure Adam effect. As a result Boston maintained the look of a British city long after the others were native in character. New England's oval parlors, spiraling staircases, and doorways with elliptical fanlights came to be known as "Bulfinchian." Bulfinch also designed the first Harrison Gray Otis mansion, where John Quincy Adams and his contemporaries found counsel and conviviality. He emulated the curved sweep of Bath in Franklin Crescent, its sixteen houses shaded by elms strung along a semioval park. He enlarged Faneuil Hall and designed the massive portico of the Massachusetts General Hospital.

Bulfinch influenced two other men who added greatly to the grace and variety of the New England scene—Samuel McIntire and Asher Benjamin. Salem, the only port not seized by the British during the War of Independence, was completely transformed by the delicate and pervasive work of McIntire. He was a wood-carver and designer whose doorframes and mantelpieces reflected the work of the English masters in this field, except that he varied the urns and garlands of the Adam brothers with strongly American eagles and shocks of wheat. His low wide cornices, slim pilasters, and exquisite rope moldings, flutings, and mantel decorations, were well expressed in the Derby House, but nearly every street in Salem had examples of his decorative skill. Although imitative and clearly derived from *Pain's British Palladio* and from his *Practical House Carpenter*, McIntire's work carried its own distinguished imprint and became famous throughout New England.

Asher Benjamin not only designed some of the most famous churches of the colonial era but his influence spread to the backwoods through his writings and the practical guidance he offered carpenters and builders in *The Country Builder's Assistant*. His simple church steeples rose all through the Connecticut valley. Successive handbooks by Benjamin showed the uninformed how to carve their leaves and volutes in the Corinthian manner, rather than in Doric or Ionic terms. He told them how to thin the fluted columns and how to build spiral stairs without visible support.

Worcester had its own Elias Carter, a builder and architect who swung from late colonial to Greek Revival style. His large square houses with continuous two-storied colonnades were significant in their time. Connecticut produced many architects during the Greek Revival era, from Colonel Belcher who designed the Old Lyme Congregational Church, to Ithiel Town, who gave New Haven in its state capitol the first Greek Doric temple in New England. It stood on the town green, in startling contrast to the simplicity of its surroundings.

The rich lumber princes of Bangor, Maine, built one fine mansion after another and encouraged churches in the classical tradition. They had Alexander Parris to add his dynamic touch to the houses of Portland. Along with Solomon Willard and Isaiah Rogers he stirred up excitement in the architectural world. These three were men without special training for their profession but, like other amateurs who edged into this field from simple carpentry and building, they became successful individualists well known in the early nineteenth century.

Providence had J. H. Greene, J. C. Bucklin, and Russell Warren. New Orleans, swinging and prosperous between 1835 and 1855, boasted the James Galliers, father and son; Jacques De Pouilly; Charles and James Dakin; and James Freret. Louisville had Matthias and Gideon Shryock, who worked also in the Ohio and Mississippi valleys. But two major stars in the firmament were William Strickland (1787–1854) and John Haviland (1792–1852), both brilliant exponents of Greek Revival architecture.

The whaling captains of Nantucket, who had seen the world, built Greek Revival houses, churches, banks, and libraries between 1840 and the outbreak of the Civil War. Rhode Islanders found the style equally good for the mansions of summer residents along its rocky shores and for its mill towns. Such was the zeal for the Palladian touch at this time that it showed up even in New England's covered bridges. Ithiel Town, already fully committed, had a hand in this, although his main contribution to the covered bridge was the lattice truss. Timothy Parker, a shipfitter from Newburyport who built the first covered bridge in America over the Schuylkill River in 1805, became a Greek Revivalist as the years went on.

The architects working in Ohio leaned less to the temple style of building and more to the simpler classicism of Boston, perhaps because so many of the settlers had come from New England. Marietta showed strong signs of the Palladian influence, but the early Virginian type of manor house was more typical of Chillicothe. The Taft Museum in Cincinnati, dating from 1820 and looking like a smaller White House, has been attributed to Latrobe, and Lane Theological Seminary, which harbored the Beechers and the Stowes, was built with a six-column Doric portico on a hill overlooking Cincinnati.

The state capitols of Illinois and Iowa, Dubuque's City Hall, and the United State Mint in San Francisco were all Greek Revival. The gold rush carried this unlikely style to the Far West, where monuments, churches, schools, public buildings, and houses reflected its free use. The small towns of Washington and Oregon, emerging from log-house simplicity, used Greek Revival details in the cornices and molding of the frame buildings that followed their earliest homes in the wilderness.

Except for its public buildings in Philadelphia, Pennsylvania stayed aloof from Greek Revival, sticking to its traditional plain house of stone or brick. The Germans, Dutch, and British preserved their own patterns throughout the state. Philadelphia, the nation's cradle, saw the birth and also the death pangs of the Greek tradition in America. It had begun with the Bank of Pennsylvania designed by Latrobe in 1798, and it ended with the Ridgeway Branch of the Library Company in the 1870s. On the plantations it had lasted until the Confederates massed for action, but it flickered out completely in the days of Reconstruction. It had been bitterly attacked as a pagan style during the 1840s and 1850s, and Andrew Jackson Downing, the protagonist of the natural and unaffected in architecture, noted cheerfully in 1846: "The Greek temple disease has passed its crisis."

The austerity of classical architecture had a swift antidote in Gothic Revival, which reflected the romanticism sweeping Europe. Rousseau had sounded the back-to-nature call in the late eighteenth century, and Marie Antoinette had built her rustic cottage with dairy and mill at Versailles. People were reading verse and hanging landscape pictures in their houses. Jane Austen and Sir Walter Scott were being avidly read, and thoughts of battlemented castles and tournaments were prevalent. The medieval influence was strong, and many Americans, doing the Grand Tour in Europe, were affected by the donjon keeps, notched battlements, and crenellated towers they saw on their travels. The Gothic Revival that took root in England when Horace Walpole settled on Strawberry Hill near London in 1751 found an echo in America in the mid-nineteenth century. And one of its leading protagonists was Downing, who fostered the Gothic Revival from a cottage of his own at Newburgh, New York.

The wave of Gothic that passed over America checkered the landscape with the most curious effects in the history of American architecture. Gothic villas rose along the Hudson, where Samuel F. B. Morse's imposing Italian mansion already stood at Poughkeepsie. W. H. Coventry Waddell built a Gothic villa on Fifth Avenue with peaks and

Charles Bulfinch drew inspiration from Federal Hall for his State House on Beacon Street, Boston. Its steep roof, porticoed balcony, and cupola became familiar to the early lawmakers of America.

View of the East Front of the President's House in 1807, with the addition of the north and south porticoes. Benjamin H. Latrobe, its designer, made many small and charming watercolors of his buildings, and this one bears his signature and the date, 1807. There have been many changes in the White House since then, but the building is still essentially Latrobe's creation.

Federal Hall: The Inauguration of Washington, April 20, 1789. Pierre Charles L'Enfant added characteristic touches here to New York's first City Hall, using stars and eagles as decorative elements in the modified Doric façade. The French influence is visible in the ironwork of the windows. Engraving by Amos Doolittle after a drawing by Peter Lacour.

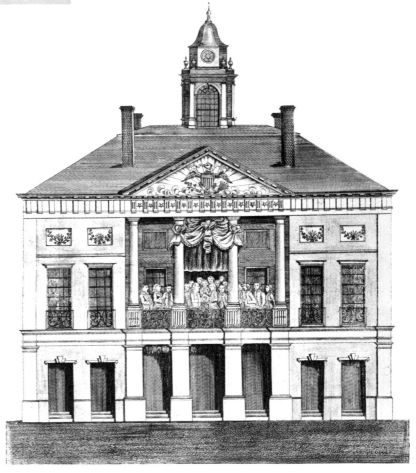

minarets that reminded passersby of a cruet. His widow took William Makepeace Thackeray up in her towers to show him her view of the Hudson, and she entertained Washington Irving, who had a semi-Gothic house of his own at Tarrytown that in 1966 was declared a national historical site.

When Philip Hone went to call on William Paulding at his house on the river bank below Tarrytown, he was dismayed by his "immense edifice of white or gray marble, resembling a baronial castle, or rather a Gothic monastery, with towers, turrets and trellises, minarets, mosaics and mouse-holes; archways, armories and air-holes; peaked windows and pinnacled roofs, and many other fantastics too tedious to enumerate, the whole constituting an edifice of gigantic size, with no room in it; great cost and little comfort." Both Hone and Paulding were mayors of New York early in the nineteenth century.

Most of the Gothic Revival houses were of wood, painted to look like stone. Domes and minarets, crenellated effects and battlemented castles were some of its choice manifestations. From Buzzards Bay to Kentucky the fashion raged, with arches and peaks, narrow windows and towers with finials pointing toward the sky. Tuscan villas and Swiss chalets, Venetian and rural Gothic buildings were a change of pace from Greek Revival. Connecticut had a Persian palace complete with minarets. The jiggy scroll-saw ornamentation was an inescapable aspect of Gothic Revival. Interiors were spacious and informal, with sundry signs of the arts and crafts fostered by William Morris in England.

Downing, lord high priest of all this irregularity, had a fixed idea that was later brilliantly realized by Frank Lloyd Wright—the need to link architecture with the natural landscape. He believed that cottage architecture borrowed its "most winning and captivating expression from foliage"; that houses should be adapted to rocks and ground, to trees and plants; that a Swiss chalet should rest on a hillside, and an English cottage in a valley. He considered white paint vulgar, and advocated the somber and offbeat hues of nature—the tints of moss and stone, the browns, dull reds, and olive-greens of foliage. He believed in painting stucco, but was all for the naturalism of a church that looked like a church, a bank that suggested a bank and not a Greek temple. The battlemented castle, pretentious though it might be, pleased him if built in an appropriate setting, like a mountain gorge. He liked the crenellated tower, the oriel window, the vine-draped veranda, and with his able assistance the jambalaya that emerged included, by his own definition, English Cottage, American Log Cabin, Farm House, Collegiate Gothic, Manor House, French Suburban, Swiss Chalet, Lombard Italian, Tuscan Villa, Ancient Etruscan, Suburban Greek, Oriental, Moorish, and Castellated styles.

*A villa in the oriental style with minaret and Romanesque
arch and dome. Designed for Godey's Lady's Book by
Isaac H. Hobbs when the craze for pagodas and
oriental teahouses was sweeping the country.*

*New York's most ridiculed Gothic villa, the home of
William H. Coventry on Fifth Avenue, was built in 1845
and demolished in 1857. The view from its tower,
however, was enjoyed by such visiting celebrities as
William Makepeace Thackeray.*

*"Ridgeview," A. C. Richards' house at Irvington-on-
Hudson, was built in the Queen Anne tradition, with
gabled roof, open porches, and dormer windows.*

In the United States the Gothic Revival had traveled some distance from Walpole's "charming venerable Gothic . . . . the battlemented towers and vine-covered walls hallowed by history." Its lath-and-plaster effects were often suggestive of stage scenery; the battlements were frequently phantom boards with scrollwork. Alexander Jackson Davis called himself the "architectural composer," and he illustrated Downing's volumes of designs for country houses. Davis was adept at combining Tudor chimneys and oriel windows, dripstone moldings and rustic balconies. He drew his inspiration from many sources and fostered the Tuscan villas that rested uneasily in the American landscape. The Waddell villa was his, and he was the architect who deplored the high stoop and introduced the typical American house with basement. Many of the Gothic houses in Kentucky show the Davis influence and the versatile Latrobe was responsible for "Sedgeley," built in the Gothic manner in Philadelphia.

A rash of books dealing with country architecture fostered the Gothic Revival, and gave it something of the do-it-yourself spirit. Edward Shaw's *Civil Architecture*, first published in 1831, was still being printed as late as 1876, and his *Rural Architecture* started many builders on their way. In 1841 Downing published *A Treatise on the Theory and Practice of Landscape Gardening Applied to North America*, followed by *Cottage Residences*. He encouraged Calvert Vaux to come to the United States and be his partner in building and park designs. Downing's *Architecture of Country Houses*, appearing at the same time, focused further attention on the Gothic style of architecture. The plans he submitted to President Fillmore for laying out public grounds in Washington came to life later in Vaux's design for Central Park, an early dream of Downing's. In his brief lifetime—Downing drowned at the age of thirty-seven in a steamboat fire—he had profoundly affected the architectural scene, so far as the average family was concerned, and inspired the style of many country homes.

Richard Upjohn, the English architect whose name is most closely associated with Gothic churches, was responsible for many Gothic villas, too, and for the spread of this curious Victorian style. Campuses as well as post offices were testing grounds for Gothic trends. Russell Sturgis, art critic and author as well as architect, gave Yale the Gothic touch, and the Smith College girls studied in a Gothic building, with lancet windows topped by stained glass, and a turreted clock tower striking the hours from a gabled fortress. While the mood lasted the brownstone row took hold in New York. In the 1850s and 1860s its deep color tones beguiled the public as wood was sanded and painted to resemble stone. By the 1880s there was even more flimflam when the monotonous brownstones were variegated with yellow brick, buff, and red or green effects. Terra cotta, resistant to weather, came to stay.

21

A New Land

The public liked the picturesqueness of the Gothic Revival. They browsed over Henry Hudson Holly's *Country Seats*, Gervase Wheeler's *Homes for the People*, and A. A. Turner's *Villas on the Hudson*. They enjoyed the stained glass, the red colonnettes, and an assortment of stripes amid the turrets. For years to come Gothic cottages might be found nestling in their woodland settings, while fashion had shifted to Queen Anne, a somewhat more sophisticated expression of the same basic idea. Wooden domestic architecture, known as the "stick style," developed steadily between 1840 and 1876, and sometimes the two were indistinguishable. Americans were introduced to this mingling of the Elizabethan, Jacobean, and "free classic style" at the Centennial Exposition in Philadelphia (1876). The half-timbered British buildings at the exhibition touched off the craze, already well established in England by Richard Norman Shaw, with the earlier infusion of Inigo Jones's baroque effects and Wren's Palladian influence. In America the Queen Anne trend was strongly suggestive of the cottage architecture favored by Downing and his followers. The public went in heavily for casement windows, Tudor chimneys, and half-timbered finish. Even before the Centennial, Henry Hobson Richardson had introduced it at Newport with the Watts Sherman house, and the style soon flourished in that fashionable resort.

The Queen Anne houses had open halls, great fireplaces, and continuous banks of windows. With bays, gables, and diamond-paned windows they introduced a fresh note that charmed many but was deplored by the classicists. A number of the colonial houses in New England were remodeled in Queen Anne style, and dormers and alcoves, Palladian windows in gables, and porte-cochères became high style with people of wealth. Autumnal colors were used for the new shingled houses, and redwood and other unpainted woods gave the interiors a rustic magnificence. The old colonial style with long, sloping roof was revived in the 1870s in Newport, when it was found that Queen Anne and early colonial were harmonious together. This union was a relief from the mansard roofs, cast-iron façades, and scroll-saw ornamentation that contributed to the *Brown Decades* defined by Lewis Mumford. Pure architectural traditions were obscured in the industrial drive that followed the Civil War, and the fortunes made at that time led the *nouveaux riches* into a forest of English Tudor, French Renaissance, American Gothic, or pseudo-Oriental mansions. However, the shingle style, at its height in the 1880s and 1890s, persisted into the early part of the twentieth century.

The Oriental trend that had spread through Europe in the eighteenth century led to exotic effects in America after it was accented at the Centennial and the Columbian expositions. In France Chinese summerhouses, mandarins, and peacocks had been woven into the rococo style. In England William Halfpenny in 1752 pushed Chinoiserie with his designs for Chinese temples, triumphal arches, and Oriental gardens, and in the 1750s Thomas Chippendale introduced Chinese Chippendale. Kew Gardens had a Chinese pagoda, a mosque, a house of Confucius, and showed Hindu, Turkish, and other exotic influences. Victorian England's close links with Egypt, India, and China encouraged this development. As Americans traveled more, as the native architects studied the English books dealing with the exotic, as the sliding partitions of the Japanese house were taken up by such architects as Frank Lloyd Wright at the Chicago Fair, a fusion of unfamiliar and highly stylized effects followed. The Egyptian influence showed up strongly in hotels, and obelisks rose over the Potomac and in Central Park. Chinese temples appeared in rural New York, and R. M. Hunt designed a green-tiled Japanese teahouse for Mrs. O. H. P. Belmont at Newport, where many of the Oriental variations had their genesis.

Businessmen, opening up foreign markets, picked up ideas as they traveled. Robert Louis Stevenson's home in Samoa whipped up discussion of tropical houses among contemporary writers. The Indian Mutiny spread interest in native ways of life, and Kipling's writings focused attention on the bungalow style of architecture. Japanese prints introduced to Americans in the 1870s by John La Farge affected various architects. All these influences combined to create talk of Chinese, Gothic, and natural grottoes, cascades, mosques, Moorish pavilions, and summer and winter hermitages. The affectations were endless, and much enjoyed on country estates during the luxurious 1890s. Soon no one was surprised to see minarets rising along the Hudson, verandas with Saracenic arcades, or green tiles embedded in colored bricks in true Persian style. The Near East influence was pervasive, but it was stronger indoors than out and was reflected largely in furnishings.

Years earlier the octagonal type of house had brought some diversion into the building field. Actually it was a form used by Thomas Jefferson, but it did not attract any attention until O. S. Fowler, the phrenologist, wrote *A Home for All, or the Gravel Wall and Octagon Mode of Building.* On a trip to Wisconsin he had seen an octagonal house that impressed him as having spiritually healing properties. He argued that since nature's forms were mostly spherical, houses should follow the same design. He already had many followers, and his theories were listened to with respect. Hundreds of octagonal houses were built, from the Hudson River valley to the Middle West, and some remain today, like Carl Carmer's home at Irvington-on-Hudson, with its dome-tiled roof, eight-sided veranda, and Roman-arched windows. On the Pacific coast the Octagon House of the California chapter of the Colonial Dames of America, built in 1861 from the proceeds of gold rush days, was one of the last houses in San Francisco to be electrified. But the most famous and lasting example was Washington's Octagon House designed by William Thornton for John Tayloe III, son of the man who had owned Mount Airy.

Fowler believed that by eliminating the corners of a square-house plan he could enclose the same amount of room space at much less cost, but builders found that the obtuse angles were more difficult to frame than the right angles of the average home. One of the charms of the octagon, however, was the all-around piazza that gave its owner a full-scale view of the countryside. Fowler's own house in upstate New York stood on an oval knoll and was built of slate mixed with gravel, an arrangement that he thought suited his own phrenological bumps.

Fowler was involved in many of the movements of the day and was full of unusual ideas that he knew how to publicize. Among other things he advocated houses with playrooms for children, dance rooms for teen-agers, and gymnasiums where the women of the family could exercise. These sheltered creatures were just beginning then to swing Indian clubs and do calisthenics. But the naïve and sylvan spirit was far removed from the balloon-frame house that dotted the prairies and sheltered many of the men who were building up the West. This flexible frame, like the skyscraper, was indigenous to Chicago, and it played an important part in the rapid growth of the city from its beginnings as a fur-trading post. The frame was put together much like a box, with nails, studs, clapboards, and a few posts for foundations. Although seemingly frail, it stood up to heat, cold, and cyclones better than more solid buildings. New cities grew like magic on the balloon principle, and the simplicity of the Cape Cod models was soon lost in the gewgaws, rosettes, and jigsaw scrollwork that traveled west and gave the frontier towns a slightly rakish air.

During the Klondike gold rush of 1897 the whole settlement was put together with the various sections of the balloon frames shipped out from New York and reaching their destination on sleds. The numbered pieces were easily put together, and farmhouses, schools, barns, hospitals, depots, and barracks fell into place with the monotonous uniformity common to the later prefabricated houses. Although its original material was wood, the balloon style continued in metal and even in stone. The first building of this kind was St. Mary's Church in Chicago in the year 1833, when Greek Revival was in full flower. Americans were being exposed at the same time to the most pretentious and the simplest forms of housing. They were also learning to worship in a new type of church.

As the simplicity of the seventeenth-century church building gave way to the sophistication of the eighteenth, stately edifices rose in various parts of the country. The shadow of Sir Christopher Wren fell across Boston in the 1720s, profoundly influencing the church architecture of the United States. William Price, a distributor of engravings in Boston, had carefully studied the Wren churches in England and those of his copyist, James Gibbs, before designing Christ Church, better known as "Old North." Translating stone into brick and wood, Price designed a rectangular church with a pitched roof, a square tower, and a spire that later was replaced by a loftier one. Although "Old South" was a meetinghouse, it had some of the same quality, and both were copied over and over again until spires rose from many New England commons before the Revolution. The steeple of Old South, with its arcaded octagon of wood designed by Robert Twelves, was copied all over the East, and the bell that proclaimed Jonathan Edwards' Great Awakening in Northampton rang from this curious type of belfry.

Various provincial builders picked up the Wren inspiration from sketches and guidebooks, and soon handsome Anglican churches stood in the leading cities. St. Michael's in Charleston, with its white stucco glistening over brick, King's Chapel in Boston, and St. Paul's in New York were striking examples of this influence. The Chapel Royal of St. Philip's in North Carolina had the Palladian window identified with Wren. Newport's Trinity Church resembled St. Bride's in London. Velvet cushions and carpets, and gold-fringed pulpit hangings, were added by degrees. The Ten Commandments, the Creed, and the Lord's Prayer in illuminated parchment were framed and hung in some of the interiors. In general, Episcopalians and Congregationalists encouraged church form and pomp. The other Protestant churches were chaste and bare of ornament while the Roman Catholic churches were traditional in all respects.

Soon Greek Revival churches, notably those in Connecticut, added an exotic touch to the landscape with their paneled pilasters and square belfreys. In the nineteenth century a strong group of American architects came to the fore, building in the Gothic or Romanesque tradition, or with the individualism of Henry Hobson Richardson, who gave Boston Trinity and the Brattle Street Church. His massive effects were more often applied to building houses for rich men. Richard Upjohn, a High-churchman who came from England at the age of twenty-seven, was a cabinetmaker before he became an architect and the designer of Trinity Church at the head of Wall Street. He was steeped in the ecclesiastical spirit and refused to submit plans for a Unitarian church in Boston. Although equally cold to Presbyterian austerity, his handbook on wooden churches guided many carpenters in country parishes as they put up simple structures. Trinity was his masterpiece and is today one of the best-known churches in America. An early colonial building preceded his design. Upjohn insisted on a deep chancel and a cross on the spire, which seemed popish to his vestrymen. Edgar Allan Poe was critical, calling it a showy building, but he expressed the hope that its tall spire would make the Wall Street brokers look up to heaven for a change.

Trinity's popularity was challenged only by Grace Church, designed by James Renwick, Jr., who was also responsible for the Smithsonian Institution and the Corcoran Gallery of Art in Washington; New York's St. Patrick's Cathedral, whose twin Gothic spires give Fifth Avenue a touch of medieval splendor; and St. Bartholomew's, the Romanesque church with columns of Cippolino marble, panels of Egyptian porphyry, and a suffusion of Byzantine influence. But Grace Church was Renwick's particular pride. Philip Hone, one of its vestrymen, characterized the church's place in the social life of the period when he wrote in his diary: "This is to be the fashionable Church, and already its aisles are filled . . . with gay parties of ladies in feathers and mousseline-de-laine dresses, and dandies with moustaches and high-heeled boots; the lofty arches resound with astute criticism upon gothic architecture from fair ladies who have had the advantage of foreign travel, and scientific remarks upon acoustics from elderly millionaires who do not hear quite as well as formerly."

The real high priest of the Gothic tradition in America was Ralph Adams Cram, who set his stamp on Princeton, Wellesley, Bryn Mawr, West Point, and St. Thomas's. His buildings were compact, without the transepts and flying buttresses traditional to Gothic architecture. St. Thomas's was finished by his partner, Bertram Goodhue, who whimsically left a message to posterity in the dollar sign over the portal that was not detected for many years. It was the church of the millionaire, of the Easter parade, of the fashionable wedding.

Farther down Fifth Avenue stood the Church of the Transfiguration, better known as the Little Church Around the Corner. Its gabled roof and haphazard towers had no architectural history, but it was known around the world as the church of brides. Its jeweled interior, with a La Farge window and many other treasures, had seen more weddings than any church in the world, and popular actors of the nineteenth and twentieth centuries had used it for baptisms, weddings, and funerals. O. Henry was only one of many famous characters whose coffin rested under the pagoda-shaped copper roof of its lich gate.

Today lich gates, like covered bridges, remain chiefly as picturesque and symbolic reminders of the past. A few are still to be found at various Episcopal churches in the Northeast and in regions where a strongly English type of architecture prevails. The earliest function of the lich gate was to provide a roof or canopy at the churchyard entrance where pallbearers might rest the coffin until the priest arrived. Later many of the lich gates were made of stone or oak, and they were frequently used as outdoor chapels.

St. Michael's Church, Charleston (1752), is built of brick covered with stucco. Its sturdy steeple soars behind a pedimented colonnade, and it shows the Palladian influence. This famous church has been attributed, but without authentication, to James Gibbs, Sir Christopher Wren's most ardent disciple.

The Peter Harrison Synagogue in Newport, Rhode Island, completed in 1762, was one of the most distinguished of the early houses of worship in America. Its Ionic columns, coved ceiling, and graceful balustrade, enclosing the Ark of the Covenant, have details traceable to the influence of the English architects James Gibbs and Inigo Jones.

Trinity Church, the Gothic building facing
Wall Street with a spire that once dominated
the New York skyline but is lost in the
1960s in a dense complex of skyscrapers. Like
the thirteenth-century builders its architect,
Richard Upjohn, planned the carved statues
and other decorative details in a workshop
behind the church. Lithographed by
John Forsyth and E. W. Mimée in 1847 from
a sketch done by Upjohn, it is now known
as "the Bird's-eye View of Trinity."

Founded in 1771 during the administration of
Fr. Junipero Serra, San Gabriel Arcangel is
the fourth oldest Franciscan Mission in
California. The church, built from 1792–1802,
is constructed of brick and mortar, and is
typical of the austerely long and narrow
structures built by Indian hands in the early
days of California. The unusual range of
buttresses was probably inspired by the
Mosque of Cordoba, and the campanaria or
open belfry has been deservedly praised.

St. John's Abbey and University Church in
Collegeville, Minnesota, reflects the
philosophy of its creator Marcel Breuer.
For Breuer, architecture must represent the
present, not the past. The towers of the
medieval churches have been replaced by a
cantilevered concrete slab, a monumental
bell banner whose trapezoidal shape is
repeated in the façade and floor plan of
the church.

The few remaining lich gates in the United States are no longer used for this purpose, except the one at St. Mary's Episcopal Church, Burlington, New Jersey, which was built in 1883. To this day the coffin is placed on the bier, and the pall is spread at the lich gate before the bearers carry it into the church. One of the most picturesque of the lich gates is at St. James the Less in Philadelphia, known as the Biddle church. The edifice itself dates back to 1846, and many noted Philadelphians have been borne under the oak beams of its lich gate. Cass Gilbert designed St. Clement's Church in St. Paul, Minnesota, which has a lich gate with a slanted, shingled roof, topped by a cross. Local craftsmen built the lich gate at the Church of Saint Mary the Virgin in Falmouth, Maine, with oaken beams too solid to take nails.

While the Gothic tradition flourished, new settlers poured in to the United States, and a variety of churches and synagogues were built to meet their needs. Social and educational activities were encouraged, and many of the churches in the Middle West were auditoriums rather than houses of worship. The Roman Catholic Church, grounded in ritual, grew ever stronger. The Mormons flourished and their great temple in Salt Lake City was a massive testament to their strength and purpose. The Christian Scientists, with growing numbers, built huge churches in the classic or Renaissance style. One of the earliest of the modern churches was the Christian Science Church in Berkeley, designed by Bernard Maybeck. By degrees contemporary architects invaded the church field, from Frank Lloyd Wright's masterpiece, Unity Temple, at Oak Park, Illinois, to the stark simplicity of the Roman Catholic St. Michael's chapel in Burlington, Vermont. By the 1960s the New England spire, the Gothic cathedral, the Saarinen synagogue were combined harmoniously on the American landscape. By the mid-sixties there were 325,344 churches across the nation, representing scores of religious beliefs and rituals.

WHEN America was settled, it took time for a unified social pattern to emerge. Inherited tastes and prejudices lived on tenaciously but in modified form after the War of Independence. Even today regional distinctions persist. Most of the colonists had come from simple homes, and their manners were not helped by the fusion of languages, the hardships they had to overcome, and their lack of possessions. They lived under primitive conditions and were subject to a stern code. Church and state determined their habits, and at first they were not free people.

The earliest and strongest influence in government was the Puritan imprint on New England, which led to the punishment of heretics, Quakers, and witches, and let loose on the land a repressive spirit that leaves some echoes three hundred years later. The early laws were repressive and binding. Retribution was swift and often grim. Transgressors were pilloried in the stocks for scandalmongering, swearing, or lying. Gossips and scolds were chastened with the ducking stool or a quick plunge into a tub of salt water. The hanging of criminals was a public spectacle. The Mary Magdalenes were forced to stand trembling in open congregation, wearing the white sheet of penitence as they confessed their sins. When the young showed signs of rebellion, Cotton

Mather observed that the "iniquities of the younger generation were causing the glory of the Lord to depart from New England." A ban had gone forth on shouting, screaming, running, riding, singing, dancing, jumping, and winding horns on the Sabbath.

But courage, enterprise, and ingenuity survived even if the civilities and the mellowing touches of social usage suffered. In course of time each group, while still responsive to inherited instincts, worked with the other to build up the new country, and from their toil, painfully wrought, came the American way of life. The polish was slowly applied as men and women overcame the forces of nature, established themselves in comfort, furnished their houses, educated their children, and found time for recreation and self-improvement. It needed the first generation of children born to the settlers to break some of the bonds and assert themselves with the buoyancy of youth.

The Quakers, who settled in Philadelphia, had a restrained but democratic approach to life, and at first they led the field in finance, trade, and lawmaking. The Dutch and the English were traders, merchants, and shopkeepers in New York, and the South reflected the more aristocratic English tradition of pomp, the leisurely life, and a show of manners. The Germans, who pushed to the frontier and settled around Ohio, were the careful craftsmen, the industrious workers who introduced new skills as well as their love of music. The French, clustering around New Orleans, added culture and cuisine to the national picture. The Italians, later arrivals who settled chiefly in New York, made their mark on the eating habits of the American people as well as introducing their own great musical tradition. The Irish, fleeing their native country at the time of the potato famine, brought their keen political insight and warmhearted wit across the Atlantic. The Jews, coming from many countries, added immeasurably to America's arts and industry. In course of time each European nation contributed something to the new country's rapid growth and development.

But the process of amalgamation was gradual. The agrarian, the commercial, and the shipping groups gained strength and grew rich in their separate ways. Settlers moving west took their idiom, customs, traditions, and religious faith with them. The Swedish tongue was heard in Minnesota, the Polish accent in Illinois, and the German in Ohio. Social distinctions were apparent from the start, however. Government officials, gentry, scholars, men of means, and the clergy were in the ascendant. Merchants, shopkeepers, and freeholders made up a strong middle class, and on the bottom rung of the ladder were the servants, slaves, and unskilled laborers. Anyone holding a university degree was considered a gentleman and was addressed as Sir. The clergy were known as Reverend Misters. The judiciary were Esquires to their subordinates. The wife of a gentleman was addressed as Madam, and the middle-class man of substance was Goodman, with Goodwife ever at his side. There was a strong line of cleavage between master and apprentice.

Although manners and social distinctions were still somewhat medieval on both sides of the Atlantic in the years that America was being settled, some of the Virginians were Oxford graduates belonging to titled families, and they quickly set up an aristocracy in the South. Cavaliers, the Roman Catholic Royalists who supported Charles I, many of whom had come to the United States, had similiar traditions. With this inheritance the planters soon established their own hierarchy, and their ways had little relation to what went on in other parts of the developing country. They lived on a luxurious scale from the profits they made shipping tobacco and cotton to London and Bristol. They dined off gold and silver plate from England, served the wines of Spain and Portugal, and went in for sports and tournaments, masquerades and great balls. Their women had large staffs of slaves to cater to every whim, from tightening their corset strings to fanning them as they lay on their piazzas. And regardless of the manner in which they used their forks, their gowns and jewels were imported, and they rode in fine chariots with liveried attendants. Many had their portraits painted when they could find suitable artists.

Early in the day the Virginians were committed to fox hunting and horse racing. In short, they lived with considerable style in their Georgian houses, perpetuating the traditions of seventeenth-century England. Shops on their own plantations supplied many of their basic needs, and Williamsburg had the best stores in the colony, stocking everything from Turkish carpets to French sugarplums. In the North life was less abundant, but the acquisition of luxuries kept pace with the growing prosperity of the new land.

Once the early groundwork was laid, fortunes were made so fast that merchants often retired before they were forty to pursue a life of leisure and recreation on their comfortable estates. Benjamin Franklin did so well with his printing that he was able to bow out at forty-two, but life held so many challenges for him that his true retirement did not come until he died. Ship captains, too, liked to retire in their prime, the treasures they had picked up on their travels arranged in their solid Georgian houses and fat accounts in the bank. The earliest fortunes stemmed from shipping and mercantile interests. Newport, remaining strongly English, developed its own maritime population, men of wealth who had traded with the West Indies and the Mediterranean ports. Boston in 1743 was ahead of all other American cities in shipbuilding, furniture and hardware manufacturing, hatmaking and the leather trade. The sons of these prospering families were sent to college to study law, theology, or medicine. In 1773 students were listed in the

Harvard catalogue according to their social rank, showing that class distinctions were alive in New England as well as in the South.

The drive for education as a civilizing force grew strong as families prospered. Both girls and boys went to dame schools at first, but while the boys studied Latin, Greek, and mathematics, the girls read from the Bible and did their crewel work, or else they knitted verses or letters of the alphabet into their mittens. All were expected to perfect their spelling and penmanship, however deficient they might be in their other studies. In Virginia small schools were conducted out-doors on abandoned tobacco fields, the children arriving by horseback or by boat, but for the most part the planters had their children tutored by parish ministers or visiting British scholars. The classical tradition took root in this fashion.

In the Bay Colony parents assumed responsibility for the edu-cation of their boys and girls until the middle of the seventeenth cen-tury, when an act required towns with a hundred families or more to establish grammar schools on the English principle. The Boston Latin School and other New England institutions still in existence had their beginnings in this way. While Boston fostered grammar and free writing schools, New York lagged behind, partly because the Dutch tongue created bilingual difficulties. Around 1820 a large proportion of the children were not being educated, either because their parents could not meet the fees or because they were unwilling to accept charity. Half the boys and girls attending Boston's primary schools in 1880, according to historian Arthur M. Schlesinger, were so much the product of city life that they had "never seen a plow or spade, a robin, squirrel, snail or sheep; had never observed peaches on a tree or growing grain and did not know an oak tree from a willow or poplar."

Although university life began to take shape in America when Harvard received its charter from the Bay Colony in 1650, it was a long time before women's education caught up. A few girls as well as many boys were sent abroad to be educated, but no one worried about the intellectual development of the girls as long as they attended to their music, dancing, and embroidery. They learned mostly by osmosis until the feminists of the mid-nineteenth century stirred up interest in their education as well as in their voting rights. Perhaps the most significant landmark was the establishment of Mount Holyoke by Mary Lyon in 1836. Otherwise, higher education was denied women until the 1880s.

Although the rich gathered first at the colleges, scores of im-poverished young men left farms and traveled far to enter Harvard, Yale, or Princeton. Many earned their way as they went along. The northern colleges suffered during the Revolutionary War, but Yale had a graduating class of seventy in 1785, twice as many as Harvard that year. Phi Beta Kappa, the first intercollegiate fraternity, later to become a scholarship honor society, was founded at William and Mary College during the War of Independence.

The spread of higher education has been one of the miracles of the ripening years. In 1950, 18 per cent of all Americans between the ages of eighteen and twenty-one attended college. In 1966 there were approximately 5,400,000 undergraduates, a 30 per cent increase in this age group. Twenty-five per cent went on to graduate work. Since 1950 American colleges and universities have spent $16.5 billion on new buildings and more than 180 new campuses were being planned in 1967. The nation's public schools are today educating a record number of students, too, with an enrollment of 44.66 million in the elementary and secondary schools, a 38 per cent increase in the space of a decade.

The drive in scholarship has been reflected in the reading habits of the nation, but many of the early Americans were scholars, too, and they liked to read. The individual read with more depth, if less variety, than the average reader does today. He had fewer books, but he knew them well. The American culture, in the years before the Declaration of Independence, was still that of the Old World, and the educated man reflected the philosophical and literary tastes of his homeland. In Virginia and New England an established literary tradition soon found roots. However, the widespread use of books developed only slowly as men and women wove and dug, cleared the land, and struggled for mere existence. At first they had little from which to choose, but soon books, pamphlets, and broadsides were sold in large numbers to country stores and schools, involving a wide dissemination of primers, Bibles, spellers, and histories. Everything of a religious or textbook nature had its following. Catalogues were sent to the taverns to incite interest, and book auctions were popular. The Bible and Prayer Book, the *Bay Psalm Book*, *Poor Richard's Almanack*, and the *Old Farmer's Almanack*, first published in 1792, were part of the furnishings in all manner of homes. The *Virginia Almanack* preceded its durable successor, still welcomed in farm homes, but it concentrated on acrostics, enigmas, and queries. Noah Webster's spelling books were vital to this generation. Early manuscripts testify to the uncertainty and confusion in this field.

The self-help idea was strong in the mid-eighteenth century, as it is today, and the Chapbooks—the tracts of their day—were devoured at the rural level. They were small, compact paperbacks that could be tucked in the coat pocket, and their enigmas, jokes, forecasts, and useful information were scattered about among people hungry for information, or were quoted around the stove in the village store. Book wagons for adults and children traveled around the countryside, their sides opening out for display like the book stacks of today. Parson Weems, the Maryland preacher who toured the South for thirty years with horse and wagon, was perhaps the most famous of book peddlers. The broadsides and public proclamations scattered around in public places spread news as television does today.

Like other luxuries, calf-bound copies of the classics were imported from England by those who could afford them. One wealthy Virginian, William Byrd, laid the foundation for his library at "Westover" as early as 1690. Other planters established private libraries, but the average citizen soon had the benefit of bookshops and lending libraries. Philadelphia had seventy-seven bookshops between 1761 and 1776; Boston had thirty-one; New York had twenty-seven; Newport had ten; and Charleston, six. Samuel Loudon, running one in 1774, found Manhattan ladies his best customers, since, he thought, they showed a "becoming delicacy of taste in their choice of books." They may also have been beguiled by the fact that the book dealers sold soap and medicines, tennis racquets, ink, stationery, and lottery tickets as well as reading fare.

Libraries that flourish today were early in the field. The ever popular New York Society Library, which had its beginnings in 1754 as a lending library, received its royal charter eighteen years later, and was patronized by the nation's founders. The Redwood Library of Newport was incorporated in 1746, and the Boston Athenaeum in 1807. The college libraries soon became powerful because of their influence on student life. Harvard in 1723 had 3,000 volumes; today it has more than 7,000,000. Yale's first catalogue in 1742 listed 2,600 books; today it has nearly 5,000,000 volumes. Cornell, Stanford, and the University of California house between two and three million books apiece. The number of volumes in American public libraries had increased from 143 million in 1950 to 210 million in 1960, and dozens of libraries are becoming mechanized, with data-processing machines and computers to cope with the avalanche of books. Together, book sales and library circulation have increased three times faster than the population in recent times. But food for the mind still lags behind the more carnal appetites, if statistics prove anything. Americans in 1965 spent a total of $12 billion for alcohol, $8 billion for tobacco, as against $2 billion for books.

Book printing in general was honored in the colonies, and early in the eighteenth century Boston had five printing presses turning out, among other things, books in the tribal languages of the Indians. Cotton Mather published 382 different works, some of which were printed in England. The earliest printing press in the English colonies and the second in North America was established in 1639 in the old village cowpen that had become the Harvard College Yard. Here the historic *Bay Psalm Book* was printed in the following year. A decade before the war broke out the New Englander was sampling Shakespeare and Congreve, Molière and Smollett, Pope and Milton. But whatever his classical reading he was an ardent student of the early press. The newspapers were effective in pushing the policies that led the nation into war.

Foreign news came in by monthly mail packet after 1756, but as early as 1743 the five cities had four-page weekly journals distributed by post riders and carriers or by boat. Peter Zenger's victory on a freedom issue in 1735 gave journalism its most lasting tradition. Benjamin Franklin was the powerful friend of early printing, financing presses and founding papers as well as selling books and almanacs. In his own *Pennsylvania Gazette* he introduced illustrations into advertising, and in 1753 was responsible for the first American newspaper cartoon, an experiment with dynamic results. The early printers were civic leaders and molders of public opinion, like the crusading editors of a later date. Books, sermons, pamphlets, magazines, and broadsides all influenced the public thinking of that troubled period, as they do even more conclusively today in their scope, number, and variety. Through it all the Bible has remained the unshakable best seller.

Potent as the written word was then, and is today, public debate was of prime importance in the nineteenth century. Wits, celebrities and savants, visitors from abroad and home-grown protagonists of vital or far-out causes toured the Lyceum circuit and always drew crowds, a fashion pursued by other lecture bureaus today. An endless dialogue was sustained on public issues and the propagandist note was sounded clearly on such diverse subjects as women's rights, slavery, temperance, free love, prison reform, dress reform, hygiene, and health. Men and women zealots projected their causes with such success that after its inception in 1827 nine hundred lyceums were in operation within five years.

Even before the war Philadelphians flocked to forums on popular science. Phrenologists analyzed the conformation of the head, and astrologists turned the eyes of their listeners toward the heavens. Whole families went to lectures as they do to the cinema or theater today, and women who were denied scholarship opportunities even at a time when bookstores were opening, libraries were being established, and intellectual interests were broadening, thrived on the Lyceum and talked for weeks of lectures by Dickens or Ralph Waldo Emerson. Boston, with its eloquent and pervasive Transcendentalists, was the intellectual center of the nation during this period, and its orators, scholars, and writers were as radical as its business community was conservative. Philadelphia prided itself on its cultural interests, too, although its strong and industrious Quaker families leaned more strongly to commerce. New Yorkers were the true hedonists, making no pretension to intellectual interests in the early days but enjoying the fleshpots to the full.

The day of the camp meeting has faded but great bursts of

The severe dame, the dunce with his cap, and pinafored girls were characteristic of the early dame schools.

"The American School." Americans sought education abroad in the eighteenth century, and these youths are studying art in Benjamin West's London studio. An American by birth, West at various times had studios in Philadelphia, New York, Italy, and London, where he was a close friend of Sir Joshua Reynolds and succeeded him as President of the Royal Academy. Painting by Matthew Pratt (1734–1805).

Higher education for women did not come into its own until the 1880s, but these Smith girls in 1889 concentrated on chemistry as eagerly as their male counterparts at Yale or Princeton.

religious fervor have continued to stir the public from time to time, most notably in the nineteenth century when agnosticism and piety were pitted against each other in a noisy struggle for principle. The Methodists held camp meetings as early as 1780. The Presbyterians picked up the torch next, and finally the Baptists outworshiped them all. The fever spread until even the more restrained Episcopalians at times were subject to fits and jerkings. The revivalist spirit was at its peak in the middle of the nineteenth century. It was rowdy, earthy, and far removed from the austere days of the Great Awakening, when Jonathan Edwards stirred men's minds to controversy and protest. Campfires glowed in forest clearings. Wagons gathered as for a carnival. Candles and lanterns swung against the dark background of the trees, as the revivalists paraded about, singing and shouting hosannas. The Shakers lived up to their name as they shook and twitched, jerked, jumped, and fell to the ground.

Parsons talked until they were hoarse, and Peter Cartwright, a Methodist evangelist, preached fourteen thousand sermons in fifty years in Kentucky and Illinois. They appeared at the Chautauqua gatherings, which were more decorous than the excesses at some of the camp revival meetings. Thousands gathered at Chautauqua centers to listen to talks on temperance, religion, and the good life in general, solemnly waving their handkerchiefs in salute. Speakers from all parts of the world pled their various causes to this responsive audience. The Chautauquans camped in surrounding tents, wandered in woodland groves—and a strong sense of religious revival dominated their gatherings. Temperance was their particular cause. But in time the movement broadened from Methodist camp meetings by the shore of a lake to a vast educational chain. Its Literary and Scientific Circle gave many isolated Americans the feeling that they were attending a good college.

Americans have always been responsive to the revivalist spirit and have given countenance to some picturesque evangelists. Dwight L. Moody, the shoe salesman who campaigned across the country and with Ira D. Sankey had thousands singing hymns, founded a Bible institute and seminaries for boys and girls. Sam Jones and Gypsy Smith both lured crowds down the sawdust trail, but the master practitioner was Billy Sunday, the Iowa baseball player and Presbyterian minister who electrified crowds with his acrobatic platform manner, and his gift for persuading hordes of "converts" to sign up for God.

Aimee Semple McPherson, founder of the Four Square Gospel, swayed a multitude of worshipers who responded rapturously to the preaching, the music, the banks of roses in which she moved, the sheaves she held in her arms, the mounting frenzy of services at Angelus Temple in Los Angeles, and her own dynamic personality. Aimee suited her times—she flourished in the 1920s, and died obscurely in 1944.

She was the saint turned sinner, the prima donna who had lost her reputation to the echo of golden trumpets from her own altar. Finally, Billy Graham, with more scholarly restraint, continues to tour the world, stirring up the peoples of many nations with his eloquence, but without the breast-beating or whiplash persuasion of the earlier evangelists.

The religious spirit has burned with a strong flame in America from the days of the Pilgrims. The colonists worshiped under trees, in tents, in rude huts, or in any shelter they could find, and the first meetinghouse in Boston had mud walls and was thatched. John Smith wrote, of the first hour of prayer at Jamestown, that in "foul weather we shifted into an old rotten tent, for we had none better." But religion was a powerful force in the life of the people from the beginning, and churches were the earliest landmarks on the horizon. Graceful spires rose from the green fields and helped to shape the cities. New York's skyline began with steeples soaring above its rooftops. The plain meetinghouses, the Romanesque and Gothic churches built as the land was settled—all had a deep and abiding effect on the social life of the nation and the conduct of its people.

The square meetinghouse of seventeenth-century New England was America's only contribution to church architecture until modern times. The Puritans would have nothing to do with cross or spire, and they spurned the word "church." A central tower that served as belfry and upheld a weather vane was the only distinguishing mark of the meetinghouse. The Society of Friends in Pennsylvania worshiped in buildings stoutly put together with good woods and careful workmanship. The Moravian meetinghouses were U-shaped, with double-hipped roofs and dormers. The Anglican churches soon were enriched with stained glass, high altars, rich vestments, and the full liturgy of the Church of England.

In Charleston the Anglican Church was dominant, but Baptists, Presbyterians, and Lutherans had their own simple churches in the nascent town. Philadelphia had its Society of Friends, which lost ground eventually to the Presbyterians and Baptists. By 1760 the Rhode Island Quakers, the largest group anywhere in the world, had thinned down, with many joining Christ Church as dissent developed over church forms and doctrines. The Catholic Church was strong in Maryland. Boston was the Congregational center, and much of the social life of the city swung around its churches. New Englanders moved west and prospered, then changed to the Anglican Church in such cities as Cincinnati. The Great Awakening by Jonathan Edwards in the 1830s shook the churches to their foundations, and again in the twentieth century the forces of Modernism and Fundamentalism tore at each other with old-time fervor. As the country grew, churches multiplied, split, feuded, and were often a divisive as well as a civilizing force, but throughout all the battles down the years people clung to their religion and filled the churches. Neither strange gods nor agnosticism shattered the image of the American's devotion to his church.

Regular attendance was one of the early standards of good churchly behavior, and in some instances it was mandatory. In New England sermons were often three hours long; prayers might last for two. In winter the congregation sat shivering on hinged benches with men and women facing one another across the hall. It was the middle of the nineteenth century before stoves were installed, and then only after a bitter battle between the antistove faction that believed in scourging the flesh and the protagonists of warmth and comfort.

The chill extended to the wedding ceremony. Puritan ministers were not permitted to marry people until the eighteenth century. A magistrate or man of affairs usually officiated and the banns of matrimony had to be read three times. In New Hampshire the Presbyterians had guns fired at daybreak outside the homes of the pair getting married. The aftermath was apt to be hilarious because of the quantities of sack posset consumed. By 1651 dancing in taverns after weddings was forbidden. The jigs and hornpipes caused as much discussion and commotion as the frug, the potato, and the watusi today. The bride usually tossed her garter, instead of her bouquet, to her attendants.

A certain gaiety surrounded funerals, too. Madeira was usually served to the mourners and there was much feasting and drinking before they scattered. In Massachusetts each town provided wine and cider for the funerals of its paupers. But the winding parade to the country graveyard, with stops for refreshments along the way, ended with the introduction of hearses. Burials were in churchyards, or in family gardens or nearby burial plots. The tombstones encompassed the parish history with their Latin and English inscriptions—sentimental, witty, grave, or reproachful. It was a highly personal record, the furthest extreme from present-day cremation, the marble vault, or the trappings of Forest Lawn. In the South planters sent messengers by boat and on horseback to round up mourners, and it was customary to sit up all night with the dead. Funeral dinners were held by the men, but prominent women, garbed all in white and with long veils, were allowed to attend the funeral and even to carry the pall. Mourning rings, gloves, scarves, and bottles of Madeira were given to the mourners. Funeral customs changed from one generation to another in the nation's evolution.

The eighteenth was essentially a man's century. Stirring events sparked its course, with the creation of a new government and the emergence of great figures on the political scene. Peace had settled over the land with the dawn of the nineteenth century, and people had more time to study, to read, to travel, to enlarge their horizons. There was a restless groping for better things as Americans sought to create a new image of themselves in the eyes of the world. They had become sensitive to the constant hammering at their supposed lack of manners and cultivation. They were tired of being told by visitors, through the press and in person, that they were noisy, boastful, uncouth, and ignorant. The recurrent attacks by British authors were particularly wounding. Without relinquishing their sturdy native spirit they took stock of the things the rest of the world had to offer. They cultivated the foreign artist and widened their vistas by travel. Their taste in music and art became more sophisticated and the rise in popularity of Italian opera and ballet was rapid. They read widely and brought objects of art into their houses. The artistic seeds planted in the early days of the republic flowered into a finer appreciation of all the arts, especially music, which was the first of the cultural graces to be enjoyed in the newly settled country.

Music was understandably introduced by the Germans, who took it with them to the frontier. But in the Puritan world music was confined chiefly to the *Bay Psalm Book*, although the Pilgrims from Leyden already knew their Bach. Aside from this the native music was of a simple sort—psalms, ballads, sentimental songs, jigging dance music, and the minstrel shows that became popular in all quarters. Fiddles scraped in a lively vein, and lutes, violins, flutes, virginals, and trumpets soon were imported, as well as the Jew's-harps that the Indians enjoyed and coveted. Women played the virginal in the seventeenth century, and the spinet and harpsichord in the eighteenth century.

After the War of Independence music festivals were established by the Moravians of Bethlehem, and church music became more impressive. Charleston, Newport, and Boston all had singing schools, and orchestras were brought together by the St. Cecilia Society in Charleston for a series of concerts. The Handel and Haydn Society was established in 1815 in Boston and the Philharmonic Society of Orchestral Players a few years later. Cincinnati and Boston were early in the field with good symphony orchestras, and the New York Philharmonic, the first professional orchestra in America, gave its earliest program in 1842.

In the nineteenth century grand opera and symphony orchestras assumed worldwide importance, and they soon raised the level of music in the United States. New Orleans had its French Opera House before the Civil War, and the Metropolitan in New York opened golden vistas in the 1880s, but imported Italian opera had already been drawing thousands of attentive listeners. In the popular field Theodore Thomas, Walter Damrosch, John Philip Sousa, and Victor Herbert became as well known as Leopold Stokowski and Leonard Bernstein are today. Musical comedy to good scores became a notable characteristic of the

Psalm singing had always held its place in American church music, but in the late eighteenth century a new spirit pervaded the colonies. Dynamic religious leaders like Jonathan Edwards and John Wesley introduced the singing of hymns, and congregations took up their lead with enthusiasm. American hymnody flowered. "New England Psalm Singers." Engraving by Paul Revere from The New England Psalm-Singer or Chorister, *composed by William Billings, 1770.*

Song, medicine, and learning were engaged in simultaneously in the Old Lutheran Schoolhouse of 1805. The hourglass recorded the passage of time. The broom and bucket were at hand. The dunce was in his corner as the schoolmaster led his pupils through their *lieder.* But the chief business of the day was medical, as Dr. John Morris and Ludwig Miller, a teacher, ministered to a boy suffering from ringworm. The unhappy pupil was taken aside and held firmly while spirits of vitriol were rubbed into his sores. Many simple complaints were treated in school, and ringworm was as common as the cold. *Photo by Bosshart. From the* American-German Review, *1805.*

American stage, bringing on a rage for sheet music that led to its popularization around the world. The gramophone with its morning-glory horn brought classical music into the home early in the twentieth century as well as floods of popular songs. Long-playing records reached the market in 1950, and stereo and hi-fi followed late in the 1950s, filling American homes with the music of the world. Recordings by the great European conductors, such as Toscanini, flowed endlessly over the airways.

America's popular-song writers rate among its foremost artists, and their work has been enjoyed by more millions than any other form of native art. But the nation's most celebrated contribution to music is jazz, which swept the world in the 1920s and at its best is major music today in any part of the world. It had its beginnings with the Negro bands of New Orleans, and reached its crescendo with the symphonic jazz introduced by George Gershwin and Paul Whiteman. The original jazz was improvised, with offbeat rhythm patterns known as ragtime, changing pitch and accent, and using blue notes at will. It differed from swing and boogie-woogie, which rely on a rolling, repetitious bass and odd chords. The ragtime and spirituals of the Negroes have become part of the American tradition, like the Indian tunes with their emphatic rhythms.

Before the major aspects of music were fully developed in the United States, or even the popular jazz, simpler forms were zealously pursued from coast to coast. While men like Andrew Carnegie, Charles M. Schwab, and Henry C. Frick were installing great pipe organs in their mansions, the average man was enjoying his cottage organ. There were fifteen varieties in 1905, ranging from the oak parlor model costing $19.90 to the Imperial Grand at $51.95. Families gathered around the organ to sing "Safe in the Arms of Jesus" or "Silver Threads among the Gold." But they soon moved on to the musical comedy hit songs, for the young had learned to rag. Meanwhile small boys scraped rebelliously on violins, and girls practiced their Czerny exercises to please demanding parents. The music teacher came and went with the regularity of the family seamstress, and the country as a whole had more pianos and organs than bathtubs at the turn of the century.

The mandolin and banjo gained great favor with the croquet and picnic set. College youths in straw hats and striped blazers twanged away in boats and on lawns, giving Stephen Foster melodies some of the spirit of the Beatles and their fellows today. Swiss music boxes, guitars, and zithers were widely circulated, and twenty-five kinds of harmonicas were on sale, some costing as little as nine cents. Guitars were named for colleges, with Harvard the most costly at $21.45 and Stanford the most reasonable at $4.24. But the gramophone, with the commanding beat of Sousa's marches, edged the piccolo, the mandolin,

"Brentano's Literary Emporium" in 1870 was a fashionable as well as a literary center on Union Square in New York City. All the world strolled by, and the famous actors of the day, on their way to the theaters south of the square, paused to thumb through the books and foreign periodicals that August Brentano imported. Their playbills were displayed outside the bookshop, an attraction in itself. Browsers and customers ranged from Charles Dickens and Ralph Waldo Emerson to Ulysses S. Grant and the sensational Lillian Russell. The famous bookstore chain began with a table of books and periodicals in the hallway of the old Revere House on Broadway. It gathered momentum when Mr. Brentano opened a shop farther up Broadway. By the time he settled on Union Square his emporium was known as the most flourishing bookstore in America.

A Lyceum Lecture in 1838 by James Pollard Espy, meteorologist, at Clinton Hall, New York. Nine hundred lyceums across the country encouraged strange cults and fed the hunger for knowledge. Men and women flocked to hear lectures on subjects ranging from free love to higher mathematics.

and ultimately the ukulele out of the running. The accordion lingered and roused nostalgia with the rich infusion of folk airs brought by immigrants from European countries. The guitar picked up popularity again with the hillbilly music of the 1940s. The barrel organ filled the streets of New York with romantic overtones until Mayor La Guardia banned it.

The player piano came rattling in during World War I with its soulless tedium and brassy racket. Soldiers and their girls danced to it, with death close by. But the versatile radio eclipsed it. By 1930 sixteen million American families had receiving sets, and new idols were on the horizon—Bing Crosby and Bob Hope, Fred Allen and Jack Benny. Opera, symphonies, piano recitals, classical music of all kinds floated over the airways, for music made up three quarters of the early programs until games, fights, soap operas, and panels cut in. But a new spirit was abroad, and fresh interest in the arts was evident, as symphony orchestras multiplied from eight hundred to thirteen hundred, and the number of children studying music at home or in school jumped from two and one-half million in 1947 to twelve million in 1964. Beyond that the public bought eighteen million classical records in 1965.

Americans now spend more than ten million dollars annually for opera tickets, mostly for the Metropolitan, which opened in a modern setting at New York's Lincoln Center in 1966, after eighty-three years in the historic old opera house that had harbored the greatest singers of the day. Viennese chandeliers sparkled in the new opera house, and Marc Chagall murals brought a contemporary note to bear on an atmosphere long associated with plush and pomp.

"The nineteen-sixties seem certain to become the decade in which the arts in this country achieved the broad, democratic base that the prophets had long talked about," commented *The New York Times* on May 16, 1966. Large sums of money are now being spent to bring schoolchildren in direct contact with music, drama, the dance, and the visual arts. Children speak as glibly now of Picasso and Chagall as they do of their comic-strip heroes. Lincoln Center, the new Los Angeles Music Center, and Houston's center for the arts are focal points of interest. An intense feeling for the arts suffuses the social body today, possibly because of increased leisure and more money to spend. Visiting galleries and museums has become a spectator sport, and museum attendance now tops 200 million a year. On a typical weekend the Metropolitan Museum of Art clocks nearly one hundred thousand visitors, the Museum of Modern Art, close to twelve thousand, and the Guggenheim, thirteen thousand. All records were broken with the thousands who paraded past Rembrandt's "Aristotle Contemplating the Bust of Homer," for which the Metropolitan paid $2,300,000.

The new push in the arts is not alone for the socially elect. As Russell Lynes, editor and author, sums it up: "We have come from the age of the drawing-room musicale by way of the recital hall to the age of the mammoth cultural center; from the individually loved paintings to the private collection to the massive museum; from the individual patron to the local committee of art lovers to the corporate board and to the National Council on the Arts." Art is available now to people of all classes. The great collections that the millionaires of the 1890s hung in their mansions—to be seen only by intimate friends—have no counterpart today. At any given moment the Metropolitan has between 16,000 and 19,000 of its 365,000 possessions on loan to other institutions. The museums are acquiring many cherished inheritances and are displaying them in a fashion that the public can afford and enjoy. A case in point was the acquisition of Joseph H. Hirshhorn's jealously guarded collection by the Smithsonian Institution, which is emerging from its turreted aloofness as a repository for such varied memorabilia as the Wright Brothers' first airplane and the Hope Diamond to become a national art center. Foundations, corporations, educational institutions, and art centers are all involved in this strong push for the dissemination of art, and hospitals and other institutions are using it for therapy. It has truly become a vital force in America's everyday life.

In 1950 there were 150 art galleries in New York and about the same number across the country. Today there are three hundred in New York and many hundreds in the nation as a whole, ranging from the quiet magnificence of such galleries as Wildenstein's, where the great masters change hands, to the picturesque little atelier in the summer resort where artists in clamdiggers and plaid shirts make sales to society girls in Lilly shifts. It is equally smart to paint or to collect, and the American home reflects the collector's craze with the originals now hanging on its walls. The "young marrieds" of substance, a breed in themselves these days, are as likely to invest in a good contemporary picture as in a new car. Cynics observe that it's all an affectation with people who don't know what to do with their wealth, or their time, or how to dazzle their associates. Few are collecting old masters today, but many are paying steep prices for Gauguins, Chagalls, and van Goghs, and in some instances are fashioning their décor around them. Their own easels are apt to be propped at the edge of their swimming pools, for to paint, to collect art, is society's latest enthusiasm.

The theater, too, is reaching more people that it ever did before. It may be languishing on Broadway, but it is flourishing on the road and in repertory. In 1963 there were 5,000 amateur theater groups, 1,250 symphony orchestras, 710 opera companies, and 500 art movie houses. In addition to this, the foundations are lavishing more money on the arts. Big corporations are fostering this interest in their employees, and the colleges are staging lectures, recitals, plays, and debates in the growing renaissance of the 1960s. Ballet, too, has become a major American art form, with eighteen professional and two hundred semiprofessional ballet companies in the country, two of which rate with the best in the world—the New York City Ballet and the American Ballet Theater.

Polls and surveys show that it is the young who are promoting the assorted arts with such enthusiasm, even while they are being pilloried as the most shiftless, rebellious, and untidy of generations. Again the young marrieds come into the picture, setting up their own standards on every front. The country abounds in these knowing young people of average income, with average homes, and the average point of view. Undoubtedly they are more typical of the nation as a whole than those who hunt in Virginia, ski in Switzerland, surf in the Bahamas, and qualify for the gossip columns as members of the jet set.

But each group finds its own, and the gregarious nature of the American, first apparent in the days of the Pilgrims, expresses itself today, as then, in a tendency to form groups based on common interests. This early spirit led eventually to clubs and the reputation Americans bear today of being the world's champion joiners. Some of it was spontaneous and social, after the fashion of the London beefsteak clubs and coffeehouses, but more often the propelling force was a mutual cause. Long before wealth, family tradition, or professional distinction became the keys to club membership, there were simple gatherings in taverns and private homes where fellow countrymen could join forces to protect their political and religious beliefs.

Charleston had a club as early as 1795, and the first of the nation's sporting clubs, which abound today, was the Fishing Company of the State in Schuylkill, founded in 1732 on a Quaker's estate. The Freemasons were parading as early as 1760, and by 1890 they had a network of 124 secret orders. Patriotic societies took root at the time of the Revolution, and more came into being with the Civil War. College fraternities fostered the club spirit on the campus. Yale's Skull and Bones and Harvard's Porcellian were among the first, and they flourish today.

Each club had its own distinguishing interest. Some were purely social, but as the country grew and scholarship assumed depth, clubs developed recognizable patterns—political, scientific, academic, sporting, Bohemian, or intellectual—like the Century Association of New York, founded in 1847, and the Tavern Club in Boston, dating back to 1884, or the New York Yacht Club. The rage for croquet, bicycling, tennis, and golf in the late nineteenth century resulted in clubs of another stripe, and the country club, a distinctly American institution, took root after World War I.

The Park Theater was New York's
lordliest playhouse in the early
nineteenth century, and a number of
well-known New Yorkers have been
recognized in this audience of 1822.
Mutton chop bones and beer bottles
were often pitched at the actors, and
things were not always as suave as they
seemed. Men could wear their hats at
will and audiences were more vocal
in their disapproval than they are today.
Many of the most famous actors of
the nineteenth century played in the
Park Theater.

Opera is as popular in the twentieth
century as it was in the nineteenth.
The 3,800-seat auditorium of the new
Metropolitan Opera House in Lincoln
Center for the Performing Arts is
sold out for nearly every performance.

The revivalist spirit reached its peak at a camp meeting of this kind, a common occurrence in the nineteenth century. Wild scenes were enacted in forest clearings as zealots twitched and shouted, fell to the ground, or danced with joy. They camped in tents, and the atmosphere was half carnival, half religious ecstasy. Lithograph by Kennedy and Lucas, ca. 1835.

Sidewalk art show at Barre, Vermont, illustrates the growing taste in the United States for the outdoor art show, no longer the special prerogative of Bohemian centers but bringing out the housewife and her family in the most conservative communities.

Abby Aldrich Rockefeller Sculpture Garden at the Museum of Modern Art, showing the sculptured figures, reflecting pools, and birch trees from the main hall—an oasis for art lovers in midtown New York. Photograph by Alexandre Georges.

The socially oriented clubs found ways of blackballing the unwanted, until the impression prevailed that they were snobbish institutions. More recently the race issue has focused attention on discrimination in this field, notably in the case of the Cosmos Club in Washington. But, generally speaking, in the 1960s all men have their clubs if they wish them, and the nation is laced with country and golf clubs, yachting, skiing, and hunt clubs, and many more for every age and social stratum. High in the mountains and close to the shore, the sporting clubs present a formidable picture of social interchange, ranging from the fieldstone mountain lodges to the streamlined showcases by the sea.

The sumptuous aspects of the clubs that flourished in the cities during the nineteenth century have declined to some extent today. The pace is brisker; some of the old rites have had to go. Men of substance, family, wealth, or reputation found quiet havens from intrusion in these institutions, designed by noted architects, adorned by Tiffany and La Farge. Their cuisine met the most exacting standards, and the members moved in an aura of inviolability, comfort, and seclusion. Through long plate-glass windows fronting on Fifth Avenue they could watch the world roll by, without losing an iota of their aloofness. America's great financial names made up their membership lists, and the first move made by the parvenu was to try for one of these stately institutions, a tradition that weakened in the 1940s when the welfare state deposed the aristocrat and exalted the common man. Yet the exclusive club remains perhaps one of the last symbols in public life of the right of a man to a niche of his own. It pained the Penguins, members of the Metropolitan Opera Club, to open the doors to women members in 1967, and to transfer themselves from the revered glories of the old Metropolitan Opera House to the razzle-dazzle of Lincoln Center. They had long abandoned their top hats and opera cloaks and remembered the Penguins' lively beginnings in 1893 as the Vaudeville Club only when they noticed their emblem—a nude girl shaking a tambourine.

When the Knickerbocker Club was established in 1871 by descendants of the first settlers in New York, its boast was that "mere membership is a passport to society." Henry Watterson, Kentucky newspaper editor, said that the Manhattan Club, known when it opened as the home of "Swallow-tail Democracy," linked the life of primitive old New York with that of the "wondrous great metropolis." Its membership included both Commodore Vanderbilt and Dion Boucicault, the actor. Thus the clubs wove together many elements in the community, particularly those devoted to arts and letters.

James Gordon Bennett noticed a serious lack in the early clubs, however, and when the Union Club was founded in 1836 he editorialized in his paper, the *New York Herald*: "What is the use of any social system in which women do not participate? In which their petticoat is not seen—where glossy ringlets cannot enter and make it Paradise?"

It took a long time for wives to gain entry even to limited areas of their husband's clubs, but their own club life was already full and satisfying when the barriers were lowered for dining privileges. Because of their exclusion from a dinner given for Charles Dickens in New York, they stepped into the club picture in 1868 and became the most irrepressible of club joiners, strengthening their influence through united action. On Dickens' second visit to the United States, New York's intellectuals turned out to fête him at a banquet given by the New York Press Club. But even the women journalists with husbands who were members were taboo, and the resultant indignation gave America its reputation as the incubator of the woman's club.

Jennie June and Madame Demorest, both of whom were outstanding editors themselves, joined with several other feminists to organize the Sorosis Club. This was the official starting point of a movement that eventually affected the status of women around the world and had a definite impact on the votes, morals, and ideals of the American people. Soon the Sorosis members were discussing science, education, art, drama, current events, and philanthropy in an upstairs room at Delmonico's. The jeweled worldlings who had late breakfasts downstairs with whiskered escorts in cutaway coats watched the Sorosis ladies on their way upstairs, surprised to find that some were modish, in spite of a general tendency to dragging skirts and hair netted in tumbling waterfalls.

The club members were beset by gibes, jokes, and cartoons, but as their first president, the poet Alice Cary, remarked in a dulcet voice but with absolute precision: "We have tipped the teapot." And indeed they had. Their strength grew until it became fashionable for men to complain that their wives were no longer at home when they arrived because they were so busy with their clubs. After he left the White House, Grover Cleveland spanked these errant ladies mildly in a piece he wrote for the *Ladies' Home Journal* in 1905. "I believe it should be boldly declared that the best and safest club for a woman to patronize is her home," he commented.

Despite such public disapproval the club movement rolled along at an irresistible pace. By the 1960s the General Federation of Women's Clubs was an international body with membership in fifty countries. In the United States alone 15,500 clubs with 950,000 members represented a mighty show of feminine influence. All were agreed that the Sorosis had opened the door to power and influence. The politicians were soon to know it, when woman suffrage was won in 1920 and the organizational strength of the women's clubs was felt at the polls. No aggregation of men's clubs today holds a candle to the drive and influence of its feminine counterpart. And their voices on the telephone, rounding up support, can help to condemn a play, kill a book, back a cause, select a President, spread succor for the ill and unhappy, and through a dense network across the country influence the everyday life of men, women, and children.

The telephone in itself has become a special civilizing force, by establishing myriad contacts and enlivening all areas of communication. It was regarded as little more than a toy when it was first demonstrated at the Centennial Exhibition in 1876 soon after the March day on which Alexander Graham Bell had said to his assistant over a wire: "Mr. Watson, come here: I want you." But it soon telescoped time and distance, brought city and country closer together, quickened social and business correspondence, and, eventually, became a key element in international relations. At the top level the telephone links the White House to the Kremlin, and the earth-based man to the man in space. Today great switchboards lace the myriad activities of the business and entertainment worlds. Wall Street beats to their tune. Million-dollar deals are confirmed over the wire. Recorded messages by strange voices render robot service, as greetings are sung on birthdays, prayers are repeated, and film schedules are rattled off. Answering services waken the subscriber, take calls, track down one's whereabouts, and function in various mechanical ways.

Americans, from grandparents who call their children across the country, to the teen-agers who monopolize the family telephone, are a telephoning race. They grasp the phone as instinctively as they rise to face the day. They like to place calls to far places, to keep a dozen telephones humming in their offices, to pursue their commercial and social life over the wire. They rely on their telephones for police, fire, and medical emergencies.

Most Americans have access to telephones today, but in 1880 there was only one for every thousand persons. By 1910 the ratio was one for twelve. The first telephone book was a vest-pocket affair containing 252 names, and the hand-cranked telephones on the walls provided endless merriment, involving furious winding and shouts to make oneself heard. In the country the party line as the rural gossip column was a favorite jest with old and young.

Long-distance communication between New York and Boston began in 1884, and soon a forest of crisscrossed wires and telephone poles marred the city streets. After the great blizzard of 1888, cables were run underground, and the poles disappeared. The first dial telephone was introduced in LaPorte, Indiana, in 1892, but it was 1919 before switching equipment was sufficiently developed to permit its installation in larger cities. In 1925 the first disk coin instrument made its appearance, although an early coin telephone had come into limited use in 1896. By 1937 the desk set familiar today had the bell at the base of the instrument, and this was the telephone used all through World War II. Since then it has become a more decorative object— produced in color, in gilt and black lacquer, as part of the décor, in French or Danish style, in the tiny Princess model that lights up at night, in the plug-in type to carry across a restaurant or from room to room. In 1964 the Picturephone brought the face as well as the voice into a room, a new development with infinite promise, or threat, for the future.

Today direct dialing and seven-digit phone numbers, as well as area codes, add to life's complexities, and the compact steel booths that dot city and country highways bear no resemblance to the early telephone booths which were large and ornate, with comfortable seats to encourage long conversations. Some had attendants, and telephoning was a leisurely social rite, but both the booths and the telephones were few in number and none needed to fear the stealthy tapping methods of today, or of being drawn into a mire of horror by evil anonymous calls.

Americans own 48 per cent of the world's 200 million-odd telephones, or 93.7 million, but on the per capita basis they take second place to Monaco, which has more than one for every couple. Princess Grace and Prince Rainier alone have more than one hundred telephones in their palace. The United States has slightly less than one for every couple; Sweden and Bermuda come next. Soviet Russia is close to the bottom of the list. Canadians do the most talking on their telephones, averaging 635.6 conversations per person annually to 620 in the United States. Today the telephone is a prime necessity, as well as being a civilizing force, in the American home and office, but it can also be a scourge to the nerve-wracked who cannot escape its insistent clamor and the demands of life that it involves.

Oɴ the whole, Americans, unlike most other peoples of the world, have never lacked food, except for the sparse days the Pilgrims had before they learned to use the plenty surrounding them. It did not take them long to become aware of the riches of sea and land on which they could draw. The woods were thick with game, and a thirty-pound turkey sold for a shilling in 1621, the year in which the first windmill went up in Virginia. The Indians offered the Pilgrims venison and other game and taught them to grind and cook corn. Hominy, succotash, and pone soon became staples of the American diet, amply filling the daily menu.

As the land was cultivated and farms were carved from the wilderness, cheese, milk, and butter abounded, and chicken and eggs became part of the daily fare. Children drank milk and helped to churn. They ate apple butter and gingerpears, broths and jellies. Apple trees grew as seeds were planted, and orchards and gardens were laid out. For those who lived by the sea there were more than two hundred varieties of edible fish to be caught. In the 1670s crabs a foot long and lobsters of fabulous proportions were hauled in by the Dutch off Nieuw Amsterdam. Sturgeon and terrapin, salmon and trout, sea bass, scallops and mussels were clumsily rounded up with frying pans, hooks, and nets. Families lived on what would pass for luxury fare today— quail and shad, snipe and plover, and a rich assortment of wild berries. Pigeon was served in every inn and home, and children thrived on the meat of deer, moose, bear, and antelope. Potatoes sold for twopence a pound and, until their true function as root vegetables was recognized, they were soaked in grape juice, rosewater, and sugar. Artichokes, watermelon, and monster strawberries were any man's fare.

The great trees of the virgin forest poured forth their wealth of sap, and maple sugar became one of the indigenous delicacies of America. Cane sugar and molasses were imported from the West Indies to sweeten further the American palate. Molasses and ginger were freely used in early American cooking, and the echo remains in New England today. John Adams, who invariably began his Sunday dinner with Indian corn pudding, molasses, and butter, and then moved on to mutton, bacon, and eggs, always maintained that molasses was a factor in American independence, because of the Molasses Act the British Parliament passed in 1733. In the Adams era dessert came first on the menu, and apple pie became well entrenched as a staple breakfast food. It was a standing jest at Yale that for more than a hundred years every supper served included apple pie. There was no accounting for regional tastes. For instance, Bostonians liked their eggs brown; New Yorkers preferred theirs to be white.

The frontiersmen clearing the wilderness were hearty eaters, and the South soon became noted for its food, with the blended skills of Creoles, Anglo-Saxons, and Negroes. The Gallic touch was introduced after the French alliance of 1778, and the restaurants of New Orleans, like Antoine's and Galatoire's, have come down in history as among the classic greats, with their crab gumbo, crawfish bisque, fricassees, and desserts heavily flavored with rum and brandy, like tipsy cake and the popular syllabub. Elsewhere in the country the new arrivals brought with them their native food tastes and inherited recipes, so that American fare was cosmopolitan first, and indigenous afterward. It had a rich and varied infusion, from French sauces to Italian pasta, but from that point on it developed a character of its own. Yet even up to the time of World War II Europeans thought of Americans as eating like savages. The interchanges of recent years, however, have persuaded the most prejudiced that Americans do not subsist entirely on hot dogs and hamburgers, soft drinks and hot breads, pancakes, corn on the cob, and baked beans. Today the food of all nations is offered in sumptuous, average, or simple surroundings across the United States, and the restaurants of New York, New Orleans, and San Francisco rate with the best in the world.

They now have the resources of the aseptic supermarket which has taken the place of the picturesque street market of the eighteenth century—bustling with life, bright with color, fragrant with meadow scents. Philadelphia had a big one on High Street from which people bought their food until 1745. New York had five, where as many as seventy-five thousand pigeons were sold in a day. Lemons and almonds, raisins and oils, wines and olives were brought in from Europe, but the small householder bought his staples in little grocery stores. Toward the end of the eighteenth century many housewives had their cakes baked in professional ovens. Caterers supplied cakes, desserts, and syllabubs for special occasions, and crumpets and muffins were served hot twice a day. Street vendors pushed their carts through the streets, ringing their bells and crying their wares above the din of the barrel organs. "Fine, ripe and red! Buy my strawberries," was a common street cry. Milk, oysters, and sweet potatoes were hawked in this noisy manner, while the butcher at his open-air stall wore a tall hat and blood-stained apron as he carved joints. "I did not dream that such a variety of sweet potatoes, peas and beans existed on the globe, as I saw in Charleston market," commented Anne Royall, a visiting journalist taking notes in the 1820s. For the first time she beheld bananas, fresh from the West Indies, and marveled at the "astonishing quantities" of oranges and "all the nuts of the globe."

A favorite street cry in the 1820s was the ice cream vendor's, "I Scream for Ice Cream." This delicacy had come within the reach of the average citizen. It was supposed to have come originally from China and was a costly luxury little used in the eighteenth century, although George Washington made it and Dolley Madison served it so often that she made it a fashion, mixing it with strawberries from her garden. At the time of the Civil War ice cream with spun sugar was molded by the caterers into all manner of forms—forts, cannon, bridges, turrets, castles, and other conceits. It was the age of the elaborate dessert—of Nesselrode pudding, trifles, custards, blanc mange, and jellies of all kinds, and these abounded in the lush days that followed the war.

In 1846 Nancy Johnson invented the hand-cranked portable ice cream freezer that spelled the doom of the pot freezer, in which the ingredients were beaten by hand, then frozen in a pan of ice and salt. Five years later the first large wholesale ice cream business in America was set up in Baltimore. Today ice cream is used in much simpler form but greater variety, and Americans eat more of it than any other people in the world. Of the 240 flavors on the market, including a mixture of peanut butter and jelly, vanilla is the favorite, with chocolate and strawberry coming next. There are well-defined regional responses to various flavors. Floridians like coconut ice cream. New Englanders have a preference for frozen pudding—tutti-frutti with a rum base,

Maple sugar is a native delicacy. Sugaring time in Vermont was the occasion for merrymaking once the hard work was done. Whole families went to the woods to watch the maple trees being tapped and to share in the proceedings.

"Good heavens, friend, how can you wear an overcoat and look so cool this warm weather?" "I always bring my overcoat down town, as I find after drinking a glass of 'Blakely's Blizzard Soda,' drawn from his 'Arctic Fountain,' that I am cold the balance of the day."

This advertisement for the Blizzard soda fountain may have been overstated, but the refreshment stands were as popular as the illustration shows.

The root-beer seller with his peregrinating stand was the forerunner of today's soda and hot-dog dispensers. The thirsty farmer paused along the way for refreshment costing three cents a glass. Watercolor by Nicolino V. Calyo.

The milkman of 1850 arrived with horse and wagon, and sometimes brought his family along, as did Henry Keim, driving from door to door with his demurely hatted daughters, Caroline and Teresa Kate. Watercolor sketch by William Gross.

traceable to the early rum trade with the West Indies. Providence gives top rating to coffee flavor, which is unpopular in the West. With good refrigeration much of the ice cream bought is now taken home to be consumed there.

The ice cream soda, first thought up by a Frenchman who spiked plain soda water with syrups, came into view at the semicentennial of the Franklin Institute in Philadelphia in 1874. The ice cream cone was romantically introduced at the St. Louis Exposition of 1904. An ice cream vendor named Charles E. Menches offered a sandwich and flowers simultaneously to his girl. Lacking a vase, he took a layer of cardboard from the wrapped sandwich and funneled it into a cone to hold the flowers. It occurred to him that the cone would also make a good holder for ice cream, and an edible cone followed. The public picked up this novelty with enthusiasm, and it became one of the vagabond joys of this happy-hearted exposition.

The sundae was created to stimulate the Sunday ice cream trade during the prohibition years. Confections were something of an antidote to the great drought of the period. By the 1930s Howard Johnson's wayside shrines, offering such delectables as passion fruit ice and sumptuous banana splits, had become a national institution. Popsicles, bars, cups, and sandwiches of ice cream picked up along the road soon were delighting the junior population, and the Good Humor man had begun his merry reign as the prince of street vendors.

Hamburger and hot-dog stands followed logically enough. The brothers Mack and Richard McDonald, who started a one-stand operation in San Bernardino in 1948, sold 408 million hamburgers in 1965, along with 120 million pounds of French fried potatoes, through 710 concessions in forty-four states. Today the country has an abundance of snack bars, juice bars, oyster bars, milk bars, and drugstore counters and cafeterias, where the hurried may snatch a meal on the run. The quick-lunch counter now takes care of much of the midday eating that once was done at home. The custom began with a restaurant that opened in New York in 1877, serving baked beans or corned beef, mush, and bread and butter, all for a penny, and for people in a hurry.

The free-lunch counter had much more epicurean significance, and free-loaders could lean on an African marble and Mexican onyx bar in the Hotel Vendôme in New York in 1892 and gorge on the "most tempting food cooked by master hands," according to *Leslie's Illustrated Newspaper*. The custom began in the West, where two-fisted drinkers were bolstered at the bar with clams and cheese, chili con carne, and potato chips. The custom spread to the East, and sustained many in times of hardship or penury. The college student could practically subsist on the generous pickings he rounded up in the saloon. The *New York Herald* noted in 1907 that a "man who would live on nothing a year . . . could study the cooking of the various chefs and learn where to find the best chicken or salad or roast, fish or oysters, and by carefully selecting his courses he could make an excellent dinner within a radius of a few blocks."

This public beneficence began to dwindle around 1910, but cafeterias and self-service restaurants like Horn & Hardart's came next to hasten the diner on his way. Childs' windows, full of pancakes, set their stamp on the national life, and soon one chain of restaurants followed another, from the most luxurious to the all-night coffee spots that live by the patronage of the truck driver and the late reveler. The variety and availability of eating places in the United States give unlimited access to food and drink.

Perhaps because of climatic conditions and restless habits Americans consume more soft drinks today than any other people in the world. The pioneers liked them, too, as well as being hearty devotees of the strongest drinks. Even the children became accustomed to cider. New Englanders preferred it, but the descendants of the Dutch and the Germans were faithful to beer. Rum was the standby for funerals, weddings, and other special occasions, and flips and punches, hot and cold, were served in mugs and tankards. Fine wines and cordials were imported from Spain, Portugal, and the Canary Islands—Madeira was considered the peerless drink. The cocktail, which made its appearance as early as 1806, has been traced to an apothecary in New Orleans, to Dutch origin, and to various other sources, but there was no doubt that shrub, the *apéritif* made from rum and red wine, was traceable to Benjamin Franklin. Roman punch was a lordly drink for banquets, and eggnog was first made with ale.

The pioneer women could face up to strong drinks more readily than the Victorians, who confined themselves to port and sherry. But except for some of the frontier women who drank as lustily as their men, even the most addicted could never match the hard-liquor tipplers of the prohibition era or of the 1960s. Americans as a whole are a thirsty race, downing fabulous quantities of sodas, soft drinks, coffee, and tea. Their nonalcoholic tastes run strongly to coffee and Coca-Cola. Coffee became the national drink chiefly because of the Boston Tea Party. Tea had reigned supreme until five hundred Boston women pledged themselves to give up this British drink, and after the Boston Tea Party there was no further question about it. Coffee was first mentioned in 1670 when a Boston woman got a license to sell "coffee and chochaletto." The inns seized on this stimulating drink, and coffeehouses were faring well in the early eighteenth century. By the end of the Civil War coffee was overwhelmingly the leading American drink, a situation that has not changed in a hundred years. But tea dances became popular at that time and again after World War I. In general, however, tea drinking became a somewhat effete custom, left largely to poets, artists, and women, except as a social gesture, or to allay a tendency to the widely prevalent dyspepsia. Meanwhile, strong dark coffee was drunk at every opportunity. Instant coffee came into use after World War II, shattering the established custom of a well-made brew, but leaving countless stand-patters in the field.

The eating habits of the nation changed radically shortly before the Civil War when Sylvester Graham (1794–1851), a frail zealot from a family of ministers, pounded home his theories on nutrition, accepted today but iconoclastic at the time. He popularized whole-wheat flour, and his name is perpetuated in the Graham bread and crackers widely consumed since his time. He made the nation health-conscious as he preached diet, exercise, and the water treatment advocated by Vincenz Priessnitz. His boardinghouses and resort hotels encouraged early rising, hard pallets, exercise, cold sponges, and abstinence from meat, pastry, honey, eggs, shellfish, milk, tea, coffee, liquor, and snacks. The public followed him slavishly, particularly the cultists of the era who had their own reform movements. He was backed by Horace Greeley, Bronson Alcott, James Parton, Amelia Bloomer, and other individualists as he lectured on temperance, preventive medicine, and food reform. Before his lifelong campaign ended the food habits of more than two centuries had been radically changed. All were cereal-conscious as Battle Creek poured out its ready-to-eat breakfast foods. Grapenuts threatened to dislodge porridge from the family table. The dieters and food faddists of today, the calorie counters and open-air enthusiasts—all are inheritors of the Graham tradition.

Up to 1900 American women baked most of their own bread, but when gas took the place of coal in heating ovens, loaves were rolled out on the chain-store plan. Graham's theories received support in the 1940s, however, when the vitamins that had been lost from the native grain had to be replaced by chemical means. Moreover, the third of a pint of milk a day ordained for children at the time of the Civil War had become a quart a day in the twentieth century, with visible results in stronger bones, better teeth, and more resistance to infection.

Today both young and old haunt the supermarket and accept it as one of the all-time great changes in the food customs of the American people. Originally it was the dream child of George Huntington Hartford, a Maine youth who embarked on a fabulous career after watching tea being unloaded at a New York dock in 1859. It occurred to him to buy a shipload and sell it on the docks. Next he moved into a little store, painted red and gold, and hung up one of the first illuminated signs, with the letter T lit by gas. Soon his red wagon drawn by eight dapple-gray horses drove through the streets advertising the Great American Tea Company with brass bands and circus ballyhoo. Coffee

60

World of Plenty

came next, and his wagons toured the country byways as well as the city streets. He opened his first economy store in Jersey City and by 1920 there were three thousand of them across the country. The Atlantic & Pacific Tea Company or, as it is better known, the A & P, became one of the great enterprises of the world, and its founders had altered a nation's food habits. Today the supermarket is a commonplace and flowering from its core is the shopping center, adding convenience, economy, and a whiff of romance to a business that greatly affects the taste and folkways of the American people.

Its ancient predecessor, the village store, was a homely and entertaining gathering place in all parts of the country. The cracker-barrel and pot-bellied-stove tradition became firmly grounded in the public mind. Like the supermarket it dealt in the essentials of life, but managed to display them in picturesque confusion—the opposite of the orderly rows of products offered today's housewives. Men haunted it more than women, for it served frequently as post office and town hall, and matters of life, death, and national policy were debated in its smoky atmosphere. Lamp chimneys, bacon, buttons, rock candy, paint and bread, bolts of cloth and kegs of nails, barrels of whale oil, and harness lay about for the farmer's inspection. The crackers were sure to be there, and the rich aroma of coffee, molasses, licorice, and tobacco were all part of its hazy charm. Often the farmers bartered eggs, butter, and milk for buckshot, a skillet, or shoes for a child.

But when the mail-order catalogue arrived from the big stores in New York and Chicago, the village store lost some of its prestige. This link with the larger world had a strong impact on the choice of clothes, household furnishings, and possessions of the American family. It retains some of its power today, but in the late nineteenth century it was almost as indispensable to the farmer as his cows. Variously known as the Farmer's Bible or the Nation's Wishbook it could not have been more treasured, for it offered all the necessities of life, from christening font to tombstone. Its pages were loaded with romance for young and old, listing everything from sheet music to phaetons, from bridal veils to rose bushes, from diamond rings to dishpans, from rocking chairs to top hats. Each issue unrolled an endless panorama of possibilities, and it found an honored place in the average household.

In the home the emphasis today in both food and drink is on health and simplicity, with the basic needs of the growing young in mind, as well as of the calorie counters of a weight-conscious age. Dining is no longer the hearty, time-consuming rite that it once was; it points more directly to the knowledgeable palate and the trim waistline. In the early eighteenth century visitors commented on the unhealthy look of the American people. It was fashionable for both men and women to be slender and drooping at that time. In 1837 Francis J.

Grund, in *The Americans in Their Moral, Social, or Political Relations*, commented on the feeble look of America's congressmen. He observed that the women disliked corpulence in their men and, indeed, "An American exquisite must not measure more than 24 inches around the chest; his face must be pale, thin and long: and he must be spindle-shanked or he won't do for a party." Dr. Oliver Wendell Holmes, a shrewd observer, found the American of that era "pale, pasty-faced, narrow-chested, spindle-shanked . . . a mere walking mannikin to advertise the latest cut of the fashionable tailor."

Things swung to the other extreme in the 1880s when women prided themselves on keeping their husbands and children hearty and well-fed. Today, of course, obesity in either sex is regarded as a social blight, a threat to health and success, and in the 1960s even from the White House came the message that everyone was dieting—one daughter taking a single meal a day, the First Lady fitting herself into a size-ten dress, the President curbing his taste for tapioca. But after the Civil War the national health improved greatly with better fare and a growing sense of hygiene. Men and women had better teeth, straighter carriage, and they lived longer. The tallest men seemed to come from Kentucky and the western states, and the smallest from New York, New England, and New Jersey. In the 1880s clothing manufacturers changed their scale of sizes to provide for the larger measurements of their customers. After 1850 not only was the population taller as a whole but longevity was becoming a problem as well as a blessing. Geriatrics is an acknowledged science today.

The great advances made in agricultural equipment during the nineteenth century soon affected the eating and buying habits of the nation. When the McCormick reaper appeared in 1832, with its wake of drillers, mowers, plows and binders, life on the farm was revolutionized. The drift west was strongest in the 1830s, 1840s, and 1850s, when New Englanders struck out for fresh land, set up in business, and spread their antislavery drive in their new environment. Canals, railroads, and highways opened up fresh markets and the Great Lakes were linked with metropolitan markets. More than twelve thousand vessels made port at Chicago in 1870, and by that time twenty-seven bridges spanned the Chicago River.

Nearly four million farms had been dug from the wilderness by the 1880s, and half the annual output of precious metal in the world was being mined in America. Chicago and San Francisco had grown up almost in one generation. Factories sprawled toward the prairie, and thousands of workers made reapers, axes, and plows; whiskey, soap, and cookstoves; shoes and watches; pianos and melodeons. Refrigeration, canning, and ice packing affected nearly every facet of handling and distributing food. Cold storage was another landmark, and this was followed by air conditioning, so that the deep freezer and cooled rooms are now accepted routinely by the American housewife. This equipment has reached its apogee in the United States, with hospitals, schools, theaters, public buildings, and private homes of the more affluent type benefiting by its use. Congressmen no longer depend on their palm-leaf fans. Diners sit in comfort in air-cooled restaurants. The tinkle of ice is an undercurrent of social life today, of cocktail parties and leisurely evenings on the patio.

In 1867 the earliest refrigerator car was used for shipping perishables from Chicago to New York, after refrigeration had proved its worth during the Civil War. The packers put drive behind this discovery and soon refrigerated cars were conveying California and Florida fruits and vegetables to New York, and seafood to Chicago. Freighters carried food around the world, bringing pineapples from Hawaii to Chicago and breakfast foods from New York to Bombay.

Fruits and vegetables were put up in glass in California around 1860, but canning began as early as 1820 and was based on experimental work in Britain and France. It was an expensive process until 1847 when tin cans were first turned out cheaply by a stamping process. Canned milk was an invaluable standby during the Civil War, and five years later thirty million cans of food were available in the United States. Canning factories opened across the country after 1878, and soon every variety of food, from lobster to curries, was subjected to this process. There was a lingering suspicion of the safety of canned foods until the Pure Food and Drug Act of 1906 removed the element of hazard. Now manufacturers turn out a total of forty-eight billion cans a year, and it is estimated that each American empties about 252 annually, with contents ranging from baby food to caviar, camera film, or missile parts. The early cans were decorative at times, shaped like lanterns, globes, roulette wheels, or Humpty Dumpty. The Boston Tea Party adorned one; a farm scene another. The folklore touch was strong, but now cans are more or less standard in shape, bearing well-known brand names.

Baby foods reached the market in 1928 when Clarence Birdseye, who had taken out a patent in 1925, set this great revolution in motion. Gerber's 5 original varieties have grown to 130, and today's baby downs approximately 15 jars a week of his assorted foods. Prebottled formulas in disposal containers are another mother's aid in the world of today. Life has been made more glamorous for mother if not for baby. Much of the early child mortality was due to tainted food. Strange remedies were first applied, but the march of medicine and scientific feeding together cut infant mortality by two thirds in the first half of the twentieth century. Children had to eat strong game and tipple a little in colonial days. They were often hung with amulets in a superstitious age, and Mrs. Thomas Jefferson's cure for the bite of a mad dog was to plunge the dog in cold water every twenty-four hours for twenty days and rub the victim as soon as possible with ashes of tree soil and hog's lard. Rattlesnake root was a favorite remedy for a variety of afflictions, including pleurisy. Pearls, white amber, and coral were powdered or dissolved, and gold and precious stones were often hung in little bags around the neck. Governor Winthrop sent to Britain for the powdered horn of the mythical unicorn. Strange elixirs, syrups, and oils were supposed to ward off death, and herb juices were guaranteed to make the dumb speak. The virtues of cod livers were detected before cod-liver oil became a family standby.

The housewife used the herbs that grew by her kitchen door, for both cooking and healing. She was the herb doctor and medicine man of her era. Living close to the earth she used roots, herbs, and molds long before penicillin became one of the miracle finds of the twentieth century. She knew how to probe for a bullet, trim a wound with a knife, and sew up a gash. With a salve of pounded slippery-elm bark or bear's grease she anointed wounds. The duties of a midwife often fell to her, and with hammer and chisel she knocked out children's teeth when they were too far gone to be treated with cloves. The farmers' teeth were pulled by traveling tinkers, and it was not until a dental college opened in Baltimore in 1840 that American dentistry, later so widely respected around the world, had its professional start.

Sassafras, rhubarb, and sweet basil were among the standbys of the early housewife, but synthetic nostrums made headway in the nineteenth century, encouraged by the success of Lydia Pinkham of Massachusetts, whose name became a household word as her tonic enlivened innumerable fainting and anemic girls. She triggered a spirited army of medicine men who touted their wares by kerosene torches on rickety wooden platforms. Some played tambourines or banjos. Dr. William A. Rockefeller, father of the great John, sold his pills in small towns all through the Middle West during the 1850s. Tennessee Claflin, with her sister Victoria Woodhull who was later to run for the Presidency of the United States, mingled spiritualism with nostrums and set up as a cancer specialist, selling a potion brewed by her witchlike mother. It was all part of the era of magnetism and mesmerism when women prepared for their evening parties with light trickles of magnetic energy, a mild foretaste of the shock treatments of today. Leechcraft and cooking were closely allied in this dim and dubious world. Bleeding and purging were applied for nearly every ill, and angelica roots with wine vinegar were used to subdue the plague. External applications of ale, herbs, and fruits were supposed to invigorate the melancholy.

Visiting doctors were often paid with a cow or a cask of wine.

They usually wore dun-colored coats and black breeches, and carried gold-headed canes and snuff boxes in colonial days. Their wigs were curled and powdered, and their visits were impressive occasions for their patients. Some had gone to Paris, London, Leyden, or Edinburgh for a medical education, and on their return they helped to offset the inroads of the circulating quacks. Dr. Benjamin Rush of Philadelphia established the first free medical dispensary in the country in 1780 and distinguished medical men emerged in all the leading cities. But charlatans abounded at the turn of the century and high-blood-pressure patients were still being bled in 1905. The alcoholic was invited to take the Keeley cure, as he is offered the support of Alcoholics Anonymous today. But the magazines started digging into the world of medical fakery, and in 1906 the Pure Food and Drug Act bore down on nostrums, and the newspapers became wary of advertising them—a movement that was renewed in a wider form in 1966.

The steady progress of medicine through research and discovery, made possible in recent years by huge grants from foundations, has changed the lives of innumerable sufferers. Pasteurization, hygiene, discovery, and prevention have cleared the boards of ancient ills. One contagious disease after another has been wiped out, leaving heart disease and cancer the greatest threats to human life. New remedies reach the market every day, and many fall by the wayside. More than 70 per cent of the drugs on sale in the mid-1960s were discovered since World War II. Among notable drugs known earlier were insulin, introduced in 1922; the sulfanilamides, in 1935; and streptomycin, in 1943. The Salk vaccine was used in 1953. Now there is concentration on birth control, chemotherapy, and microbiology. With it all, health-conscious Americans spend more than $375 million a year for vitamin pills, enriched cereals, and fortified breakfast drinks. According to a Senate report at the end of 1966, half of all Americans are chronically ill and the national death rate is rising steadily. It is estimated that 87.3 million persons suffer from at least one chronic condition, but the great age to which many live is a factor in this. More cases are diagnosed, thereby swelling the totals. The suicide rate is rising, too. There were 20,588 proved cases of suicide in 1964, and it is now the ninth cause of death for American men. But the statistics of today cannot be accurately measured against the less searching records of the past. The restless march goes on. Advances in medicine keep more people alive to a later age, and food and drink, as always, play a heavy role in their medical history.

With it all, life in some ways has been made easier, with such accessory benefits as credit cards, part of a $633-million-a-year business. With these a man can order a choice dinner, charter a plane, or go on a safari if he is so inclined, without an immediate pull on his pocket-

A New England country store in 1898, as elsewhere throughout the nation, was the trading center for everything from buttons to kerosene, and from kegs of nails to banjos. It was also the favorite gathering ground of the local wits and sages, who settled around the pot-bellied stove to discuss the state of the nation as well as the cross-roads gossip. For generations this farmers' parliament was an integral part of American rural life. These sturdy New Englanders reflected the larger world in the cut of their whiskers—the storekeeper favored the imperial of the professional man; the shoppers sported sideburns and an echo of Dundreary. Chase & Sanborn advertisement, 1898.

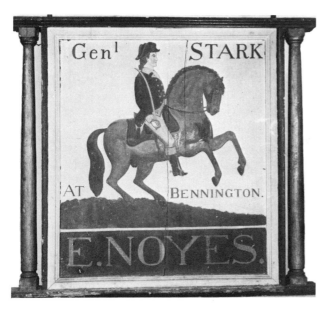

The swinging signs of the taverns were welcome sights to the dusty and thirsty traveler along the roads of New England.

The Tontine Coffee House at the corner of Wall and Water streets, New York, was built in 1792 and soon became part of the financial history of the nation. It housed the Stock Exchange and insurance offices, and here merchants, traders, and bankers chaffered over their transactions. Big deals were frequently made over the coffee cups at Tontine's. Painting by Francis Guy.

book. An endless variety of places to eat besides the home are at his command. The catering system has been revived with mobile pizza trucks. Chicken Delight dinners are left at thousands of homes in forty-four states. The entire family is frequently in motion—the car or station wagon always ready to take the children to school, father to the train, mother to her job or to a community meeting. With all this restless flitting about, families eat at odd hours and in unconventional ways—in the dining room, the living room, the porch, the kitchen, the garden, or the rumpus room. As often as not they use television trays, paper mats and napkins instead of linen, and synthetic cutlery in place of silver.

The scarcity of maids has much to do with this. Whereas in the eighteenth and nineteenth centuries all but the most impoverished families could afford a maid, every class suffers today from the lack of servants. The frilly parlormaid, the aproned cook, the uniformed nurse, the regal butler, and the good general houseworker are equally elusive. The unlimited supply of European maids who once passed through Ellis Island and gladly worked for fifteen dollars a month with room and board, tapered off as they found employment in factories and shops. Now the Negro girls who have been invaluable aids for a century are finding more satisfying jobs. Thus the American housewife today, like her colonial ancestor, has to do her own providing, cooking, and cleaning, but she is helped to an uncanny degree by electrical appliances and the wonders of the supermarket.

Not until World War II did the present revival of fine cuisine take place, but at various periods taverns, hotels, and restaurants have been a sure index to the eating habits of the American people and to the extent of their travels. In the 1840s New York had ten thousand strangers passing through the city in a year; there were sixteen million in 1965. Today there are 22,692 hotels in the United States, and 62,014 motels, tourist courts and camps, fashioned to all financial circumstances, from the great spa hotels to the inns that still dot the land. Their history is that of the growing country, its changing interests and increasing sophistication.

The hotel of today may represent the quintessence of luxury and convenience for the traveler, but it was preceded by that much more picturesque institution, the tavern, which for a century and a half welcomed the early sojourners and offered considerably more than today's snack bar or roadside stand provides. It served as countinghouse, trading post and news agency, circulating broadsides and proclamations in the days before the Revolution. The innkeepers often conducted auctions or arbitrations, and the opening of the mailbags was a social event. In fact, the tavern predated the country store as a community base of operations, and was variously used for court hearings, civil and military trials and, occasionally, as a prison or a hospital. More often it was the scene of weddings, parties, and dances.

Its swinging signs, many with the heraldic touch and bearing such names as "The Harp and Crown," "The Bunch of Grapes," or "Ship Aground," were welcome beacons along the way. Taverns were dotted a mile apart on the Mohawk turnpike between Albany and Utica. Before 1750 Philadelphia and New York had three coffeehouses apiece. Later New York's Tontine Coffee House became famous for its stock transactions, and Fraunces Tavern for George Washington's farewell to his men. Some of the inns had distinguishing characteristics, like the Indian Queen in Baltimore, which boasted a bell in every room, something that Abigail Adams had failed to find in the President's House. At the Ship Tavern in Salem, singing, dancing, and games were forbidden, but lodging and drinks could be had for three shillings a day.

Alighting from his sleigh or coach, warmth and comfort soon enveloped the traveler as he entered the tavern and found his way to the bar where Medford and Jamaica rum, cider, Madeira, or hot spiced drinks awaited him. After 1830 cocktails and juleps were added to the fare, and toasts—so named because of the hot toast floated in wine or spirits to warm a drink—had been in fashion since the seventeenth century. The most famous was Stephen Decatur's in 1816 at Norfolk, Virginia: "Our country! In her intercourse with foreign nations may she always be in the right; but our country, right or wrong!"

Toasts were encouraged in the taverns, where the atmosphere in general was conducive to relaxation and interludes of backgammon, dice, cards, or ninepins. Pewter shone faintly against the walls. Copperplate prints linked the New World taverns with the old British pubs. A touch of history often clung to these early inns, since they were the resting places of the great as well as of the raffish. "The Sign of the Buck Horn" on the Bloomingdale Road in New York, with antlers over its doorway, was called the last stopping place for codgers, old and young. This post tavern had a set of rules not uncommon at the time:

> *Four pence a night for Bed*
> *Six pence with Supper*
> *No more than five to sleep in one bed*
> *No boots to be worn in bed*
> *Organ Grinders to sleep in the Wash house*
> *No dogs allowed upstairs*
> *No beer allowed in the kitchen*
> *No Razor Grinders or Tinkers taken in*

In Charleston the early inns had summerhouses in their gardens for outdoor dining. But the reign of this type of hostelry began to dim with the opening of the Tremont Hotel in Boston in 1829. Designed by Isaiah Rogers, an exponent of Greek Revival architecture, it made a deep impression, with its Ionic columns, fine rooms and service, and plumbing arrangements of a new order. Instead of meandering corridors it had straight passageways, and an air of space and order, in place of the odd nooks and corners associated with the early hostelries.

Even Dickens, as caustic about the early hotels as he was about other American institutions, commented favorably on its "galleries, colonnades, piazzas, and passages." The Tremont, with its marble and plush, pier mirrors, gilt, heavy carpets, and carved walnut furniture, set the pattern for the hotels that followed. Nothing like its drawing rooms, reading rooms, and upstairs parlors for ladies had been seen before in America. Ceilings were high and vistas long, and the hall, ancestor of today's lobby, had a desk and a room clerk. Rogers next applied his architectural talent to the Greek-colonnaded Charleston Hotel, the second St. Charles Hotel in New Orleans, the Astor House in New York, and the Burnet House in Cincinnati, where Presidential history would be made.

The importance of hotels as political centers was established at an early date. The introduction of macadamized roads had speeded the flow of traffic, and politicians flocked to urban centers to voice their views. Such hostelries as the Ebbitt House and Willard's in Washington, the Fifth Avenue Hotel and Astor in New York, the St. Charles in New Orleans, the Spotswood in Richmond, the Palace in San Francisco, and Chicago's Palmer House made political as well as social history, for they were closely identified with men of power in the fast-growing country. Caucuses involving Presidential elections were held in the gold-fringed red damask hotel parlors, and political banquets flourished under the shimmering candles of pillared dining rooms. Lincoln was identified with Willard's, the Fifth Avenue Hotel, and the Astor House, where a special parlor was reserved for him, just as the Hotel Carlyle in New York became associated later with John F. Kennedy and Lyndon B. Johnson.

The luxury hotel quickly took root in a nation where people traveled freely and visitors came from different parts of the world. By the late sixties there were fortunes to be spent, architects to design big hostelries, and visitors to fill them. The Palmer House and the Palace soon ranked among the premier hotels of the world. "It is more like an elegantly appointed home than a mere resting-place for such birds of passage as ourselves," wrote Lady Duffus Hardy after a visit to the Palmer House in 1879. The halls were lined with *fauteuils*; the suites had private baths; the electric bells and lights invoked all manner of service; and the main floor, with its Egyptian touches, had a network of shops, a ten-pin alley, a bar, and restaurants. Beyond that it had its roof garden, its famous barber shop with silver dollars set into the floor, and a prize collection of guests from Sarah Bernhardt to Rudyard

Saratoga Springs was the most fashionable nineteenth-century spa in America
and the United States Hotel was one of the huge caravanseries that housed its
visitors. When Albert Berghaus made this sketch in 1859, the Southerners
who made up much of its summer population, driving north in great coaches
laden with trunks, were heading toward war. Fashionably dressed men and
women paraded on the hotel's wide piazzas, and a constant whirl of vehicles

stirred up dust around the hotel as stagecoaches, victorias, landaulets, and other carriages came and went. After the war its character changed. Financiers, gamblers, the bonanza kings from the West, carpetbaggers, war profiteers, and the theatrical and social celebrities of the era filled its rambling hotels, drank the mineral waters at the Springs, and enjoyed horse racing, gambling, regattas, great balls, and diverse forms of entertainment.

Kipling. It must be said that Kipling deplored the hotel, describing it as a "gilded and mirrored rabbit warren." But farm boys and girls from the prairies saved up money for a few days of its glory on their honeymoons, to dine on boned quail in plumage, and to parade with celebrities among the palms of the roof garden.

In San Francisco the Palace Hotel outdid all the other hotels in cost, nearly five million dollars going into its construction and appointments—a massive sum for the 1870s. It had thirty-four elevators and its chief fascination was its Grand Court. Crowds lined its tiered galleries to watch the four-in-hands disgorging celebrities or to catch a glimpse of Sarah Bernhardt's puma. Its original magnificence and rose bay windows were wiped out in the Great Fire, but it continues today as the Sheraton Palace and is still a focus of social life on the coast. The same sense of tradition, elegance, and opulence has been sustained at the Plaza Hotel in New York, one of the few surviving examples of the plush Victorian era. Chains of hotels in the streamlined pattern now cater to growing hordes of transients.

The Waldorf, which has housed most of the world's celebrities at one time or another, was called the largest in existence when it opened in the 1890s. Its Peacock Alley, its thousand bedrooms and 750 private baths, its Sèvres china, fine cuisine, and fleet of green and red carriages awaiting customers, were far removed from the spit boxes and trundle beds of the early hostelries. China and silver had taken the place of pewter and wood. The lumbering carriages and coaches had been replaced by simpler vehicles and fleet sleighs. New standards in service and equipment had been established, a tradition maintained in the building that replaced the original Waldorf-Astoria, one of the few historic hotels surviving the general demolition of today.

A tradition of fine cuisine, which was to affect the food habits of Americans as a whole, was fostered in the Waldorf and other great hotels, some of which became as well known for their restaurants as for the glittering air of luxury that pervaded the public rooms. Great restaurants flourished in the nineteenth century, as people prospered, traveled, and developed epicurean tastes. Hotel czars like Paran Stevens of Boston's Revere House, who is regarded today as the earliest operator of a hotel chain; the great Oscar Tschirky, whose reputation as the Waldorf chef is inseparable from the best in American cuisine; and the Delmonico brothers revived the gourmet interest that had flourished in the time of Thomas Jefferson. Oscar created stunning effects for every President in his time as well as for rulers from all parts of the world. J. P. Morgan would have no one else supervise a meal when he dined at the Waldorf. When it became the fashion to name new dishes after celebrities—a custom that persists at Sardi's, Reuben's, and other restaurants today—Oscar gave this custom the classical role by initiating the popular Caesar salad, which has been freely used to control the waistlines of Hollywood celebrities.

Lobster Newburg, an all-time favorite, owes its inception to Delmonico's. It was known first as Lobster Wenberg, in honor of Ben Wenberg, a popular patron of this restaurant. But when stocky, genial Lorenzo Delmonico quarreled with Wenberg, his devastating revenge was to rename his famous concoction Lobster Newburg. Chicken à la king became a popular dish when Foxhall Keene, son of a Wall Street operator named James Keene, suggested the creamed dish that has been the standby of women's luncheons ever since. Parker House rolls were first introduced by Harvey D. Parker of Boston, who also did much to break up fixed hours for meals in the restaurant he opened in Boston in 1855, featuring à la carte fare at any hour.

Filet of sole Marguery à la Diamond Jim was named in honor of the leading trencherman of his day—Diamond Jim Brady—who thought nothing of breakfasting on a gallon of orange juice, beefsteak, hominy, eggs, flapjacks, chops, and fried potatoes. He snacked on oysters and clams in midmorning and by lunch time was ready for two broiled lobsters, deviled crabs, salad, and several varieties of pie. Toward evening he coped with a fifteen-course dinner. He was the champion, but he was not alone in this type of gorging, which was encouraged in the great hotels of New York and Saratoga in the 1890s.

In this era the cosmopolitan influence was being felt in urban centers, and the habit of dining late was gaining ground. Americans had always preferred early meals, and the hotels had catered to this taste, which had its roots in the necessities of rural and farm life. They were slow to abandon the early pattern, and fixed-style menus may be found today in various parts of the country, but usually along with à la carte fare. However, from the 1830s on the à la carte European system had been gradually replacing the American plan, which entailed ponderous meals at fixed hours. At the close of the nineteenth century the hotels, while still serving enormous midday meals, were adding dinner dishes to the supper menu. Catering was a well-established institution because of the great number of people who lived in boardinghouses or hotels. In the cities breakfast and dinner were served piping hot in silver-plated dishes kept in steamheated copper containers and conveyed by hand wagon. Many businessmen started their day with catered breakfasts, where today they might stop at a drugstore counter or snack bar. Even the most traveled remained immune to the Continental breakfast, and continued to down fruit, cereal, ham and eggs, pancakes, chops, hot breads, and, in New England, apple pie.

The speakeasy decade, with its hidden restaurants and scarcity of good liquor, inevitably dimmed the enthusiasm of hotel and restaurant owners, with few exceptions, to aspire to Brillat-Savarin standards. The Depression vitiated the restaurant business still further, and World War II led to a tightening of purse strings everywhere. But the 1950s and 1960s brought a great resurgence of the culinary art, and a diversity of restaurants without parallel in American history. Even the early taverns are being reproduced in a widening string of pubs across the country, from Dawson's English Pub in New York to the Fox and Hounds in St. Louis, where chess is played as of old against highbacked niche seats. San Francisco's White Horse Taverne is a copy of the Edinburgh original. The Golden Bee of the Broadmoor Hotel in Colorado Springs is an authentic 150-year-old English pub dismantled and shipped across the Atlantic. Ye Mucky Duck in Los Angeles features a dart board, and horseshoes are pitched at the Saucy Swan in Costa Mesa, farther down the California coast. Thus history repeats itself.

Cuisine is still one of the guidelines of civilization. On some occasions it has also been used in the appraisal of a President. The White House fare has always been discussed by the public and the earliest Presidents had epicurean tastes not equaled until John F. Kennedy became President. In general the tendency was to stick to the traditional pattern and set a good example by using native fare. Public funds were involved, and critical congressmen took note of what they saw as they paraded through the President's house. George Washington, who had a French chef, liked shad, shrimp, and oysters, and usually had herring and corncake for breakfast. But he dined on a single course, with beer or wine. Martha Washington whipped up forty eggs and brandy with a bundle of twigs for her Great Cake. Thomas Jefferson, an authentic gourmet, delighted his guests with French dishes and his "Pannequaiques," now known as crêpes or pancakes. He also served a dessert of ice cream in hot pastry comparable to today's baked Alaska. Dolley Madison popularized ice cream, and Abigail Adams' strawberry flummery became as well known as the scrambled eggs Eleanor Roosevelt cooked for her guests at Sunday night suppers.

President Van Buren caused a rumpus in Congress over squandering public money on strawberries and raspberries, an uproar aggravated by the fact that he ate them with his much criticized gold spoons. William Henry Harrison liked steak tartare and was also credited with introducing charlotte russe, one of the favorite nineteenth-century desserts. President Buchanan gave sauerkraut suppers in the Pennsylvania tradition. Abraham Lincoln ate like a Spartan—small portions and always the same: corned beef and cabbage, blackberry pie, and corn cakes or gingerbread. General Grant could not bear the sight of rare meat or fowl in any form. He stuck to his rice pudding, and for breakfast, instead of the cucumbers and coffee of his army days, he took filet of beef done to a crisp, buckwheat cakes or fish, and boiled hominy. Mrs. Grant was prone to offer her guests twenty-five different dishes, al-

Log cabin in which Lincoln was born.

Typical banquet menu of the 1890s. Dining was a serious affair in this era of opulence, and twelve-course dinners were commonplace. The bon vivants kept the old gourmet tradition of Thomas Jefferson alive, but public figures suffered at times from the many rich courses offered them. William Howard Taft, battling everlastingly to stay below three hundred pounds, was dismayed by the riches of this characteristic menu.

The Tropical Garden on the roof of the Palmer House in Chicago was a fashionable promenading ground in the 1870s and 1880s. The idea spread to hotels in the East, and Americans became familiar with the flora and fauna of distant places through the conservatories and roof gardens of the late nineteenth century.

Menu

Astrakhan Caviar

Celery   Olives   Almonds

Smith Island Oysters

Clear Windsor Soup

Terrapin Union League

Bouche au Capucine

Roman Punch

Canvasback Duck

Wild Rice Croquettes   Baked Stuffed Potato

Tomato Andalouse

Assorted Cheese

Fancy Ices and Strawberries

Cakes

Coffee

COCKTAILS
RHINE WINE
MADEIRA
CHAMPAGNE
CIGARETTE
CIGARS
CORDIALS

TROPICAL GARDEN ON THE ROOF.

though her husband was certainly a moderate and fastidious eater.

Theodore Roosevelt liked plain food, but in quantity, and a suckling pig was frequently served at Sagamore. His bounding energies were often sustained solely by bread and milk. The mightiest feaster of them all—William Howard Taft, who at times weighed three hundred pounds and more—was a generous host, serving Lobster Newburg, salmon, steaks, chicken, fruits, and confections of all kinds. Calvin Coolidge liked roast beef and baked beans, corn muffins and custard pies. Mrs. Coolidge had a New England taste for coffee and doughnuts. Woodrow Wilson was indifferent to food. Franklin D. Roosevelt favored New England salmon with egg sauce. President Truman liked simple American food and not too much of it, and President Eisenhower had a special fondness for charcoal-broiled sirloin steaks, beef stew, his own soup recipe, and lemon meringue pie. President Kennedy liked fish chowder, steak, and potatoes, but Mrs. Kennedy saw to it that the White House table was a model of French cuisine. Several of the Presidents have chosen to do some cooking on their own. Jefferson liked to cure hams and season his own salad. He experimented with macaroni, whipped up "French fries" with beefsteak, and when he returned from France, Patrick Henry found him so Frenchified "that he abjured his native victuals." In more recent times General Eisenhower has shown a taste for brewing his soup in a chef's cap and apron, and President Johnson's Texas barbecues have become recurrent events with a strong regional association.

There were always Presidents who served good wines, like Jefferson and Van Buren, the Grants, the Tafts (who invariably served champagne), the Hoovers, and the Kennedys. Theodore Roosevelt discouraged champagne and veered to juleps made from mint grown on the White House grounds. Rutherford Hayes had a special problem because his wife, the serene and well-liked Lucy, was so devout a temperance advocate that she was known as "Lemonade Lucy." However, the President fooled his guests on at least one occasion by serving Roman punch oranges, strongly flavored with synthetic rum. In recent years the White House custodians have made their bow to native wines.

Although the early First Ladies affected the social mores of their times, this did not extend to food. The Presidents were more potent in this respect. But a flood of White House cookbooks in recent years has set women to sampling favorite White House recipes, from Martha Washington's to Mrs. Johnson's pet dishes. Between four and five hundred varieties of cookbooks may be found today on the American market, proclaiming in themselves the changing pattern of American cuisine down the years. The first one that related directly to American taste was issued in 1742 by William Parks, public printer at Williamsburg. This was followed by many more until a high point was reached with Fannie Farmer's classic, which affected the eating habits of the nation. Red-haired Fannie, who spent her last years in a wheelchair, was identified with the Boston Cooking School that trained many maidens of the 1870s in the culinary art. Her books, her lectures, and her articles spread knowledge and skill in this field, and shook many housewives out of a deadly rut. From then on cookbooks were published in a steady stream. Fifty-two came out in the autumn of 1965, ranging from Siamese, Balkan, and American Indian cooking to such oddities as *Saucepans and the Single Girl, I Hate to Cook Book*, and *Cooking in a Castle*.

More leisure has whipped up a new kind of energy in this field. Just as the business girl serves her escort a gourmet dinner assembled from the exotic sources she has today in fresh and frozen foods, the bachelor prides himself on his planked steaks and salads, and the family man wraps his chef's apron around his middle and goes out to direct the barbecue. The perfectionist may pass up the supermarket for the little shop around the corner, where he can buy his spices or a special brand of bread, for he lives in a land of natural abundance. In addition, the foods of every other country are his to command.

4　*A Sporting Nation*

However repressive the Puritan spirit, the instinct for fun and games quickly burned its way through the growing population, although New England was the last to surrender its restraints and echoes of Puritanism remain today. In all the colonies cockfighting, gambling, roistering, and drinking were indulged in to some extent, as well as churchgoing and public debate. All were committed early to dancing, and they played simple indoor games as zestfully as they developed their winter sports. Their recreations set the basic pattern for the sports-loving nation of today. The more primitive pursuits of the pioneer days mellowed into the organized sports of the nineteenth century, and Americans now spend $22 billion a year on recreation. The nation has 26,755,737 acres of public parks, which were used by 111,386,000 people in 1965.

But at first each entertained himself according to his inherited pattern, his prosperity, and the conditions under which he lived. The trappers and hunters, out for blood, seeking food, blazing trails, showed a primitive streak as they hunted wild horses with dogs, and baited bears, wolves, and even bulls with hounds. Cockfighting and gander pulling came naturally and had such status that a clergyman would attend a cockfight after his Sunday morning service. At the country fairs people danced lustily and feasted on wild turkey or venison. They drank from gourds dipped in tubs of native whiskey. Men pitched horseshoes and shot tin cups off their companions' heads, for guns were lightly drawn by those who had only recently learned to hunt.

Before the circus became standard entertainment, wild animals were exhibited in public and crowds flocked to view a lion or a bear in a padded oxcart, or a chained leopard outside a tavern. A white bear from Greenland was a drawing card at a Boston tavern in 1733, and Salem had a dog that was heralded as knowing how to read, write, and tell the time of day. In 1809 one of Salem's taverns was the scene of a bullfight. Sport was a catalyst in the social order, for the impoverished as well as the rich hung around the taverns, watched cockfights, played billiards, and went fishing and skating. Boston boys played rounders on the Common, and many went out in whaleboats when there were races. All turned out for historic spectacles and made great occasions of them.

For entertainment indoors they had cribbage, backgammon, whist, quadrille, and billiards, played in a tavern in Charleston as early as 1722. All efforts to stifle interest in cards and gambling met with resistance. Cards were pilloried as the devil's own picturebooks, and their sale or importation was forbidden. The sin was compounded when their errant possessors wrote party invitations on the backs of the cards, a social custom of the period. George Washington, who had gambled and played cards himself, banned all such games for the Continental Army, and after the Revolution royalty was effaced from the playing cards. George Washington was the new king of hearts; John Quincy Adams, the king of diamonds; and Thomas Jefferson, the king of clubs. The Indians were jacks; Minerva was the queen of spades, and Venus the queen of hearts.

During the years of stress all extravagance and roistering were suppressed. Playhouses closed, and Congress in 1774 recommended that racing, gaming, cockfighting, and similar diversions be stopped. But long before the Revolution, card playing and throwing dice on the Sabbath were forbidden, even in Virginia. Similarly none might travel, transact business, or load ships on that day, and the sinner who failed to attend church had to forfeit fifty pounds of tobacco. The Virginians lost no time, however, in engaging in a constant round of racing, card playing, hunting, and dancing, while the men who trekked west caroused and danced at country fairs, barn raisings, and other activities linked to their hard work in the wilderness. New England had its corn huskings, apple parings, sugaring off, and log rolling. Vermont, Connecticut, and Nantucket made great occasions of the annual sheep shearings. Even such natural events as shad and salmon coming up the river occasioned community feasting. Fiddlers and peddlers congregated at the slightest hint of merrymaking, tents appeared, and people sought brief surcease from their strenuous labors. Lotteries, introduced around 1719, proved to be great moneymakers for the colleges and public works. Schools were endowed; turnpikes were improved; bridges were built on the lucky numbers. The pioneers were true gamblers at heart.

Rural visiting back and forth by stagecoach was popular with the more prosperous. They rose at four in the morning to set off on a turtle frolic, forerunner of today's clambake, barbecue, and corn roast. When West Indian turtles were towed in from the Caribbean the frolics were held with feasting and dancing. New Yorkers also liked to go oystering, and many small craft assembled by the river's edge for this purpose. They frequently drove to the river banks in Italian chaises, each of which held one couple. There they fished, until it was time for tea and a drive home in the moonlight. Parties of fifty joined in these expeditions. The people of Maryland did much of their visiting by barge, with colorfully dressed Negro boatmen rowing them on the Chesapeake.

Philadelphia's mixed fishing parties were most famous of all, and exclusive little groups went to the Schuylkill to fish, boat, or stroll along its banks. They drove to the country estates of their friends, to spend a day in conversation, drinking cider, and sampling the syllabub. On their way they passed a good many burghers sitting on benches in front of their houses, gossiping and contemplating passersby. Life was intimate, friendly, measured in its course. But there was also much work to be done. Once the land had been cleared and homes established the more boisterous spirit of the frontier subsided. The average settler was a strenuous worker who had little time for recreation of any sort, and rowdiness was far from dominating the picture. The well-off might dawdle about in their coaches and spend entire days in conversation on their estates, but this was not the lot of many. Visitors from abroad were struck by the industry of Americans, and the small degree of leisure or instinct to play that they had. All seemed to be intent on business as the country grew, and their only amusement, in the opinion of their more scathing critics, was to make money. Many commented on the lack of public parks and pleasure resorts. Mrs. Trollope, who was apt to sling her arrows haphazardly, wrote that the only "rural amusement in which we ever saw the natives engaged was eating strawberries and cream in a pretty garden about three miles from town." Washington Irving observed the Dutch tea parties, which were heavy feasts of fried pork swimming in gravy, served from a huge earthen dish, with the inevitable Delft teapot for a centerpiece.

In 1821 Timothy Dwight, the Congregational clergyman who was President of Yale, listed the prevailing amusements as visiting, dancing, music, conversation, walking, riding, sailing, shooting at a mark, draughts, chess, cards, and dramatic exhibits. A half century later Joseph

Bennette, visiting from London, observed in his diary that American women were "indulging every piece of gentility to the height of the mode and neglect the affairs of their families with as good grace as the finest ladies in London."

However, with so many servants to attend them, the children were not often neglected, and even in colonial days children did not lack toys. Many were made at home, and they gave great delight to their owners, who were not satiated like the modern child with an overabundance of playthings. The Williamsburg shops carried tea sets for little girls, as well as jointed dolls and a runaway boy with a toy watch in his pocket. The miniature pieces of furniture were delicately made, and in sewing for their dolls they copied the fashions imported for their mothers' dressmakers.

Both boys and girls played singing, kissing, and counting games. Blind Man's Buff, Fox in the Corner, and Prisoner's Base were other favorites. They liked to munch on angelica candy, marzipan, and caraway comfits as they dutifully read Cotton Mather's *Good Lessons for Children, in Verse*. They gave themselves heart and soul to the public holidays, which took root slowly in the new land. The Pilgrims were as cold to Christmas as the Dutch were reverent. Neither Christmas nor Thanksgiving loomed large in the social structure of the seventeenth and eighteenth centuries. The first harvest festival held by the Pilgrim fathers in 1621, with Indians as their guests, was primarily a three-day feast, and it was some time before it became a fixed religious observance. Although associated from the first with New England, the idea spread west and south, and finally Thanksgiving became a national holiday. Christmas was first observed in Virginia, and Southerners cultivated the tradition. Today the nation sparkles in December with Christmas trees, indoors and out, ranging from the tall, swaying beauty in Rockefeller Center to small silvery novelties in countless shop windows.

The Pennsylvania Dutch were the first to popularize the Christmas tree in America, and in the early nineteenth century candlelit trees were first seen sparkling behind the windowpanes of Philadelphia. The Moravians were in the habit of building pyramids of cookies before the Christmas tree proper was introduced. The crèche, the gingerbread figures, the popcorn streamers, and German baubles are traditional, but many new and arty effects have come into fashion in recent years—pink and blue trees, silver and plumes, gold birds of paradise, and even a blue tree trimmed with white kid gloves and champagne glasses.

Besides encouraging the celebration of Christmas, the Dutch, merrymakers at heart who, in spite of their staid exteriors, liked to dance, garden, bowl, and jaunt about in boats and carriages, also initiated the custom of paying calls on New Year's Day. They kept open house and served cherry bounce, mince pie, and rum-flavored honey cakes, as well as their famous Springerle cookies, made with anise seeds. George Washington observed this custom, and it became a White House tradition, the one day in the year when all and sundry may stream through the Executive Mansion and be greeted by the President and his wife.

Election Day and college commencements were among the most popular celebrations in the early days of the republic. Crowds converged on Harvard, Yale, Princeton, and William and Mary, but not necessarily because their sons were there. They made these gatherings the occasion for drinking and dancing, horse-racing, and games to such a degree that the colleges changed commencement dates from autumn to spring, in the hope that some of the roisterers would stay at home and attend to their planting. Yale students gave theatrical performances during Election Week, and the colleges in general provided intellectual stimulation at a time when lectures and sermons were about the only public entertainment available. The stage lacked official sanction until the end of the eighteenth century, but playlets called "drolls" were presented in Boston in 1713 and puppet shows were always popular. English strollers gave dramatic readings in a Boston coffeehouse, but all these interests languished during the Revolution, and the *Boston Gazette* in 1767 was scathing about "persons of fashion" who unashamedly went to balls, assemblies, plays, and card parties. Soon after the Revolution imported companies staged plays, and eventually the American theater acquired a character of its own.

Long before it was established as a major form of entertainment, dancing was the most generally accepted form of recreation, shared in by all social classes, in all the colonies, and enjoyed just as much in the backwoods as in the bewigged and satin-clad circles of the city assemblies. Dancing schools were forbidden at first by the New England authorities, but dancing teachers were hovering around by 1716. No amount of repression served to stamp out the zeal for a pastime that the Puritans considered "wanton and unseemly" and the Quakers thought "frivolous and idolatrous." Prejudice wore thin in time, until even the Connecticut ordination balls lasted most of the night, helped on by quantities of spirits supplied by the tavernkeepers.

Philadelphia's dancing assembly, created around 1747, became as noted as its banquets and fishing parties. It was composed of eighty of the most fashionable young men and eighty debutantes, and there was no crashing this tight line of defense. They met regularly in halls, and admission was by playing-card tickets. New York's dancing assembly was formed in 1758, but the Boston girls had already sprinted ahead. Balls were held to celebrate military victories, royal birthdays, and significant historical events. They usually began with a minuet, and then came jigs and cotillions, ending with the Sir Roger de Coverley or the

Virginia reel. Powder flew in all directions as wigged partners threw themselves into the spirit of the dance. In the cities dances lasted from seven in the evening until four in the morning.

Men rode up on horseback early in the day, with mud protectors covering their satin breeches. Women drove by coach to the taverns, huge handkerchiefs covering their towering wigs, and linen overpetticoats protecting their satin and damask gowns. But at the frontier men more often rode to dances with women behind them on the saddle. They had neither satin nor wigs, but they danced with verve in their dimities, and coped dexterously with the plank dance, not unlike today's watusi, since there was no bodily contact. Partners faced each other on a plank set on two barrels, and kept on dancing as on a seesaw.

Among the colonnades and magnolias of the South it was another story, for here the minuet and the gavotte prevailed. The assembly rules were so fixed that only subscribers could enter, and no man was admissible in boots, colored stockings, or informal dress. Just as the South moved toward war the polka came into fashion, and James Gordon Bennett, the articulate and scrappy founder and publisher of the *New York Herald*, backed up Queen Victoria in condemning it as an immoral dance. He found the polka, as it was danced at Saratoga and Newport, more indecent than the "most disgraceful exhibitions of the lowest haunts of Paris and London." However, in ballerina skirts and with heelless shoes, the girls bounced through the polka with spirit. It took time for the waltz to win its way in Puritan America. Strauss's music had opened up a fresh chapter in the history of the dance, and while all Europe was waltzing, unmarried American girls were solemnly warned against engaging in this loose dance.

Harper's Magazine primly pointed out that no pure woman would let a man hold her hand in his, much less strain her to his breast publicly for a quarter of an hour at a time. The etiquette counselors reminded the hapless girl that a "gentleman never encircles the lady's waist until the dance begins, and drops his arms as soon as it ends." By the late 1880s waltzes, polkas, quadrilles, redowas, and the Sir Roger de Coverley were on every program. The two-step was being danced furiously to Sousa's enlivening marches, and the German cotillion, with its costly baubles handed out as favors, was the debutante's delight.

The next great change in the tradition of the dance came at the time of World War I when the tango and the maxixe, two of the most sensuous dances of all time, came into fashion by way of Irene and Vernon Castle. Then came the bunny hug, the grizzly bear, the lame duck, the monkey, and others as odd as the tango was seductive. Tea dances and wartime romance flourished when Irving Berlin's ragtime swept the field, and when big bands purred out "Tea for Two" and

"Everybody's Doing It." When jazz was introduced around 1914 with Dixieland jazz bands it was played so universally that the 1920s became known as the "Jazz Age." It brought the nightclub and dance hall to the fore, and young Americans rolled up the rugs and danced at home to this strange new music. Radio fed the flame, and America and jazz became synonymous in the eyes of the world. From jazz the move was to swing, to rock and roll, to cha-cha, the watusi—and the slow beat, the throb, the discothèque, and partners swaying, writhing, and doubling up, but rarely touching.

Paralleling the popularity of dancing indoors in the early days were the two great outdoor sports—fox hunting and racing. Hunting started in a simple way with farmers running foxes with hounds at night. When it gained ground in Charleston in the 1750s, Philadelphians took it up with enthusiasm, but not until after the Civil War was hunting in the English tradition introduced, with pink coats and specially bred foxhounds. Whereas hunting became the pastime of the privileged, racing was enjoyed by all classes from the nation's beginnings down to today. Everyone went to the races, from the President to the peddler, and horse racing flourished all over the country. Trotting matches were the chief attraction at country fairs; thirty thousand Bostonians would turn out for a trotting carnival and horse show before the Civil War. The devotion to riding and racing became a fixed tradition, and 6,500 of the new generation of children belonged in 1966 to 143 pony clubs in suburban and rural communities across the country. The pioneer children rode from necessity; their twentieth-century descendants ride for exercise and recreation, even in a land overwhelmingly committed to wheels.

As the world of outdoor recreation widened, one of its delights was the winter round of sleighing and skating. Early in the eighteenth century, girls wrapped in cloaks trimmed with swansdown were pushed over the ice on sledge chairs, holding huge muffs of chinchilla or fox against their faces. Skating was still too venturesome for them, but they glided happily in brightly colored sleighs, with bells jingling and buffalo robes to keep them warm. Sleigh bells were mandatory by law, and chimes echoed through the silent woods and city streets alike as musical effects were devised. They were so much the racing cars of their day that Sarah Kemble Knight noted in her *Private Journal* of the 1860s: "They fly with great swiftness and some are so furious that they'll turn out of the path for none except a Loaden Cart."

Once the early prejudice was broken down skating was the first sport in which women indulged as freely as men. By midcentury they were zooming over country ponds and city rinks. Excursion trains carried Bostonians to Jamaica Pond for skating, old-fashioned versions of today's "ski specials." The skaters did the double roll, the Dutch

Customs and manners in the home and on the highroad have found their miniature counterparts in the toyshop. The toy horse-drawn hook and ladder is made of iron and dates from about 1888.

Thanksgiving Day dinner in 1858. By the mid-nineteenth century, Thanksgiving, first celebrated by the Pilgrim Fathers in 1621, had become an annual event second only to Christmas. Families gathered from distant quarters to share in the feast—particularly in New England and Virginia, where the tradition was founded. Father carved the turkey; toasts were drunk; and the children, often seated at adjoining tables, shared in the quiet rejoicing, hearty repast, and good fellowship of the occasion. From Harper's Weekly, *November 27, 1858.*

Peddler dolls delighted grown-ups as well as children in the late eighteenth and early nineteenth centuries. Although increasingly rare after 1825, this one was made about 1870. The girls bore packs stuffed with pincushions, baskets, feather dusters, fans, satchels, sachets, lace, and teaspoons, mimicking the popular peddler wares of the era but with the added charm of the miniature. The boy peddlers carried baskets with tiny bottles, knives, mirrors, watches, books, and sheet music.

Interior of Dance House on State Street in the mining town of Leadville, Colorado, in 1879. Known as "a new Eldorado," Leadville, which was almost two miles above sea level, was coming to life in the boom developing from its gold, silver, and molybdenum mines. The bearded men who worked all day in the mines often chose to squander their gold nuggets in the saloons and dance houses that flourished in the little town. There was always a fiddler at hand to play the lively airs of the frontier and girls to swing in their arms. Fifty cents a dance was the fee in this early version of the taxi dance hall. The floor was of planks, the men wore their mining boots and often their hats, for these were roughshod, carefree days when American fortunes were being made. Woodcut from Frank Leslie's Illustrated Newspaper, 1879.

The Polka. This gay, stamping, robust dance, frowned on by Queen Victoria, was introduced in America in the 1840s and quickly became the rage. Lithograph by Pinkerton, Wagner, and McGiugan from Ladies' National Magazine, July 1844.

A sleighing scene outside Barnum's Museum in 1855. Trumpets blared and horses reared as visitors shrank in terror from the plumed white chargers and circus excitement so readily whipped up by the nation's most successful showman. P. T. Barnum was still reaping a harvest from the introduction of Jenny Lind to the American public in 1850. The carnival spirit and constant uproar were customary in and around his New York Museum. From a lithograph by Thomas Benecke, 1855.

"*Vive La France,*" a lithograph by Alfred E. Baker, shows a satiric view of indoor games. Edward Dechaux, a prominent art dealer in the 1840s, is playing battledore and shuttlecock with two ladies in his studio. The birds are cupids.

A New England husking bee. The seasonal events of pioneer life were greatly enjoyed by country people who flocked to local fairs, sheep shearings, apple parings, logrollings, and barn-raisings. Working hard, indoors and out, they celebrated their festivals with exuberance. Fiddlers appeared; tents welcomed itinerant visitors; dancing, drinking, and courting were indulged in. From Harper's Weekly, *1858.*

Connecticut was as noted for its fine county fairs a century ago as in the 1960s, and the Fairfield County Agricultural Society awarded its coveted diploma for this one in 1856. It had all the elements common to the early county fairs across the nation— the flagged tent and covered wagons, the produce carts and stock, and the crowd in its Sunday best. Geese and sheep, roosters and cows bumped against crinolines, and men wore their high hats to the fair as to church.

roll, and the figure eight. In the country there were frozen streams for skating and snow-covered hills and dales for coasting. Today more than sixty million Americans skate, and there are nine hundred rinks in the United States, ranging from the glittering showplace at Rockefeller Center to a rink at one of the world's largest shopping centers in Portland, Oregon. Six thousand skaters turn out in New York City on a winter Saturday afternoon to skate in parks and rinks. Ice sparkles on artificial rinks at motels, colleges, civic auditoriums, and arenas across the nation. Small plastic rinks, like garden swimming pools, are used at home for skating.

Roller skating was introduced in 1863 and soon there were rinks from coast to coast where the young did the Richmond roll, the picket fancy, the Philadelphia twist and duds-on-wheels. Skiing, a familiar sport in Europe, reached America by way of Norwegian settlers in 1883, when the country's first ski club was founded at Red Wing, Minnesota. But not until the 1930s were city dwellers drawn to the ski slopes of New England and the West. The Depression had forced New Englanders to develop "home" attractions as manufacturers moved south in quest of cheaper labor and business languished. Department stores whipped up interest by installing borax-covered slides and importing Austrian instructors to give the customers lessons in skiing. Railroads ran special trains and organized weekend excursions. Sears, Roebuck supplied Tyrolean jackets and ski pants for a fraction of the sum the more affluent skiers spent at the boutiques in St. Moritz and Sun Valley.

Today four million enthusiasts crowd into 1,200 ski areas, to spend more than $750,000,000 a year. In Squaw Valley, Nevada, gondolas skim through the notch of a granite cliff and hover over white-pine forests. There is dancing outdoors among the pines and crags, with all the trappings of a Bavarian beer garden, even to the Swiss recordings made popular by the Trapp family and *The Sound of Music*. Teen-agers have a milk-shake bar and Ping-Pong tables at this resort, and children from two to twelve are offered creative arts, music and dancing, snow games, skating and ski lessons. The wintertime ski lift in summer becomes the world's highest nightclub, with a view of Lake Tahoe. Sun Valley, Idaho, the country's oldest ski resort, draws Hollywood stars; the New England resorts catch the college crowd. Miniskirts and stretch pants, plastic boots, vinyl and silver metallic suits, bright colors and strange furs enliven the slopes, and the après-ski attire is as carefully devised as high fashion in urban settings. Today skiing is not just the rich man's sport, but is a family recreation reaching a wider section of the community. With more leisure and mobility parents and children alike take to the slopes.

Like all other wars, and to a greater degree, World War II left its mark on fashion, architecture, manners, entertainment, and education. The Civil War disrupted all aspects of daily living. The Spanish-American War worked less profoundly on the everyday life of the people. But two world wars initiated a revolution that proceeds in widening circles—shorter working hours, higher pay, more time for recreation, international interests, man's concern for his fellow man, a whole new world in the making.

Things have changed dynamically since there were torchlight processions at election time, talks on the village greens of New England, fireworks shot off from amusement parks, and simple country pleasures when the visiting circus was the annual excitement. In the nineteenth century the young liked to play charades and parlor games, sing Gilbert and Sullivan melodies, and congregate at one another's houses for Welsh rarebit parties. But the rise of the colleges figured strongly in the development of sports and recreation. Rowing was the one competitive sport that was organized before the Civil War and students were deeply involved, with their college crews and skulling races. Track and field events led to a grand climax in 1896, the American team winning all along the line at the Olympic Games held in Athens. Rugby, first played in America during the Civil War, became intercollegiate in 1869. Football was revived at Harvard and Yale around 1872, after a ban for roughness, and the autumn games of the big universities became sports events of major importance. Four thousand spectators watched the first Princeton-Yale game in 1878, but 100,000 watch the games in Pasadena's Rose Bowl today, and additional millions view them on television. Most professional sports have great new audiences today—not only on the screen but in restless thousands seeking recreation. A World Series game, a Davis Cup match, the Walker Cup, the Olympic Games, a big prizefight, a championship golf game, the autumn football games—all draw spectacular crowds.

But now the major excitement centers on the heavens. Even in the early nineteenth century, men had begun moving toward the space age, with balloon ascensions an attraction from time to time. The balloons were variously known as Archimedial Phaetons, Vertical Aerial Coaches, or Patent Federal Balloons. It was considered healthy to go up in them, the theory being that the motion expelled strange humors from the bloodstream. In the 1830s Charles F. Durant charged fifty cents admission to show the crowd how it was done, and some time later John Wise staged his embarkation scene before twenty thousand onlookers. The public grew sky-minded. A growing feeling for speed developed, as horse-drawn cars went rollicking through the city streets, flags flying and bells clanging. It was only a matter of time until young and old went storming along the roads on bicycles. The nation's full bicycle army was estimated at two million and in

"The Bathe at Newport," as drawn by Winslow Homer, shows bathers of both sexes dressed to the teeth while gamboling in the water. As early as 1858 they were breaking down the old convention that men and women, even husbands and wives, should not bathe together. Instructors wearing wide-brimmed hats are giving swimming lessons. One of the men is playfully squirting water at a protesting girl. A bather is just about to make her modest descent from a bathing machine rolled to the water's edge. Several of the women are wearing rubber life belts, and their petticoats whirl around in the water. There are children here and there but the grown-ups seem to be having all the fun. From Harper's Weekly, 1858.

A Sporting Nation

International regatta at Saratoga Lake, 1874. The Columbia boat has just crossed the line and won the university race, leaving the crews of Harvard, Yale, and other colleges trailing. The spectators assembled in the arbor and grandstand are showing a mixture of excitement and grief. Men wave their hats; a few of the women dare to flutter handkerchiefs; but the little girl in the foreground, clasping her hands and looking stricken, must have a brother at Yale. The annual regatta was one of many attractions Saratoga offered in the nineteenth century, but it drew more of a family crowd than Canfield's Casino, for the students' families attended en masse and the college spirit prevailed. Close to the grandstand was the country home of Frank Leslie and his famous wife, a Swiss chalet where all visiting world celebrities were entertained. From Leslie's Weekly, *1874.*

1895 there were forty thousand women cyclists whooping it up in long jackets with leg-of-mutton sleeves, short skirts, gaiters, and equestrian tights. They wore soft felt hats with protective brims, or gay little jobs with birds' wings and upstanding quills that slipped off base when the pace grew frantic.

"You cannot serve God and skylark on a bicycle," one despairing clergyman remarked to the remnant of his congregation. Sunday was the big day for bicycling breakfasts and luncheons, and cyclists responded automatically to the bugle call of "Boots and Saddles" for parade. Wall Street bankers attended a bicycle school so that they could wheel rhythmically to band music on their organized outings. The Josephine was matched with the Napoleon bicycle when men and women went wheeling together, as they sometimes did. The bicycle races were known as "Scorchers," although the pace was mild compared with the popular six-day bicycle races of the twentieth century. Bicycle polo tournaments were held at Newport and Bar Harbor.

For a time bicycling was the most popular of all sports and it created many problems along the highways. When nine hundred bicyclists, representing the forty-five different clubs of the League of American Wheelmen, pedaled solemnly down Fifth Avenue in 1883 a crowd of ten thousand gathered to cheer them as they got under way with a flourish of bugles. They wore bright uniforms, caps and insignia, and pitched large tents in a city street to protect their bicycles until they were ready for the signal to start. But the automobile squeezed the bicycle off the highways until it reappeared in the 1960s, not only on college campuses, but on country roads and city streets. Bicycles were seen again in Central Park, as in the old days when they curvetted in solid masses around the park and chickens darted from the road as they pedaled majestically into the country.

Croquet gripped the public with even more speed than the bicycling craze, and at about the same time. It was introduced from England in the late 1860s and became the favorite evening game when someone thought to light the wickets with candle sconces. Old and young enjoyed the game, and it brought them into the open. Women played in shirtwaists and gored skirts, with flat sailors or ruched white muslin hats. The National Croquet Association held its first tournament in the 1880s, and there were many hard-fought contests on the croquet lawn. Homesteaders in the West played it on rough grass. The fad faded around 1905, as the young turned to tennis and more active sports. But Alexander Woollcott gave it life again in the 1920s, and here and there an enthusiast sought to revive it. Vincent Astor turned an indoor tennis court at Rhinebeck into a croquet pitch, and Darryl Zanuck converted his Palm Springs lawn to the same end. The game is still played on Long Island and in California. Down the years it has

Union Pond in the Williamsburg district of Brooklyn, New York. The crinolined ladies of 1863 did well with their skating, giving observers occasional glimpses of white stockings under tilting hoops. Their tippets and muffs kept them warm, and their hoops, like sails, seemed to speed them over the ice. Union Pond was opened as a skating rink during the early days of the Civil War, and with many men in the army the girls took over, using the Grand Street ferry to get from Manhattan to Brooklyn. Since skating was one of the few sports in which they could indulge without a loss of modesty, they flocked to rinks all over the country and became champion skaters. It was an old game, however, for the male of the species. Those in mufti wore their top hats and linked arms with their partners. The effect was panoramic. Lithograph by Thomas & Eno, 1863.

Twins were not uncommon in the 1890s, but a special tandem bicycle was a conversation piece when it showed up in Central Park as a variation of the Brewster or rattan perambulator. A nursemaid, riding in the center with cap ties streaming behind her, steered the twins in their rattan baskets poised on linked bicycles. The rage for bicycling had reached a point where anything was conceivable, and frilly babies were in their heyday. From Harper's Bazar, 1896.

Croquet was a gentle family pastime
introduced from England around 1860
and enlivening American lawns just as the
Civil War was about to start. This family,
living in Norwalk, Connecticut, were
learning the game in 1860, and the rough
grass did not seem to hamper their moves.
Grandparents enjoyed the leisurely pace of
the new game, and three generations
frequently aimed at the wickets. Wartime
courtships flourished when evening croquet
took hold, romantically lit by candles in
sconces. A few enthusiasts keep the game
alive today, but tennis, motoring, and the
fast pace of life doomed croquet early in
the twentieth century. It was inseparable
from the age of plush, hammocks, and
the stereopticon.

Roper's Gymnasium in Philadelphia, about 1830. Accused of
being pale effigies and of losing the sturdiness of the frontier
days, Americans became gymnasium fans early in the nineteenth
century. They fenced, boxed, vaulted the horse, climbed ropes,
and chinned themselves on parallel bars, developing muscle.
Later in the century women had their gymnasiums, too,
where they swung Indian clubs and did calisthenics to offset
the burgeoning curves of the 1890s. The habit persists with
American men and women, in spite of the wealth of sports at
their command. Athletic clubs, gymnasiums, and spas are
used by many besides professional athletes. Lithograph by
Childs and Inman.

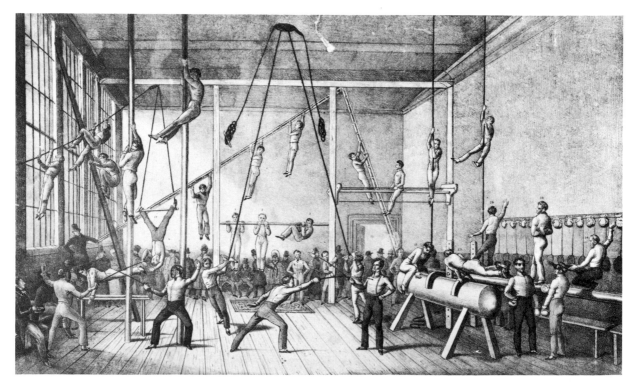

had some of the dilettantish quality of cricket, which was introduced in New England in 1833 and was pushed from time to time by English settlers on Staten Island and elsewhere. Cricket never really won its way as bowling did. One of the earliest pastimes, much indulged in by the Dutch, its popularity has been renewed from time to time. Perhaps it has never been more widely played than now by both men and women. It goes much further back in American history than baseball, the nation's leading organized sport.

This all-time favorite has been traced back to the early game of rounders, otherwise known as town-ball. Abner Doubleday has been credited with using the diamond formation at Cooperstown, New York, in 1839, but the organization of the Knickerbocker Club by Alexander J. Cartwright in 1845 is more generally recognized as the official starting point of organized baseball. A group of business and professional men had been playing the game at the Elysian Fields in Hoboken for the three preceding years. The early Knickerbockers were men of wealth, garbed in blue trousers, white shirts, and straw hats. The umpire sat in the field near first base, with an umbrella over his frock coat and stovepipe hat. But as baseball took hold across the country to the Pacific coast, less exclusive clubs were formed, and it became the national game, as it remains today.

Tennis was introduced from Bermuda in 1874, and was mildly played at first by club members wearing high silk hats, and girls who merely patted the ball as they hung on to their trailing skirts. In the 1880s they were frozen out of the open tournaments lest their modesty suffer, but they went right on skipping rope in a great whirl of petticoats. Once the bars were let down, they played tennis with zest and skill, and it became a sport rather than a pastime in 1900, when the International Davis Cup matches were introduced. In the 1920s such stars as Suzanne Lenglen, Helen Wills, Molla Mallory, William T. Tilden, and Jean Borotra, playing with ferocious drive and placement skill, ranked as tennis greats. By the 1930s the game had become professional; the nation had from three to four million tennis players. Today more people play tennis than golf. The Davis Cup tournaments are among the most popular of all spectator sports, but it might be noted that "gouff clubs" and "racquets for tennis" sold along with cork swimming-jackets, battledores, and shuttlecocks before the Revolution, even though golf and tennis were not acknowledged sports in the United States until the nineteenth century.

Golf, which was played by the French in the fourteenth century, and by the Dutch some time later, was thought to be imported from Scotland when it reached the United States in the 1880s. It took hold gradually, but more convincingly as men had more leisure, as well as automobiles to take them to golf courses. It began as a rich man's game, but in time came within reach of everyone through municipal golf courses. By 1910 it had ceased to be a fashionable fad. There were hundreds of courses and half a million players. In 1928, at a time when men were going around the course in baggy plus-fours, with tasseled wool stockings, and were spending $200 million a year on the game, Grantland Rice wrote in the *New York Herald Tribune* that the "democracy of golf today has gone far beyond that of any other sport." Spectacular as well as simple courses are part of the national picture now, from the dramatic ones on Monterey Peninsula to the crab-grass greens of Cape Cod.

All classes can enjoy this healthful sport, which is also the favorite game of rulers and kings. Two American Presidents—William Howard Taft and General Eisenhower—have been enthusiastic golfers, but a great variety of sports have entered into the lives of White House families. Theodore Roosevelt's game was tennis, a fact that he played down for the public, since it was then regarded as a sissy sport, a rich man's pastime. Alice Roosevelt, an enthusiastic horsewoman, made headlines by galloping her horse up the White House steps. Calvin Coolidge rode an artificial horse before beginning his day of silence, and he was much addicted to cruising on the *Mayflower*. Franklin D. Roosevelt chose boating and swimming in the days of his infirmity. Margaret Truman sang, while her father played the piano, took brisk walks, but showed little interest in sport. John F. Kennedy favored sailing, a moderate amount of golf, touch football, swimming, and most other sports; the White House resounded to the games of the Kennedy clan. Mrs. Kennedy dances, skis, rides, goes cruising, surf bathing, and hunting, but avoids touch football, having broken her ankle in a Kennedy scrimmage. President Johnson leans to riding, dancing, swimming, and barbecues. His daughter Luci frugs, and Mrs. Johnson has ridden the rapids. The Presidential families in recent years have moved closer to the public insofar as sports and entertainment are concerned.

Few Presidents have enjoyed yachting except as a means of getting away from people, but regattas and boat races have always drawn the public. Excursion steamers and small craft filled the harbor for a regatta held by the New York Yacht Club, which was organized in 1844. Up to the time of the Civil War this was the only yacht club in the country, but by 1885 there were fifty, scattered from Portland, Maine, to Milwaukee, and crowds turned out for their regattas.

The steam yachts that took American millionaires across the Atlantic and cruising in the Mediterranean slid into view in the 1870s. The most famous were J. P. Morgan's three consecutive *Corsair*s and William Astor's schooner, the *Ambassadress*. Yacht races became the most fashionable of spectacles, as the gilded set converged on Newport to watch the fun. The America's Cup races, with Sir Thomas

Lipton whipping up competitive interest with successive *Shamrocks*, brought this diversion to its peak. The regatta fever spread, and all along the New England coast, in San Francisco Bay, Puget Sound, and the Chesapeake, small boats were used for races, for fishing as in the old days, or for family excursions.

Since yachting began and ended as the rich man's ultimate gesture of luxury, when the costs became prohibitive for all but millionaires and even they found them steep, a lesser form of cruising, reaching a greater variety of people, became popular. The new yachts do not travel far, in the tradition of the *Corsair*, but the waterways are crowded today with small craft and an army of amateur sailors. Power-boat makers find that 70 per cent of their customers want twenty-eight-foot motor yachts and that they are often more concerned about the accessories than the seafaring qualities of their craft. They frequently haunt the inland waters, but sometimes they merely hook up at yacht club docks and imagine themselves at sea as they enjoy the latest electrical equipment, air conditioning, television, a deluxe hot-water system, and ample supplies in the freezer.

One firm that built clipper ships before Benjamin Franklin flew his first kite has had its sales soar from one to fourteen million dollars since it started installing luxury equipment. The outboard motors served for a time, but now power boats and cruisers of all kinds are in demand. A fifty-three-foot motor yacht with television and bathtub is the businessman's *Corsair* today. But true sailors still abound, and may be found every summer weekend bouncing along in a variety of craft, with wives now as expert as their husbands at reefing sails.

Canoe races and riding the rapids, familiar sports to the colonists, go along with sky diving and gyrocopting in the twentieth-century manner. Dune-buggying involves whole families who scuttle and slide in the sand from Cape Cod to California's Imperial Valley in caravans of high-wheeled buggies. In or out of the water Americans are a sports-loving people. The strong summer sunshine, the winter snows, the low rainfall for the country as a whole are conducive to outdoor life. Health clubs and gymnasiums foster the philosophy of fitness, but many of the games played by the colonials are in high standing today—horseshoe pitching and bowling, archery and badminton. Field hockey, squash, rackets, handball, and volley ball have not lost their earlier magic. Prizefights have dimmed in popularity, but summer theater and opera flourish. Drive-in movies have caught the younger generation. The cinema is recovering some of its lost glory, and there are more radio receivers in the United States than there are people. Television has become the passive sport of millions. But there are still country fairs and church socials, strawberry festivals and clambakes. Boys still fish in country brooks, and girls still make daisy chains in meadows.

5 *Fashioning the Home*

 EARLY American homes, lacking the importations and the work of native craftsmen that later enriched them, were hollow shells until the settlers overcame the forces of nature, established themselves in comfort, and furnished their barren rooms. The battle for survival long preceded the drive for comfort and luxury that characterize the American home today. It took time and infinite effort to create settings with furnishings beyond the primary needs of life. The polish was slowly applied as a second generation of children born to the pioneers asserted themselves with the buoyancy of youth, and laid the foundation for the great assortment of styles cherished by Americans in the last three centuries.

Household possessions were so sparse at first that family life focused around enormous fireplaces. The first seventeenth-century houses, built with the native woods by yeomen used to farming and handling simple tools, consisted of a single room, with a chimney at one end. The next step involved a second chimney at the other end, and finally one great central chimney became the heart of the home.

While the men coped with a primitive world outdoors, the women by degrees beautified their houses with their spinning and weaving. But at first they slept on straw pallets before the fire, warmed by deerskin, and they rose each day to face a world devoid of the barest necessities. It was 1640 before a family of substance could boast of blankets, rugs, six stools, and six chairs, andirons, and a dozen spoons. Often whole families drank from one bowl and ate from one trencher. Cream was skimmed with wide clam shells, and gourds served as bowls, dippers, and bottles. They ate with their fingers and pocket knives, and mopped up with napkins.

Their varied inheritance soon asserted itself in the furnishings they devised for their houses. They had brought a few simple tools as well as a wealth of memory and association, which soon served them in putting together their homes and in meeting everyday needs. The British colonists in New England, Virginia, and Maryland; the Dutch who settled along the Hudson; the Swedes who made the Delaware their base—all dug deep roots that flowered with the growth of the Republic. Once they had broken land, coped with the Indians, built simple houses, and strengthened themselves with the produce of land and sea, they set about creating a new civilization, instinctive and derivative at first, with much that was imported, but acquiring in time a patina of its own—the American way of life.

As towns and villages took form, craftsmen and artists sprang up like magic to copy, to create, to beautify, to adapt. There were joiners and coopers, wheelwrights and carpenters, butchers, tanners, shoemakers, and blacksmiths. These men stood next in importance to the farmers and merchants who were building up the communities. Soon they were designing carved brackets and nail-studded doors; making weather vanes, grave and gay, like the grasshopper over Boston's Faneuil Hall; turning out American pottery, crudely shaped but beautifully colored; and copying the elegant eighteenth-century furniture of Thomas Chippendale, George Hepplewhite, and Thomas Sheraton.

When the eagle was adopted in 1782 for the great seal of the United States, it was pounced on as the motif for all manner of decorations—carved, painted, engraved, embroidered, or stenciled on such trivial items as butter molds and such major pieces of furniture as highboys, mirrors, and beds. The carvers, coppersmiths, iron and tin-plate workers flourished as they designed tin chandeliers, created eerie headstones decorated with skeletons, fashioned urns, and made plaster figures for garden walks. They made sturdy furniture, hammered plain silverware, often from coin, fused their own glass, forged tools, and built carriages. They had black walnut and white pine for furniture, cedar for shingles, and sturdy oak to build their houses. Many of the early trenchers were made of poplar, and they used bottles and drinking cups of wood before pewter came into general use. Buffed to the sheen of silver, pewter soon became the pride of every housewife who

Before 1800 there was little change from the lighting devices used by the first settlers in the colonies. Candles, an open lamp, or a pine splint answered all purposes, but early in the nineteenth century various new devices were used to light homes, shops, and ships. Pictured from left to right: (1) the Cape Cod spout lamp—a tin cylinder with a spout for the wick and a drip pan beneath; (2) the whale-oil lamp mounted on a tin pan for reflector; (3) the sheet-iron betty—a cruse with wick supports; and (4) the nineteenth-century whale-oil lamp made in Hartford along classical lines.

Weather vanes whirled swiftly or with slow majesty on the American landscape as the early craftsmen fashioned roosters and eagles, butterflies, centaurs and mermaids, peacocks and Indians with bow and arrow. Some were made of sheet copper; others, of pine. A mermaid combed her flowing hair, meanwhile admiring herself in a mirror, over a barn in Wayland, Massachusetts. But the best known of all was Shem Drowne's grasshopper installed in 1742 on top of Boston's Faneuil Hall, a landmark familiar to the orators and politicians who made history in this public forum.

One of the arts the young girl of early America was expected to master was crewel work. Pillow covers and bed hangings in various hues and designs added color and charm to the home.

Metal of any sort was not plentiful in the rural communities of early America, and what was available was usually devoted to practical purposes that wood could not serve. This deep pewter dish is of American make, bearing the touch of Thomas Danforth III, of Stepney, Connecticut, and Philadelphia (1717–1818).

Glass did not become common in America until the late 1700s, but by 1815 molds designed to hold quarts and pints were perfected. This three-mold cobalt glass creamer has diamond diapering and sunburst motif.

This rough-hewn wooden tankard, thought to be of cedar, is a rare reminder of the hearty drinks quaffed by the settlers of the eighteenth century as they cleared the forests and built their homes in the wilderness. Wooden trenchers, scoops, and spoons were the earliest kitchen utensils, and the hard maple of New England lent itself readily to carving and simple decoration, such as the eagle motif on the butter stamps. After the War of Independence the eagle was the favored symbolism in architecture and furniture. The carved maple utensils were known as "treenware."

Walnut dresser in the Pennsylvania Dutch style, Manheim, Pennsylvania. The open chest with shelves for china and decorative pieces was characteristic of the early eighteenth century in this area. Lusterware and pewter spoons, usually arranged with perfect symmetry, were the housewife's compromise with the square, sturdy look of these highboys.

The painted chest was not only an object of beauty in the eighteenth-century home but it also served as clothes closet, linen chest, and repository for the silks and fine stuffs imported by Americans for their wardrobes. Sunflowers and tulips frequently figured in designs of the Dutch variety. This yellow-pine and poplar chest, dating from about 1780 and known as the Berks County type, also shows heralds and unicorns in the medieval tradition.

owned it and a favorite gift for brides. In Dutch households the pewter plates and earthenware were neatly arranged in open cupboards.

So suave had Boston become by the early eighteenth century that David Neal, after a visit to the Massachusetts metropolis, noted in his *History of New England*: "A gentleman from London could almost think himself at home in Boston, when he observes the numbers of People, their houses, their Furniture, their Tables, their Dress and Conversation, which perhaps is as splendid and showy, as that of the most considerable Tradesman in London." And some years later John Singleton Copley left living evidence on canvas of the great ladies of the period and their opulent attire.

Philadelphia was the fountainhead for the skilled craftsmen. There they fostered an American look, even while drawing inspiration from English design books. The Newport cabinetmakers avoided fads and stuck to earlier designs. They favored the classical shell, the fluted column, and Chinese fretwork. Craftsmen soon penetrated all the growing centers, but the less skilled simplified the designs characteristic of Philadelphia and Newport. Shells became fans; rosettes dwindled to pinwheels. Leather and stone cutting flourished in New England. Charleston turned out china and pottery, a craft that soon developed everywhere, since china was scarcely known in America before the Revolution and earthenware or Spanish platters served for general usage.

The homely word "cupboard" began to be heard around 1647, and it took many forms, but meanwhile the chest had been firmly established as the receptacle for personal belongings. It became an ornamental as well as a useful article of furniture. The Dutch chose to paint their chests, cupboards, and mirrors with bright colors. Many were carved and paneled, with molding and pendant drops. The Connecticut chests had sunflowers and tulips. Brides cherished dowry chests, often done in polychrome. Witty sayings and historical allusions were sometimes buried in the fruit and flowers, the parrots and thistles of the painted chests. When one drawer was added, the chest of drawers came to life, to be followed by highboys and recessed shell cupboards. Built-in cupboards with latticed glass doors were often installed at the recessed windows, or else there were wide window seats under the arch. Corner fireplaces, lined with gay Dutch tiles, added interest to the informal room.

The scalloped open cupboard was distinctly American in origin, and ship captains' wives from New England who sailed the seven seas with their husbands brought home Chinese porcelain and lacquer as well as British glass and silver to display on its open shelves. Japanese prints were used with lacquered furniture in the early 1760s. After 1810 the pure colonial style was freely mixed with imports from the Orient as well as from Europe. Gorgeous fabrics came from India and

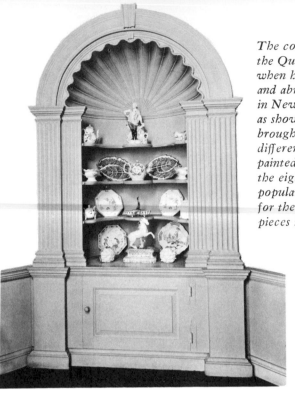

The corner cupboard flourished in the Queen Anne and Gothic periods when houses were built with niches and abrupt angles. They were popular in New England in the whaling days as show cases for the ornaments brought back by sea captains from different parts of the world. This painted pine specimen, dating from the eighteenth century, illustrates the popular shell pattern as a background for the decorative oriental porcelain pieces it contains.

Oriental influences appeared early in the American home as the whaling captains traded in the East. This eighteenth-century maple and pine New England highboy was japanned, a process used by the English in imitation of oriental lacquer. Japanning soon found its way into American cabinet-making and was a favorite form of decoration for many years.

The eighteenth-century Chinese parlor at the Winterthur Museum takes its cue from its brilliantly patterned wallpaper, illustrating the Chinese life of the era and giving its Chippendale furniture an appropriate background. The sofa was finished by Adam S. Coe in 1812. The lacquer screens in black and gold came from the famous Elias Hasket Derby mansion in Salem. The shell-carved open cupboard contains Chinese porcelain and a tea service of the exotic "Jesuit" china, a Chinese porcelain decorated with biblical scenes from European engravings. A garniture of Derbyshire spar adorns the mantelpiece and the chandelier has engraved hurricane shades.

China, brilliant with foliage and exotic birds. Wainscoted rooms were hung with tapestries or Spanish leather. Suits of armor and coats of mail brightened dark, small rooms in early Jamestown.

Cabinetmakers were arriving from England all through the eighteenth century and setting up in business in the larger centers. By using the abundant white pine they were able to undercut the imported pieces. Their work furnished many of the early houses, for itinerant cabinetmakers traveled west and south with carts, taking orders. But among them a few native cabinetmakers of distinction emerged, the most remarkable of whom was Duncan Phyfe (1768–1854). In his New York workshop he made furniture that survives today, notable for its delicate carvings of acanthus leaves and the lyre, its subtle varnish, characteristic dog-paw feet, and the Grecian curve of chairs and sofas designed originally for Greek Revival houses. Phyfe used only choice woods and studied contemporary taste. He worked in Regency style and late in life concentrated on decorative Empire pieces. At one time he employed a hundred workmen. In his own era American householders could buy his sofas for $122, his chairs for $22, and a pair of card tables for $140.

Down the years beds have been important furnishings in the home. Some of the early beds were imposing objects, standing well off the floor to allow for the trundle bed to be rolled beneath them. Twin beds under one canopy had curtains designed to keep out the "unhealthy" night air. But before beds of any kind were available, many of the colonials were forced to sleep on pillows, bolsters, and bed ticking stuffed with straw. Tired from their day's exertions in the woods, they often threw themselves down on the floor or on raw boards. Long before woven wire mattresses came into use around 1870, making way for the compressed-spring and foam-rubber models in use today, wool, feathers, sea-moss, paper shavings, straw, and hair were used to stuff mattresses. Hemlock boughs and sponge mattresses were thought to encourage fertility. Featherbeds brought warmth and comfort, however unhygienic, and the Dutch liked to shut themselves up in a curtained alcove bedstead, closely resembling a closet. New Englanders preferred the bedstead that they could hook to the wall with a network of rope, making way in the daytime for the spinning wheel, the wool winder, and the cradle.

In the 1850s two major improvements were made in sleeping arrangements—the use of leather thongs to support the featherbed mattress, and the swing bed that folded up into a cabinet or couch—forerunner of the Murphy bed and the Castro Convertible. In the nineteenth century the convertible craze evolved a bed that looked like a spinet and held a bureau, two closets, a basin and pitcher to boot. The infinite variety of design in this era and the freakishness of some of the built-in beds led to a general simplification in the twentieth century. Americans did not adopt the rococo French beds except in professionally decorated houses, but they used tall four-posters in their Greek Revival houses and were much addicted to the colonial canopied bed and the spool bed of New England. The Lincoln bed in the White House, made of rosewood and nine feet long, is known around the world. During the Victorian period the huge carved cherry and walnut bed reached by ladder was popular. The brass bed, the painted bed, and the plain mahogany bed all had their day, and by the mid-twentieth century pale woods and streamlined effects had invaded the American bedroom. The Hollywood bed, vast and symbolically shaped, luxurious, satiny, and much advertised, achieved a rakish fame.

At the turn of the century the twin bed came into favor. It was considered essential to good living in the next fifty years, but has lost ground recently to the ancient belief that husband and wife should share one large bed. Brides now are apt to stress the point. Their beds are often the product of personal design, with headboards, side cabinets, and all manner of paraphernalia at hand, from books to radios. Studio couches and similar subterfuges are the twentieth-century variation of the colonial's desire to have the bed roll into smaller compass to make room for other objects of furniture in crowded living quarters.

Sheets, once made of coarse Osnaburg, or trimmed with Elgin lace, then of the purest linen, are apt now to be delicate, of nylon or percale, often with printed floral designs. Fine monogramed linen, crimson damask spreads, quilted crewel work, and crocheted spreads have acquired the interest of period pieces, as lustrous synthetic silks or trim tailored effects in linen or corduroy cover the contemporary bed.

Only slightly less important than the bed were the trestles, stools, and benches that preceded chairs and tables. The earliest dining tables were long, narrow boards, often only three feet wide, supported on trestles. They were frequently made from the packing boxes and chests coming in with stores from England. But late in the seventeenth century, dining, serving, and tea tables supplanted the trestle, and in many homes fine linen and lace took the place of the early tablecloths made of Osnaburg, Holland, or huckaback. The tiptop table with pie-crust edge soon added grace to innumerable rooms. The writing table —a bureau that had evolved originally from the wall desk of the monk— carried the Renaissance influence into many American homes. From this came the commode, a dominating piece of furniture in the bedroom, converted into a washstand, with a marble top. The chaise longue, which in time became one of the most rococo pieces in any house, actually developed from the simple settle, but it was never a prime favorite with the energetic American people. It vaguely suggested idleness and dalliance, the French court, and the courtesan.

By the end of the eighteenth century highboys, lowboys, desks and chairs, cupboards and assorted tables, many with scrolled pediments, pilaster treatment, or carved relief, were the accepted furnishings in graceful surroundings. John Adams, visiting the home of his friend Nick Boylston in 1766, was struck by the elegant dinner, the Turkish carpets, the marble tables, the rich beds with crimson damask curtains and counterpanes, the painted hangings and spacious garden—"the most magnificent I have ever seen."

The Bostonian's love of books was reflected in the glass-fronted library bookcases derived from Chippendale, and the need of flat surfaces for study resulted in the large library tables that abounded all through the Victorian era. Chippendale built a bookcase with library steps folded inside it during the era when everything had to be enclosed. But many years earlier Benjamin Franklin had put a stepladder with hinges underneath his *fauteuil*, and he liked to show his visitors how he forked down books from the upper shelves with calipers at the end of a pole.

Nowhere was there greater variety than in chairs, and here the native American cabinetmaker made a solid reputation of his own. His chair backs were sturdier than those of the Sheraton and Hepplewhite style. A certain simplicity was characteristic of the native furniture, like the American Shaker pieces, which were practical, well built, and devoid of ornamentation. In fact, imagination was first brought to bear on simple carpentry through the creation of good chairs. From the day when public attention was drawn to Lord Delaware's green velvet seat in Jamestown Church, consistent efforts were made to provide comfortable resting places in the early American homes. At first chairs were reserved for the master of the house or the honored guest, while lesser mortals used settles, stools, or benches. They were sturdy before they were graceful, and the first, or "wainscot chairs," were of solid oak with square backs, occasionally carved or paneled. Thin cushions covered with damask added a touch of ease as time went on.

The next variation was an oak chair with a high back and cane seat, cane having come into fashion during the reign of Charles II. Next came the slatback chair, usually with a leather seat, followed by the rush-bottom Windsor chair. It was more popular in America before the Revolution than it was in England, and it sold in quantity. Easy chairs appeared early in the eighteenth century, and the winged fireside chair with shell-carved knee and deep cushions had the place of honor. It was often upholstered with the Turkish or Irish stitch, and the colors usually were red or green. The early Dutch chairs, forerunners of the Queen Anne and Chippendale styles, had a provincial charm of their own, with Spanish feet and rush seats. The Dutch, above all other settlers, paid attention to warmth and physical well-being, with their warming pans filled with hot coals, their huge painted *kases* and kaleidoscopic tiles spreading color in all directions. The claw-and-ball feet of the bow-legged Dutch chair led to their being known as "crowfoot" or "eaglesfoot" chairs. Bedroom easy chairs done with brocatelle to match the bed hangings and curtains could be found in most of the prosperous homes during this period.

Between 1720 and 1750 the delicate Queen Anne chairs were turned out by native cabinetmakers, with the cabriole leg and slippered feet of Danish origin. By this time the classic Chippendale, Sheraton, and Hepplewhite styles were affecting all manner of household furnishings, including chairs. The native craftsmen became successful imitators, and soon a great hodgepodge of chairs were scattered around the American home, some of local production, like the Brewster and Carver chairs. A sale in 1817 noted an "elegant assortment of curled maple painted, ornamental landscape, sewing and rocking chairs, lounges, settees, sofas, music stools, etc."

The rocking chair became more or less a national symbol when President Kennedy took office, but it has been part of American life since the 1770s when slat-backed chairs were first converted into rockers. They made an early appearance in Philadelphia, and Benjamin Franklin has been credited with their invention, but the point has never been proved. In the years that followed, the rocking chair gained great popularity in America, but after a century and a half of widespread use, it degenerated into a sign of the humdrum, unsophisticated home—until President Kennedy gave it fresh interest.

Since nearly all the earliest models had been converted, they were strongly suggestive of cradles. Then Lambert Hitchcock, noted for the excellence of his chairs, turned out stenciled rockers that were cheap and sold well early in the nineteenth century. A variety of models soon flooded the market until the rocking chair became a symbol of simple family life in America, as grandmother drowsed to its motion, father read the newspaper, mother nursed the baby, and the young made it sway and swing. In buying her furniture a bride thought first of the family bed, then of a rocker for the parlor. The "rocking settee," a combined bench and cradle that enabled a mother to rock, knit, and read was a popular novelty for a time.

The brightly painted Windsor rocking chairs, with comb-backs and stenciled vines and garlands, were short and bumpy in their motion. Longer rockers were tried for a more satisfying swing. The tall, straight models without arms were soon abandoned in favor of the fiddlebacks of New England and the Dutch rockers with upright stiles and block-turned front legs. The cabinetmakers of New Hampshire and Vermont made chairs with wider spindles than the Windsor type, and some were of bamboo, tulip, ash, or maple. But the factory principle was brought to bear on the rocking chair by the middle of the

The evolution of the chair is a good index to changing styles in American furniture. The chair-table, ca. 1675, is an ingenious variation on the imported pieces that early American cabinetmakers copied.

The Windsor settee was an American adaptation of the Windsor chair that came from England about 1725. Instead of using the wide splat of the English models, American cabinetmakers substituted spindles in a variety of effects—the hoop-back, the fan-back, and the comb-back, which extended the top rail until it looked like a large comb. This settee, popular with courting couples, illustrates the comb effect.

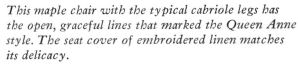

The decorative touch favored in Pennsylvania is apparent in this side chair of maple or ash designed in 1796. The oval-backed painted chairs made by expert cabinetmakers in Philadelphia for the early Salem mansions featured a peacock and bow-knot design, and the foliage is typical of painted Dutch furniture. (Below left.)

The American variation of Hepplewhite's shield back flourished during the Greek Revival period, and this side chair, suggestive also of the lyre motif favored by Duncan Phyfe, has the strength common to all the furniture of this period. It is painted and gilded, and has a stout rush seat.

This maple chair with the typical cabriole legs has the open, graceful lines that marked the Queen Anne style. The seat cover of embroidered linen matches its delicacy.

nineteenth century and the Lincoln, Sleepy Hollow, and American Standard rockers became the popular makes. The Lincoln rocker was upholstered in crimson damask, but the fussiest and most Victorian was the Standard, done with plush, tassels, and fringe, a clumsy rocking chair that lingered in American homes until the twentieth century. The Boston rocker showed a touch of Empire influence, with ebullient curves. At no time in its history did the rocking chair add grace or style to the surrounding décor, but the better examples were well adjusted to the human frame, and its soporific quality soothed several generations before the automobile whipped up the craze for speed.

The rocking chair has been traced back to the late Gothic cradle, and to the nursing chair used around 1750 in Lancashire, England, but the principle was extended in the United States to a series of chairs adapted to the business world. The rococo period tended to induce ease with wider and deeper seats, and people were beginning to lounge in comfort after the Spartan slat-back and Windsor chairs, when the principle of the spring that had given Thomas Jefferson his revolving chair was applied to piano stools, library chairs, and high-backed easy chairs. Movable railroad seats added to the comfort of travel early in the 1850s. Two decades later the sewing-machine seat was introduced, to ease the aching backs of innumerable housewives. In the 1890s the typewriter chair, with its resilient back rest, became part and parcel of the business world. Finally the surgeon, the barber, and the dentist had adjustable seats that could be locked at will.

The wide-armed chair used in lecture halls today goes back to the medieval practice of using a combined adjustable writing board and seat. But the desk chair remained heavy and clumsy until the metal-based furniture of the 1920s—and particularly Mies van der Rohe's tubular chair—hit the market with the speed and intensity of a summer storm. His Barcelona chair has been described as the perfect model of its kind, preceded though it was by the remarkable Thonet chair of 1900. Marcel Breuer's cantilever furniture was followed in 1945 by the Charles Eames chair of molded plywood, rubber joints, and steel tubing. Eames then moved on to a wire-frame chair, a molded plastic, and a cast-metal chair. Laminated wood and steel tubing changed the interior scene of the great office buildings of the nation, removing the chair to its farthest point from the Duncan Phyfe tradition. Unmistakably the functional age had set in, with modern chairs giving a light and uncluttered aspect to a world without decoration. For the hostess who must have everything, a stainless steel dining room set was devised that could be packed away neatly after dinner. Such novelties left the general public untouched, however.

But even in the modern décor the landscaped and Chinese wall-papers of an earlier era combine harmoniously with the stark lines of the furniture. They are among the most interesting reminders of

The eighteenth-century American Chippendale mahogany
wing chair has never lost its popularity. This one is
remarkable chiefly for its printed cotton upholstery.
The design, known as "the Apotheosis of Franklin,"
symbolizes the deification of this gifted American.
A patriotic medley of flags, stars, soldiers, and other
symbols of independence made a popular decorative motif
after the War of Independence. It was customary then
to use historical themes in textiles as a change from the
tropical birds, animals, and flowers of the oriental
garden scenes.

Long before the days of John F. Kennedy the rocking
chair had an honored place in the White House. Abraham
Lincoln had a comfortable rocker in his bedroom, with
a wide swing that suited his long legs. It was the lounging
type that preceded the fiddlebacks of New England and
the gaily painted Dutch rockers. Upholstered in crimson
damask, this style became popular after the Civil War
and was known as the Lincoln rocking chair. Although
rocking chairs had been in American homes from the
1770s, they were hand-fashioned until factories after the
war turned them out in various styles—the Windsor,
the Sleepy Hollow, the Boston, the Standard, and many
others. The monstrosity of the late Victorian era was the
Standard, a stubby rocking chair smothered in plush,
tassels, and fringe that swung in the parlor or on the
porch of countless American homes.

colonial days, when they adorned the drawing rooms and dining rooms of town and country houses. The Chinese and flowered wallpapers accented the Chippendale furniture turned out by Philadelphia cabinet-makers. The Oriental trade had brought this influence to bear on furniture, porcelain, and the wallpaper that came in scrolls on rollers. Glazed English wallpaper, with exotic birds painted separately and applied to verdant backgrounds, enlivened somber rooms, and Italian landscapes done on sepia paper, with classic ruins in the background, adorned many a dining room.

Although white paint is usually associated with the colonial scene, it was not used to any extent before the nineteenth century. Pearl and cream were applied to the dining room and parlor of the Governor's Palace at Williamsburg in 1727, but the "bluish or lead color" used at Yale College in 1738 was more characteristic of the period. Painters used a wide range of colors, but the New Englanders leaned to yellow ocher and a deep crimson made from red lead mixed with lamp black. Prussian blue, Spanish brown, Venetian red, and a dull green appropriately known as verdigris were widely used before the Revolution. Years earlier the pioneer women had dyed their homespun with the colors squeezed from roots and herbs—brown from butternut hulls, red from ground madder root, yellow from onion skins, beige from sumac.

In the more sophisticated age ceilings had tinted plaster or papier-mâché finish, and staircases had elaborately turned balusters. Fluted pilasters were intrinsic decoration in many homes. The sunflower design was common on stairways and highboys, particularly in Philadelphia. Walls were often hung with damask, velvet, or satin, and rooms were named after the color of their hangings rather than their paint. Curtains and valances were heavily lined and fell in rich folds with the lambrequin finish, or they were of calico, lightly strung from rings on a rod. Fringes, ropes, and swags abounded down to the twentieth century when the true Oriental silks, Genoa velvets, and Nottingham lace were followed by a period of synthetics, of chintz and cretonne, of oatmeal cloth and fiber glass, of abstract designs and geometric patterns, of cheesecloth and brocade, ninon and printed linen—something for every taste. But calico, chintz, and copperplate linen were popular in 1765, and history was repeating itself when the yellow satin and red brocatelle of the romantic past came to life again in the 1960s. A dash of Victorian plush was revived by smart hostesses who had tried everything else. They even trafficked in horsehair, the sepulchral upholstery that first made its appearance in the early nineteenth century as "flowered horsehair" and "fancy haircloth."

But the porcelain, china, and silverware of the early days gave subtle coloring and glow to the dullest rooms. Late in the seventeenth century the decorative value of Chinese pottery was apparent to the

When Charles Eames designed this molded plywood chair with polished chrome steel legs and frames for Herman Miller in 1946, he initiated a revolution in furniture design. The airy look belies an engineered ruggedness that has made it a staple item in offices and auditoriums across the country.

The Barcelona Chair. When Mies van der Rohe's tubular chair reached the market, it was described as the perfect model for the human body. It was part of the revolution in modern furnishings that followed the introduction of metal-based chairs and tables in the 1920s. Homes, offices, clubs, patios changed radically in appearance as chairs by Thonet, Eames, Mies van der Rohe, and others became an essential part of the glass houses, the copper skyscrapers, the banks and offices of the 1960s. Heavy, old-fashioned furniture disappeared like magic in the business world as the tubular chromium effects took hold, with a passing nod to posture, health, and fatigue.

traveled and the stay-at-homes. The American eagle and old Cantonese symbols decorated punch bowls and ornaments. Delftware was popular in all parts of the country but particularly in New York and Pennsylvania. And china poured in from the Chelsea factories in England. Where once the potter's wheel had been used in the home soon every American city had pottery factories. The native silverware acquired distinction of its own. It was heavy, substantial, and plain. As homes were built by the men who had prospered in the new land the silversmiths became important members of the community. There were twenty-four of them in Boston, Newport, and Williamsburg by 1680, and the goldsmiths of Charleston were as well known as its landscaped gardens. Yet only sixty families owned silver in the seventeenth century, and it was early in the eighteenth century before silver and china were generally available, and the Dutch introduced their delftware in America.

The dram cup made in 1651 was the oldest piece of colonial silverware, but the tankard, soon in general use, was often an imposing piece of silver, with a crest or coat of arms. The caudle cup with tulip decoration was a valued family possession, and a large silver saltcellar often occupied the center of the dining table. Spoons for the most part were of pewter, alloy, or wood. The better shoebuckles were of silver, displaying the American eagle or the profile of George Washington.

There was little tin in the seventeenth century, but the iron age brought in pots and pans, firedogs and candlesticks. The early foundries of New England and Pennsylvania turned out toleware, or painted tin. Brides collected tinware for their hope chests, and the tin dipper at the pump and well became traditional, if unhygienic. The peddlers' wagons jingled along with the rattling tinware and tinkling bell that announced their arrival in country hamlets. Candle molds and sconces were made of tin, and japanned ware was immensely popular for trays.

Native brass was not produced in America before 1800, but it was soon in demand for kettles, lamps, and buttons. Most of the sleighbells came from the early brass factories, as well as the cowbells and handbells that brought children into the classroom and the farmer home for his dinner. Brass was also one of the prime needs of the clock industry that flourished after Connecticut became the heart of the clock trade. One of the most interesting of the early clocks came from Pennsylvania, where David Rittenhouse, expert in astronomy and mathematics, made the grandfather clock a dependable and inexpensive timepiece for colonial homes in the 1790s.

Boston was still without a clock in 1657, and neither a clock nor a watch could be found in Newport in 1672. Lynn had a celebrated clock that struck the hours. But the sundial stood in gardens amid the flowers, and hourglasses and an occasional waterclock kept

The rug is a bear skin, clothes are hung on wall pegs along with the tools, and the child's toys are as crude as the hand-hewn furniture. Though roughly furnished, the one-room log cabin provided all the essentials for life on the frontier.

Seventeenth-century parlor, originally in the Job Wright house built on Long Island soon after 1667 but now known as the Oyster Bay Room at the Winterthur Museum. Family life focused around the great fireplace with its unique lintel of diamond-shaped points. The ceiling illustrates the Dutch and Flemish treatment of beams and framing, with supporting posts for the narrow summer beams. The Cromwellian chair in the foreground has its original upholstery of Turkey work, and the slatbacks include a typical New England Carver chair. A Bible box dated 1664 stands on the carved Ipswich chest.

The sala of the Hugo Reid Adobe built in 1839 resembles, in homely comfort, the early New England rustic farmhouse living room, translated into the architectural idiom of the Spanish-Mexican period of "Alta California." Many of the articles in the room are of Mexican origin: the wall box, probably used for housing a santo, the ladderback chair against the wall, the Alpujarra rug beneath the table, and the woven blanket covering the spool bed. The chairs are an excellent example of Spanish colonial furniture. Other articles such as the whale-oil lamps and the American Empire drop-leaf table of mahogany were shipped from the East. The Hawaiian tapa cloth hanging above the bed was originally used for bedding.

This New England William and Mary daybed with its handsome Spanish feet might have been found in a Federal parlor. Uninviting as it may appear, it was the forerunner of the comfortable chaise longues of the late eighteenth century.

This mahogany Sheraton-style sofa (1795–1800) has none of the lounging possibilities of the Madame Récamier directoire models, but many great American ladies of the post-Revolutionary days chose it for their Greek Revival drawing rooms and sat on it with stiff spines, entertaining the statesmen of the day. The swags and classical decoration gave it a unified effect with its surroundings.

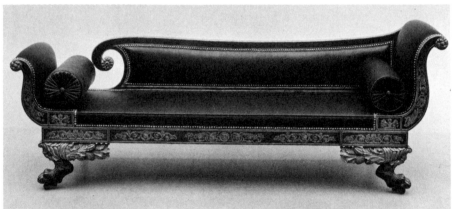

This painted and gilded cherry Empire-style sofa (1815) suggests the workshop of Duncan Phyfe. It shows the deplored horsehair upholstering at its best. The claw feet and thistle-and-rose decoration are typical of the work of America's master cabinetmaker.

The Oxford rooms of Old Salem are Federal in style. The furniture was made in Virginia and South Carolina. The mahogany Pembroke table, the Chippendale armchairs, and the little mahogany settee are from Charleston; the Hepplewhite tall clock was made in Chester. The wallpaper is a fox-and-rooster design inspired by the fables of La Fontaine. The rug is an early nineteenth-century Aubusson.

The Empire parlor, dating from about 1830 and originally in a house in Albany, is a choice example of Greek Revival style, with its purity of line and formal spaciousness. It has Greek honeysuckle pilaster capitals on its tall windows and doorways, and the Aubusson carpets show the Greek motif. The columns of its pier tables and the oversize lion-paw feet can be traced to ancient Greece. The mantelpiece is flanked by carved caryatids and a Girandole mirror hangs above it, a characteristic Empire touch. Some of the marble-topped tables with gilded carving suggest the work of the French emigré cabinetmaker, Charles Honoré Lannuier. Portraits of American heroes are painted on the French porcelains. The cut-glass and bronze chandelier makes a perfect finish for this stately room.

Two phases of American Gothic taste are represented in the dining room at Lyndhurst, a Gothic revival mansion in Tarrytown, New York. The group of smaller chairs ranged around the table and the table itself (based on a Pugin design) echo A. J. Davis' monastic design for the first part of the house built in 1838–41 for William and Philip Paulding. The total effect of the room, however, is late Victorian Gothic, the style of the second wing built in 1865–67. The three varieties of marble in the fireplace are repeated in the marbleizing of the columns and arches; the textured floral pattern of the walls and its gold centers are glazed a rich raspberry red; the pine ceiling is painted to imitate oak and cedar. The elaborate table settings represent the taste of the third owner of the house, financier Jay Gould.

people in tune with shifting time until a great wave of clocks appeared early in the eighteenth century. Some came from England and had japanned or walnut cases. There were hour clocks, week clocks and month clocks, chime clocks, church clocks, and spring table clocks. Wall clocks came from France at about the same time, graceful models designed by master sculptors, and contemporaneously the tile clock arrived from Holland. The American clockmaker established himself firmly in the eighteenth century, however, with everything from the Wag-on-the-Wall clocks to stately grandfather models. The banjo clock was adapted by Simon Willard of Boston from an English wall clock, but the carved and gilded eagle and its glass paintings recording naval successes gave it a strongly native touch. The classical period in architecture found expression in its clocks, too, with an acorn clock made in Bristol, Connecticut, showing on its case its maker's Greek Revival house. He was Gideon Roberts, an enterprising man who, by using wood instead of brass, was able to sell his clocks for twenty dollars, without cases.

Eli Terry of Plymouth, Connecticut, was a pioneer who made his first all-wooden clock in 1793 and traveled on horseback with hang-up clocks in his saddlebags. Seth Thomas and William Clagge were two other great names in the world of clocks. Thomas bought the patent to the wooden movement used by Terry, started a factory of his own, and his clocks became nationally known. Although the clockmakers after the Civil War tried to make grandfather clocks with some of the skill and care of the colonials, they merely succeeded in putting ordinary works into tall cases.

Clocks and candles were among the early possessions of value and interest, and after Newporters started whaling in the 1730s, factories for spermaceti candles flourished in New England. The first settlers used pine knots for lighting, and Governor Winthrop had to send to England for tallow and wicks. The Betty lamp, pear-shaped and filled with tallow or whale oil, was the earliest lamp. It came in tin, and in pewter for those who could afford it. The Phoebe lamp, which closely resembled the Betty lamp, had a shallow cup to catch loose grease. Families made their candles in autumn, or they used the services of traveling candlemakers who had molds to shape them. The green wax of the bayberry was decorative, and fragrant bayberry candles are still on the market in the twentieth century. The first chandeliers were roughly made with strips of metal or crossed sticks.

At the close of the seventeenth century one lantern hung on a pole served every seven houses for lighting. A watchman with rattling kloppers patrolled the streets with a black, brass-tipped stave, calling out at intervals: "Lanthorn, and a whole candell-light. Hang out your lights." New York had only ten watchmen for its police force at that

The Queen Anne bedroom of Old Salem, Inc., has the
fresh charm associated with this style that brought a
new sense of comfort, liveliness, and grace to domestic
interiors in the early eighteenth century. The cabriole
leg and pad foot are hallmarks of this curvilinear style,
though the mahogany bedstead has unusual hoof feet.
A Cucena and a smaller Kulah rug in yellows and
greens complement the greens and yellows of the
crewel-embroidered linen hangings and the
linsey-woolsey coverlet.

Many New England homemakers preferred the rich
and decorative background provided by French and
Chinese wallpaper. The wallpaper in the Haverhill
Room, in the Metropolitan Museum of Art, designed
by Jacquemart and Bénard of Paris, complements the
ornate carved bed and its elegant silk hangings, the
embroidered rug, and the Chinese cabinet.

The English influence on furnishing remained strong
through the early centuries of our nation. Often the
well-to-do who traveled in Europe preferred to send
home furniture and furnishings that they had
purchased abroad. The nursery at Villa Boscobel at
Garrison-on-Hudson, New York, with its Sheraton
child's bed with canopy and coverlet in a floral print
and miniature Liverpool tea set, looks very much like a
child's room in a house in the English countryside.

time. But things changed by the eighteenth century, and Philadelphia in 1751, with its whale-oil lamps, was considered the best-lit city of its time. Newport put glass lamps outside houses and shops, and New Yorkers were heavily fined for tampering in any way with a hundred lamps, fifty feet apart and ten feet above the street, installed by private citizens in the mid-eighteenth century.

But in the 1750s, when whale-oil lamps were in use, the streets were even less safe than in the 1960s. Today's marauding had its counterpart in the violence and disorder of a sparsely policed age. Footpads who sneaked up on their victims, muggers, and pickpockets abounded, and all manner of transgressions were reported, from highway robbery, rape, assaults, and murder to petty thievery, counterfeiting, and housebreaking. People were warned to lock their doors and windows at night, and shops and warehouses were looted regularly. Many of the entries were made in broad daylight. A bunch of keys found in Boston in 1768 would open any lock. The thieves on Murray Hill at a later date worked with skeleton keys, revolvers, and bowie knives. Few people would walk the more fashionable streets alone at night lest someone leap out at them from dark porticoes or badly lighted basement steps. Pennsylvania had the strictest criminal laws, but from the beginning New York had the most crime. In 1749 a newspaper commented: "It seems to be now become dangerous for the good People of this City, to be out late at Nights, without being sufficiently strong or well armed, as several Attacks and Disturbances have been lately made in our Streets."

Fire was a constant hazard, and a system of bells alerted the community. Families frequently were warned to take care of their sooty chimneys. Nevertheless major fires continued to plague the cities: New York was all but wiped out in 1835, and Chicago barely survived the Great Fire of 1871. In each case a new type of city was built on the ruins, with larger shops and wider streets. The eighteenth-century stores were more picturesque than convenient. Their swinging signs resembled those of the taverns, and sometimes the names of the establishments were placarded in giant letters. New York had more than two hundred tiny pane-glass shopwindows by the middle of the century, and lighting improved steadily with the years. The first practical matches, Congreves, came from England in 1827. They were made of wood and cardboard treated with sulphur, and a box of eighty-four sold for twenty-five cents. But before matches were in use the tinderbox was a household essential in every home. Flint and steel stirred up a spark, sometimes on old linen, but Dickens complained that it took half an hour to get a light.

This era ended suddenly when Thomas A. Edison lit up the world in a dramatic new way. Things moved slowly at first, even in his own country, but in 1879 he took out his patent for an incandescent bulb and in 1880 he gave a demonstration at Menlo Park, New Jersey, with three hundred lamps. There were not more than five thousand electric lamps in the United States in 1881, when J. P. Morgan became the first New Yorker to have his house illuminated in this fashion, but five years later two hundred thousand were in use. When Welsbach brought out his popular gas mantel in 1885, gaslight took on a new flourish, and it was not until electrical energy was dramatized at the Columbian Exposition in 1893 that the public showed warm interest in the new form of lighting. Today American electrical effects are among the wonders of the world, and the gaslit era lies in the misty past.

Perhaps no one has benefited more than the housewife in the three hundred years of the nation's growing up. From the austerity and privation of the simple cabin she has moved into a world of electrical and other conveniences. The fireplace today is a luxury touch, but it was the very focus of family life in the days of the colonists. It swallowed logs so large that sometimes they had to be dragged to the door by horse and chain. Much of the heat went up the great open chimney and was lost to parents and children. But the joys and defeats of family life lay close to the hearth, with the bed, the cradle, the spinning wheel, the cooking and eating utensils around it. Early inglenooks were sometimes built within the chimney proper, and the bare walls and rafters were brightened with strings of dried peppers, apples, and pumpkins dangling from poles over the fireplace. The saltbox hung by the fire, and trammel rods and swinging iron cranes suspended huge cast-iron pots at differing heights. The skillets and trivets made a merry clank as game was roasted, to the delight of the watching children.

The Dutch oven or roasting kitchen was an early feature of the colonial home. Bread and rolls were baked on pans, or even on large oak leaves. Iron griddles, tongs, and pokers hung on the wall, and an iron fork was used for toasting bread. A popular gift for brides was a long-handled shovel to take food out of the oven. Andirons were an important fireside tradition, and as people prospered, those useful items became elaborate, representing human figures or dogs, which gave them their colloquial name of firedogs.

Early in the eighteenth century the stove, already in use in Europe, was introduced in America. The Germans of Pennsylvania were the first to use the sheet-metal stoves and hot-air drums that passed muster for a time. Soon china stoves were being advertised, as well as the "Philadelphia fire stoves" that came into fashion when Benjamin Franklin in 1742 devised an early variation of what later became known as the Franklin stove. It burned both wood and coal, and in its ultimate form met the needs of thousands of early American families.

At first it was regarded as Franklin's "Pennsylvania fireplace,"

121

Fashioning the Home

and it caused some merriment. He had observed that with the German stoves "a man is scorched before, while he is froze behind." He decided to move the fireplace away from the wall, so that it would radiate heat all around, and he devised his iron fireplace with the chimney going through the old flue. Franklin was pleased with the effect. "How warm our stove rooms seem in winter," he told a friend, "and yet the highest they ever rais'd my Thermometers was to 56." But the founding fathers were used to having their ink freeze, and John Adams remarked that he longed to "hibernate like a dormouse from autumn to spring."

The Franklin stove held its ground, although many other varieties reached the market—round, oval and, finally in the 1840s, the flat-topped model that presaged the modern cookstove. At this point the kettle was detached from its crane to sit on a cast-iron surface, and the housewife had found a major convenience. Many of the colonial stoves were inscribed with the Ten Commandments, the miracles, or with floral and other worldly designs. Although most of the fireplaces were boarded up at this time, a good many women still liked to cook at the open fireplace, roasting their meat on spits and baking their bread in brick ovens. They no longer had to cope with unwieldy iron pots that sometimes weighed as much as forty pounds. They now had lighter ware of coated steel, and a reservoir of heated water with which to wash up after meals. They had kerosene or "coal oil," as they called it, to serve many household purposes. Parlor stoves of many kinds appeared during the Civil War era, but the visitors from England and France who traveled in America during these troubled years complained that they could neither keep warm in winter nor stay cool in summer.

The cast-iron range that dominated the kitchen from 1840 to 1880 was an American invention, perfected by Benjamin Thompson, Count Rumford, who was born and grew up in colonial America. The gas range made its initial appearance in the 1880s, but it was considered dangerous and housewives were afraid of it. However, it survived, with a succession of improvements, and although it began to lose its primacy in 1930 it holds its own today in the electrified kitchen. The revolution in the kitchen had its first reverberations at the Columbian Exposition, when a clumsy electric range held women in rapt attention, though it was not the streamlined enamel object it is today, smoothly merged with other kitchen units into a harmonious whole. By 1945 architects had given unity, compactness, and a clinical efficiency to the kitchen, and few women hankered any longer for the size, warmth, and homeliness of the old-fashioned kind. Iron, zinc, copper, and finally porcelain and steel had replaced the early wooden sink. The icebox, with its old drip pan, had given way to the electric refrigerator. The broom and the carpet sweeper had yielded to the vacuum cleaner, and the laundry tub and washboard to the electric washing machine.

Fashioning the Home

In the mid-nineteenth century 85 per cent of the population lived in the country, but by 1940 only one in four lived on farms, and life became easier for everyone as a succession of irons, toasters, wringers, and fans; eggbeaters and waffle irons; broilers, ice cream freezers, and coffee percolators; Mixmasters and nursery bottle warmers; electrical appliances, such as blankets, shoe buffers, hairbrushes, and toothbrushes, fulfilled their various functions for the householder. The deluge started after World War II; there were nineteen electrical appliances on the market in 1930, thirty-six in 1940, fifty-six in 1954, and eighty-nine in 1966, ranging from television sets and air conditioning to ice crushers, can openers, apple parers, and sweater driers.

The first American washing-machine patent was taken out in 1797. Many hopeful inventors soon picked up the trail and patented their machines. Fifteen patents for the gyrator type widened the field by 1929. Although the first of the electric dishwashers went on the market around 1910, they were not in general use before 1930, and it was 1956 before the present combined washer and dryer appeared on the scene. When the sadirons faded and electric irons showed their cheerful glow, the housewife had taken another step toward nirvana. She could do her laundry, clean her house, and cook without the back-breaking effort that the women's magazines had been deploring since 1912. Actually, Catharine E. Beecher, antisuffragist but propagandist for advanced education for women, had outlined home arrangements in the mid-nineteenth century that took into account the human being as well as the work to be done in the kitchen. Miss Beecher advocated scientific kitchen and bathroom arrangements well ahead of her time as well as careful planning to simplify household tasks.

The electric refrigerator, one of the greatest improvements of all, first came on the market around 1913 and cost nine hundred dollars, but each year models changed and prices were modified. Finally the Deep-freeze was added to all the other perquisites, a touch of paradise for the suburban housewife and the large-scale entertainer in any sphere, enabling her to bring to her table at a moment's notice an endless variety of fare. In 1966 one leading electric company showed thirty-three brightly decorated refrigerator fronts, with designs ranging from a brilliant red Pennsylvania Dutch hex sign to pop art jack-of-hearts playing cards. Color had conquered the clinical neutrality of the icebox.

The vacuum cleaner, based on a principle evolved in 1859, became practical in 1908, but at that time it was still a clumsy object used chiefly in hotels and mansions. When the Hoover appeared in 1915 it was still unwieldy, but a source of immediate joy to the housewife. As vacuum cleaner models improved, their mechanism was tucked out of sight, and they moved on compact trolleys. Only the sloppy house-keeper lets dust gather on her possessions today. She does not have far

The Calvin Coolidge kitchen at the Coolidge Homestead in Plymouth, Vermont, is a typical old-fashioned kitchen of the nineteenth century, and nothing was added to it when Coolidge became President. He washed his hands at this sink before being sworn in as Chief Executive by his father. The pipe ascending from the cast-iron stove warmed his bedroom, and he raised a storm if the lamp chimneys were not crystal clear. The dipper, simple basin, pepper and salt, and assorted tins were the same kind as those used by farmers across the country. The coffeepot and iron always stood on the stove, and the big iron pot held the President's favorite mush. Towels dried on a rack behind the stove. Calvin Coolidge preferred his farmhouse kitchen to those of the White House, but his wife did not agree.

The modern housewife's kitchen may not be as large as her colonial ancestors', but in a compact area she has every convenience—tile working surfaces, chrome stainless steel sink and stove surface, refrigerator, freezer, storage space—even a dining counter.

to walk from one point to another in directing her household operations. The combined efforts of industrial designers, architects, engineers, decorators, and nutritionists have brought her kitchen and all its activities into focus, with separate working sections for storage and preservation, for the preparation and cooking of food, for dining and family life.

The components of home life are now as they were in the beginning, but with a world of difference. The hearth does not glow—it glitters as austerely as ice; the spit is electrically run; the vegetables do not hang on strings but are tucked out of sight and frozen; the chicken and steak are in the Deepfreeze; milk is in cartons, not in great wide pans. But parents and children gather in the modern kitchens as they did of old, to eat in dinette areas with Formica-topped tables instead of trestles; or in dining nooks with colonial touches; or on the patio, a kitchen annex where metal furniture picks up the contemporary mood.

The housewife can watch her baby at play as she cooks, launders, irons, or dines. All around her are wall cabinets, sliding doors, working surfaces, broom and china closets, shelves easy to reach, disposal units, and every possible convenience. In addition, she has the inestimable boon of air conditioning that came into popular use after World War II, although under trial since 1905. Household air conditioners may now be matched to the décor—colonial, traditional, contemporary, or provincial. Only a certain percentage of the population lives within this glossy framework, however. There are still old-fashioned kitchens, even though few today are without an icebox and shining stove.

Next to the kitchen, the bathroom perhaps has undergone the most dramatic revision down the years. The ubiquity of the American bathroom has been a matter of comment around the world, and Americans are perhaps considered the most tubbed and scrubbed of mortals. Not only do they have the greatest number of bathrooms, but theirs are the best equipped. Nevertheless, bathtubs were not in general use, even in America, until the twentieth century, and tenements suffered a lack of this convenience down to the 1960s. As late as 1959 a million more Americans had television than had bathrooms.

A century ago no special room was allotted to bathing. The zinc tub in front of the kitchen fire or in the bedroom involved the Saturday night ritual of the weekly bath. One or more of the family washtubs were lined up behind a screen while the children splashed and cavorted as water trickled over their soapy bodies. It was always a problem to have enough heated water to go around. The pump and the kitchen sink did service, too. But a man who bathed every day would have been considered slightly mad, since even in the 1870s frequent bathing was considered a menace to health, encouraging inflammation of the lungs.

Bathing was something of a public rite until the eighteenth century, but never in America, where the Puritan spirit made it a secret ritual. The leisurely hours passed in the marble baths of Greece and Rome, the Turkish baths of the Crusaders, the seventeenth-century Frenchmen and their ladies who entertained while bathing and even had their portraits painted in their tubs, bore small relation to the quick showers of today.

The bathtub was regarded with suspicion when Latrobe designed the first complete bathroom in American history. He put the tub, water closet, and basin in the same room in a Philadelphia house as early as 1810. But it was not until the 1880s, when five out of six Americans were still washing with pail and sponge, that bathtubs began to be discussed in the newspapers. Presidents and millionaires had become interested. President Millard Fillmore had caused an uproar in 1851 by installing the first bathtub in White House history, a move as unsettling as the addition of President Truman's balcony. The tub was considered a case of "importing a monarchical luxury into the official residence of the Chief Executive of the Republic." President Fillmore did not live long to enjoy it, but William Howard Taft got the full benefit of his mammoth tub while he was President. His girth created special problems, and the tub he ordered was large enough to hold four average-sized men. He had another in the Philippines that could swallow six. His sister-in-law, Mrs. Charles Phelps Taft, installed an enormous $1,500 bathtub for his use at her home in Cincinnati, but it could not compete with the sixteen-by-ten-foot tub used by the Prince Regent, later George IV, in the Royal Pavilion at Brighton.

The bathrooms of famous men and women became matters of public interest in the 1890s. J. P. Morgan, also of giant build, had a bath twelve feet long—with gold taps—housed in the library he had built adjoining his house on Murray Hill. He had to travel by an underground passage to reach it. Mrs. John Jacob Astor's two-ton bathtub was fashioned out of a solid block of marble. George Vanderbilt's Fifth Avenue bathroom, with exposed lead plumbing and nickel-plated pipes, was considered a marvel of luxury and modern plumbing in 1885. It had the same sort of double-shelled porcelain tub used in rajahs' palaces and at the court in St. Petersburg. The subject of even more comment was Mrs. Potter Palmer's sunken swan-shaped tub, her oval basin, and the delicate floral designs on all her bathroom fixtures, a fashion that became widespread in the more luxurious homes at the turn of the century.

England led the field for plushy bath arrangements in the nineteenth century, but the United States forged ahead in the twentieth century. The hotels helped to popularize the functional bathroom, still an American tradition. The Tremont House, Boston's four-story Greek Revival hotel built in 1829, set the pace with eight bathing rooms in its cellar and cold water coming from cisterns for its 170 rooms. It was the first hotel to have inside closets. The Astor House, opening seven years later opposite City Hall Park in New York, had eighteen bathing rooms with hot water. Cape May's Mount Vernon Hotel in 1853 boasted a bath with hot and cold water for every bedroom. The idea spread west, and there were bathrooms for suites if not always for individual rooms. But Ellsworth M. Statler's Buffalo hotel that opened in 1908 with the slogan "A Room and a Bath for a Dollar and a Half" established a tradition that spread like wildfire.

The other factor that sparked the full development of the American bathroom was the nineteenth-century rage for spas and their mineral waters. There was nothing particularly new about the spa idea, since the Cretans, Egyptians, Arabians, Greeks, and Romans all had cultivated their healing springs, some of them bathing together in their finest attire, dining on floating tables, and playing cards while musicians twanged their lyres. The nineteenth-century spa was named after Spa, a Belgian resort, at a time when hydropathy was in full swing in Europe. Travelers enjoyed the vapor and sulphur baths, the Finnish sauna, the Siberian hut, the Russian and Oriental baths and, most of all, Vincenz Priessnitz' spa in his native Silesian woods. Priessnitz advocated a Spartan diet, vigorous exercise, spring water, and full exposure of the body to the sun and the cascading water from woodland rocks. Tales were brought back to America of the nymphs who sported in the spray more seductively than the members of today's nudist colonies. As Priessnitz preached and practiced hardening of the body the cultists and reformers, already a large and noisy group, flocked to his spa. Others followed the sun worship of Arnold Rikli, a Swiss, who tipped his patients on inclined boards and let the sun toast them until they were bathed in sweat.

This popularized the home steam bath, and soon many portable and collapsible varieties appeared on the market. From the 1870s until the close of the century the folding type of bathtub was popular in the United States. Showers either in the open or in the collapsible cabinets were available to people of limited means. In 1895 they were known as "rain baths" and by that time Americans were well on their way to being the world's greatest devotees of the quick shower. The custom was introduced in schools as athletics gained ground and a new generation of bathers was born. Moreover, the Turkish bath of the 1850s and the sunbath of the 1870s have their counterpart on American beaches today, and the men who tramped through the Silesian forests hatless, barefoot, wearing short trunks and open-necked shirts are close to the nomads and nature lovers of today.

The luxurious life of the American spa encouraged this developing taste for mineral waters and the back-to-nature spirit. But the colonists were not dead to the values of the waters that the Indians had so long considered sacred. The Pilgrims sought health in the seventeenth century at Stafford Springs in Connecticut, and Philadelphians in the

127

Fashioning the Home

George W. Vanderbilt's bathroom was considered sybaritic
when the public learned in 1885 of its double-shelled porcelain
tub, known only to Rajahs and the Czar of Russia; of its
stained-glass windows, hand-painted oriental screen, flowered
wallpaper, and tiled floor covered with woven rugs. Although
its toilet was festooned with roses, its exposed lead plumbing
and nickel-plated pipes were slightly disturbing to perfectionists.
This problem had not yet been solved.

More ornate than functional, the novelty toilets of 1900
included geometrical designs and the pop art of the period, as
well as delicate Dresden china flower patterns. The plumbing
catalogues at the turn of the century outdid one another in
luring the public into dashing experiments of this sort, with
the porcelain dolphin leading the field in luxurious homes.

A contemporary bathroom designed by
Edward Durell Stone is typical of the
style used in certain fashionable suburban
homes, where indoors and outdoors
flow into one another. The enclosed
garden and sunken tub, the marble statue
and climbing vines, suggest the outside
world. The sun lamp poised over a cot,
the long tiled vanity table, and tall
closet with rows of shelves supply the
functional touches in this spacious
bathroom.

eighteenth century drank "iron water" from a spring close to William Penn's country house. Ben Franklin took baths, hoping to prolong his life, although this was considered a dangerous practice at the time. George Washington tried Warm Springs, near Staunton, Virginia, for his rheumatic fever in 1759. But Saratoga became the queen of spas, the focus of fashion, gambling, and political villainy. Presidents and millionaires sampled the waters; gamblers and courtesans haunted the race track and the gaming tables. By 1870 every state and territory in the Union but South Dakota had a spa. Medical progress and new forms of transportation changed this picture at the turn of the century, and the old resorts, with their deserted bathhouses and empty rocking chairs, took on the look of ghost towns.

With a turn of the wheel the spas revived again in the 1960s, no longer the playgrounds of only the well-to-do. Diagnostic centers and national baths with physiotherapy under Federal regulation opened at some of the old springs, and again the spas were in business. But long before there were spas or bathtubs in America, the colonists used their streams and lakes for washing, and they dug shallow wells into which they lowered wooden buckets. These were drawn up by pole until the 1850s when the chain pump was introduced. The village pump became a social center long before the country store. Some houses had pumps in their cellars or gardens, a distinction that meant as much as the possession of a good carriage. But frozen pumps, both in city and country, were a winter problem, and blankets, straw, and wrappings of all kinds were used to protect them. Everyone just assumed that the water in his pitcher would be frozen solid by morning, and it usually was.

Philadelphia from the beginning had a good water supply, with the city corporation overseeing the public pumps. The Fairmount waterworks became one of the sights for travelers as water coursed through wooden pipes from the Schuylkill River. New York was backward by comparison. It was 1842 before the Croton Aqueduct was completed—the great reservoir that stood, like an Egyptian temple, where the New York Public Library stands today—and was used as a parading ground. Its granite walls were more than forty feet high, and it held twenty million gallons of water. Before then the city water was so tainted that those who could afford it preferred to buy their water from vendors coming in from the country, and the "Tea-water Man" with his rattling cart was a familiar sight on the city streets. The Common Council of New York tried to keep the public pumps in good repair and to have new wells dug periodically.

With ample water supplies many of the bathing problems were solved. Farmers took to a folding bath that looked like a wardrobe when not in use. Mail-order catalogues pushed it as the counterpart of the folding bed. The wardrobe tub that had a gasoline heater was only one of many bathing devices offered the public late in the nineteenth century. Running water first reached the kitchen sink, then the washbasin, and finally the bathtub, and America pioneered in piping water to the basin. The hot-water boiler came into use in the 1870s and it sometimes caused a scare by exploding. The rainwater barrels and cisterns were purified by charcoal.

It was considered a mark of distinction in the country to have a bathroom and a cookstove. The zinc- or copper-lined tub of black walnut usually had a water tank overhead, which was pumped full each day from cisterns in the cellar. Washbasins were fitted with faucets as far back as the 1850s, but the water was still drawn by hand pump. The showers that rose in cascades from the bottom of the basin to splash the face were playthings of the 1890s. But by 1900 the public was being offered sunken tubs with ornamental tiles, and the enameled bathtub was firmly established ten years later, a great advance over the old wooden box lined with sheet lead, or the roll-rim tub poised on iron claw feet. It took another half century for Hollywood to dramatize the bathtub with freak effects, from Liberace's piano-shaped to Jayne Mansfield's heart-shaped tubs.

The early bathrooms were often large, with furniture and space enough for ambling around and relaxing. They had massage tables, sofas, and a variety of sitz baths, showers, and other fanciful effects. Stained-glass windows were part of the picture. All this helped to bring an end to the passion for encasing and disguising sanitary fixtures. The Victorian tradition involved monstrous hooded baths concealed in carved wardrobes, washbasins hidden in bureaus, toilets sunk in all manner of commodes, a throwback to the time when Sheraton, Hepplewhite, and the French cabinetmakers did some of their finest work on this article of furniture. At the court of Louis XIV baths were hidden in sofas, washbasins in pianos, and toilets in carriages. Isaac Singer, founder of the sewing machine family business, drove in the Bois, dressed all in red, in a huge carriage with a dressing room and lavatory at the back. Small libraries of dummy volumes sometimes camouflaged the commode. Ermine and mink, crests and flower designs surrounded the throne.

A musical chamber pot was a popular novelty. Hetty Green's son, Edward H. Green, became the proud possessor of a jeweled example of this to add to his collection of erotica. Medallion portraits of Benjamin Franklin on Sèvres chambers were on view at an exhibition of china at Versailles in 1776. Arabesques, windmills, and all manner of floral designs and solid colors were used to beautify this homely object, and the same idea was carried over to the toilet when it became a fixed part of the bathroom ensemble, often as a sculptured porcelain dolphin holding a shell in its mouth. The "Victoria and roses" washbasin, a reigning favorite, brought the rose theme strongly to the fore, and basins, ewers, and chambers were splashed with cabbage roses or delicate Dresden china designs.

It was not until 1966 that American papers boldly advertised the bidet, although it had found its way into many private homes. The Ritz Carlton had been forced to abandon it after a brief try in a less sophisticated age. Actually, the bidet was first mentioned in 1710 in connection with the Marquis d'Argenson, and was advertised after 1739. It turned up in England in the 1890s, surprisingly enough while Queen Victoria still reigned. There was some disapproval but the bidets survived, and traveling Americans became used to seeing them in London and Paris. Madame Pompadour had hers encased in rosewood, with floral inlay and gilt bronze legs, but the model finally appearing in America was austerely clinical, with no suggestion of sybaritic trappings except for color introduced in 1966. Some Americans living in Paris now collect antique bidets and use them as tables with the lids down or to hold flowers or plants when they are opened.

The outhouse preceded the commode, the bathtub, and the lavatory in the United States, and from the earliest days it was as traditional a feature of the landscape as the barn. Often it stood in the garden or in a nearby field, with sunflowers, rambler roses, or honeysuckle giving it a picturesque rusticity. Trellises and arbors screened it at some of the early mansions, and a lilac-and-syringa-bordered walk with trellised woodbine overhead, a brook blue with forget-me-nots, and a rustic bridge leading to the privy made a pretty picture, but cold-weather scampers were the other side of the coin, and part of the outhouse lore.

Generally the outhouse was a bleak, weathered structure, tall and narrow as a Puritan pulpit, punctured with stars, diamonds, or crescents. It had community elements in the early days. James Buchanan's house at Lancaster had a brick outhouse with separate rooms for "him" and "her," and seats in each partition for half a dozen. Newspapers and comic books, the early paperbacks, magazines, old catalogues, and a few pinups were the interior decoration. In the late 1920s the privy became a national topic when nearly a million copies were sold of Chic Sale's *The Specialist.* Charles Sale was a Dakotan, a vaudeville actor who seized upon this topic by chance and told the story of Lem Putt, a privy builder who tinkered with the star, diamond, and crescent cutouts in the walls, tried to pitch the roof at the proper angle and to provide a latch and string, or hook and eye, for the doors. Chic Sale jokes became current coin as successful men harked back to their early days of hardship on the farm.

When the Federal government in the 1930s supplied thousands of outhouses designed by sanitation experts as part of its rural rejuvenation campaign, the old lean-to practically vanished from the landscape. Though the privy no longer seemed to matter, except for its period

131

Fashioning the Home

interest, the chamber held on, and thousands continued to be sold in china or enamel. The old ones became prized items at auctions, and decorators put them to sundry uses for which they were never intended.

New York had 10,384 water closets in 1855 and 1,361 bathtubs at a time when its population was 630,000. In 1857 Boston had only 6,500 water closets for a population of 165,000. New sanitary standards were set up during the Civil War, and the two world wars brought about great changes in America's bathrooms. Hotels, tall apartment houses, and housing developments all had their effect on plumbing arrangements, and in the 1920s colored tiling and modern decoration broke the austere pattern of gleaming white. Wallpapers with birds and fish, dolphins and mermaids, brought back the early Chippendale touch. Decorators experimented with fantasy and functionalism, designing floors of vinyl, marble, plastic, tile, linoleum, or carpets from wall to wall. Mirrors and glass makeup tables, divans and baskets of ferns and flowers, vistas of the outdoors, and sunken tubs or circular pools have made bathrooms the decorative annex of the house. Headrests, reading stands, and telephones have invaded the tub itself, and gold dolphins sometimes serve as taps. But these luxurious effects are by no means usual.

In general, bathrooms have taken on life and color, with matching sets of everything from bathmats and shower curtains to flowered toilet paper, cut-glass bottles, and odd-shaped soaps. Even in the simplest homes there is now a dash of color in the bathroom, if not a Plexiglas dome over a sunken pool, radiant heating underfoot, warmed towel racks, music drifting from the walls, jeweled fittings, perfumed sprays, "his" and "her" tubs and basins, or the sauna and steamrooms that often accompany the more luxurious bathrooms. All this is a long way from the primitive equipment of the colonists. A poll taken in 1966 showed that Americans are still the most scrubbed people in the world; that 98 per cent of the grownups bathe at least two or three times a week and 75 per cent daily. Fifteen per cent read in their bathtubs and only 20 per cent will interrupt their bath to answer the phone, if it isn't at hand.

However, the vaunted elegance, variety, and efficiency of the American bathroom came under heavy attack in Alexander Kira's book *The Bathroom*, a 1966 report based on a six-year survey done for the Center for Housing and Environmental Studies at Cornell University. He found the American bathroom minimal in "terms of contemporary knowledge, technology, values and attitudes." Tubs were too small and uncomfortable, basins too small and too low, toilets too high, showers awkward, and the fixtures in general unsanitary, dangerous, and not well adapted to the body. This bold critic of one of the nation's most cherished institutions could think of innumerable amenities to make the American bathroom safer and better.

6   *Plush and Pomp*

THE Victorian style ran wild in the American home after the
Civil War. The quiet distinction of the eighteenth century
at its best was giving way to a period of plush and pomp. Fortunes
multipled but taste developed slowly, and furniture was bought for its
bulk, its carving, its ornamentation. The craftsman was being supplanted
by the manufacturer, and the guiding hand of the professional decorator
had not yet touched the land. Flowered carpets, towering black-walnut
beds and sofas smothered in patterned tapestry were found in countless
homes. It was the era of the monster wardrobe, the washstand set with
pink rosebuds, and the hatrack and umbrella stand. Double parlors and
high-ceilinged rooms with long pier glasses were often the setting for
all this bulk.

No sophisticated drawing room was complete without a few
French period pieces, an ottoman, or a Turkish divan. Five periods were
often represented, but without the knowing juxtaposition of today.
Gradually the public moved deeper into a forest of bric-à-brac, with
console tables and whatnots heaped with statuettes, Dresden china, and
conch shells. Busts of Homer and Socrates on marble pedestals, and
paintings casually displayed on draped easels, were as common as heavy

bronze ornaments and towering vases. Funereal velvet curtains, fringed and roped, hung from gilded lambrequins. Nottingham lace kept the sun from shining through glass. Ancestral portraits in heavy gilt frames crowded the walls, and in simpler homes the chromos of the Silesian lithographer Louis Prang hung haphazardly—"The Maiden's Prayer," "After the Storm" and, in particular, "Home Sweet Home."

However, the world of decoration was stimulated by the Centennial Exposition of 1876, which not only projected the aesthetic principles of Charles L. Eastlake and William Morris but brought the Oriental touch strongly into the American home. The carpets, hangings, furniture, and fine arts of China, Japan, Turkey, Egypt, and the Near East were on display. Almost at once teakwood and Indian brass, inlaid tables and wrought-metal hanging lamps reached the market and were bought enthusiastically by Americans beginning to tire of cumbersome tables and flowered carpets. For a million dollars William Sloane bought all of the Oriental rugs shown at the Centennial. Alexander Smith Cochrane, manufacturer and philanthropist, paid $75,000 for one of the Centennial rugs, and his fellow financiers became heavily committed to the Oriental craze. Soon the familiar Axminsters and black carpets patterned with golden arabesques and scarlet geraniums gave way in the statelier houses to the glowing rugs of Persia and Smyrna.

The Saracenic look, with dim interiors, metal work, stained glass, and the pouf or taboret, prevailed for two decades. In the 1890s Turkish Corners followed as the night the day, and most fashionable families added a few Oriental pieces to their drawing rooms, or staked out a cozy corner. Pierced metal lamps shed a dim light over masses of embroidered pillows and small tables inlaid with mother-of-pearl. Spears and peacock feathers, taborets and tiger skins made the Turkish Corner an ideal set for the film industry soon to be born. Young romantics and middle-aged sirens sought to encourage these harem effects, but the result was grotesque, and out they went, along with much of the dust-catching bric-à-brac of the period. However, Moorish, Turkish, and Chinese rooms of some distinction were installed in the houses of the Rockefellers, the Havemeyers, the Vanderbilts, and other wealthy families. Well into the twentieth century, with a strong revival after World War I, the brass tray, the inlaid ebony table, and the teakwood chest were honored pieces.

The décor of many of these houses was encompassed in the history of the most noted of all—the Potter Palmer mansion in Chicago, considered the last word in Victorian magnificence, or chaos, depending on the point of view. Architecturally it was variously described as being English battlemented, castellated Gothic, or Norman Gothic in style. Mrs. Palmer's three-story octagonal hall had Gobelin tapestries and a marble mosaic floor laid by imported Italian craftsmen. Her music room was Spanish, her dining room English, her library Flemish Renaissance, her drawing room and small white-and-gold salon pure Louis XVI, with a tiled floor inlaid with a pattern of pink roses. Her picture gallery, with its strong array of Impressionists, was hung with rose-red velvet and Tiffany chandeliers. A Moorish passageway led to her ballroom. She slept in a Louis XVI bed, ten feet high with Nattier blue-taffeta draperies, installed in a Moorish bedroom, all ebony and gold. Her salon cabinets held rare Chinese porcelain and jade.

But this was not the way that most Americans lived, and the average household welcomed another offshoot of the Centennial—the simplifying and cooling influence of Eastlake and Morris, who had tired of too much pattern in design. This dissipated a good deal of the Victorian excess, but it also led to wholesale and eventually tawdry reproductions at Grand Rapids and elsewhere of some of the better furniture of the past. Eastlake, who had studied dyeing and carpet weaving, encouraged a single style throughout a house, instead of a different style for every room. He deplored gilded tin lambrequins and windowshades stenciled with ruined castles and glossy milkmaids. He was the advocate of buff wallpaper between a wooden dado and a decorative frieze. His influence had its critics, too, but it helped to thin out excrescences and to subdue the gaudier patterned effects. His *Household Taste in Furniture, Upholstery and Other Details* went through seven printings between 1872 and 1883, spreading the gospel of Ruskin and Morris.

Even more widespread was the influence of Andrew J. Downing on the architecture and decoration of the mid-nineteenth century. His books were widely read and he advocated the sturdy native touch in furniture and an end to importation. He stood for neutral tones, for quiet dadoes of green, maroon, or brown, for floor coverings in solid colors instead of the "abomination of flowers" that Edgar Allan Poe had said "should not be endured within the limits of Christendom." He disliked frescoed ceilings and rosewood cabinets with tapestry panels.

Another new touch in decoration after the Centennial came with the popularity of the Queen Anne style house. The Tudor feeling was revived in low ceilings, wainscoted panels, English prints, and small windowpanes. Country houses had deep window seats, floors painted green, high mantelpieces, and huge chimneys. Vines and plants filled the fireplaces, and the tropical-garden effect was sustained with birds singing in gilded cages and fountains splashing. Lampshades were trimmed with silk and lace, and wicker wood baskets had bows. Sideboards were laden with silver and cut glass. Ottomans and wicker chairs abounded, the occasional tables held the stereopticon, photograph albums, and limp leather books. The accompanying gardens were rich in old-fashioned flowers and the lawns were velvety.

One of the most significant changes was the passing of the parlor —the musty, funereal monstrosity that had discouraged family warmth

Although not altogether the Turkish corner fashionable at the time, Mrs. Leonie's parlor is typical of the clutter of the 1890s. Fringed shawls draped her piano and dangled from her mantelpiece. A rosy glow spread from the deep taffeta ruffles of her lamps. Cushions, ornaments, and flowery upholstery were all in key, and the tea table was ever ready for the chance visitor.

The domed stained glass lamp designed and popularized by Louis Comfort Tiffany at the turn of the century had a revival in the 1960s. The Tiffany range in lamps was wide, from tulip-shaped chandeliers to the wisteria, pansy, or lily-of-the-valley designs used most frequently in library lamps.

The scalloped-edged plate is an acid-frosted "Classic" pressed-glass pattern issued by Gillinder & Sons of Philadelphia in the 1870s. The ornate design, a naked warrior on horseback spearing a lion, is suggestive of mid-Victorian taste, and its like probably found its way into parlors across the country.

The thirteen-foot mirrored plateau with vermeil decoration has been one of the treasures of the White House since President Monroe imported it from France. It has been used by a succession of Presidents for the most formal dinners. The vermeil figurines have added grace to many official occasions, but at times First Ladies have found it baffling for their pet flower arrangements.

for years. All over the country, and particularly in rural houses, the parlor had been sacrosanct, to be used only for ceremonial occasions. With the Eastlake and Queen Anne influences, windows were flung open, casement curtains fluttered in the breeze, dust covers were removed, and old and young could at last enjoy what soon came to be known as the living room. Life became more fluid and vigorous. Children no longer were afraid to sit on yellow damask or red brocatelle chairs; the antimacassar age had ended. Parlor games still flourished but there were more outdoor sports. The slippery horsehair furniture had gone, and though plush was in, with tassels and fringes, fresh air was blowing on the clutter that reached its zenith in the 1890s.

The mansions of the millionaires from coast to coast were the most expressive of this trend. On their trips abroad these nabobs picked up paintings and massive objects of art, since they had become the natural quarry of the dealers of London, Paris, and Berlin. Art masterpieces flowed regularly into America, first in the classical tradition, then Impressionists, and finally modern art. Great collections were in the making; it was the era of acquisition.

In simpler homes Hudson River School paintings hung over black marble mantelpieces, draped with scarves on which rested heavy onyx clocks, wax flowers under glass, and a scattering of photographs. The carved mantelpieces made famous in Cincinnati by Henry L. Fry and his son, William Fry, were passing from the scene, although those in the homes of Nicholas Longworth and Alphonso Taft were noted in their time. Steel engravings hung somberly in the dining rooms that had baize or flower-stamped plush covers spread over the table between meals. Japanese storks in flight and hunting scenes were themes for friezes.

Rusticity was fostered when Elbert Hubbard founded the Roycroft School at Aurora, New York, in 1895 and spread the gospel of mission furniture, sturdy and unpretentious, with straight lines and plain forms. People flocked to the workshops where artisans labored with principles made famous by Eastlake and Morris. As the simple mission chairs, tables, and chests found their way into countless American homes, their owners soon were reading Elbert Hubbard's writings on all manner of public issues. His workshop was named for the seventeenth-century English printer, Roycroft, and its purpose was to revive the old handicrafts, and especially artistic printing.

Closely akin to the Hubbard ambience were the Craftsman homes that flourished briefly early in the twentieth century and were fostered by Gustav Stickley. They were built like the mission houses of California, low and wide, with arches and thick cement walls. The roofs were covered with glazed red Spanish tile. Built-in furnishings glowed with color, and a great many families across the country responded to the appeal of these comfortable and durable houses. The Craftsman workshops encouraged home crafts and amateur cabinetmaking, but in a civilization growing more industrial by the day, the movement languished and died around 1910.

Meanwhile, in the West new processes were devised for art metalwork in bronze and iron. The granite quarried in Wisconsin, the sandstone of Michigan, and the jaspers and marbles of Colorado and California were beginning to show in the home. Glass had come to figure strongly in the decoration of the 1890s and its undisputed priest was Louis Comfort Tiffany, who called himself the first American industrial artist to design for the modern age. His ten glass windows and twenty pieces of blown glass shown at the Paris Exposition of 1895 were linked with jewelry by Lalique, paintings by Toulouse-Lautrec, sculpture by Bourdelle and Rodin, and prints and drawings by Mary Cassatt and Whistler. Tiffany became the American symbol of *art nouveau*, as the modern movement in art took shape and form.

Glass did not become common in America until the late 1700s, and even then it was used only in the East. Glassblowers worked near a silicon deposit in New Jersey around 1740 and they produced rum flasks, windowpanes, and tableware. But in 1815 molds designed to hold quarts and pints were perfected. The log cabin flasks filled with liquor made by a Philadelphia distiller named E. C. Booz introduced the word "booze" into the common speech, although in *The American Language* H. L. Mencken traces it back to the fourteenth century. In any event, it came into use in America when the Booz flasks, adorned with eagles, flags, and other national symbols, were fashioned to represent the supposed birthplace of William Henry Harrison. They were made in Glassboro, New Jersey, the small town where President Johnson and Premier Kosygin had their historic meetings in the summer of 1967. By 1835 a Pittsburgh glassworks was producing opaque glass, and soon the country was flooded with glass doorknobs from New England. Another factory in Sandwich, Massachusetts, turned out the streaked, translucent Sandwich glass that is sought and treasured today. Bristol glass was used for candlesticks and salvers, pickle and syllabub dishes, sugar bowls and cream pots. Glass, like pewter, became popular for wedding gifts. Much of it was embellished with names, dates, or verses from the Scriptures. Bit by bit, the bubbles and flaws that had plagued the early glassmakers disappeared and by the turn of the century the creation of apple green, opaque turquoise, sunburst and peachblow glass dovetailed into the "art glass" period.

Louis Comfort Tiffany moved into this world with unmistakable authority. He worked with such men as Stanford White, John La Farge, and Augustus Saint-Gaudens on churches, men's clubs, and the mansions of the rich. Drawing inspiration from Byzantine chapels and the Doge's Palace, his own chapel at the Columbian Exposition was a sensational success. Like White, he used the peacock theme in his neo-Byzantine ecclesiastical interiors, working with mosaics of iridescent glass, mother-of-pearl and transparent tesserae backed with gold or metal leaf. His opalescent glass involved new processes for making stained glass, and he experimented with chemicals to reproduce the tints of ancient cathedral woods. At the turn of the century he was regarded as the most successful American decorator working in the medieval style. Much of his work had the Islamic East Indian flavor. He blended the decorative art of East and West—in rugs, wallpapers and armor, using exposed beams and hanging lamps with cone shades of opalescent glass. He was largely responsible for the wave of Oriental ceramics and textiles, brass and bronze, silver and dull gold that dressed up the libraries and drawing rooms of famous American houses. His exotic lamps hung harmoniously in the Turkish Corners; and the metal-bound cassone, the carved settle, the sword with jeweled scabbard, all bore the Tiffany stamp. He set up his own workshop in New York and ran it like a Florentine *bottega*, surrounding himself with artists in many fields. All worked together on wallpapers and murals, tapestries, books and draperies to produce a unified effect.

Tiffany, who called himself a rebel in glass, was descended from a Massachusetts family noted for its silver and jewelry making. In 1870 he was the youngest member ever elected to the Century Club in New York, and he became one of the founders of the Society of American Artists. John La Farge preceded him as a designer of stained glass, however, and as early as 1876 was responsible for the opalescent windows of Trinity Church in Boston. Even after Tiffany had added drama with the brilliance of his colors La Farge continued his careful work, represented today in many colleges, clubs, and churches, such as St. Thomas's and the Church of the Ascension in New York City.

The Tiffany touch in the American home was expensive but it was new and different, so it was quickly acquired by those who could afford it. His Byzantine desk sets and ashtrays, enameled boxes and agate and malachite paperweights became instantly recognizable from his pine-needle and grapevine designs. His chandeliers and dome-shaped lampshades were almost a trademark. When he turned his attention to costume jewelry his Queen Anne's lace, peacock necklace, clover-blossom tiara, Etruscan metalwork, scarabs, lorgnon chains, and gold repoussé were enthusiastically welcomed by American women early in the twentieth century. Those who had Tiffany pieces in their drawing rooms also wore Tiffany jewelry on their persons.

By the 1930s Tiffany's work was scorned and then discarded by a generation cultivating a taste for plain glass curtain walls and the stark use of natural materials in furniture. It came into fashion again with a revival of interest in Victorian pieces, and the name "Tiffany" never fails to arouse response at an auction.

With all these luxurious forces at work Elsie de Wolfe stepped into the picture—spare, sophisticated, knowing. Cecil Beaton said of her that she "was a *religieuse*; fashion was her god." She was the first of the modern type of interior decorator who has helped to shape the American home. Her style was clear, cool, and anti-Victorian. She revived the Chinese wallpapers of earlier days, the *toile de Jouy* of Marie Antoinette, the printed linens of old England, and the newer ones of William Morris. She became known as the "Chintz Decorator" as homes all over the country were freshened with chintz and cretonne. Miss de Wolfe went in for white and pastel paint, for molding on plain walls, for simple white muslin curtains, and painted furniture. She popularized the triplicate vanity table with chintz ruffles, as well as soft pastel carpets, and lamps made from good jars and vases to replace those with cabbage roses and dragon designs.

Working with simple materials Miss de Wolfe gave interior decoration a sophisticated twist. She made careful use of stools and benches, and played up indoor fountains and little pools bordered with plants and glittering with goldfish. Women followed her work with enthusiasm after she finished her masterpiece, the Colony Club in New York, where she used the trellis to good effect, an old Oriental trick. Her style was opposite to everything that Tiffany had introduced. She lightened up rooms that had been heavy and dim, and concentrated on flowers and sunshine. "Light, air and comfort—these three things I must always have in a room," she said. "You can take your indiscriminate inheritance of Victorian rosewood, of Eastlake walnut and cocobolo, your pickle-and-plum-colored Morris furniture, and make a civilized interior by placing it right, and putting detail at the right points."

Miss de Wolfe brought this artful simplicity to bear on the scene at a time when pebble-dash walls, coarse wrought iron, and orange light created a pseudo-Spanish effect, and a heavy Hispano-Moorish patina lay over Palm Beach. California, too, reflected the curved arches and grillwork, the terra-cotta floors and Alhambra touches. Long after she left the United States and settled in Fontainebleau, her influence was felt. She had set the stage for the group of men and women decorators who now give infinite variety to the interiors of the mansions, hotels, and offices of the United States. With the combined influence of the magazines, newspapers, department stores, and television, new horizons have been touched in the tasteful, exotic, fantastic, or far-out aspects of twentieth-century interiors, down to the whims of college students who are prone to adorn their dormitory rooms with posters, Japanese kites, traffic lights, pinups, or beer cans.

Housewives in the most remote parts of the country learn quickly today of the calf rugs and suède sofas, abstract paintings and Japanese rock gardens, of the gem-encrusted silver platters and Meissen china of well-known hostesses. They get intimate glimpses of the interiors of towering duplexes and converted barns, of French châteaus in

The Turkish-style room from John D.
Rockefeller's house on West
Fifty-third Street, New York City,
reflects the passing taste of the
late nineteenth century for oriental
rooms and Turkish corners. The
Centennial Exposition of 1876 added
Near East and oriental influences to
Victorian opulence, and the most
fashionable mansions had Moorish,
Turkish, or Chinese rooms. Oriental
carpets supplanted Axminsters,
and Byzantine friezes and peacock
feathers were part of the décor.

Elsie de Wolfe (later Lady Mendl), living
in Washington Irving's house in New York,
applied her own cool decorating touch
in 1898 to her diningroom. She gave up
the stage for interior decoration and set the
pace for today's decorators. Known as
the Chintz Lady, she went in for painted
furniture, pastels and lilies, catering to a
generation satiated with Victorian excess.

Ancient art blends harmoniously with the
contemporary décor of this pavilion
designed by Melanie Kahane. The mood
is oriental: on the right are two rare
thirteenth-century Chinese figures; the
chaises have brass frames in a bamboo
design and the chairs are in bleached teak.
An early Chinese leather map case mounted
on a platform serves as a table. Two
unusual touches are the precast stone
fireplace with its cantilevered stone bench,
instead of a conventional hearth, and the
ceiling striped in Hungarian ash and
black cork.

Florida, stables in Greenwich Village, or a lighthouse on Cape Cod. Every day the papers pinpoint some startling new décor or a Victorian revival of plush and pomp. A giant philodendron stands at one corner of a fashionable swimming pool, and an Italian *cassone* on the loggia of another. A Japanese house, all glass and sliding doors, glitters through the woods, and the fame of Philip Johnson's glass house at New Canaan, Connecticut, has spread around the world. This debonair architect dines off Limoges, with pistol-handled silver, on a marble table, while seated in a Meis van der Rohe steel-and-leather chair. An art gallery, a swimming pool, and the green world of outdoors are part of the composition.

The simplicists in furnishings have had their effect on flower decoration, too. Just as she streamlined the general décor Elsie de Wolfe brought a fresh note into use with the madonna lilies she arranged in black-and-gold drawing rooms. They matched the austerity of her interiors at a time when concentrated masses of flowers in assorted colors were the favorite effect. Florists now go to great lengths to match the room décor as well as the color of party gowns. Salmon-colored roses, green carnations, turquoise daisies, and black orchids no longer seem like hybrids among the natural blooms. Double snapdragons are developed with the drug colchicine, and other exotic flowers are flown in from all over the world—orchids from New Zealand, birds-of-paradise from Hawaii, and carnations from Colorado.

The nation's twenty-two thousand retail florists have now branched out in all directions, selling ceramics, crystal chandeliers, bronze sculpture, and stuffed animals in the 3,500 suburban garden markets across the country. More offices and public institutions display flowers than at any time in the past, and they are lavishly used for landscaping purposes around apartment buildings and housing developments, on penthouses and terraces. "Say It with Flowers," the slogan of the Society of American Florists, has helped to whip up $50 million worth of business done annually by telegraph.

The rose is still the perennial favorite for the house, according to a breakdown of the $800 million sale of flowers a year in the United States. The purple orchid, the clubwoman's delight and Hollywood's trademark, has fallen from grace in favor of the greenish-brown cymbidium varieties, if one chooses orchids at all. The space-age girl seems far removed from the world of the corsage—a Cardin bride in 1966 wore a cabbage rose on her head as part of her wedding attire.

The use of fresh flowers with the costume became fashionable in the eighteenth century when women wore them on their shoulders, attached to ribbons round their throats, and in small vials covered with the silk of their gowns and tucked into their bosoms. The Federal breastknot made of black ribbon with a white button was widely worn. During the Civil War festoons of fresh flowers streamed over billowing crinolines, and garlands decked the hair. Camellias, violets, and carnations were the choice of the Victorian girl and she often held little frilled bouquets of sweetheart roses, or carried a single flower with her to the opera. Her beau would send her one stately American Beauty rose in a vase of Austrian glass or Dresden china, and his own boutonnière would be large and arresting perhaps a chrysanthemum. Gardenias scented a girl through the years of World War I and the 1920s; the showy orchid came next.

If Elsie de Wolfe championed the lily two other women have profoundly affected American taste in flower decoration. Irene Hayes, a Kansas actress who became one of the country's leading florists, has dramatized flower arrangements for balls and banquets, for debutante parties and television programs. She changed the corsage from the right to the left shoulder so that it would not be crushed, when dancing was still a cheek-to-cheek affair. Her colleague, Constance Spry, introduced a fresh note into flower decoration on both sides of the Atlantic with exotic combinations of lilies and grasses, thistles and pampas grass. She nursed along the Victorian revival of wreaths under glass, and with this development waxed flowers of greater subtlety than the sad poppies of the nineteenth century invaded the American home, becoming more realistic and inexpensive each year, so that now they are available in the five-and-ten as well as in the most exotic florist's.

All through the 1870s and 1880s dinner tables were lavishly decorated with flowers, and various Presidents' wives had to figure out ways of having their guests see one another through the forest of blooms arranged on President Monroe's long mirrorlike plateau with its vermeil ornaments. Styles at the White House have changed from one administration to another, from the stiff palms and ferns of the conservatory era to the more natural effects of today; from the massed impact of formal flower arrangements for diplomatic dinners, and the bouquets of wired japonicas with huge lacy frills favored at the time of the Civil War, to the knowing simplicity of Mrs. John F. Kennedy's field-flower combinations. Although the flower arrangements for the White House are more or less automatically managed behind the scenes today, occasionally a First Lady shows a personal interest in the choice of flowers, and expresses her own taste in the matter. Some, like Grace Coolidge, have gone straight to the pantry and have done a little clipping and arranging on their own. But flower arrangements on a massive scale figure among the big industries today. This was equally true of the 1890s when ballrooms were converted into the gardens of Versailles, and arbors, trellises, and trailing vines were an inescapable part of the formal entertainment. It reached such a point of satiation that hostesses broke with tradition and concentrated on daisies and Queen Anne's lace by way of relief. Flowers, like furnishings, have reflected the changing tastes during the ripening years in American history.

From the colonnades of Mount Vernon to the patio of today, the porch has played a significant role in American family life. It has figured in the architectural evolution of public buildings as well as of average dwellings. Variously known as portico, gallery, piazza, loggia, balcony, or veranda, it has linked the outdoors with the inner citadel of the home, and all through the nineteenth century it was the indispensable addition to a house, grotesque or full of grace, as the case might be. Even in the skyscraper age the balcony, used also by George Washington, has its place—a swing from the level of the earth to the dizzy peaks and towering masses of the 1960s.

But in its original form, designed primarily for creature comfort and cool breezes, the porch died a slow death. The automobile in the twentieth century finally drew young and old away from its familiar shelter. Changing social customs and the stripped nature of modern achitecture made the old-fashioned porch anachronistic. Yet for two hundred years the gregarious habits of the American people were fostered on the piazza, with its open door to the public, its vista of life flowing by, its charm for all members of the family, from grandparents to two-year-olds.

Traditionally the porch has been identified with the leisurely hours of the day, with romance and family gatherings, with naps and cool drinks on hot nights, with political discussion, gossip, knitting needles, and parlor games. It has ranged from the homeliest lean-to on a remote farm to the sweep of glassed-in porches overlooking the ocean at Newport, or club verandas on the California coast.

Regional weather conditions influenced its development, and the sunny North American climate gave point to its ubiquity. Until air conditioning made indoors more comfortable than the outside world in hot weather, the piazzas' cool breezes and shady vines were part of summertime, in city or country. The first porch-sitters occupied benches at either side of the entrance to their Philadelphia houses, and shopkeepers sought shade under painted cloth awnings over their stores. The Dutch burghers liked to sit outdoors in small, tidy gardens. But the porch took on its stately lineaments around the time of the Revolution when colonnaded loggias in the Jeffersonian tradition were added to the mansions of Virginia and Maryland. The four-column portico of Monticello was a significant factor in this development and later, during the Greek Revival period it was natural for the South and Southwest to adopt an architectural style that gave room for promenading and wide, open spaces for coolness.

In the 1840s iron porches abounded in New York, Pennsylvania, Ohio, and the South. Their lacework effects adorned early Charleston and made New Orleans the picture city that it is today. Some reminders of this period may be seen in Gramercy Park and other parts of New York today, where the cast-iron porch with lacy supports, open brackets, and curved roof still survives. Verandas on the balloon houses of the West in the 1860s had fanciful railings cut by scrollsaw. In his constant drive to promote the simple country house Andrew J. Downing said that "verandas, piazzas, bay-windows, balconies . . . are the most valuable general truths in domestic Architecture." He insisted that the principal entrance to a house should never be directly into an apartment, but by way of a porch, a lobby, or special entry.

The Gothic Revival and Queen Anne styles were well adapted to porch life and structure, and they flourished during these periods. The Gothic houses had picturesque balconies looking down on gardens and rustic summerhouses. During the Queen Anne period the balconies and porches were recessed into the house and sheltered by its eaves. The railings were spindled and the porches were roomy and irregular, like the houses themselves. They served as sitting rooms, and much of the family life was conducted from the back and upper galleries, as they were then known. The rage for cottage architecture led to flowery vines and creepers, rambler roses, and convolvuli decking the porches with captivating effects. Here and there it looked like a revival of Tudor England, even though it was clearly the Middle West. Calvert

Vaux, a thoughtful observer, said in 1857 that the veranda was perhaps the "most specially American feature in a country house, and nothing can compensate for its absence."

O. S. Fowler, the phrenologist who pushed the merits of the octagonal house, favored verandas that ran all the way around allowing one "to choose sun or shade, breeze or shelter from it, as comfort dictates." But whatever the style, from the 1840s to 1910 the porch was a family institution, a symbol of American life in more leisurely days. North, south, east, and west, along quiet village streets, families gathered at the end of the day to talk, play their Victrolas, dance or dine, play cards or entertain. Countless marriages were nurtured on the porch, and moonlight was insidious from this vantage point.

Sleeping porches came into fashion as the nation became health and diet-conscious at the turn of the century. The drive to end tuberculosis encouraged this trend, and the sick and the well inhaled hearty draughts of frosty air with the enthusiasm shown for sunbaths half a century later. The introduction of mosquito netting soon after the Civil War made life more comfortable for all porch dwellers, but the piazza reached its zenith at the spa hotels, where guests promenaded ceaselessly at Saratoga, Atlantic City, or on the Venetian red loggias and Florentine balconies of the Antlers Hotel at Colorado Springs. When they did not walk they rocked in long rows of swaying chairs, but porches had their historic moments, too. The public read of President McKinley on his porch at Canton, of President Taft being notified of his nomination on the porch of his half-brother's house in Cincinnati, of President Truman causing an uproar with his insistence on an upstairs balcony for the White House.

But the veranda as an important aspect of family life died with the coming of the automobile. Social life moved to the country club, the beach, the tennis court or golf course, the soda fountain, the cinema, the baseball game, the drive-in movie. Family unity dissolved as the young freed themselves from their elders' close observation. Churchgoing declined. So did jokes about father waiting for the visiting Romeo to leave the porch and go home. No one wanted to sit and rock any longer except the aged, who still found the porch a comfort. In 1916 Mrs. Lillian H. Tryon, in *House Beautiful*, wrote: "I hate to see these desert wastes that were once piazzas. House after house along any great summer highway, shows its porch, gay with all the trappings of outdoor elegance and vacant. They have hung their harps upon the willows, and gone a-motoring . . . ." By the 1930s many of the old porches remained, but new ones were not being built and they all seemed deserted. The bungalow type of house had cut deeply into the need for porches.

The hammock was not only one of the favorite objects on the

porch, but it had its own romantic interest. It was linked with lazy afternoons, siestas, croquet, and romantic dalliance. In the nineteenth century it usually swung between trees or in gardens, but in the twentieth century it became more of a fixed object, still swinging, but lacking its loose-roped instability. These rope couches were sketched and pictured as often as the hansom cab. There was nothing new about them. Hammocks are older than the nation itself, for Columbus saw them on his first voyage to the Bahamas. They were known as Brazil beds and entire families slept in them in the tropical islands. But it was not until the 1880s that patents began to circulate and Americans took them up with enthusiasm.

Like the piazza, bay windows or oriels were part of the architecture of the nineteenth century, and rows of identical houses, all jutting out in concert, might be seen on any city street. They flourished along Commonwealth Avenue in Boston, usually with begonias and geraniums lined up close to the Brussels lace curtains that fell to the floor. Passersby used to pause at Mrs. Jack Gardner's bay windows on Beacon Street to study her seasonal displays of flowers, or perhaps to catch a glimpse of the chatelaine herself. In Chicago during the 1870s the segmental bay, carried to the roof and embracing three stories, was the favorite style of oriel. Some were octagonal; others were square. Libraries and parlors were brighter and larger for their bay windows, and hanging plants and cushioned window seats created attractive effects. But in time the bay window seemed as Victorian as the red-plush sofa and architects would have nothing more to do with it.

However, the geraniums, aspidistras, and hanging plants that went with porches and bay windows were missed by city dwellers, and the more the massed façades of the skyscrapers hemmed them in, the more people longed for flowers, parks, and glimpses of greensward. It was an ancient and instinctive hunger. As Mrs. Lyndon Johnson traveled across the country promoting the idea of national beautification, each city in its own way sought to recover some of the verdancy lost through its buildings and roadways. With penthouse and backyard gardens, trees and flowers planted along the streets, fountains playing in the shadow of skyscrapers, formal plantings ranged close to apartment houses, the garden theme is pushed for all it is worth, even if somewhat artificially, in the modern city. The horticulturist seeks fresh ways to humanize the solid blocks of masonry, and the vest-pocket park is a contemporary development in New York.

The colonial towns took civic pride in maintaining a certain verdancy in their communities, and trees, flowers, and grass soon transformed the five early cities of the new land. Thomas Hancock planted lime trees in front of his mansion on Beacon Hill to add to the green look of Boston Common, which was one of the earliest pleasure grounds of America. At town meetings a favorite subject for discussion was how to keep Bostonians and their cattle from using it as a parading ground. The fourteen-hundred-foot walk known as the Mall on Boston Common was constantly used from the old cowpath days. Hollyhocks, stocks, and Canterbury bells flowered in Boston at the time of the famous tea party, and the countryside throughout New England was rich with rambler roses and field flowers. Although wildflowers already checkered the land and seeds blew wild in the wind when the Pilgrims landed, it rarely occurred to a colonial wife to bring in an armful of blossom from the outdoors to adorn her house or her person.

Philadelphia had its commons, too, where citizens relaxed in a small grassy area, with trees around them. Here they often shared in one of the grim public rites—watching criminals being hanged on the gallows. New York had Bowling Green, which soon became famous for its gardens, its carriage drives, and promenading beauties. Generations of New Yorkers strolled through this early vest-pocket park at the tip of Manhattan Island, from the men in satin breeches and powdered wigs, who were building up the political and commercial structure of the city, to the nineteenth-century titans of Wall Street. Like Boston Common, Bowling Green survives amid a network of skyscrapers.

Pierre du Simitière, a Swiss artist who visited New York in 1767, was charmed with the city's four squares—Hanover Square, St. George's Square, the Commons before the New Gaol, and Bowling Green, "a beautiful ellipsis railed in with solid iron." Union Square in New York went through many phases from its early fashionable days until it was taken over by the labor forces. In 1887 pond lilies and lotus flowers floated in its fountain, but it also had bonfires, skyrockets, and steam whistles when Henry George led men through the square singing the "Marseillaise." But Union Square saw much more than political uproar. Nursemaids haunted it with their small charges in the days when the Rialto was its south boundary, and the great stars of the stage and opera walked through it to visit the theatrical agencies and costumers' shops. Madison Square Park, Gramercy Park, and Washington Square Park were all closely identified with the city's social history.

The man who made the United States as a whole park-conscious was Frederick Law Olmsted. He was largely responsible for Central Park in New York, and he also laid out four town sites and twelve suburban districts in the last two decades of his life. Until he became active in designing parks, the United States was singularly devoid of cultivated beauty spots except for the commons in New England, and such well-known areas as the Battery parks of New York and Charleston. Olmsted had farmed on Staten Island and was familiar with rural life. As he watched industrialism crowding out the city dweller, he encouraged the whole idea of parks and joined forces with Calvert

Porch life flourished in the city, as in the country, and this family group sought fresh air on the back porch of their New York home in the summer of 1875. Hanging plants, climbing wisteria, and wicker baskets of flowers were as typical of the period as the women's molded basques and the men's beards. Young Dr. I. W. Drummond, boater in hand, is surrounded by his family, but the house, built in 1825, had earlier been the home of Edwin Forrest, the actor.

The hammock was not only one of the favorite objects on the porch; it had its own romantic interest. It was linked with lazy afternoons, lawn tennis, and dalliance. The young lady in the advertisement looks somewhat dreamy-eyed. She certainly isn't interested in her book.

Gramercy Park West, November 1935. These twin houses, dating from before the Civil War, have handsome wrought-iron work reminiscent of the French-inspired New Orleans style. "The Mayor's Lamps" to the left were installed in 1848 when James Harper, whose home it was, became Mayor of New York City.

Vaux and Richard M. Hunt in the development of Central Park, first envisioned by Andrew J. Downing, who drew his inspiration from the parks of Europe. Before it was finished in 1876, Central Park covered 843 acres and bloomed with half a million trees, shrubs, and vines. Its grottoes and rustic houses, bridges and picturesque nooks, delighted old and young. Dodworth's band played in an Oriental pagoda and pantaletted children chose between goat carriages or camel rides, swings or small boats on the lakes. They played first on the greensward, then in cement playgrounds as New York grew up around them—a picture that was repeated in other cities across the nation. Today Central Park seeks to revive its faded image with bands, dancing, bicycling, skating, an annual Shakespeare festival, and community sprightliness in general—the theme song of Fun City.

From Central Park to Golden Gate Park in San Francisco, Olmsted spread the park tradition, fostering a system of small recreation parks, like the vest-pocket ones of today, in addition to his major efforts. At a time when landscape architecture was scoffed at as being a European affectation, Olmsted gradually demonstrated the importance of separating footways from roadways and bridle paths, and respecting the natural topography. Like Robert Moses more recently, he battled with politicians in order to carry out his dream of using the landscape creatively. His mind ran to verdancy and garden effects as Moses' did to highways, traffic communication centers, and such appealing playgrounds as Jones Beach. He encouraged the whole idea when industrialism began to crowd out the city dweller and anticipated the town planning that was tried later in many parts of the country, beginning with Pullman's disastrous efforts in the nineteenth century and spreading far afield in the New Deal days. His work between 1872 and 1895 had a permanent and beneficial effect on the American landscape.

The cultivation of fields and gardens was well established in the United States long before the planning of parks, which Europe already had in abundance. In the early days the President's House in Washington had what was then described as a grass common, with ambling walks and herds at pasture. Temporary tents and booths were put up for special occasions. By the end of the nineteenth century Washington had 150 varieties of trees and shrubs, with the silver maple, American ash, pin oak, and Norway maple predominating. And the White House conservatories supplied a succession of First Ladies with greenery.

In recent years both city and country dwellers have become strongly garden-conscious all over again, and although there are fewer landscaped gardens than in the last century small ones abound. There are more flower and vegetable plots than at any time since the mid-nineteenth century, and it is estimated that forty-four million American gardeners spend nearly five billion dollars a year on garden supplies, from peat moss to rosebushes. The Garden Clubs and flower shows that gain ground each year are social catalysts, like charity balls. New York's annual flower show draws some 300,000 flower lovers, to wander through lush gardens with brooks and log benches, dogwood trees and primrose plants. Kansas City has its annual "Circus of Flowers" under a striped circus tent. In Milwaukee, Detroit, and Cleveland, the flower shows spread their annual enchantment for those who love the earth. And Americans in general still love the earth, as they did when the Pilgrims landed. Quite early in its history New York had clipped box hedges, lilacs, roses, and snowballs in small gardens, while Dutch housekeepers in prim caps weeded their flowerbeds and dropped cut roses into their painted baskets. It is an inheritance that still haunts the city dweller. In fact, it was first in the cities, where people had always aired themselves on the front stoops in congested quarters for lack of any other breathing space, that a new type of porch appeared, high in the sky, narrow, precipitious, flecked with dust, furnished with canvas and chromium chairs, but often giving its owners a breathtaking view of the city. By the 1950s the roof garden at the top and the patio at the foot of a building had made the old-fashioned porch, however secure and comfortable, seem strangly dated, and builders let it drop from sight. They concentrated on flowing units of house and patio, with walled-in courtyards, little fountains, flowers and pools close to the kitchen or the living room. Instead of being an extension of a house the porch became an integrated part of the general building plan, a development that kept pace with the fantastic changes that began early in the twentieth century as modern architecture spread its shadow across the land. At that time draftsmen busied themselves with Utopian plans for tunnels, aerial bridges, and tiered colossi, most of which have come to fruition in the last half century.

The change came sporadically at first, beginning in Chicago, but by the 1920s there were soaring skylines from Dallas to Buffalo, and from New York to San Francisco. They had changed the look of the land and the life of its people. It was a new America, with a native architecture expressive of aspiration and purpose, and the word "skyline" came into appropriate use in the late 1890s as poets and artists heralded the new architecture, and photography carried the story around the world. Chicago's tall buildings were gracefully strung along its lengthy lakefront, giving an impression of space as well as of height. New York's skyline of necessity assumed a dense pyramidal form, first at the tip of Manhattan Island, then in the midtown section, and finally with another massive grouping uptown.

Although international developments influenced American architecture, the skyscraper was of truly native inspiration, differing from anything that had gone before in the world of building, and leaning

Old and young, shopping at Lord & Taylor's in 1870, marveled at the rope-operated elevator that took them aloft. Wood engraving from a drawing by Hyde in Frank Leslie's Illustrated Newspaper, 1873.

The first cast-iron building, pointing the way to today's steel-and-glass architecture, was designed by James Bogardus, a pioneer in iron construction. It stood at Center and Duane streets in New York City, and its significance in the evolution of building techniques was overlooked by contemporaries, who referred to Bogardus as the manufacturer of "the Eccentric Mill." Lithograph by Ackerman.

Boston Common was one of America's first pleasure grounds. It was filled with strollers on ordinary days, and holidays or special occasions, such as the water celebration of 1848, brought out great crowds. Bostonians rejoiced in the city's first pure water supply. Among the celebrants in the foreground are Henry Wadsworth Longfellow and Daniel Webster. Lithograph by F. Rouse, after a drawing by B. F. Smith, Jr.

Americans were inveterate excursionists in the nineteenth century, whole families traveling by steamboat or chugging train to their favorite seaside resorts. Locust Grove and Coney Island were the favored spots for short excursions and Brooklyn was always good for a day's jaunt. Lithograph by Chas. Hart.

strongly on the nation's vast steel resources. After a century of groping through an assortment of styles and during which they covered the land with everything from Greek capitols to balloon-frame houses, American architects found in the skyscraper a fresh interpretation of the national life as well as a new way to house the ever growing population, and to give light, air, and efficiency to their offices and workshops. The majority liked it but some felt the chill of its massive impersonality.

The new architecture was closely linked with the social turn-over of the twentieth century and the industralization that swept the country, plus the power and the range of the new metals, alloys, plastics, and glass brought rapidly into use once the pattern was set. As turrets soared skyward, creating a vast gray fresco tipped with silver and gold, shaded with black and beryl, people felt the magic of this new development. It became the distinctive note in American city life and its contribution to world architecture.

Chicago was the cradle of the skyscraper. The tall buildings that rise today in their infinite variety of design, composition, and material may be traced back to the group of brilliant architects who started this movement in the late nineteenth century. With versatile skill the same men built mansions for the new millionaires, and planned the factories, warehouses, and stores from which they drew their wealth. Hotels, railroad stations, churches, and public buildings all reflected the inspiration they brought into the world of commerce and everyday life. Louis Sullivan and Frank Lloyd Wright determined in the 1880s that American architecture should spring solely from native sources, with complete freedom from the European influence that had tinged all its earlier developments. "Arrange your architecture for Democracy because a certain function, democracy, is seeking a certain form of expression, democratic architecture," said Sullivan.

By 1900 nearly one-fifth of the population lived in cities of 100,000 or more, and the frontier was shrinking fast. People were on the move. Railroads were booming. Factories were meeting new consumer demands. The cast-iron building, which paved the way for the skyscraper, had come on the scene in 1848 when James Bogardus used iron columns instead of masonry to support his five-story factory building in New York. From then on he built others on the prefabricated idea of the balloon-frame house. The cast-iron front gave a certain uniformity to such cities as Cincinnati, St. Louis, and Louisville, but it was used for bridges, cotton mills, and factories rather than for residential purposes.

Brooklyn Bridge, with its gala dedication in 1883, drew attention to dynamic construction principles. Built by John A. Roebling and his son Washington, this suspension bridge with towers 276 feet high and a central span of 1,600 feet, was regarded as one of the most dramatic engineering feats of the century. It was an engineer, too, who was responsible for the first skyscraper—Major William Le Baron Jenney, who designed it quite by accident. Because of a bricklayers' strike, the ten-story Home Insurance Building, which he finally completed in Chicago in 1883, was at a standstill, and since neither reinforced concrete nor Portland cement was available at the time, he put a skeleton framework of iron inside the masonry to take the load off the walls. This was going one step further than predecessors who had used cast iron in their masonry as well as wrought-iron floor beams.

Major Jenney's priority claim was questioned by a Minneapolis architect named L. S. Buffington, a Phileas Fogg character who as early as 1880 was drawing innumerable sketches of buildings as tall as a hundred stories. Other dreamers had thought along the same lines but Buffington felt that he was the originator of the whole idea. However, the architect more generally thought to have been the father of the skyscraper was Louis Sullivan, who settled in Chicago after the Great Fire of 1871 and set his stamp on the Loop, the Stock Exchange, and the Auditorium Building.

The Tacoma Building, completed by Holabird and Roche soon after Major Jenney's production, went one step further; it was the first building in which the outer wall had no burden to carry. Its steel skeleton supported the brick and terra-cotta walls that served merely as a curtain against the elements. One skyscraper followed another in Chicago, with master architects enhancing their reputations with this new development. In 1889 the Rand McNally building designed by Daniel H. Burnham and John W. Root established the fundamentals which have remained unchanged in the construction of tall buildings. A year later they finished the Masonic Temple, twenty-one stories high, the tallest building in the world at that time.

It had taken less than a decade for the skyscraper to reach maturity in Chicago. St. Louis was quickly in the field with Sullivan's Wainwright Building in 1890, and Buffalo with his Guaranty Building. New York made a slow but striking start in 1902 with the Flatiron, designed by Burnham. This curious building on Fifth Avenue became a landmark of great interest until Cass Gilbert's Gothic Woolworth Building, 792 feet tall, became one of the wonders of the world. In the spring of 1913 Woodrow Wilson threw a switch in the White House that lit up eighty thousand lamps in the Woolworth Tower. For two decades this "Cathedral of Commerce" held its primacy as the tallest of buildings, and a trip to the top was the first objective of visitors from all parts of the world. But it seemed puny after the bulletlike tower of the Empire State Building rose 1,250 feet into the air in 1931, encompassing 102 stories.

By 1966 tourists headed first for this tall citadel, for the newly opened Lincoln Center, or for Rockefeller Center, already much loved for its many charms—a building development that humanized the skyscraper scene in New York and affected the tall buildings that came later. The Center set a pattern for grouped masses around open plazas; it also made fresh use of the slab.

In 1917 the Bush Terminal Tower Building in midtown Manhattan repeated the Gothic effect of the Woolworth, but in 1925 Raymond Hood's American Radiator Building, described as "one big cinder," made a breathtaking debut, black as night, with beveled corners and vertical piers tipped with gold. It was considered dramatic and daring, but more soothing to observers was the silvery stainless steel spire of the Chrysler Building. Opened in 1929 and soaring 1,046 feet in the midtown area, it stood aloof from the growing piles of cubistic forms. Two years later the Empire State had topped it, after much rivalry and speculation about the comparative upward thrust of the two buildings.

As the United States moved into the Depression following 1929, its cities had 377 skyscrapers more than twenty stories high. Of New York's 188, fifteen were more than five hundred feet tall. A long hiatus in building followed, through the 1930s and early 1940s, and by the time it was resumed the world had changed. The international style was in full flower, with cantilevered steel skeletons enclosed in transparent sheaths of glass. Lever House (Skidmore, Owings & Merrill, 1952) and the coppery Seagram Building (Philip Johnson, 1957) were early examples of this influence and both were considered lineal descendants of the Crystal Palace and the Eiffel Tower.

Even railroad stations, often monuments from the past, were affected. In 1914 the *Architectural Record* pointed out that they were the second most important symbol of the Imperial era after the skyscraper. Until the 1870s most of them had been shabby wooden shelters or brightly painted balloon-frame buildings. But as more people traveled and saw what Europe had to offer in the way of stations, the most noted architects were commissioned to design great terminals. The railroads had become a powerful and penetrating factor in public life. Burnham designed Washington's Union Station early in the twentieth century, giving it the classic air and a Romanesque waiting room. Stanford White's Pennsylvania Station (1903), modeled after the Baths of Caracalla and a gem of its kind in the eyes of traditionalists, fell to the wreckers in the 1960s. Its Roman Travertine waiting hall had impressed—and sometimes chilled—many millions of travelers in more than a half century.

New York's Grand Central, opened in 1913, set a new standard for warmth and activity in a station, with its lively concourse and the variety of shops and restaurants in its arcades. More than 500,000 people pass through it each day but when the New York and Harlem Railroad—later part of the New York Central system—ran its first train, drawn by a team of horses, Park Avenue was a wilderness. William H. Vanderbilt had his favorite horse, Maud S., in a little pasture surrounded by a picket fence, where he could watch her from his office. The newspapers were full of worried letters about the danger of having trains run through the streets. There were mass meetings, and a group of cab drivers tore up a section of the track. But the public soon liked the merry jaunts by train to sights nearby. The first terminal was completed in 1871—a somber building with red brick walls and cast-iron trimmings. Today's concourse is roofed inside with a zodiacal mural of 2,500 stars in gold leaf, and the skyscraper touch has been added with the Pan-American Building that now soars behind Grand Central.

The modern mood shown in many of the stations built in recent years stems from the international style which crystalized in France with the work of Le Corbusier, in Holland with J. H. P. Oud, and in Germany with Mies van der Rohe and Walter Gropius. When Gropius was asked to organize a German art school after World War I he named it the Bauhaus and created a technical school of design with concentration on the industrial arts and the use of modern materials. Like Ruskin and Morris, he sought to break down the cleavage between artist and craftsman, and this led to industrial design of a new order. In architecture, by the use of steel, glass, and bronze, internationalists aimed to incorporate in their buildings the simultaneous realization of outer and inner space.

With the influx of some of Europe's most notable architects the new buildings in America were profoundly affected by the Bauhaus tradition. Le Corbusier preferred American grain elevators to Gothic cathedrals and ridiculed early railroad stations disguised as Roman temples. He lifted buildings on stilts, in the fashion of Lever House, designed chiefly by Gordon Bunshaft. Interior walls were eliminated and stairs spiraled over the exteriors, to preserve the sense of pure space within. Wright, Mies, Le Corbusier, and Gropius each cast the world in his own image, one organic, one structural, one primitive, one mechanistic—as the *Architectural Review* pointed out in 1960.

Between 1933 and 1960 American architects were evolving a more advanced type of modern architecture by absorbing what they wished from the Bauhaus school and other European sources, and adapting it to native taste and requirements. Gropius and Marcel Breuer joined the Harvard faculty in the late 1930s; Lazlo Moholy-Nagy established the new Bauhaus in Chicago in 1937. Philip Johnson, designer of the Seagram Building, became the leading exponent of Mies van der Rohe's techniques. But however strong the Bauhaus influence, individualists found new ways to match environment, notably in the

Rockefeller Center, New York. The skyscrapers of the world's largest privately owned business and entertainment center rise dramatically in midtown Manhattan. Its seventeen buildings dwarf the Gothic spires of St. Patrick's Cathedral, which looks down on the flower-filled channel enjoyed by thousands of tourists sauntering through the plaza to the towering peaks beyond.

Lever House, designed by Gordon Bunshaft of Skidmore, Owings & Merrill. A glass curtain wall sheathes the 3,499-ton steel skeleton of this dramatic New York City landmark, a "small" skyscraper which uses open space as significantly as closed space.

The TWA terminal at the John F. Kennedy Airport echoes Eero Saarinen's intention "to take the discipline imposed by the concrete shell vault and give it a non-static soaring quality."

case of Edward Durell Stone, whose United States Embassy rose like an Arabian Nights' dream in New Delhi in the late 1950s. Bizarre and beautiful in its setting, its gold-leaf columns and lacy grills made it the most discussed embassy building in the world. When asked to reflect Islamic architecture within the structural limitations posed by a reactor he drew up designs for the Nuclear Research Center in West Pakistan, setting the swimming-pool reactor beneath a mosquelike dome in gold mosaic, close to a minaret-style exhaust tower—perhaps the last word in adapting an ancient culture to the requirements of the space age.

Some of the same spirit was expressed by Eero Saarinen in the TWA terminal at the John F. Kennedy Airport in New York City and in the David S. Ingalls Hockey Rink opened at Yale University in 1959. A master of engineering problems, he struck a fresh note on the campus with a Viking design. His father, Eliel Saarinen, designer of the Cranbrook Academy at Bloomfield Hills, Michigan, set his stamp on church architecture, and started fountains flowing at Cranbrook, at the Metropolitan Museum of Art, and in front of the Union Station in St. Louis. The Saarinens were no more committed to the Bauhaus than a number of contemporary American architects today engaged in building great art centers, libraries, memorials, and all manner of public buildings across the country. Wallace K. Harrison, a key architect of Rockefeller Center and the United Nations Secretariat building, is a plain-spoken New Englander who regards architecture as a "whole society of people working together." Both he and Philip Johnson, among others, joined forces in the complex of buildings known as Lincoln Center. Walton Becket, of California, deep in industrial and hotel architecture, designed the Eisenhower library in Abilene, Kansas; and Gordon Bunshaft, who did Yale's rare book library, is also involved in the L. B. Johnson library proposed for the University of Texas campus, a monumental building with curved slabs bracing set-back façades. The Viennese Victor Gruen, of Beverly Hills, designs department stores, apartment houses, and manufacturing plants keyed to the contemporary mood in architecture that is changing the traditional pattern of the industrial world. Glass and metal cover rectangles of steel and concrete. Sparkling domes and arches appear in fantastic combinations, where once the drab factory marred the countryside.

Although individualists now loom large in the experimental world of architecture, the greatest of all was Frank Lloyd Wright, who had his early training in Sullivan's office. He created his own organic architecture and scoffed at the Bauhaus. His houses were built into nature's own conformation, as he made use of boulders and foliage, of waterfalls and crevices, of diffused light, rough terrain, or any advantage he could gain from nature itself. "Go not to the ribbon counter for your color scheme," he wrote, "'but to the autumn woods and fields, develop what is the natural texture of wood or plaster, brick or stone; make use of the machine, for it is the normal tool of our civilization; give it work that it can do well."

Wright found inspiration in Mayan architecture and its concrete temple masses. Above all, he extended the range of materials that the architect might use, experimenting constantly himself with steel, copper, concrete, glass, brick, stone, and wood, and sticking close to the colors of the earth. The succession of prairie houses he built between 1900 and 1910, such as the Ward H. Willetts house in Highland Park, Illinois, the F. C. Robie house in Chicago, the Darwin Martin house in Buffalo, and many more in the Middle West, entranced their owners. His long horizontal roofs and broad spread-out masses fitted almost imperceptibly into their setting in the Japanese fashion. Wright had been much influenced by the years he had spent in Japan and he brought the Oriental influence strongly to bear on his own two homes in Wisconsin, "Taliesin East" and "Taliesin West," and on "Falling Water," which he built in 1936 for Edgar J. Kaufmann at Bear Run, Pennsylvania. This house creates an effect of singular beauty, because of its dramatic site, cantilever construction, and natural waterfall.

Although skyscrapers were less close to his heart than his prairie houses, Wright was responsible for one of the most dramatic of them—the Larkin Building of Buffalo, planned around an interior court and surrounded by balconies leading to offices. Most of the furniture was designed by him to blend harmoniously with its setting. The hermetically sealed building kept out noise and dirt, yet was bright and well ventilated. After a period of withdrawal from the competitive market the master architect emerged in the 1930s with a new synthesis of design, and startled the public with his controversial Guggenheim Museum on New York's Fifth Avenue considerably later. Its spiral, windowless shell of reinforced concrete, with a cylindrical center core surmounted by a wire-glass dome, is either admired or detested, but it never lacks for curious crowds who come to stare at the building itself, if not always at the art it contains.

Although Wright had little to do with the Columbian Exposition held in Chicago in 1893, beyond commenting favorably on its Japanese exhibits, his fellow architects were deeply involved. It was the most ambitious world's fair held in America up to that time, and its emphasis on architecture and the arts profoundly affected the country as a whole. The nation's leading architects, sculptors, and painters worked under the direction of Burnham. Saint-Gaudens called it "the greatest gathering of artists since the fifteenth century," as a snow-white city rose like a mirage along Lake Michigan's south shore, dedicated to the classic and Renaissance tradition. Plaster of Paris palaces were mirrored in the lagoons, the spires and domes were alternately Roman, Greek, or in the style brought back to America by students at L'École des Beaux-Arts in Paris. The Women's Building overlooked the lagoon and was Italian Renaissance in style, with balconies, loggias, and touches of gold to relieve its snowy interior. It was largely Mrs. Potter Palmer's creation, and the board of women she directed passed up the chance to have Richard Morris Hunt design it in order to show their confidence in the ability of their own sex. The Hall of Honor, unbroken by supports, rose seventy feet high and was inscribed in gold with the names of women great in art, letters, music, science, and the theater. Mary Cassatt, an American artist not yet well known, did one of the murals.

But the architects from the East crowded out the strong men of Chicago, like Wright, and the traditional touch of McKim, Mead and White was omnipresent. Saint-Gaudens' statue "Diana the Huntress" was transferred from Madison Square Garden to the Fair, in spite of waves of protest from the puritanical and a strong defense of it by Mrs. Palmer. The public enjoyed it all, from Venus de Milo molded in chocolate to the Yerkes telescope, from Edison's Kinetoscope to Columbus' contract with Ferdinand and Isabella, from Impressionist art to the hootchy-kootchy dancing of Little Egypt. Charles Eliot Norton thought the Fair a "superb and appropriate symbol of our great nation . . . in its refinements, cheek-by-jowl with vulgarities, in its order and its confusion, in its heterogeneousness and in its unity."

In many ways this particular fair left a greater impression than any of the others down the years, although each has evoked its own nostalgic echoes. The influence of the Columbian showed up in Roman temples and triumphal arches, in Gothic churches, in French châteaus and Florentine villas, since the men responsible for the buildings of the Fair were soon commissioned by the newly rich to build their city and country mansions. Root who, with Burnham, had designed Chicago's Rookery in 1885, was scornful of it all. He called the Victorian Era the Cathartic; the Romanesque, the Dropsical; the Queen Anne, with its wens, carbuncles, and pinworms, the Tubercular style. But he died before the Columbian Exposition was fully built, and had little chance to stamp it with any of his own characteristics.

By the close of the century most men of wealth had country estates or seaside villas, a trend that had started before the Exposition and dated back to the Queen Anne manor house that the mighty Henry Hobson Richardson had built for Watts Sherman in Newport in 1874. Famous for his beard, his yellow waistcoats, his love of good food and champagne, and the surging strength and vigor of his style, Richardson worked in the Romanesque tradition. In Lewis Mumford's opinion his buildings, including the Marshall Field store in Chicago, looked as if they were put up for eternity. His country houses were unpretentious but had the same air of strength. He used the autumnal

The William K. Vanderbilt
mansion on Fifth Avenue, finished
in 1881, was designed by Richard
Morris Hunt, with architectural
detail ranging from late Gothic
to the castles along the Loire, and
particularly the Château de Blois.
The craftsmanship of the interior,
the plain walls, oriels, and turrets,
all done in gray limestone, were
much admired by connoisseurs
who preferred it to the more
florid and pretentious Vanderbilt
houses farther along the avenue.
From Century Magazine, 1883.

The Frederic C. Robie house on Woodlawn Avenue, Chicago, designated a
historical landmark in 1966, is one of Frank Lloyd Wright's masterpieces.
Finished in 1909, its long decklike balconies, massive masonry, and intersection
of planes in space made it the most discussed building of the period. The lift
of its balconies and eaves seems suggestive of the airplane. Wright also designed
its furnishings, with chairs like ancient thrones, cabinets built into the masonry,
and lights raised on columns. Its somewhat ecclesiastical interior was preserved
by the Chicago Theological Seminary. The house is now owned by the
University of Chicago and is occupied by the Adlai E. Stevenson Institute.

*Courtyard of Fenway Court, the
Venetian palace built outside
Boston by Mrs. Jack Gardner,
patron-collector of the arts. The
building, now known as the
Isabella Stewart Gardner Museum,
was designed by its owner and
shows a mingling of Roman,
Byzantine, Romanesque, and
Gothic influences.*

*The residence of C. C. Moseley in Beverly Hills
—Wallace Neff, architect. The architecture of the
missions and the spacious informality of the
"rancho" are an abiding influence in southern
California architecture.*

*Modern community life and rustic surroundings
are combined at Reston, one of the New Towns,
eighteen miles from Washington. Townhouses by
Charles M. Goodman are reflected in a quiet
Virginian pond in Reston's first village of
Lake Anne. The woods are at hand but life is
brisk and avant-garde along the waterways.*

tints of sumac and red oak with his weathered shingles. Much of his work was done in New England, and he introduced native sandstone with the granite to brighten his buildings in the cold gray of the North.

But the two architects who worked most intensively in the field of ornate design were Richard Morris Hunt and Stanford White. Hunt designed the William K. Vanderbilt château that became a landmark on Fifth Avenue. It was called a "singing marriage of the Château de Blois and the Jacques Coeur house at Bourges" when the first guests gathered for a fancy-dress ball in March, 1883, and saw Mrs. Astor eat humble pie in the home of a Vanderbilt. Hunt designed the Marble House at Newport, and he gave Château-sur-Mer, George Wetmore's house at the same resort, a French ballroom, an Eastlake library, an Italian dining room, and a stone porte-cochère. Always versatile in his work, he designed the classical pedestal for the Statue of Liberty.

Stanford White, working closely with La Farge and Saint-Gaudens, became famous in the 1890s for his Renaissance effects. He designed the Washington Arch, and the mansion he built on Madison Avenue for Henry Villard was patterned after the Cancelleria in Rome. Sullivan and Wright called it imperialistic planning when the Baths of Caracalla became the model for the Pennsylvania Station, and J. P. Morgan's library was strongly suggestive of the Villa Medici. White and his partner, Charles F. McKim, designed Robert Goelet's house and the Casino at Newport. They fostered a revival of Georgian and colonial style, studying the houses at Newburyport and other New England landmarks, but "Ocher Court," the Goelet house, had a painted ceiling and gold encrustations reminiscent of the Paris Opera. Hunt remodeled the Breakers as a mammoth Italian villa with a loggia floored with mosaic.

In northern California Mark Hopkins, Charles Crocker, and Leland Stanford built palaces of brick and wood on San Francisco's Nob Hill, and later, above San Luis Obispo, William Randolph Hearst created San Simeon, a medieval fortress filled with Old World treasures. Etruscan-style colonnades, backed by a Greco-Roman temple surrounded the 104-foot Neptune pool, last used as a set for the film *Spartacus*. Hearst spent more than $30 million furnishing La Cuesta Encantada (the Enchanted Hill). Mrs. Jack Gardner built a Venetian palace on the Fenway outside Boston and Henry Frick a Louis XVI mansion in New York to house his art treasures. Andrew Carnegie gave the gold key of the mansion he built on Fifth Avenue to his daughter Margaret. E. T. Stotesbury had a miniature Versailles outside Philadelphia, and Harold F. McCormick built a Renaissance villa at Lake Forest, a suburb of Chicago. Eugene du Pont's choice was a slate-roofed Tudor house in Delaware. Addison Mizner built the J. S. Phipps house at Palm Beach in the early 1920s, and it and "Viscaya,"

James Deering's Florida villa, presented a dazzling if somewhat jumbled array of terraces, fountains and parterres, sculpture, obelisks and gondolas, along with waves of tropical foliage. Between 1918 and 1929 the range was wide, from the colonial mansion, Gothic manor, and Norman farmhouse to the central-masted "Dymaxion House" of R. Buckminster Fuller, who later designed the American pavilion of Expo 67.

Ranch houses and villas dotted the Southwest as the pueblo tradition was revived, and the architecture of the missions and churches came to life again, this time with all modern conveniences. The feeling for the ranch house spread across the country. Fieldstone, hand-hewn wood, title floors, lustrous metals, and polished woods were freely used, and plastics entered all spheres of homemaking. Richard J. Neutra experimented in California with a modified skyscraper design for a house.

The Depression and the New Deal brought waves of low-income housing developments, model villages, and public buildings with murals. America welcomed an infusion of artists in various fields who had left Europe as the dictators rose to power. Mass production prevailed and building was carried out on a colossal scale. The greenbelt towns had their day until William J. Levitt came along and established himself as the Henry Ford of the home-building industry. During the 1920s and the 1930s the big automobile companies brought in top-flight architects to design their showrooms. Maybeck, who had designed the Palace of Fine Arts in San Francisco, introduced Pompeiian effects in California. Albert Kahn designed the type of factory that was all under one roof. His buildings of reinforced concrete and steel sash tidied up and dramatized areas once devoted to meaningless factories and shabby warehouses.

By 1929 the fourteen largest cities showed that three apartment houses were being built for every single- or two-family house. This had been reduced to a formula. But in the 1960s a swing back to blocks of one- and two-story units in the suburbs resembled the old row-house style. Chicago, Washington, and San Francisco showed this trend as new towns sprang up, exemplified best in Reston, eighteen miles from the capital. The architectural planning and community spirit of these developments were widely praised, and an effort was made to extend them to low-income units.

Town houses were again in demand in New York in the 1960s, in spite of the well-established taste of its citizens for apartment-house life, a tradition dating back a hundred years. When a group of French flats first opened on Eighteenth Street critics complained bitterly about people living in boxes piled on top of one another. But by the time the House of Mansions, or Spanish Row, opened at Fifth Avenue and

Forty-second Street in 1855, they had become used to the idea, although still convinced that this way of living would ruin family life. Some of the early apartment houses rose to eleven stories and had balconies on the upper floors. The more luxurious had timbered ceilings, tiled fireplaces, paneled walls, deep window seats, and built-in cupboards in the Queen Anne tradition. In the course of a century these miniature developments pointed the way to New York's most magnificent cooperative apartments of today. And in 1857 the world's first passenger elevator paved the way for the skyscraper. The one supplemented the other.

The first elevator came from a small factory in Yonkers and was installed in the store of E. V. Haughwout & Company in New York. It was the invention of Elisha Graves Otis, who died as the Civil War was beginning. His sons, Charles and Norton, incorporated the business in 1867 and from then on Americans took to being hoisted in the air—in shops, in hotels, in factories, in private homes, and finally in skyscrapers, which would not have become a reality without the indispensable elevator. Five- and six-story "elevator" buildings began to supplant low-hung offices and stores, and the skyline soared.

Hotelkeepers were enraptured, making the upper floors, once relegated to the servants, the choice ones of the house. The fascinating new "vertical railroad" was something to advertise, a drawing card for new hotels. Crinolines jostled against one another as their owners lounged in comfortable velour or padded-leather seats, and before long the question arose as to whether men should remove their hats in this intimate setting. The most discussed elevator in fashionable circles was the steam model installed by Lord & Taylor in the 1870s. A solemn youth controlled it by rope while a row of women breathlessly shared in the perilous ascent.

The steam elevator was followed by the hydraulic elevator, which made better speed and had a safety device to use in case of emergency. The first elevators in the White House were installed in 1881, and by that time high-speed types were in use in many commercial buildings. A few were also to be found in private houses, and a popular advertisement showed a little girl running one by pushbutton for an elderly lady and saying: "Now, Grandma, no more stair running."

In 1900 the first escalator, an Otis product, was awarded a grand prize at the Paris Exposition, and traveling up and down on the moving stairway became a popular sport. Ten years later elevators reached a speed of seven hundred feet a minute, or eight miles an hour, which was then the maximum allowed for bicycles on city streets. By that time plunger elevators were in use for buildings twenty-five or thirty stories high. The much-loved porch or piazza was on the decline; the skyscraper age had dawned.

8 *Eve's Daughters*

F ashion" was an unfamiliar word to the founding mothers
of America, but their inherent instinct for style and adornment came quickly to the fore. Repressive measures in New England
did not snuff out their vanity, although men were the peacocks of the
era and women the brown wrens. The clothes worn by women in the
new land soon ceased to be dull and dowdy. Color, particularly scarlet,
blazed in the colonies at an early date. Women wore silks and Tiffany
hoods in spite of cautioning laws and injunctions, laying the foundation
for America's strong fashion-consciousness today.

Since these early gropings, styles in fashion have zigzagged, repeating themselves at times and invariably stirring up interest, from the
towering wigs and floor-length dresses of the eighteenth century to
the startling hair arrangements and seminudity of today. Fashions have
lent color to the nation's history, inciting argument, stimulating competition, encouraging trade, and creating great fortunes. Today America's dress business is estimated as $18 billion a year. It is the eighth
largest manufacturing industry in the United States, and the leading
one in New York State.

Even three hundred years ago the imitative spirit developed
rapidly, as women escaped from their Puritan fetters and fashions became kaleidoscopic, moving first toward the show and extravagance   167

Mary Duncan Ludlow (1713–1779) by John Singleton Copley (1738–1815). She was one of many New England women who posed for this famous Bostonian. A Copley portrait became a status symbol in the nineteenth-century home. Brilliant, realistic portraits came regularly from his studio on Beacon Hill until the time of the Revolution, when he settled in London. He was one of the sharpest observers in colonial America, and he painted the shrewd, strong New England faces with understanding. Mary Ludlow was a case in point. She was less decorative in her attire than many of his subjects, but she wore what countless other American women of seasoned age wore at that time—the simple lingerie cap, the multiple ruffles known as engageantes at her wrists, the crossed fichu, and fine cashmere shawl.

Mrs. Peter Beckford (Bathsua Hering) by Benjamin West (1738–1820). The "Queen's Cap" affected by many great ladies of the period framed Mrs. Beckford's face with an all-round ruching when she posed for West, the self-taught artist from Pennsylvania who set up studios in Europe and followed Sir Joshua Reynolds as president of the Royal Academy. Mrs. Beckford, who spent much of her life on her husband's large plantation in Jamaica, is dressed in Pompadour taffeta, with yards of crushed gauze forming a chemisette.

Martha Washington (1732–1802) by Rembrandt Peale (1778–1860). Poufs of lace or gauze closely framing the face followed the towering coiffures of the mid-eighteenth century, and Mrs. Washington, always meticulously fashionable, is here shown wearing a guipure cap with ribbon bow and the soft, puffed fichu popularized by Marie Antoinette. George Washington was in the habit of ordering these caps—"lace-head, ruffles and lappets"—for Martha. The high girdle of her gown reflects the Greek Revival influence then taking hold. The full-length fitted sleeves had not been worn since the fifteenth century but were coming into fashion again. Peale, who had painted George Washington from life in 1795, was still quite young when he made this portrait of Martha. One of Charles Willson Peale's three artist sons, all named after painters—Raphael, Rembrandt, and Titian—he was best known for his paintings of historical scenes.

Mrs. Thomas Brewster Coolidge (Clarissa Baldwin) by Chester Harding (1792–1866). This portrait was painted around 1828 when Clarissa, the daughter of Colonel Soammi Baldwin of Boston, was thirty. Harding, in turn a cabinetmaker, house painter, tavern keeper, and self-trained portrait painter, had a studio in Springfield, Massachusetts, and among his subjects were Daniel Webster and John Randolph. He painted Mrs. Coolidge during the era of mad hats, towering structures with all manner of frippery, but hers is a comparatively modest version of the plumed hat, slightly tilted, with the lace ruche around her chin. Capes had become fashionable because sleeves were too ballooned for fitted wraps. This taffeta cape is edged and collared with ermine, less of a luxury fur then than it is today.

Amelia Palmer by Charles Cromwell Ingham (1796–1863). "The Flower Girl," painted about 1829, shows the adolescent of the period in a soft classical gown with drooped shoulders and wide, scooped neckline. Amelia, daughter of Amos Palmer, a hardware importer living in Stonington, Connecticut, is showing her pantalettes beneath a scalloped and embroidered hemline. The classical influence was declining at this time, and the Empire genre was reflected in the gowns of American women. Amelia's hair, parted in the middle, was softly arranged in long curls on her shoulders. Ingham, who came to America from Dublin when he was twenty, was known as a "ladies' portrait painter" because of his highly polished work. Woodland scenes as background were used increasingly at this time by the growing body of portraitists in the United States.

Kate Lyon Cornell (later Mrs. Dabney William Diggs) by Theodore E. Pine. At fifteen Kate, as caught by this artist, seemed already a mature adolescent in an age when girls married even younger than they do today. She wore her ringlets in the spaniel fashion made popular by Elizabeth Barrett Browning in the 1840s. Her closely fitted bodice and full skirt with low waistline were fashionable at this time, and the lace undersleeves and lateral neckline were a departure from the puffed sleeves of the classical period. Kate's cameo necklace and bracelet were characteristic of her day, and she followed the custom of wearing a ring on her forefinger.

of the eighteenth century, and then to the dramatic crinolines of the Civil War era. The Pilgrims who arrived in Plymouth in 1620 were as simple and austere in their garb as in their convictions, but the voyagers who came on the *Arbella* with John Winthrop were a mixed company, with worldly elements among them. Inevitably vanity and show touched Boston and Salem before Plymouth was affected by the rise of fashion. But as the Pilgrims prospered their simplicity waned. Some of the women were arrested at Newburyport in 1653 for appearing in public with silk hoods and scarves. It was considered indecent for them to sit in meeting with bonnets on their frivolous heads. John Cotton thought that they should show their faces, but Rogers Williams urged the women of Salem to wear veils in public. In the end they did what their instincts dictated, depending on the treasures they could accumulate after they escaped from the simple homespun that was practically the uniform of the early days.

The Quakers as well as the Puritans found much to censor in the growing worldliness of the colonists. They seemed to be "launching into finery" and dressing their children more elaborately than the young in England. Their own women in Pennsylvania were warned against scarlet shoes and frivolously dressed hair at a time when New York women were flaunting gauzes, silks, and laces. But in spite of these injunctions Philadelphia at the time of the Revolution outmatched the other cities in luxury and high living. Things were little different in Boston; a British observer in 1740 noted that the men and women there were as flashily dressed as British courtiers at a coronation. Even the little girls went skipping around in stays and lutestring coats, with flowered-damask shoes and brightly colored dresses.

The Dutch *frauen* in New York could not be deterred from wearing innumerable fancy petticoats, and gold and silver girdles, with bunches of keys dangling on their chatelaines. They were not unduly fashion-conscious, but they firmly believed in comfortable and seemly living. Separate sleeves trimmed with gold lace, fur caps, waistcoats, and aprons were their daily dress. They lived by their own style, so that they stood out in the community, like a race apart. Women wore waistcoats as universally as aprons at this time, and in the 1760s beaded stomachers and spangles caught on with the more fashionable Bostonians. In fact, the vain creatures were caught applying as many as seventeen black beauty patches to their persons, and dampening their ball gowns to make them cling to their figures. They whisked their fans at parties and wore feathers in their towering headdresses, which made a visiting Englishman, viewing their patches and gay apparel, call them the "foolish virgins of New England." The ladies of Annapolis and Charleston were equally noted for their style and embellishments, and their storage chests brimmed with imported materials.

Until the Revolution nearly every business letter from merchants and planters contained orders for bolts of cloth, kid gloves and worsted stockings, silver shoe buckles, aigrettes, masks and mittens for their wives and children. George and Martha Washington were among the most lavish buyers of silk and velvet gowns, greatcoats, and riding outfits. From France Benjamin Franklin sent his daughter Deborah white cloaks and plumes, satin cardinals and paste shoebuckles. During this period American women reflected to some degree the lingering influence of Madame de Pompadour, princess of fashion as the delicate baroque merged into the rococo mood. Fantastic combinations of garlands, bows, and magnificent silks prevailed through the era of Marie Antoinette and until the tumbrel sounded. The elliptical hoop skirt, the pannier, the pouf polanaise dominated fashions in the 1770s and the bustle was briefly revived.

Englishwomen of the period were committed to simple muslin gowns in the pastoral tradition of knotted fichus and heelless shoes. Nothing English was in favor in the United States, but the Greek Revival in architecture and philosophy was reflected toward the close of the century in clinging gowns with high waistlines and short puffed sleeves, not unlike the shepherdess muslins. The classical period in America was a soothing one in fashions, with girls moving freely without stays or chemises. Their sheer gowns, held at the neck by drawstrings, flowed softly from the armpits to the floor and were not unlike some of the fashions of 1966. Their hair was cropped in the classical tradition and their shoes were purple or green.

But this simplicity soon went into eclipse and a top-heavy look followed, with leg-of-mutton sleeves and gowns expanded with whalebone. The scooped décolletage held its ground until the mid-eighteenth century, when the neckline squared and widened. American women were apt to tuck lace in their bosoms, since vestiges of the Puritan spirit remained. They took up riding, creating a new image of themselves, as they posted sidesaddle, wearing tricorne hats, long habits, strapped riding breeches, white cambric vests, and top boots.

New styles were quickly noted across the Atlantic, and within a few months the colonists would be wearing the same hats, gowns, and shoes as Londoners. The news was transmitted by the model dolls known as "Babies." Mantua-makers and seamstresses studied the diminutive garments and copied them faithfully. Although the "Babies" came originally from England, after the Revolution they were brought from France, until Madame Demorest and Ebenezer Butterick flooded the country with paper patterns in the 1870s. This development, closely following the introduction of the sewing machine, profoundly affected the world of fashion. By the end of the eighteenth century 75 per cent of the population made their own clothes.

The sewing machine is still a valued object in countless homes, although inexpensive ready-made clothes have made it impractical to spend time on home dressmaking, and the seamstress who once went out by the day is a rare find in the 1960s. But simple, chic patterns have taken the place of the complex array of segments that often baffled the nineteenth-century home dressmaker. Even by present-day standards the colonists had a wealth of materials to choose from, with sailing vessels arriving from Europe and later from the Orient, bringing brocades, damasks, and the finest silks. The opening of the East Indian trade led to the use of nankeen, a standby for sturdy wear, as well as the fine shawls, calico, dimity, chintz, and other simple materials, to be used along with satin, plush, and velvet. The hard-wearing Osnaburg linen, Holland lawn, and German serge were popular on all social levels, and in course of time Spanish poplin, Irish linen, and Scottish tartans were packed into the family chests, the clothes closets of their day.

This, too, was the era when widows hid themselves from head to foot in bombazine and crêpe. Their faces were screened with heavy veiling flowing free from tiny crêpe bonnets. Their handkerchiefs and gloves sustained the funereal note. Dull ornaments might be worn after six months, but nothing that glittered for a year. By degrees the fashionable woman muffled her grief in a smarter use of black, moving as soon as she could into white, lavender, or gray for half mourning. The enveloping veil, if worn at all, became a shadowy fiction. Mourning jewelry, black-edged notepaper, and sable trappings faded gradually, like chaperones and fans. The business and professional world demanded a more realistic approach. Life went on, without the interminable round of black plumes, opaque veiling, of crêpe armbands for men, and the total immolation of the widow. Today there is little about the attire to indicate, even at a funeral, that death has visited a family. Black veiling may be worn briefly by the immediate mourners, but next day they return to their accustomed wear—one of the many contemporary modifications of ancient customs.

Each war has left its imprint on fashion. The Italian war of independence in the 1840s inspired the Zouave jacket, Garibaldi shirt, and braided pillbox cap. The Crimean War in 1854 brought the burnoose, a hooded mantle linked with the Near East. The trenchcoat and wristwatch took hold after World War I, and the Eisenhower jacket after World War II. But wraps in general changed radically in style between the seventeenth and the twentieth centuries. The crimson-hooded cardinal cloaks and the shawls of colonial days made way for the redingote, the spencer, the pelisse, the pelerine, the mantle, the dolman, the fitted coat, the sports coat, the trenchcoat, the guardsman's coat, and many others linked to current events, like the popular caftan and the African ajellabah of 1966.

Fitted cloaks first made their appearance as the Civil War began, and many women wore Talma cloaks of velvet or merino during this somber period. The spencer was a gay little wrap made of muslin and gingham, as well as of satin and velvet. It came in many colors but white was the choice for formal wear. The dolman of the 1870s was fringed, braided, and forbidding. Plush coats were fashionable at the close of the century, and silk jackets and long silk coats came in with the Gibson girl.

The redingote, an English riding coat dating from the late eighteenth century, presaged the smartly tailored coats of today—double-breasted, gold-buttoned, with swinging lines. Capes were introduced early in the nineteenth century, but the handsome Indian shawl, appearing at about the same time, continued as a favorite for another century. Along with Paisley shawls from Scotland, embroidered shawls from China, and Chantilly stoles from France, it showed up at the opera and the races, as well as on the home porch. But fringed velvet or flowered satin and moire cloaks were the diehards for formal occasions.

The trenchcoat for women came on the scene by chance when Wells Peck, one of the six Pecks who run a chain of sixty-five stores across America, found while on a buying trip to Europe that small boys were wearing the wartime trenchcoats. He brought one home for a young son. When his sister-in-law, Mrs. Carleton Peck, slipped it on, all the Pecks liked the way it looked on her. Another classic fashion was born when they introduced trenchcoats for women in tan gabardine.

While sealskin may have been the indispensable fur at the beginning of the twentieth century, and broadtail, ermine, beaver, fox, and muskrat the winners in the 1920s, furs bear strange labels today and are tinted in many colors as they move away from the fixed orbit of sable, mink, and ermine. Chinchilla jackets are worn with chinchilla boots. Zebra dresses are fashioned from Italian lamb and Russian broadtail. Australian kangaroo and Wyoming bison, Algerian sand rat and Mongolian pony team up in bizarre combinations. The costliest furs come in pale mutations, and mink is used impartially on wedding gowns, culottes, and pajamas. And as if to mock the traditional coat the beatnik generation digs up a mixed bag of black-leather hoodlum jackets, jean jackets from the Army-Navy stores, orange-leather coats adorned with geometric inlays, plaid evening coats, and even a frowsty Dalmatian-spotted coat with ostrich ruchings.

But American fashion took an odd twist in the mid-nineteenth century with the introduction of the Bloomer costume at the same time that one brainy woman, neatly packed into a trimly tailored suit, was nominated for the Presidency. Victoria Woodhull, the sister of Tennessee Claflin, whose macabre influence over Cornelius Vanderbilt through spiritualistic séances was well known, battled Ulysses S. Grant for the nomination and went down to defeat with Horace Greeley.

Victoria, a swan among the ducklings, was a coquette impeccably arrayed in becoming clothes and she scorned trousers but watched the fate of the controversial bloomers with interest.

They came into view quite suddenly when Amelia Bloomer, a temperance lecturer, wore them with considerable grace. Although her name will be forever associated with the divided skirt she was not responsible for its introduction. Elizabeth Smith Miller, daughter of a well-known abolitionist, had designed the costume for land workers at Oneida Colony, a communal experiment that drew a radical element. She had noticed that Fanny Kemble had copied the Empire pantalettes worn by little girls for one of her own mountain-climbing expeditions.

Several of the feminists agreed to wear them at a woman's rights convention held in Seneca Falls. Amelia, something of a beauty, wore them so becomingly that everyone took notice. She strolled about in Turkish trousers nipped in at the ankles and billowing under a knee-length skirt, all topped with a blouse and belted jacket. The absurd outfit immediately became identified with the beautiful Mrs. Bloomer when Horace Greeley, ever ready to beat the drum for an eccentric new cause, gave the costume his own personal brand of publicity. P. T. Barnum promptly staged a Bloomer parade at his museum, and Amelia found herself a celebrity. She made full use of the publicity, and it not only helped her career as a lecturer, but gave her name to posterity and initiated a fashion that persists in many forms today.

Susan B. Anthony and Mrs. Elizabeth Cady Stanton soon decided that they could not weather the ridicule, since no fashion in American history has been so thoroughly held up to scorn. When lean-limbed Susan showed up in black satin trousers, topped with her usual bonnet and shawl, her good friend Mrs. Stanton wrote of her: "I have seen scarecrows that did credit to farmer boys' ingenuity, but never one better calculated to scare all birds, beasts and human beings." The campaign for dress reform went down to defeat and did not cause a ripple in the world of true fashion. It was merely another of the eccentric causes that stirred up Americans in the mid-nineteenth century. But it was not the young, as today, who tried these experiments. Mature women were groping for political rights.

Although the Bloomer fad died before the Civil War, the idea was by no means lost. Divided skirts flourished in the bicycling era and became fashion incarnate in 1966. For several years slacks and shorts had been gaining ground on every front—at home and outdoors, in the supermarket, the patio, the kitchen, and on the street. But the 1960s brought variations—new, dynamic, startling or appalling, according to the point of view. Women went overboard for skintight stretch pants; Levi's; leopard-skin pants; bell-bottom pants; harem pants; hipster, chiffon, denim, and sailcloth pants; piazza pajamas; and palazzo pajamas.

The trend reached its climax in an outcropping of sleeky tailored pants-suits in 1966, with its gentler variant, "le smoking," introduced by St. Laurent in velvet and lace for evening wear.

Bizarre effects loomed in view on every front, from the bedroom to the ballroom. Reluctantly the older generation took note, and in time the most conservative designers bowed to the trend, thinking to help it with their telling cut. The films played up svelte lines, and dieting helped but did not altogether cure the rearguard view of the trousered girl. Men for the most part regarded Mrs. Bloomer's offshoots with suspicion. However, pants had become big business in the fashion world, and were dear to the feminine heart.

The Bloomer flurry was followed by the graceful crinoline age that had the Civil War for its grim background, though the aura of moonlight and magnolias has surrounded it ever since. The hoop and its offspring the crinoline have held a romantic place in fashion history, although women have never had more trouble with any type of skirt than with the treacherous, tilting balloon that flew into the air, caused traffic jams, impeded their progress, and exposed their ankles and calves in a strictly covered-up age.

The crinoline is usually identified with the Civil War period, but the bell or dome-shaped hoop came long before. The farthingale of Queen Elizabeth's time involved an intricate series of hoops. The French picked up the idea from the English and inflated it to fantastic proportions, so that women sailed about like galleons in the 1740s. The belles of New York, Boston, and Philadelphia, alert to European fashions but not yet deeply committed, made cautious use of the elliptical hoop, wide at the sides, flat in front, and compressed toward the back. They were glad to abandon this court costume for the rounded crinoline, having heard enough of the monstrous hoops that inspired the ridicule of Hogarth and other satirists. The wired structures and stiffly starched petticoats were so uncomfortable that eventually Princess Metternich, a fashion leader of the era, pushed the short puffed skirt of the ballerina.

In 1853 the crinoline proper took hold and by the time the Civil War broke out it was approved and worn by the most fashionable women. In general it was a provocative if cumbersome fashion, the extreme opposite of the spare look of 1966. It concealed a multitude of bulges and figure flaws, and made a deep secret of coming maternity. Men complained that it was difficult to embrace their girls when courting, or to fit them into a sleigh. Again the cartoonists went to work, showing hoops tilting at ridiculous angles. But in spite of the drumfire of criticism they had won the day by 1862, and rich taffeta and glacé silks kept them in full sail. Although the most drastic of all fashion innovations, the touch of scandal about them subsided by degrees

175

Eve's Daughters

Julia Gardiner in 1840. Known as "the Rose of Long Island," Julia, who married John Tyler and became one of the most fashionable of First Ladies, was always attired in the height of fashion. She is shown here parading in the streets of New York as a model and advance agent for a local drygoods store. Her velvet walking costume, edged with fur, flounced at the hem, with deep revers and swelling bustle, was the last word from Paris. So was her bonnet, with its diaphanous veil and long plume unfurling below her shoulders. Julia wore embroidered gloves, carried a lace-trimmed handkerchief the size of a scarf, and whirled a tiny parasol in the face of her mustached and fur-coated escort.

"The Breadth of Fashion. Fifth Avenue, 1865." The crinoline lent itself readily to the acid touch of the cartoonist, and this lady hurrying home in her cone-shaped costume, her pagoda sleeves edged with ruffles, her bonnet almost falling off the back of her head, is here lampooned.

Summer fashions of 1871 in Central Park. By the 1870s crinolines were on the wane, and these fashionable ladies, gathered around the lake, were beginning to bulge in different areas, notably to the rear. Hoops had dwindled; stomachs had flattened; but the polonaise and the bustle, with a great deal of fringe, ruching, flutings, and drapings, were creating a complicated fashion picture. Swags were draped at odd angles and pleated flounces abounded. The hats and bonnets, however, were small, feminine, and universally becoming, with lace, ribbon, and flowers discreetly arranged on their tilted surfaces. Not until the 1880s did the more formidable high crown appear. From Butterick & Company's Quarterly Report of New York Fashions *for Summer, 1871.*

TO M⁼ LYDIA BLOOMER.

THE NEW COSTUME POLKA

COMPOSED

FOR THE PIANO
by
MATHIAS KELLER.

Philadelphia, Lee & Walker, 162 Chesnut St.

SUCCESSORS TO GEO. WILLIG.

NEW YORK,
Wᵐ HALL & SON.

MEMPHIS TEN.
P. FLAVIO.

NEW ORLEANS.
Wᵐ T MAYO.

Amelia Bloomer was a beauty who wore her Turkish trousers so becomingly that they were soon named after her and the word "bloomer" was added to the English language. Actually the bloomers of the 1850s that evolved into the pants of 1967 were designed by a plain Jane named Elizabeth Smith Miller. But Amelia, a fellow feminist, was persuaded to wear them at a women's rights convention held in Seneca Falls, New York. She sauntered about with such grace and modesty that she became their natural promoter. Horace Greeley spread her name and fame, and this helped her as a temperance lecturer, but no one was more surprised than Amelia to find her name firmly embedded in the English language.

as their wearers learned how to dance with grace, to sit down with propriety, to board a train in safety, and to climb into a carriage without mishap. But they never learned how to avoid a tangled jam when shopping and traveling, or how to pack their gowns for Saratoga in fewer than fifteen trunks.

When Madame Demorest introduced her small Quaker hoop skirt, it achieved immense popularity with the average woman, who was content to exist outside the aura of high fashion. It was neat and graceful, took up little room and seemed to assist, rather than impede, locomotion. This fashion pioneer added the Imperial dress elevator, with weighted strings to raise or lower the skirt at will, and keep it clear of the sidewalk, thus offsetting the tilting that plagued the hoop brigade. Toward the end of the Civil War the crinoline began to shrink in size again, until it disappeared altogether. It had done one good thing in divesting women of the heavy load of petticoats they had previously carried. In its dying hours the crinoline had been flattened in front, with the skirt fullness pushed backward, and this led to a revival of the bustle, creating a monumental distortion of the feminine form.

But while the indelicacy of the crinoline was still under fire in Europe, American women were more censorious of the low-necked and high-waisted Pompadour bodices popular in France. Puffed lace chemisettes were added by American dressmakers to give this neckline the decorum required by the more straitlaced children of the Puritans. It was not until the 1960s that a neckline slashed to the waist, and with the bosom revealed from various angles, side and front view, passed muster on the social scene, for by then the topless era had dawned—in theory if not in fact.

Necklines and skirt lengths have been key factors in the fashion spectrum throughout the ages, and often they have been linked with the social outlook of the period. "The length of the train no longer marks the lady," Madame Demorest ruled after studying the Paris scene in 1869. Valenciennes flounces, white ostrich feathers, and diaphanous gauzes were beginning to pall. Sleek heads had smooth bandeaus, waists had diminished, but the bustle gave a pompous look to its wearers. Muffs had shrunk to minute proportions, basques were pointed, panniers were ruched, and cuirass bodices were fastened tightly from waist to neck. But all this armor gave way briefly to the princess, or tubular, effect. The 1880s were strictly the years of form, not eccentricity, although there were variations, from Highland costume, showing the Victorian influence, to Worth's elaborate creations. He had become the rage with American women who could afford him, and the great beauties of the day wore his gowns at Saratoga, at Newport, and in the ballrooms of Washington and New York. Before 1850 women alone had been the dress designers. Worth was the first of the long line of men who rule the fashion world today on both sides of the Atlantic, along with a lesser number of gifted women. But nineteenth-century fashions were also profoundly affected by portrait painters like Watteau and Gainsborough, and later Boldini and Sargent.

Waves of pearl passementerie, draped bodices, and balloon sleeves came next, and by the turn of the century feather boas swirled around pearl-laden necks, cartwheel hats sagged beneath their burden of plumes, flowers, and birds; and bosoms and posteriors were well defined in the Grecian bend. The fin-de-siècle girl was also the froufrou girl, all lace and taffeta, with petticoats coyly displayed as she raised her skirt. Waistlines were pinched; skirts were gored; hip and bust pads were in demand, or stockings were stuffed into fitted bodices to ensure a molded effect. These variations all evoked contemporary comment.

The fuss and feathers of the 1890s, however, were only half the story. A new kind of girl hove into view—the athlete who rode a bicycle and leaped at a tennis net. She was lovingly enshrined by artist Charles Dana Gibson as the Gibson girl, noted for her classic profile and hourglass figure. Her appearance on the scene made sports clothes an important part of the fashion picture, and in this field American styles have played a distinguished role. The tailor-made swept suddenly into view in the United States when Redfern & Company of London opened a branch adjoining Delmonico's, and the fashion-conscious woman sped there for the new streamlined cut. The long Boldini line had taken hold, but the suit, which would flourish in a thousand different guises in the next half century, was an awkward costume in the beginning. However, it was a fashion landmark that soon led to the shirtwaist, an austere touch matched by the glazed sailor hat. The cyclists, the skaters, the tennis and croquet devotees—all sought escape from shackling skirts and overpowering hats. The cyclist adopted the divided skirt. The croquet enthusiast wore a Breton sailor and trim shirtwaist as she whacked the ball with her mallet. The tennis player, with a sailor collar and tight belt, clung to her skirts with one hand as she leaped at the net. The skater alone achieved a seductive and wholly feminine effect with her close-fitting costume, her tiny muff and tilted fur cap. She was the forerunner of the ski-minded girl of today, who wears a fox hood with stretch pants and plastic boots.

But the shirtwaist, above all, had become an established factor for sports, office, or home wear. In 1899 it kept 83,000 men and women busy in the garment center, and New York's twelve shirt shops in 1890 had become 231 by 1900. Eleven years later the fire at the Triangle Shirtwaist Company, which resulted in the deaths of 145 employees, highlighted the conditions under which the shirtmakers worked, and so forced reforms. The shirtwaist went hand in hand with the suit but it was not until the 1920s that women agreed on their greatest suit

Sports costumes of 1896. By the end of the nineteenth century the sports girl had come to stay. She assumed many guises, and she still took up a lot of room, with her leg-of-mutton sleeves, gored skirts, wide shoulders, and high-rise hats. The bolero jacket was considered smart for tennis. The tweed skirt and shirtwaist freed her for golf. She was magnificently tailored and straight as a ramrod when she went driving. The wand was a help with the outing gown, and for mountain climbing the alpenstock, a great big bow at the neck, and skirts that cleared her ankles were dashing. She fished quite happily in high collar, gigot sleeves, long skirts, and ribboned hat. In the gym she was neatly belted and wore knickers that were met by stockings at the knees, thus preserving the status quo. But her bathing suit was her greatest triumph—a long tunic with bloomers, a wide fringed scarf, the traditional sailor collar and anchor, and the inescapable stockings and laced shoes. From Harper's Bazar, *1896.*

Yachting costume of 1894 by Worth. When yachts were at their most magnificent in the 1890s, their owners' wives and daughters dressed up to the image, and it was strictly a spectator effect. In this case a ruffled cape with wired ruchings flared out over a tight bodice and wide skirts that swept the deck. Flyaway winged hats rested on the women's tidy chignons, and they wore gloves for good measure. They bore small resemblance to the bare-footed girl of today in bell-bottomed pants who can reef a sail or run a cruiser, but they could cheer from the sidelines for the cup races. From Harper's Bazar, *1894.*

"Ah There: Coney Island," 1897. This merry view of the
frilled and stockinged bathing girls of the 1890s was a
favorite stereopticon slide, although wives discouraged
its use in the family parlor. The junction of stockings and
bloomers is dimly related to the more subtle and
seductive pantystocking of the 1960s. The girls were
also showing their fashion sense by practicing the
prevailing Grecian bend. Or were they just being naughty?

Sports costumes of the 1870s. An enterprising lot of girls
tore loose from the conventional moorings during this
decade and cavorted around in what were then laughingly
known as "sports clothes." They could even skip rope—
and did—in their absurd long skirts. The slim silhouette
was coming into style after the billowing crinoline and
bustle, but a few frills and flounces remained, even with
the sports-minded. Their pancake hats, planted squarely
on neat coiffures, had forsaken the feminine image and
sported forbidding quills and stiffened ribbon, pointing
skyward. For their country walks the girls relied on
their wands, the long shepherd's crook that had become
high fashion from Newport to San Francisco.

designer—Gabrielle Chanel, the black swan who dominated fashions from 1919 to 1938, then faded from view, only to return with renewed inspiration in 1954. Without peer in her field she gave simple, boxy suits their place in the sun, used English tweeds and jersey for the one-piece dress, and scented generations with her perfume, Chanel No. 5. Her designs, said *Vogue*, showed an "understanding of the times and the unusual necessities of present day life." She proved it for close to a half century as other fashions came and went, leaving her suits recognizable wherever sophisticated women gathered. "Coco Chanel and Madeleine Vionnet can claim to be the creators of modern fashion," said Christian Dior in 1957.

Her style from the beginning was far removed from that of her contemporary, Paul Poiret, who led a generation of women into a thicket of tassels and barbaric jewels. "I freed the bust, but I shackled the legs," he announced as he imprisoned women in wired tunics that resembled lampshades, and crippled them with the hobble and harem skirts. They were smothered in furs and ospreys, and wore chinstraps of pearls. But World War I put an end to this Turkish interlude, gave status to uniforms, and left its echoes in the wild and flashy 1920s, which paved the road to the still more uninhibited 1960s. The last stray suggestion of the Puritan influence wavered if it did not die altogether before the onslaught of Freudian revelation, the demoralizing impact of prohibition, and the recurrent discontent of youth. Fashions reflected the trend. Skirts got shorter until by 1926 the outcry against them was deafening. Flaming youth with its bathtub gin and skimpy garments became as world famous as the Beatles and beatniks today. Figures were flat, before and behind. The waistline sagged to the hip. Beads and paillettes flew in all directions as girls pounded out the Charleston. Vionnet's bias cut, deep-set bows, and black satin gowns encouraged the vampish look. Cloche hats screened the eyes, and boop-boop-a-doop had all the insistence of the Beatle throb.

Elsa Schiaparelli was the fashion bombshell of the 1930s, with her poufs and aigrettes, her shocking-pink effects and heavily padded shoulders. She dyed furs in bright colors and tricked up the sweater for formal wear. Her stockings swept the market, and she pushed the stretch idea, but no one wanted it then. However, she was a pacemaker, and today's boutiques may be traced back to Schiaparelli, who set this fashion thirty years ago.

The New Look by Dior followed, in 1947, swinging and billowing, with rounded shoulders, nipped-in waistlines, and long skirts. The chemise came into view in the 1950s but faded fast in its original form. It sparked a historic change in fashion, however, with the treasured waistline, which had sagged to the hips in the Charleston era, now disappearing altogether in the artful shapelessness of the shift, the sheath, the sack, the nightgown that walks by day and, finally, the baby-doll look, marking a dramatic swing of fashion emphasis from maturity to youth. The shorn 1960s, more sparc, more eccentric, more extreme than anything in fashion history, followed. If the 1890s was the period of fuss and feathers, the 1960s inevitably rates as the era of nudity. The first significant sign was the bared bosom of Christina Paolozzi in *Harper's Bazaar*, a gesture which soon enveloped her in a social chill. This was followed by a rash of fashion pictures carrying out the all-revealing theme. Rudi Gernreich splashed the market with transparent blouses, and St. Laurent, laying claim to originating the nude look, showed a definitive gown in 1966, with the figure clearly outlined in flesh-colored chiffon, and a diamond design camouflaging breast and hips.

It had been coming on gradually—the cut-outs at odd angles, the Mondrian and trapeze effects, the tent, the cage, all with the merest whiffs of lingerie underneath. Halters, suspender straps, and deep arm-holes shouted their message and models strolled into view with neck-lines slashed to their navels, a style quickly adopted by society. A belly button, briefly exploited, carried little conviction as a fashion note, in spite of all the publicity it garnered. In this it shared the fate of the topless bathing suit (more myth than fact), the topless dress, and the topless nightgown. So far only a few shoeshine girls, nightclub waitresses, and one bride can lay claim to the topless dress.

Silver jumpsuits and plastic garments flashing like gold seemed to draw their inspiration from the astronauts' space suits. Racks of metallic dresses appeared overnight along with gold-trimmed vinyl shifts. Their wearers completed the picture with silvery lipstick, silver eye makeup, silver mittens, stockings and boots, strange goddesses of the space age. A six-hundred-dollar backless gold-lace dress found competition in sexy black-chiffon gowns that spread their old-fashioned charm and femininity. Lacy angel dresses were offset by butcher-boy pants, and Granny Gowns by pastel sequins and plastic disks strung on wires. The Granny Girls wore their ankle-length dresses with pride, and in defiance of the space girls in their bright leather helmets and chinstraps. This style was inspired by the muu-muu which, in turn, was fashioned on the old Mother Hubbard that the early missionaries in-flicted on the South Sea Islanders.

But 1967's newest whim was the paper dress—a disposable trifle selling for small change and catching the attention of women in all social circles. When the Duchess of Windsor bought Adolfo's custom-made flowered paper caftan and John Weitz predicted paper shirts and suits for men the stage was set. The top fashion writers gave status to

The social call was an occupation in itself in the 1890s, and cards were dropped by the thousand. The well-dressed caller of 1894 wore a cuirass bodice nipped in at her tiny waist, and her embroidered skirt ballooned at her feet. Her sleeves were enormous; her parasol was ruffled and beribboned; and her bonnet was tightly lashed to her chin. If the day was cold, she donned a basque coat and the merest whisper of a hat, with bows and ties. The day of the hourglass figure had dawned. From Harper's Bazar, 1894.

Mourning costume of 1896. Mourning was a well-observed social rite in the 1890s, but fashionable widows were shedding the enveloping weeds made popular by Queen Victoria. They no longer screened their faces from view but wore smart black toques with upswept trimming, and long veils in the back, which could be swung into use upon occasion. This walking dress of bombazine has wide ruchings of crêpe, crêpe ruffles down to the knuckles, and leg-of-mutton sleeves. From Harper's Bazar, 1896.

Summer costume of 1896. Plumes, lace, and fans went happily together in the Gay Nineties, and the American women who could afford it pounced on this Worth model of 1896. The sleeve had ballooned again and reached its maximum volume. The bustle had had a revival, too, but emphasis was now on the bodice and sleeves, and away from the skirt, which swung in widening arcs to the ground. The lace peplum and boned ruff suggest the Elizabethan mood, but the pancake hat and stand-up ostrich plumes are strictly end-of-the-century touches. From Harper's Bazar, 1896.

the paper trend as soon as well-designed models reached the market, and mothers across the country thanked heaven for a fashion that lightened their labors. Children's designs were quickly worked out, and manufacturers dealing in a cellulose non-woven fabric derivative found themselves millions of yards behind on orders.

Here was a fashion that took fire, and had a good send-off in Hartford, Connecticut, when a hundred and fifty socialites wore paper gowns to a ball held at the Wadsworth Atheneum. But nothing in fashion is new, and as long ago as 1867 Madame Demorest gave a paper-dress masquerade in her fashion emporium on Broadway. Prevailing styles for three hundred years were faithfully reproduced, to the last ruff and plume. Her two hundred guests rustled like falling leaves in October as they danced. The new paper gowns are silent, svelte, and are picking up style as they go along. They match the informal, outdoor life of the current generation, particularly the hours spent by the sea.

The water has never ceased to interest successive generations of Americans, although they had no inkling until the eighteenth century of the delights of swimming, or the opportunities that their own beaches offered them. The rites of the Greek and Roman baths and the medieval custom of men and women bathing naked outdoors were matters of historic interest only when the beaches along the New England coast were finally put to use early in the nineteenth century. It took another hundred years to adapt the swimming suit to the contours of the body. Dowdy-looking, voluminous attire prevailed long after the natural beaches had become popular playgrounds. Now the pendulum has swung from the cumbersome costumes of the nineteenth century to the bikinis and fishnet beguilement of the 1960s.

When the pioneers forded rivers, petticoats did not daunt them as the water roared over wagon wheels, but swimming was strictly for fish. The young may have splashed in lakes and swimming holes, but with no inkling of the pleasure their descendants would find in the water. John Quincy Adams gave the subject a fillip when he found himself trapped in the Potomac River by Anne Royall, a termagant newspaperwoman who sat on his clothes until he had given her the interview she had been seeking for some time. Like later Presidents, Adams liked the water and chose to bathe in the raw to prove his hardihood. He was one of the first to take lessons at a "'swimming bath" that opened in Boston in 1827.

By the middle of the nineteenth century a great many other Americans had learned to swim, and in the 1890s it was a fashionable and universal sport that could boast of special "bathing machines" which rolled down to the water's edge and allowed the modest maiden to slip unnoticed under the waves. Cartoonists took delight in sketching her coy descent and her quick submersion up to her neck, although she was amply attired in blouse, skirt, pantaloons, stockings, shoes, and hat. *Godey's Lady's Book* took note of the bathing machines in 1849, but they had been spotted on Long Island as early as 1794. By the end of the nineteenth century resort hotels kept small fleets of these wobbling cabanas as a major attraction.

There was scandal at Newport and Nahant in the 1830s when some daring matrons bathed with their husbands. But Charles Augustus Murray, a British visitor who left his impressions on record, pictured a convivial scene with men "handing around their pretty partners as if they were dancing water quadrilles." Like the girls, the men were modestly covered from neck to toe. They stayed as remote from one another as in the frug, and it was considered rowdy to squeal, splash, or throw water at one's partner. In 1853 a *New York Herald* reporter, studying the situation at Newport, found the "blooming girl, the matronized yet blushing maiden, the dignified mamma, all playing, dancing, romping, and shouting together, as if they were alive with feeling." He noticed that they were done up in green, blue, orange, and white, although their garments were so enveloping that he could not appraise the shapes within. There was nothing startling about appearing on the ballroom floor with bare shoulders and exposed bosoms in their Empire gowns, but it was unthinkable to sport in the water in broad daylight in anything less than full attire. The bold girl who went for a swim on her wedding morning in 1887 was the Bardot of her day.

The story was much the same at Atlantic City and Cape May, at Southampton and Virginia Beach, with men splashing about in horizontal stripes and looking like sad ducks when they emerged from the water, their waxed mustaches all awry and their pantaloons sagging.

The girls had little taste for lolling about on beaches to sun themselves. They considered the sun death to their porcelain complexions, and the wary tied Nantucket hats of white chip straw to their chins and used mobcaps to save their abundant hair from the waves. It took hours of preparation to get ready for the plunge. Jennie June, the energetic social commentator for the Demorest publications, observed that it was more troublesome to dress for a swim than for a ball. The swaddling process involved corsets to be donned, strings that had to be tied, and pads to be adjusted. The girl of today, oiled and lotioned, can don her tiny bikini with two whisks and head for the surf. The influence of the Bloomer costume was felt at the beach when the girls took to wearing crimson Turkish coveralls. Seen in groups, an observer noted that they looked like a parade of flamingos. When they escaped from this transfiguration they became strongly naval, wearing square-yoked blouses in blue twilled flannel or serge, trimmed with black alpaca braid and stars. Others buckled themselves nattily into gray moreen suits, anchored at the ankles with plaid bands. A smother-

Striped gowns, trailing skirts, and monster hats were not unknown to the woodland in the first decade of the twentieth century. The mature woman was not rushing out to buy sports clothes, like her daughter. The gigot sleeve was in process of deflation, but the waistline was smaller than ever. Skirts fanned out from a series of gores, and a fur stole and muff completed the formal costume. From a Lord & Taylor advertisement, 1907.

By 1904 the Gibson girl had become an accepted type, and here she is in playful mood—long and lean, in tailored costume, with high collar, pompadour and Trilby violets. She had become so much the girl of the day that other artists had picked up the Charles Dana Gibson image. Sketch by Clarence F. Underwood, from Harper's Bazar, 1904.

ing black wool poplin with soutache braid, and a cape of plaid home-spun, was the height of fashion at the time of the Civil War. Later the Garibaldi fad reached the beach. All were remote from today's jeweled bikini for the moonlight swim, the beach pajamas of 1967, or the transparent vinyl-and-plastic nothing worn by day. But in the 1870s yards of flannel meant little to a girl accustomed to crinolines.

Luxuriant hair gave monstrous aspects to the hats and caps used for bathing—tasseled, knitted, or of straw. The girls wore sand shoes with crossed straps, high boots, lacing shoes, or white sailcloth models with scarlet rosettes. Black lisle stockings were as inseparable from bathing attire as sugar from cream. It was 1907 before women appeared on the beaches without stockings, and this piece of boldness was considered questionable even then. But the bars had begun to lower slightly around 1886 when the girls at Narragansett showed up in sleeveless black silk bathing suits, their skirts shortened and an inch or two of neck on view. They were lavishly padded, for the curvaceous effect was taking hold, and the skinny were as unseemly on the beach as the obese are today. They now lay on the sand and courted the sun in a discreet way, with shady hats and swirling parasols. Sunglasses were still unknown and sun umbrellas did not dot the beaches. The awninged cabana had yet to appear, but the girls sought shelter by the rocks. They were daring, too; some puffed cigarettes.

Although beach bathing was identified with the fashionable set at first, it soon became a truly national pastime, and early in the twentieth century the Sears, Roebuck catalogue advertised for a mere $2.98 bathing suits with braided sailor collars and bloomers attached. By this time the Steel Pier had opened at Atlantic City, ushering in a new era in bathing, with gaslight, banjos, bands and, finally, the bathing beauty contests of today. Coney Island was becoming so much the haunt of assorted classes that it lost the fashionable aura it had had in the 1880s when the Coney Island Jockey Club was established, and Vanderbilts and Belmonts raced their horses at Brighton Beach, Sheepshead Bay, and Morris Park.

By 1903 Henry M. Flagler had converted Palm Beach into a fashionable playground, and California was awakening to the promise of its beaches. Yachts lay at anchor in Florida and along the New England coast, and the seacoast rivaled the mountains with holiday-makers. But women were still bathing in twill, foulard, or flannel, with sunbonnets and mobcaps on their heads, when Adeline Trapp Muhlenberg swam the East River in 1909 wearing a one-piece bathing suit. Annette Kellerman, an Australian-born girl, caught the public fancy even more convincingly when she was arrested for swimming in a single garment sewn to long black stockings. The symmetry and grace of her figure so simply clad was indisputable, and by 1913 Jantzen was manufacturing one-piece suits for daring swimmers. "The Suit that Changed Bathing to Swimming" became a well-known slogan as women grew more athletic and took pride in their swimming grace and skill. Annette's one-piece suit caused more talk in its day than Rudi Gernreich's topless bathing suit that appeared in 1964 and died overnight.

The 1920s experienced the first decline in standards of modesty that led gradually to the nudity of the 1960s. Fashion had swung from encumbrance to simplicity. Sunbathing became a popular diversion, and Hollywood helped to scatter old traditions with its bathing beauty contests. Women's clubs protested but by 1925 the bathing beauties paraded with bare arms, knee-length bathing suits, and rolled stockings. They were obviously more fully clad than their landlubber sisters in sheathlike dresses and skirts above the knees. Yet the Mack Sennett girls, with every strategic area covered, were once considered risqué.

By the 1940s women's backs were bared at the beach, the bust took shape again as in the 1890s, stockings disappeared, and rubber helmets clung tight to bobbed heads. But Americans remained cold to the bikini until 1965, when it swept the beaches. The mesh and fishnet suits, however, were thought to have greater allure, as designer Cole of California turned out more than 200,000 in the summer of 1965. No girl needed to bulge any longer in the wrong places, or to be more shapeless coming out of the water than when going in. Controlled Lastex, instead of whalebone stiffening, enabled her to twist and turn without discomfort and, finally, she was supplied with body and face makeup that did not wash off in the sea.

Beyond doubt the beaches have become the brightest of playgrounds. California designers have set their stamp on fashions for yachting, cruising, surfing, diving, and other deep-sea sports. Their beach wraps, hats and bags, fantastic beach dresses and sunglasses, as well as their assorted swimming suits, are known around the world. Yet conservative women continue to appear in skirted affairs with decorous necklines, and many men stick to simple dark trunks, with or without tops.

Although the young are dominant in beach fashions, as in all else, the aged and the cloistered have their innings in this most healthful of sports. Eleven grandmothers in Worcester, Massachusetts, organized a lifeguard swimming club with the slogan "Life Begins at Fifty," and in the summer of 1965 the Sisters of Charity of St. Elizabeth wore bright bandanas, sandals, dark sunglasses and colored beachrobes in walking from their convent to a private beach on Long Island. One chose a fuchsia muu-muu; all swam in simple black bathing suits.

Nowadays a designer creates a style and the fashion writers exploit it but, historically, new styles generally have been linked with a ruler, a celebrated beauty, an actress, a courtesan, or a painting.

The long tailored suit was gaining ground by 1909. This one was trimmed with soutache braid and strategically placed buttons. No one thought it odd that ostrich plumes should soar above this severe ensemble, or that a Gainsborough hat was offbeat with a tailleur. The buoyant curves of the 1890s were flattening out, but even a walking suit had a lengthy train to trail in the mud. From Theater Magazine, 1909.

Paul Poiret, like Chanel, was one of the great innovators, introducing the oriental influence in costume that rages today. He used bold, curving lines and substituted lamé for the heavy eighteenth-century brocades. Women dressed by Poiret moved with mobility, after the rigid postures induced by tight corseting, until he tied them up again with the hobble skirt. He introduced the fringed, irregular hemline and made cagelike gowns, hanging heavy ropes of pearls on their wearers. From Harper's Bazaar, 1920.

Marie Antoinette was responsible for seventeen changes in women's hats within two years' time. The crinoline came into being to conceal the fact that the Empress Eugénie was pregnant, and Charles Frederick Worth, the earliest of the noted French designers, pushed it although he disliked this style. Gainsborough's famous portrait of the Duchess of Devonshire gave plumed hats their accolade. Queen Victoria inspired the tartan fad that swept the United States, and she emphasized the taste for profound and lasting mourning—the enveloping widow's weeds and layers of crêpe that were characteristic of the nineteenth century. Queen Alexandra's dog collar and Queen Mary's firmly planted toques had their effect on American dowagers of the old school.

Today's paillettes and spangles, popular also in the 1920s, were first introduced by Worth when he copied a picture of the Empress Josephine that hung in the Louvre. He devised the kimono sleeve when the brother of Emperor Komyo of Japan visited the Paris Exposition in 1867, and this led to the dolman and other variations of a fashion that became popular in the United States. American women first started going outdoors without wraps after Madame Worth appeared in public with a wisp of lace on her hair, and no shawl or mantel to cover her gown—an act as startling as if she had gone to the races in a bathing suit. Thus fashions are born, by chance or inspiration, like the geometric Mondrian prints that St. Laurent introduced—a fashion that flared and quickly died on the American scene.

The White House has not been noted until recent years for setting styles. Abigail Adams, listened to with respect on all manner of subjects, did not influence fashion, but Martha Washington and Dolley Madison did. Even as a child Dolley Payne had worn white linen masks to protect her complexion, as well as a sunbonnet sewn to her hair by her mother each morning as she left for school. During her White House years she popularized the turban, just as Julia Gardiner, the "Rose of Long Island," who paraded in the streets of New York with a sign swinging from her arm advertising a drygoods shop, established her own style of feathered headdress when she married President John Tyler.

Harriet Lane, President Buchanan's niece, gave the bertha prestige in Washington society before the Civil War. Alice Roosevelt was as strongly individualistic about fashion as about everything else and she lent her own particular style to anything that she chose to wear, from a cartwheel hat to a batik smock. She had many copyists and the shade Alice blue was commonly seen in Washington ballrooms. Mrs. Calvin Coolidge was addicted to the becoming picture hats that her husband made her wear in the days of the cloche, and Mrs. Eisenhower's bangs were as distinctive as her softly feminine clothes and careful

Trains were seen again in the long, swinging lines of the filmy hostess gowns of the late 1920s. The influence of Madeleine Vionnet was making itself felt at this time. The bias cut that gave gowns a softly molded look, and her deep V-necks, and large bows, made her models popular. *From* Harper's Bazaar, *1928.*

This Jay Thorpe model shows off the close shingle, short skirt, and graceful swing-back typical of the mid-twenties. From Vogue, *1925.*

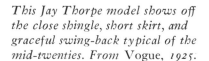

The narrow, svelte gowns of Lelong clung to the figure and gave grace in the 1930s to those who could wear them. From Harper's Bazaar, *1934.*

grooming. American women have been prone to pick up some characteristic touch from the much-photographed First Ladies, with or without the feeling of high style, but Mrs. John F. Kennedy was the first President's wife to give fashion genuine impetus, both in and out of the White House.

To meet the great and sudden demand stores rushed out copies of her pillbox hat, her Somali leopard coat, her mink sweater, her fox fur hood for skiing, and her gown draped over one shoulder. She dramatized in her own person the sleeveless, hatless effect; the simple sheath cunningly fashioned; the casual suit, the guardsman coat, the windblown hair, as well as the soft and breathless voice. Designers and the fashion press alike recognized her as an authentic fashion leader, perhaps the first in White House history, because she influenced public buying in a convincing way. Mrs. Johnson and her daughters have created their own fashion images, and the traditional feeling that a First Lady should be well, if not conspicuously, dressed has given ground to a more personal pattern. Jonquil yellow, because of its Texas association, was Mrs. Johnson's choice for her inaugural-ball gown and again for the dress she wore at Luci's wedding.

But long before the time of Mrs. Johnson, Rachel, the actress, made yellow the rage when an impoverished woman brought her some yellow material and begged her to use it on the stage. Stage stars, dancers, and current celebrities, more than ruling families, have been responsible most often for fashion innovations. The sweater girl of today has Lily Langtry to thank for the jersey she introduced when she was the favorite of the Prince of Wales, later King Edward VII. This fashion swept England and reached its apogee in the United States, where it became the indispensable garment, from conservative cardigans to the glittering and body-shaping sweaters of the film stars. It served as a uniform on the college campus, at country clubs, in offices, and on the suburban lawn long before it became a sex symbol.

The Trilby legend, linked to the stage and fashionable life by George du Maurier's novel and sketches of 1894, soon spread the violet cult across the United States. Lillian Russell started a craze for Irish lace in 1905 when she appeared in the costliest gown of the theatrical season—a two-thousand-dollar model made completely of lace. Her matching lace hat sported a blue aigrette, and she carried a huge muff made of blue ostrich tips. Fortuny created the first of his pleated gowns for Isadora Duncan, to conceal the fact that she was pregnant as she started a tour of the United States. But Isadora's influence extended beyond pleats, and her Greek sandals and tunic turned up in Bohemian circles as inevitably as waves of iridescent chiffons were let loose in this area by another dancer, Loie Fuller, whose flame effects with shifting colors inspired designers. Mary Pickford's curls and dimples, like the Irene Castle bob, had a transient influence on fashion. Jean Harlow's seductive gowns and ways, repeated even more convincingly by Marilyn Monroe, became as legendary as Gloria Swanson's tiger skins or Greta Garbo's pirate hats and haunted eyes. The denim craze broke loose when Valentina, asked by Marlene Dietrich to design some clothes for her daughter, advised her to wear denim slacks. "Nothing has the simplicity and majesty of denim," said Valentina, adding a man's shirt, chopped off, with collar open and sleeves rolled up. Blue jeans, worn with stiletto heels, became a passing fad in 1952.

But these were the evanescent touches, not the solid fashions born of an era. They were the innovations—if anything is new in fashion. Every style repeats itself. The John Held, Jr., girl of the 1920s, with her clanking beads, short skirts, and head-hugging helmets, was the prototype of the girl of today; the low décolletage of 1966 was matched in the Empire period.

Down the years bridal attire has changed less in its fundamentals than any other type of costuming. The traditional white satin has had a long reign. The inherited lace veil, the bridal bouquet—frilled nosegay, sheaves of lilies, or cascade of orange blossom—the prayer book, rosary, fan, or muff have been more or less constant features. But now the picture is being transformed. The focus is on the bride rather than on her gown, veil, or flowers.

The brides of long ago were voluminous figures, wearing heavy satin trains with silks so stiff that they seemed to stand by themselves— a long way from the simple shifts of the 1960s, the pillbox coronet, the modest cascade of lilies of the valley, the airy mist of Stephanotis, the tilted profile. Infrequently in the past, color has impinged on white satin and an occasional Victorian bride has moved down the aisle in lilac or gray, colors favored by colonial girls. Martha Washington was married in yellow brocade, with a slit skirt over a silvery petticoat. Her high-heeled slippers were of lilac silk, and pearls were twisted on her powdered hair. Brides proceeded from the eighteenth-century panniers, and the simplicity of Greek and Directoire gowns, to the short puffed sleeves and low décolletage of the early nineteenth century. They dressed their hair flat over their ears, and their bridal veils reached to the hem of their skirts.

When Julia Dent of St. Louis married Ulysses S. Grant by candlelight in 1848 she wore a white gown of watered silk with cascades of lace, caught with cape jessamine. The ceremony was held in her home, but by the time the Civil War began the church had become the approved setting for the fashionable wedding. Brides wore embroidered satin, and bows and garlands adorned their ever widening crinolines, but their bridesmaids walked demurely in tarletan, with the broad ribbons of their Quaker bonnets bowed under their chins. Ushers

The 1930s was a decade when femininity was emphasized, with frilly tulle evening gowns, feathers, and bows. After the flapper era and the depression, skirts reached to the mid-calf; décolletage was low; jackets and capes were swingy, and detachable sleeves in the early Dutch fashion had a brief revival. Paillettes glittered on many of the evening gowns. Close-fitting turbans were worn over softly curled hair. The stark shingle of the 1920s had had its day until it was revived again in the 1960s. From Vogue, 1935.

The legendary flapper of the 1920s, with her cloche hat, big fox collar, knee-length skirts, and curving posture, was immortalized by Hemingway and Fitzgerald, and caricatured by John Held, Jr. She opened the door to the Mod fashions of the 1960s. She was Flaming Youth in a more shockable era, and although her skirts just covered her knees, she seemed incredibly daring to her elders. Fashions for the young were never the same again, after the flapper established herself as a separate image, a trend that today is overwhelming, as the mature dance to the tune set by their juniors. From Vogue, 1928.

By the 1940s "the little black dress" had become the hallmark of the American woman, at home and abroad. Young, middle-aged, and old wore it with flair for all manner of occasions, and its popularity flagged only briefly and was strongly revived in 1967. Nettie R. Rosenstein, a favorite American designer, gave the slim black dress all manner of variations, such as a tracery of finespun lace to soften its severity, but the distinction of the little black dress always lay in its cut. From Vogue, 1944.

soon to be on the battlefields wore frockcoats and light pantaloons, with lavender gloves and large boutonnières anchored to rosettes.

The graceful crinoline girls were followed in the 1870s by brides in heavy faille, with bustles, pointed basques, fringes, and ruchings. Their rosepoint veils fell in heavy folds to their ankles from orange-blossom wreaths. Bridesmaids wore fringed or beaded tippets and formidable Victorian bonnets. The brides of the 1880s were stately in Whittingham white satin gowns with pearl trimming. Their waists were pencil-thin, their hair was dressed in the waterfall, and most of them carried fans. In summer they were wrapped in clouds of illusion, and the favorite bridal bouquet was white roses mingled with geranium leaves in gold holders set with pearls. They wore white satin boots and six-button white kid gloves, and their orange-blossom wreaths were finished with three large bows. Groom and groomsmen sported blue coats with brass buttons, over fancy waistcoats, with ruffled shirts and white satin stocks.

But weddings reached their sartorial peak in the 1890s when crowds gathered outside fashionable churches to observe what they could of the nuptials of such social celebrities as Consuelo Vanderbilt and the Duke of Marlborough. Trousseaus and jewels ran into fortunes, and the Sunday supplements gloried in minutiae on the flowers, costumes, and noted guests. But brides in general at the turn of the century were imposing, with their high pompadours, hourglass figures, and the forward-slanted posture of the Grecian bend. Their curves were accented by bridal costumes with tucked bodices, pinched waistlines, and sweeping gored skirts. Their veils were enveloping, but their nosegays were apt to be tiny, round, and frilled. Their bridesmaids wore stiff dark silks and picture hats with ostrich tips, tilted far back on their heads. The next generation of bridesmaids shunned dark colors and wore lace, chiffon, or organdy, with horsehair or leghorn hats—a bridesmaid fashion that lasted for several decades.

World War I affected traditional bridal costuming and brought the informal note into the marriage ceremony. As in all wars there were hasty marriages, the guests quickly assembled, the wedding gowns often improvised. New brides, like divorceés, wore afternoon gowns and were married in chambers, hotels, or registry offices. The more formal brides of this era were hampered by hobble skirts as they made their way to the altar. Their sheaves of lilies and huge bouquets of roses, crysanthemums, and ferns half covered their gowns of white satin or moiré, and their veils were traditionally festooned with orange blossom. Then came the flapper of 1925 with skirts barely covering her knees, a fashion she did not often take to the altar, however—unlike the bride of 1966.

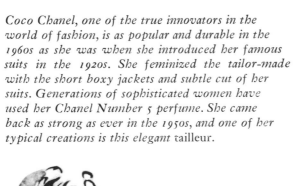

Coco Chanel, one of the true innovators in the world of fashion, is as popular and durable in the 1960s as she was when she introduced her famous suits in the 1920s. She feminized the tailor-made with the short boxy jackets and subtle cut of her suits. Generations of sophisticated women have used her Chanel Number 5 perfume. She came back as strong as ever in the 1950s, and one of her typical creations is this elegant tailleur.

White House brides have had their own whims from time to time. Alice Roosevelt, a dramatic bride simply attired, decided to do without bridesmaids. Luci Baines Johnson settled for ten and a full cathedral service when she married Patrick Nugent. In 1874 her predecessor, Nellie Grant, had the showiest wedding, as well as the most famous father, in White House history until Luci outmatched her. Her bridegroom, Algernon Charles Frederic Sartoris, nephew of Fanny Kemble, startled Washington by carrying a bouquet of orange blossoms and tuberoses, with a small flag inscribed with the word "Love."

Some of the most fashionable brides of the 1960s have cut away from tradition entirely, and have chosen to be married in a state of sophisticated simplicity. "Our brides are less interested in tradition and more interested in fashion nowadays," explained the bridal buyer of a leading Fifth Avenue store. "The big-skirted dresses with yards and yards of fabric and lace over layer upon layer of petticoats is as old-fashioned in the wedding gown as it is in any other kind of dress." Old family veils have not lost ground, even when affixed to Oriental crowns, fezlike and embroidered, or flowing down past skirts cut well above the knee, but they now contend with such oddities as a Swiss lace baby bonnet, a visor crowned with gardenias, a white fox parka hood, a white bunny-fur baby helmet tied under the chin, or a fountain of plastic strips cascading from the head. The swing is away from veils, wreaths, and crowns that detract from the gown and conceal the wearer's natural grace.

The bridal gowns of recent years have shown some fantastic variations—a costume of white lace culottes, a silver lamé gown with slit skirt and silver veil, a short dress glittering with plastic spangles and topped with a visored helmet, a white broadtail wedding gown with a ten-foot train, a white lace cage worn with white tights and lace gaiters ruffled at the knees, a tent-shaped gown with mini skirt, and an all-enveloping garment made of white turkey feathers. Palazzo pajamas were worn at a candlelight wedding ceremony in the Plaza Hotel, but St. Laurent's transparent bridal gown of organdy over a body stocking did not get beyond the stage of a fashion showing, although it made its viewers sit up and take notice. So did an all-vinyl transparent costume, topped by a vinyl space helmet.

The camp element has invaded this most conventional of social institutions. Elopements, early marriages, war marriages, mixed marriages, and divorces have confused the established picture. But still across the country brides in great numbers cling to conventional white satin and ancestral veils, to their mothers' gowns made over, to decorum in all respects, with only a slight nod to fashion in the cut of their gowns and the flowers they carry. The wedding day remains the most ceremonious event in the life of the young.

In 1947 Christian Dior, fresh from the army, revolutionized the fashion world with the New Look. He thought that wartime uniforms had turned women into Amazons, so he designed clothes with rounded shoulders, full bustline, and willowy waists above long spreading skirts. He emphasized the width of the hips and revived the old tradition of cambric and taffeta linings. The New Look flashed around the world like lightning and Dior emerged as an important new designer. He was quick to admit, however, that "from quite different points of view Chanel and Vionnet can claim to be the creators of modern fashion."

St. Laurent's oyster-and-black wool three-piece vest suit is worn with polka-dot necktie and beige felt fedora, typical of the slouch hats of 1967. The skirt is mildly mini above textured stockings. The cufflinks are a businesslike addition.

The girl of 1967 strides boldly into the water in anything from a mini bikini to a suit composed of triangles. This geometrical design is done in kaleidoscopic colors and it follows the peekaboo trend in contemporary fashion.

Mollie Parnis, eminent American designer, has been a favorite of First Ladies through several administrations. Never extreme, Miss Parnis excels in the classic look here embodied in a white silk crêpe evening dress with a diagonal neckline that bares one shoulder and drapes the other in a wide sleeve that falls gracefully to the floor. The costume jewelry is typical of the 1960s when massive effects were in vogue.

"Le Smoking," a variation of the popular pants suit, was fashion's latest twist in the spring of 1967, and it took many forms, from velvet suits with lace ruffles to this tailored model by St. Laurent. Modeled after a man's dinner suit, the wide-legged, straight trousers have satin stripes down the side.

Bridal gown of the 1880s. The figure is firmly outlined in this white satin gown lavishly encrusted with pearl trimming. The bodice is tightly buttoned down in the basque effect. Overskirt and train are heavily seeded with pearls and the elbow-length sleeves drip with them. The train has a wide border of fluted silk and tiny satin bows trim the bodice. The bride's coiffure is not unlike the hair fashions of the 1960s.

Bridal gown of 1775. White satin was not always the bride's attire and this early bride wore taupe silk woven with a large-scale floral motif. Material counted more than cut at this time, and a girl was apt to settle for something embroidered with polychromatic silks in balanced floral designs. The pannier was beginning to make itself felt, although American women avoided the extremes common in France.

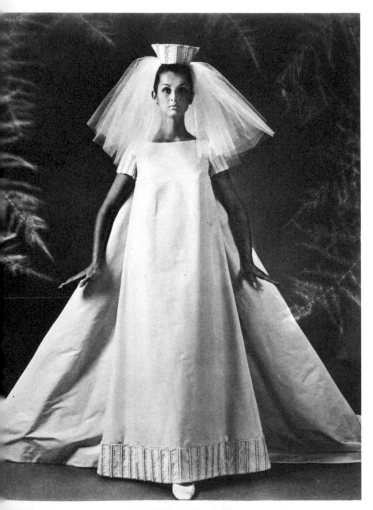

A bride of the 1960s. This dramatic gown is called the Egyptian silhouette by its designer, Priscilla of Boston. The shape is simple, high-fashion A-line, the material silk cloud peau de soie. The sleeves and hemline are heavily embroidered in pearls, as is the high open crown. The train creates a pyramid behind the bride.

It was late in the nineteenth century before children escaped completely from the thralldom of looking like their parents. From the earliest days they had worn the same clothes in miniature. The boys found freedom first and made the most of it, spurning the Little Lord Fauntleroy push staged by ambitious mothers, in favor of the Huckleberry Finn tradition of tattered caps, feet bare and fishing rod in hand. Helped out by Mark Twain, a strongly native tradition centered on the American boy. It was somewhat out of focus, and removed from reality, but except at prep schools and fashionable resorts, English shorts, blazers, and Eton caps were never the favorite garb of the American boy. He chose to stand out in the community as a roughhewn individualist until college, or life itself, smoothed out the raw edges and taught him to conform.

The emancipation of the little girl took longer, but she gradually escaped from poke bonnets with ostrich tips, too-tight shoes, and burdensome petticoats. She was geared to chasing butterflies rather than balls, and only by slow stages in the twentieth century did she proceed to simple dresses and plain leghorns with streamers, to sailor suits, jerseys and, finally, blue jeans and shorts. No longer did she look like her mama; not even mother and daughter dresses could sustain this fiction. She ran free and untrammeled as the wind, but could show a doll-like façade with Mary Jane shoes, white gloves, flowered dresses, or party velvets when the occasion demanded it.

The baby, an infant encased in lace and satin, resting on frilled pillows in a Brewster pram or being pushed along in a rattan-and-wicker carriage, was the real doll at the turn of the century. His layette would support a small army of the babies who now loll around in wisps and scraps of clothing. This Fifth Avenue child and the infant of the tenements had little in common beyond the fact that both were smothered in wrappings.

Teen-agers scarcely existed as personalities in the early days, except as small reproductions of their mothers. Today they crack the whip on fashion, a revolution closely tied to the outlook and social goals of the day. Historically, clothes have reflected the contemporary mood—from the austerity of the Pilgrims to the extravagance of the 1890s, and now to the unrest, rebellion, and untidiness of the 1960s. But freak fashions aside—and usually they are ephemeral—the American woman has gradually gained a commanding place as the exponent of high style. She has created a special look that knows no social barriers and is always recognizable as her own. No longer is she merely the showcase for Paris fashions, since American designers now strengthen her image with the sure touch of their own creative gifts.

The international note is ever present because of the speed with which fashion moves. The lines of communication are now so swift that Paris, London, New York, Chicago, Hollywood, and all points between are alerted almost before the fashion showings end. Copies are rushed out within a matter of weeks, so that business girls quickly pick up $29.95 versions of St. Laurent's thousand-dollar originals, and the seasoned observers of *Women's Wear Daily* note that it "becomes harder and harder to tell the original from the copies." Nor is anything more "in" socially than the top-designer fashion show, the ultimate drawing card for philanthropic causes. The most aloof dowagers turn out for these events held in the mostly unlikely places, all in the name of charity. This attitude has penetrated every part of the country. Churches in small towns raise money with fashion shows. High schools stage them. Hotels enliven the luncheon hour with runways. Thus fashion is not only one of the great industries of the country—it has become part of the everyday life of the people and is approached with professional understanding.

A straw in the wind in 1965 was the selection of a young matron as the best-dressed woman of the year, a distinction traditionally reserved for the mature. Another was the Coty American Critics Awards to nine little-known American designers for their "youth-oriented, popular-priced clothes," a significant bow to the native designer, and a double tribute to youth. The élite of the fashion editors, strong individualists themselves, have cultivated this emphasis on youth. The models, the photographers, the writers are all attuned to this new conception of fashion. Artful camera work has succeeded still-life effects, false props, and carefully posed figures in period settings. Now they find their backdrops in spontaneous situations—in the rush of travel, in a tangle of wires backstage, in a strikers' march, in the rapture of tearing across sand dunes, or frugging in a discothèque. As photographer Richard Avedon, an experienced observer of this world, puts it: "The picture of the woman of fashion in the mid-sixties is frantic, probing, and technically expert, if sometimes alarming in its determined grotesqueries." The model's face is cast in a new mold, too. The heart-shaped image of the Nell Brinkley girl, all curls and rosebud mouth, has given way to the somber type, angular but with grace, her sulky face ridden with hollows, her lips parted and about to speak, her eyes sunk in a thicket of false eyelashes. Or else she is a bright young thing with a new stance—a panther about to spring.

The contemporary picture is showy, and magnified through a constant flow of imaginative photography that rarely takes note of the innumerable young who abide by the rules of common sense, and lean to good manners, traditional clothes, and a sense of fitness in the midst of confusion. All is not as kooky as it seems in the world of youth. Meanwhile, the *haute couture* remains inviolable in its strength and variety—and brides for the most part maintain the historic pattern.

Of all the vanities, hairdressing has been perhaps the most consistently cultivated from the early days of the Republic. It has reflected the political tone of the country, the manners and ideals of each period, the fashion whims of celebrities, and today it is consciously influenced by the fashion designers and a small group of hairdressers linked to the "Beautiful People" and the stars of stage, screen, and television.

The same cycle has repeated itself from time to time—long hair, short hair, elaborate or simple, classical or curled, piled up or streaming in the wind. Today both men and women do their hair in styles closely resembling those of the eighteenth century, although the wigs of the 1960s are minor in size and idiosyncrasy compared with those of the 1760s, when they reached their ultimate extravagance. At first they were more closely identified with men than with women, and it was not until the eighteenth century that women wore exaggerated wigs, spurred on by John Still, who had come from London to New York to promote the use of all manner of wigs, and in particular his "Ladies Tatematongues and Towers."

The tower and comet effects deplored by Increase Mather were a pale copy of the fantastic commode wig worn by Frenchwomen.   203

Godey's Lady's Book reported in 1776 that Marie Antoinette had to have her wig removed so that she could get into her carriage, and women doubled up to step into their sedan chairs, after which their wigs protruded through the top. Doorways were enlarged for their passage and hairdressing appointments were usually three weeks apart. The hair could not be taken down in the meantime, and women slept on wire structures, with a mess of wool stuffing, ribbons, and gauze more or less glued to their heads. Much symbolism was associated with the more extreme wigs worn by women. They were mounted with coaches and horses in blown glass, with reproductions of landscapes and waterfalls, and the most discussed of all in the United States was a ship in full sail signifying a naval victory during the War of Independence. Although Americans never quite touched the extravagant height and decoration of the court monstrosities, social leaders did their best to follow up until the French Revolution curbed all vanity for the time being.

As women escaped from the torture of the crimping and frizzing connected with wearing fantastic wigs, they adopted the easy and graceful style of hair brushed back from the forehead, with curls softly arranged behind the ears, an approximation of the later bob. Madame de Pompadour's influence led them through a variety of French curls, scallop-shell curls, and natural effects. They continued to powder their hair and they dressed it in simple loops and braids. Finally, loose curls dangled at either side of their cheeks, suggesting spaniel's ears, a fashion adopted briefly in the United States when such British writers as Elizabeth Barrett Browning and George Sand gave it stimulus on both sides of the Atlantic.

The chignon of the Civil War era followed, with the waterfall, meshed snood, garlands of flowers, and quantities of false hair. After the war, women dusted their hair with gold powder, for it was a period when everything shone and glittered, as in the 1960s. The blonde tradition, later fostered in the fashion world, grew strong at this time. High tortoise-shell combs held pouf bonnets in place. Ornamented with heather, mignonette, or tea roses, they rested precariously on Alpine peaks of false hair.

By the 1890s the natural hair was stiffly curled and bolstered with rats and wire structures known as transformations. But early in the twentieth century the pompadour look came into style, springy and comparatively simple with the hair combed high over the forehead. The marcel wave kept the hair in order through World War I, aided by curling irons, hairpins, combs, barrettes, and impedimenta of all kinds. The wistful psyche knot, beloved by poets and girls with delicate profiles, had a brief run before masses of little puffs known as French curls enveloped the head. But curls and elaborations came to an abrupt end in the 1920s when the bob, the Eton crop, the shingle, or whatever one chose to call it, took the feminine world by storm. There was nothing historically fresh about this fashion. The Egyptians wore short hair, the Phoenicians offered theirs to the gods when someone died, and the Greeks went in for closely sculptured effects. The colonial women at times sacrificed their hair for wigs, and short hair was worn intermittently in the seventeenth century. Nell Gwyn was a lively example of this style.

Nothing as sharp and angled as the Vidal Sassoon cut of 1966 disturbed the 1920s, but short hair was as much discussed as miniskirts today. The uproar came from the press, pulpit, and men in general, as girls invaded barbershops and pranced about in their tight helmets, turbans, and cloches. The cropping had begun in 1918 but it took many forms before the wig craze was revived in the 1950s. The windblown effect flourished in 1928, just before the Greta Garbo look of the 1930s, followed by the slanted pageboy coiffure of Lauren Bacall. Veronica Lake introduced the shaggy sheepdog fashion with her hair drifting over one eye. Brigitte Bardot touched off the all-over-the-face craze, and a long-haired Mia Farrow first did much for the Alice-in-Wonderland look that flourished in 1966 when many of the young covered their heads with kerchiefs and wore fat braids down their backs, or carried the air of innocence further with long, straight hair screening their eyes or flowing to their waists without restraint. But Mia gave fashion another twist with her close-shorn hair, elfin on her, but suggesting the Greek goddess when Sassoon coated the same coiffure with bronze for more exotic customers.

The girls committed to the geometric cut of this new hairdressing czar are the daughters of the women who kept their hair trimly cropped during World War II, as they worked in factories, drove ambulances, or engaged in other public services usually performed by men. During the Vietnam war hair for the most part has been teased, lacquered, blown up in beehive or bouffant effects reminiscent of some of the eighteenth-century styles. By the summer of 1967 curls and soft waves had returned, along with the youthful emphasis of the swinging fall. Wiglets, braids, pony tails, bangs, and Grecian cascades gave infinite variety to the feminine parade. Wigs have come into general use, and are commonplace now for professional women, lecturers, and entertainers. A half-million women spend more than $25 million annually for wigs. Many are dyed to match evening gowns, another exotic link with the eighteenth century. Four out of ten women tint their hair at home, but with more subtlety than the results of henna and raw peroxide in the 1920s.

In the pioneer days they used herbs for this purpose—elderberry juice to dye it black, butternut to dye it brown. Red hair was unpopular until the twentieth century, when it became the symbol of passion and hot temper. One New York bride in 1868 had her own and her bridesmaids' hair dyed red, as a novelty. She was the talk of the town for several days, but lavender or green hair passes almost unnoticed today in a world where far-out coiffures are an essential part of the "in" look.

One of the major changes in fashion of the mid-twentieth century, along with extravagant hair styles, has been the decline of the hat—the added touch that sets the final seal on a woman's appearance. Lingerie, jewels, cosmetics, and all the aids on which she has traditionally relied are at a high pitch, but the woman of today on all social levels chooses most often to go her way bareheaded, a fashion revolution of the most drastic kind.

Historically, hats have been as diverse as the costumes they have matched and they have always been of prime importance. They were of such consequence to the early settlers that they were bequeathed in wills as valuable objects. The most characteristic hat for men was the beaver, but it was taboo in Massachusetts in 1634 for any but the affluent, just as cocked hats with metal lace and cockades were kept within the charmed circle of the privileged. In the southern states the beaver was known as the castor hat and it sometimes had feathers as well as gold or silver hatbands. But palmetto hats were preferred in hot weather.

Women wore beaver hats occasionally, too, but bonnets and hoods were their customary millinery. All through the eighteenth century they clung to their frilled caps, wearing them indoors and out. Some had aigrettes; others were wisps of gauze strapped under the chin. But the calash was the bonnet most generally worn by the country woman. This enormous creation, usually made of green silk, shirred over rattan or whalebone, hid all the hair and most of the face. It was drawn close in the back with strings and in some ways suggested an accordion. The Tiffany hood, made of gauze or silk in summer and felt in winter, was more cherished by the feminine population.

The rage for hoods lasted a long time. They reappeared at intervals, too, notably in the Victorian era when little girls as well as their mothers wore them in velvet, silk, or straw, and again in the 1960s, as part of the mod fashions, but also more traditionally for the ski run, opera, or theater.

Another enduring fashion came into view in the early 1760s when a Boston paper advertised silk and silver turbans. Sometimes they were fashioned of gauze and plumes, and it became fashionable for women to have their portraits painted wearing these turbans. Dolley Madison's devotion to the feathered turban later established its popularity. Like the hood, it has reappeared repeatedly on the fashion scene—strongly in the 1920s and again in the 1960s.

As the turban gained ground another fashion, rooted in Italy but developed in the United States, revolutionized the millinery trade. The straw bonnet was an instant success after two rival creators and a number of other contenders learned to plait straw and make bonnets of it. Betsey Metcalf (Mrs. Obed Baker), of Providence, and Sophia Woodhouse (Mrs. Gordon Welles), of Wethersfield, Connecticut, were the two young women who gave this new twist to the hat trade. In 1797 Betsey noticed an imported straw bonnet in a Providence shop. After studying its weave closely she asked her father for some straw from oats. When she split it into six strands, the magic was missing, but with seven strands she caught the effect she wanted. She bleached and braided it and made a few bonnets that were so much admired that the local milliners copied them. Betsey soon lost interest in her straw bonnets, but many New Englanders took up straw braiding, among them Horace Mann, the pioneer in progressive education, who paid in this way for much of his schooling.

Sophia was more persistent after experimenting with field grasses from near her home. She twisted and braided them, boiled the stalks, bleached them in fumes from burning sulphur, and plaited the strands like leghorn braid. Her bonnets made a hit. She won an award from the Hartford County Society and another from the Society of Arts in London. She and her husband patented them in 1821 and continued manufacturing the straw poke bonnets until 1835. Meanwhile, the straw bonnet, from the most fashionable New York models to the big straw calash, was a substantial contribution to the millinery tastes of early America, something of a feat at a time when all inspiration in the fashion field came from England or France. Hats of various kinds poured in from Paris at the time of the Napoleonic Wars. They were loaded with feathers, ribbons, pompoms, and cascades of decoration. On the simpler side plush caps, muslin turbans, velvet berets, Polish toques, and tall shakos mingled with the flyaway monstrosities. The military mood was reflected in enveloping helmets, which appeared again in the 1920s and in the space age of the 1960s.

The romantic mood was somewhat restored in the 1830s and 1840s with wide, low-crowned hats, soon followed by the popular bonnet, knotted under the chin and becoming to all types of women. Hats were tiny and charming during the Civil War period but the bonnet was considered more formal. When the war was over, round hats trimmed with gauze ended with long veils looped around the neck like a hangman's noose. High-crowned hats came next, with streamers flowing down the back and plumes drooping over the chignon. Plumes reached full estate in the 1880s with the Gainsborough hats, their clustered feathers in rainbow tints giving an extra dash of romance to coaching parties and the races. Long gloves picked up the shrimp pink, gray, and lilac shadings of the plumes. Feathers found their way to the farms, too, as a relief from percale sunbonnets and straw pokes.

The fashionable little cap, worn with or without the hat, had a

The Added Touch

The charming folk-art watercolor is called "Girl with Corkscrew Curls." In the mid-nineteenth century, locks of hair were brushed around wooden sticks to make tight curls like these.

Eighteenth-century wigs reached fantastic proportions. Some were three feet tall; others were adorned with miniature gardens or landscape scenes. One famous wig bore the ship of state, a French gesture to American independence. From Le Magasin Pittoresque, *1841*

The soft curls of the Renaissance were back in fashion in the spring of *1967*, flowing in wide arcs at the sides and lying close to the nape of the neck in the back.

long life. Women liked these frilled and lacy bits and wore them into the twentieth century. By that time they had come to be associated with old age and the fireside, but in earlier days they sat becomingly on matrons of all ages. The nightcap was another matter, worn by both men and women until the late 1870s. The nightshirted figure with stocking cap invited ridicule, but women managed to turn theirs eventually into a frivolous asset, with colored silks and laces. They were never able to abandon them altogether, since beauty routines involved net caps, chinstraps, and other swathings for bedtime wear, right into the 1960s. Only in the 1920s, with the simple Eton crop, could girls go to bed without fear of spoiling their hairdos. Even today's seemingly artless effects involve a surprising amount of shaping and setting to hit the happy mean between chic and disarray.

Toward the end of the nineteenth century hats moved on from Gainsborough plumes to birds, poised at various angles in the midst of feathers and ribbons. Wings projected perkily, and whole birds seemed to be nesting on the head, a habit nipped in the bud when the smuggling of aigrettes was prohibited in 1913. The slaughter of these birds was finally outlawed by Federal law in 1922. The cartwheel hat created another sort of problem at the turn of the century and became the subject of lively discussion as a nuisance in the theater. The "roof gardens," as they were called, were formidable when perched above gigot sleeves, making a girl quite unapproachable.

During World War II women wore trifles of net and veiling, or tiny flowery hats at off-center angles, but by degrees the hat began to vanish altogether. The pageboy cut took over, good coiffing became important, wigs reappeared, and finally the girl with free-flowing hair strayed through the city streets and country byways. The young world adopted eccentric creations in vinyl and plastic, with gleaming visors. The mature were offered great loopings of silk, soaring turbans, paisley prints, and stripes but, as always, the average American woman, if she chose to wear a hat at all, could find something with grace and taste to cover her intractable head and still have an authentic air of fashion. By the spring of 1967 the slouch or mannish hat was in the ascendant and girls flaunted fedoras, sombreros, and softly dented bowlers.

Just as important down the years as the tilt of her hat has been the span of a woman's waist. Stays have been part of her costume from the earliest days in America. The echoes of Elizabethan customs were not yet distant, and although the more rustic types in rough homespun had little chance to worry about their waistlines, the city women strained to keep up with European fashions in this, as in all else. Whenever they could, however, they removed their stays and relaxed in sacques and trollopees.

After the French Revolution stays and stockings were abandoned in a burst of democratic sympathy by all but the aristocracy. But not

The Added Touch

Brown silk calash. This bonnet, fashioned much like an accordion and anchored in the back with a drawstring, was the sturdy headgear of many American women in the early part of the nineteenth century. It enveloped and sometimes hid their faces, serving as an umbrella on rainy days and a parasol in the sun. The calash was usually made of brown or green silk and was shirred over rattan or whalebone.

The calash might serve for country wear, but this black velvet bonnet of 1835 was a formal affair, with lace ruching, organdy bows, and plaiting at the hairline.

The first straw bonnets made in America caused a furore, since two New England girls claimed to have introduced the process, but Sophia Woodhouse, of Wethersfield, Connecticut, patented hers in 1821. "Up with Leghorn bonnets, down with Corsets" was the song of an amateur poet as the battle raged.

for long, and the iron corsets of the previous century merely gave way to tight lacing, sloping shoulders, and the low décolletage of the Empire tradition. Corsets became works of art, intricately put together with whalebone, silk, and cambric instead of the cages of steel which enabled some of the Elizabethan women to shrink to a shallow core of thirteen inches. But the feminine population in Queen Victoria's time was as rigidly encased in whalebone as their predecessors had been in steel. Fifteen pounds of skirts and petticoats dragged them down, and doctors blamed this for 90 per cent of feminine ills, and especially for the vapors, fainting spells, headaches, and indefinable malaise that beset them.

The battle was an ancient one, but it became a hot issue when the feminists campaigned for dress reform in the nineteenth century and, above all, for escape from the encompassing corset. Legs might be covered up but bosom, waist, and bottom were emphasized with tight lacing. The issue was hotly debated from pulpit and platform, and women's groups condemned as immoral an exhibition of the controversial garments in A. T. Stewart's shopwindows. The worst of the sinners fell flat on their faces from sheer compression, and there were those who charged that they died of suffocation. Boarding-school girls were first advised to sleep in their corsets to restrain their burgeoning shapes, but the head of Vassar took a bold stand and outlawed corsets when the college gymnasium opened up and the athletic life began. However, this pragmatic stand had no effect on the social leaders or stage stars of the era. It was the boast of such women as Lillian Russell and Mrs. Frank Leslie that they could encircle their waists with their necklaces, and a span of sixteen inches seemed ideal.

By the Gay Nineties waists reached their narrowest point, with the hourglass figure. The Gibson girl struck a refreshing note with a longer, more graceful line as corsets wandered lower on the hips. They were boned, and laced or hooked in front, creating an effect of lengthy grace for those who were tall and well proportioned. By degrees stays began to loosen up, and by the time of World War I they allowed for considerable spread. From 1903 on they had served a useful purpose in holding up stockings with fancy ribbon suspenders. The garters so universally worn in the Victorian era faded into the background except as period pieces and expensive wedding gifts. One bride received a $1,500 set of garters with her monogram in pearls and a motto in diamonds, and jeweled garters became a fad with courtesans.

The war years completed the cycle as uniformed girls and a myriad of office workers strode forth with relatively unhampered contours. In the 1920s, with the free and easy spirit of the Jazz Age, girdles were left in cloakrooms at parties and in nightclubs, when girls bothered to wear them at all. An entire generation reached the nadir of visible femininity with flat, attenuated forms, back and front, while their mothers wore prim foundations, firm but relaxing—a plain corselette combining brassiere and corset. By 1925 the rubber corset was luring many down the path to promised slenderness. From then on the process was progressive—less and less confinement for the body; softer, shorter girdles, helped along by stretch materials that fitted like gloves, gave with the body, but lent it shape. The climax was reached in the 1960s with the nongirdles, transparent bras and the irreducible body stocking.

Generally through the years fashion has allowed the bosom to keep its contours, though in the early 1960s its outlines were exaggerated. Actually, artificial padding goes back in history as far as the corset itself. At the close of the eighteenth century women of meager proportions added delicately veiled false bosoms made of wax. In the nineteenth century the women's magazines boldly advertised all types of aids for bust expansion—exercises, creams (forerunners of today's hormone preparations), a bust developer shaped like a bell, Madame Demorest's spiral-spring bosom pads, and her "improved breast protector with hinges." The "bust bodice," first popularized by Dr. Jaeger in 1904, was the earliest intimation of this accessory as it is known today, but the word "brassiere" (literally, "arm protector") did not creep into the English language from France until 1916. Whatever claims have been made in this field, the idea evolved gradually from the Elizabethan cage, the steel corset of the period.

Some of the early variations were such instruments of torture that women gave up in disgust and simply stuffed their bodices with stockings or frills, but a well-molded bosom was essential to the close-fitting gowns of the nineteenth century. At any rate, hip pad, bustle, and bosom aids were worn even with bathing attire at the turn of the century, and young men had the wit to know, long before the highly advertised falsies of the 1960s, that things were not always what they seemed. In Hollywood, bust building in the Sophia Loren or Dagmar tradition has become a big cosmetic industry, a complete reversal of the flattening process undergone by the stars of the 1920s. But not all are show girls. Housewives, college girls, and teen-agers are succumbing to the craze known as the "Samurai Formula," in deference to the Japanese doctor who introduced the silicone technique for beautifying the bust.

When Rudi Gernreich launched his "No Bra" look, with transparent materials, a rounder look was achieved, and halter styles and cutaways partially exposing the breast from the side came into fashion. Stretch fabrics, power lace, and pliable straps gave unity and movement to the figure only half hidden by the short, short dress. Petticoats shrank from 24 to 16 inches in length. Stockings, patterned, striped, polka-dotted, grew ever longer, to meet the ascending miniskirt.

Lingerie has reached its present transparent and abbreviated state by a circuitous route, from the heaviest swathings to filmy nothings.

The Added Touch

No one could wear ostrich plumes like Lillian Russell, who had the curves and swagger to match them. Feathers and diamonds were her *best* friends long before the age of Anita Loos. She sparkled with jewels, synthetic and real, and the pearls trimming this dress were the size of peas. Her tilted hat had roses above and below the brim, as well as billowing ostrich plumes. She was never afraid of a low décolletage at any hour of the day and, because she was Lillian Russell, no one minded.

Dolley Madison's turbans popularized a fashion in America that has had many revivals, notably in the 1920s, 1940s, and 1960s. Her turbans, worn indoors and out, were often feathered, but this one is fringed and matches her heavy Paisley shawl. With it she wears the separate lace ruff of the period. Engraving by Jolin Sartain.

The Centennial hat was one of the joyous by-products of the great Exposition at Philadelphia in 1876. It was a saucy sailor with red, white, and blue hatbands and streamers, and boys and girls could be seen skipping about in this snappy number.

Underwear in the modern sense was unknown in colonial days. Even the nightgown had no identity of its own, and was as much used as a dressing gown as for sleeping. The petticoat, then known as a petty-coat, was, as its name implies, a small coat that was worn with a skirt on stormy days. The Dutch treasured their petticoats as they did their velvet and gold-threaded aprons, and often had as many as twenty—quilted, fringed, flowered, ruffled, and elaborately embroidered. They came in a great variety of styles, and in such combinations as a scarlet taffeta trimmed with gold lace, or an Indian silk with heavy beading. Linen, mohair, changeable silk, Holland, and calico were among the materials preferred for this garment. Actually, the petticoat often outshone the gown; and a multi-petticoated figure was a woman of substance.

In the Gay Nineties petticoats again provided a touch of glamour and romance. The rustle of taffeta was considered so aphro-disiac a sound that girls who could not afford silks tried newspapers instead to create this provocative whispering. But by 1905 lacy ruffles were on their way out and silence reigned as the age of synthetics was born. The more everyday world of flannel drawers and union suits, of camisoles and combinations has left no trace. The long flannel petticoat first gave way to silk and rayon, and then to the nylon slip and half-slip. The bouncy drawers with pink and blue ribbon looped through eyelets have no counterpart in the skimpy briefs of 1966. Batiste and torchon lace seem as archaic as the stereoptican. The nightgown is apt to be as transparent as glass, or perhaps more pro-voking in Puritanical simplicity, with long sleeves and high neckline. Sleep-shifts look like daytime frocks. Pajamas come long or short, warm and boyish for the college dormitory, swank for public display, kittenish with puffed sleeves for elfin moments. The leading designers have moved strongly into this area—Pucci with palazzo pajamas and Turkish harem pants, Princess Galitzine with a sarong and bra for sleeping, Norell with slacks and double-breasted tops for bedtime.

All types of accessories have changed more than stockings, which alone bear any resemblance to their forebears. The nation's $600 million hosiery industry has features now not unlike those of two hundred years ago, when bright-colored stockings were worn, and stripes and patterns were in fashion. Many of the colonists wore with their doublets long Florentine hose, much like modern tights. In the 1650s their stockings were apt to be russet, green, or blue, but requests for pink and yellow hose also appeared in the orders sent abroad. White silk stockings with buckled shoes were worn by men, women, and children. In cold weather cloth and felt were used for hose, and William Penn and his associates wore leather stockings much like leggings. The stirrup hose worn by riders were protection for their other garments as mud splashed up and rain came down. They, too, were of soft leather and were wide at the top.

Before the Revolution women's stockings were much like today's, except for the sleek modern fit. They were clocked, ribbed, patterned, dyed, and covered with strange devices. But they vanished from view under the long skirts of the eighteenth century and were not closely observed again until the late nineteenth century, except for occasional glimpses, when hoops tilted, of the white stockings worn by the crinoline girls. But the popularity of the theater focused attention strongly on legs and stockings, and in the 1880s there was wrangling over the aesthetic effect of black stockings with a pink tulle dress. Special imported stockings with pink and brown stripes were considered the height of chic with summer gowns at that time. But only those who could afford it bought imported stockings that often had to be sent back to Paris to be rewoven and darned. The others did the best they could with lisle and cotton, which were on the market for ten cents a pair.

In 1900 twelve thousand pairs of silk stockings were sold in the United States, but with high boots and long skirts it took some time for them to be noticed. Things moved ahead during World War I, with some slight show of leg, and the 1920s found women sleekly clad in beige or gunmetal silk stockings, or in the new rayons, rolled and often gartered. By 1930 stocking sales in the United States had risen to 300 million pairs a year, and when the nylon craze gripped the fashion world before World War II, stockings, like cigarettes, became prized possessions. They were scarce, with nylon needed for parachutes and other war supplies. Sales reached fantastic proportions when the war was over, and by then nylon was worn by women of all classes and income. The famed American legs were shown off to the best advantage with these subtly fashioned stockings in a wide range of tints. This was as true in the country as in the city—uniformity prevailed, perhaps more than in any other article of clothing.

With the 1960s the lacy leg, the patterned leg, the medallioned leg came into view again, to be adopted enthusiastically by the young, both on college campuses and in more conservative haunts. The mini-skirts strengthened this trend, and the white stockings of the colonial era were again high style; so were long heavy woolens for winter wear, but with a novel touch—the high crushable kid boots by Mancini, as soft and clinging as gloves, and Courrèges' white boots, swaggering and infantile at the same time—perhaps the true guideline to the eccentricities of the era.

Stockings are cheap today compared with the luxurious hose sold at the turn of the century. Long before Peck & Peck became distinguished for sportswear they were selling stockings to Mrs. John

Jacob Astor, Mrs. Jay Gould, and Mrs. Cornelius Vanderbilt; and Lillian Russell was cheerfully paying five hundred dollars for imported hose with lace insets. Their stocking trade led directly to the wholesale introduction of the sweater in the United States. In 1914 a hosiery man dropped in at the Peck & Peck Fifth Avenue store with a batch of knitted silk sweaters costing fifty dollars each. A good customer who came in spotted them and bought all the samples on the spot. The Pecks cabled their buyer at once to bring back Scottish sweaters. They were snapped up so fast that the brothers went one step further and matched them with skirts. At this point, after a long history as dealers in hosiery, their specialty stores were born. They introduced their famous Braemars when women began to covet the sweaters men were wearing for golf in the 1920s. They also popularized the Tattersall checked vest for women, and they were the first to open women's shops in Palm Beach and Newport. Their city, suburban, resort, and college shops may be found across the country. Like Brooks Brothers in the men's field, the long-established Peck & Peck has special influence with the young set at college and resorts, and with smart young suburbanites.

Many of the specialty shops today concentrate on stockings, gloves, and lingerie, catching the busy woman who has little time to shop. Still richly alive, although less imperative in their usage than they once were, are gloves, which have held their own through every fashion cycle. Clasped, buttoned, gauntletted or fringed, embroidered, plain or adorned, they have given their own distinctive touch to every change of fashion, arriving at length at the sleek simplicity and easy cleaning preferred today. The earliest gloves made in the colonies by seamstresses were as shapeless as the early shoes, but the imported gloves of the late seventeenth century were svelte and well fashioned. They were in great demand in the mid-nineteenth century. Mary Lincoln and her contemporaries stocked up on dozens of pairs of long kid gloves. In the 1890s lilac, gray, and pale yellow shoulder-length varieties, with innumerable small pearl buttons requiring buttonhooks to do them up were unquestioned favorites. Sarah Bernhardt made twelve-button gloves the rage for a time, and black kid gloves were worn dramatically with white gowns. Alexandre, the premier Parisian glovemaker of his day, reigned supreme in this field. Gloves were worn both indoors and out and even at the dinner table until etiquette advisers drummed home the message that this habit must be dropped. One of the diplomat's wives in Washington, however, insisted on eating her asparagus with her gloves on, even when the other women guests pulled theirs off and tucked them under their table napkins.

Long kid gloves declined in usage as women converged on the workaday business world. Fine suèdes and kids lost ground to the doeskin, fiber, and washable varieties. In all lengths and styles today's gloves may be found in bright colors, as in the seventeenth century when they matched the multicolored shoes. The beatnik generation bypasses gloves as it does well-coiffed hair, but American women as a whole stand by the old tradition of the right glove for all occasions, and they have never had a greater variety or better fit from which to choose. They are even offered—rather whimsically—Rudi Gernreich's "glittens," a combination of gloves and mittens to be worn with visor caps.

Mittens, which had a long and romantic run, went out of fashion early in the twentieth century. They were used originally for warmth and to hide the scars of labor in the Bay Colony. At that time they were made of deerskin or heavy cloth. But soon women were knitting their own. Girls were mittened from their earliest years and remained so until they died. By the 1840s black silk mittens were as inevitable at a party as cap and locket. Delicately colored silk mittens were often inset with medallions of lace or flowered designs, and for heavier wear kid or lambskin was used. As time went on they became lacy, diaphanous, frivolous rather than utilitarian, and the mittened hand, presiding over the teacups, was regarded as a social grace. But the turn-of-the-century girl abandoned them along with the lace cap.

Muffs, too, have reappeared from time to time down the years. They were as important as gloves in the early days of the colonies, and big bearskin muffs were carried by both men and women in icy weather. The heavy gauntlets of the Cavaliers were the showiest gloves men in America have used, but gold lace and fringe flourished before the Revolution. The average man kept warm in deerskin, but these gloves were rough and untanned, in no way resembling the deerskin ones that are popular even today. In the 1880s men went in for fine kid gloves in bright colors, showing up at formal receptions in lavender or canary effects. White kid gloves alone remained in good standing for ceremonial occasions down to the 1960s. Men today favor gloves made of buckskin, capeskin, pigskin, or mocha.

As their husbands prospered, colonial wives ordered their muffs from abroad, along with their fur tippets. The imported ones were often made of velvet, fur, or swansdown. As time went on they shrank in size until the skaters of the 1890s were seen most often with tiny sealskin muffs, occasionally adorned with Trilby violets. But they expanded again to dramatic proportions in the era of cartwheel hats, disappearing altogether soon after World War I.

Boots and shoes have followed much the same course as gloves. They were heavy and misshapen at the start, then became ornate and fanciful, and finally the emphasis was on perfect fitting. Farmers were prone to go barefoot in summer, and hunters wrapped their feet in deerskin in winter. Shoes looked as if each were cut for the same foot. But as early as 1670 cobblers were turning out stout double-soled shoes of cowhide. Rosettes preceded buckles on the dressier shoes and it was 1730 before the silver, brass, copper, steel, and pewter buckles so long associated with the Puritans came into general use. Children wore black-and-white calfskin boots, copied from models imported from England. Early in the day planters' wives had the journeymen cobblers make their French heels. Silk or damask was then glued over them to match their party gowns.

As the toes of men's shoes became more rounded, buckles were fashioned to follow the curve of the instep. Some were set with jewels and were prized possessions. But pointed shoes and high heels became fashionable for women in the middle of the eighteenth century. They were usually made of prunella, satinet, flowered damask, or morocco, and their evening shoes were richly brocaded to match their costumes. Everyday shoes at that time were more varied in color and shape than at any later date, and since women wore colored stockings and gloves to match their shoes, the total effect was bright and sometimes startling. A typical slipper of 1840 had chain-stitch embroidery, cut-steel beads, a ribbon bow, and a silver buckle. Russet-and-white striped leather was another popular combination. Children wore morocco, satinet, and prunella-topped shoes as well as their white calfskin boots, not unlike the Courrèges models of today. The smallest children danced about in purple satin, or gold-embroidered shoes, but by the 1840s they were wearing heelless slippers tied with ribbons crisscrossed around the ankles. Like their fathers, they wore splatterdashes in rainy weather— leggings made of glazed linen, covering the leg up to the knee, in the fashion of the gaiter that followed. Men wore oilcloth capes with them to keep out the rain, and women threw heavy petticoats, called weather skirts, over their gowns to protect them in bad weather. Riders sported highly polished jockey boots with tops turned down.

After the Revolution heels flattened and the brogue made its appearance. Buttoned boots became popular during the Civil War and by the 1880s, with the crinoline out of the way, women wore sensible walking boots in winter, with thick cork soles to make them water-proof. For really rough weather they had Balmoral clumps, with triple soles and double uppers. In the evenings they wore tinted kid, with velvet bows to match their gowns, and large steel buckles. White satin slippers were a hard-and-fast rule for weddings. Elastic-sided boots reached the United States when Queen Victoria's shoemaker made her some after the coronation. These hung on to the end of the century, a comfortable choice for gouty men, but the young bloods liked them, too.

The hourglass figure and the Grecian bend of the late nineteenth and early twentieth centuries involved some classic tussles in tight lacing. Corsets came in various styles, sizes, and colors, but one factor remained the same—the nipped-in waist. Lacy camisoles, floor-length petticoats, and bloomers were all part of the lingerie picture, but no lady stepped forth until she was laced as tight as a drum. From "Book of Styles," B. Altman & Company Catalogue.

The "robe intime" fashioned like this was the favorite boudoir garb in 1919, as World War I came to an end. It was usually made of Georgette crêpe or chiffon and was apt to be embroidered with beads or edged with marabou. The chosen colors for these carefree moments were orchid and coral.

In the 1960s Pucci pajamas were good for bedroom, boudoir, or ball. This "villa pajama" is fashioned in a brilliant abstract printed chiffon. It has a short jacket, an overblouse, and bell-bottom trousers.

When the tailor-made costume caught on, women carried pearl-handled knives with two buttonhooks attached, one for their gloves and one for their shoes. In the 1890s shoes, like all else, reflected the luxury of the period. Velvet carriage boots were edged with fur and lined with quilted satin, and everyday shoes had kid tops and patent leather vamps. Bronze kid slippers with or without cut-steel beading were worn by children as well as by their mothers. But sports had brought a sturdier calfskin walking boot into usage as well as light tan shoes for golf and a "bicycle boot of American kid." In their boudoirs women wore scarlet Turkish slippers, fur-bordered pantoufles, or satin mules.

The shoe industry grew to impressive proportions in the twentieth century, as it ran through a series of saddle shoes, loafers, pumps, high heels and low, sports shoes and ballet slippers, gimlet toes and square toes. In the 1960s it reverted to some of the earliest styles in American history—buckles, bows, and the low heel, bright colors like hot pink or scarlet lacquer, two-tone leather effects and baby boots in white kid or suede. Wedgies, sling-backs, and jeweled types were seen again. Men's shoes have plied a steady course but they, too, have been mildly affected by the mod world. The monk front, the two-eyelet chukka boot, the high slip-on have been added to the traditional brogues, moccasins, fringed-tongued golf shoes, saddle-straps, and the conventional black and brown city shoes.

The Dutch pattens worn in the early days went with aprons, which were an intrinsic part of the costume and were fashionable long before they were associated with kitchen drudgery and the care of children. Like many of the early styles they flashed back into view in the mid-twentieth century as airy whiffs of net, lace or plastic, covering a small area of a career girl's dress as she whipped up dinner for her beau, or being hastily donned by a hostess making last-minute preparations for a dinner party.

It has again become a decorative garment, as it was in the days of the settlers, when it was regarded as the finishing touch to any costume, not to be whisked off as guests arrived, but to remain as part of the ceremonial costume. The substantial housewife kept them in dozen lots, both long and short, bibbed or simple, lacy or braided. But aprons moved from the parlor to the kitchen when crinolines and bustles came into view, nor did they have any place in the world of the feminist with her Bloomer costume. Instead they took on new and useful functions in the kitchen, and soon the image of the farm wife baking bread or bending over the cradle with a large apron covering her dress became a reassuring symbol of maternity and a well-kept home. Little girls wore aprons to school well into the twentieth century under the name of pinafores. They dressed their dolls in tiny aprons with true housewifely zeal. The nurse or maid, wrapped in a large enveloping apron or whisking about in a frilly, diminutive trifle, was part of the domestic picture at the turn of the century.

As slacks and shorts became popular, aprons lost ground. They no longer seemed to match the spirit of the times unless they were decorative accessories, in the mood of the décor or the wearer's personality. The apron is by no means dead. It has its place in a changing civilization, but it is no longer indispensable in kitchen, nursery, or parlor. It still has its uses, however, for men superintending the barbecue in clouds of smoke and spattering fat.

Shawls, like aprons, ran their course from the decorative to the practical, with diminishing significance. After the early cardinals and cloaks of one kind or another, the shawl became the conventional wrap, reaching the height of its popularity in the nineteenth century. When trade opened with the Orient, Indian and Chinese shawls brought a new and exciting element into the fashion picture. The women of Salem in the 1780s strolled about in fine Kashmirs and heavily embroidered Canton shawls. After 1810 the spencer, redingote, and mantle took over, and by the time of the Civil War bonnets rather than shawls were used to cover the head. But the Indian shawls were still prized and were often made into gowns. Small ones were used as stoles. The average woman kept several plain shawls on hand, usually fringed with tassels. Their popularity dwindled after the Civil War, and by the end of the century they were used chiefly by the aged or the invalid—soft shetlands for chilly nights, a protection for flying hair during buggy rides, a shield against neuralgia. But back they came into full estate in the 1950s, dramatic and jewel-studded, supplying decorative touches for the hair, providing gossamer veiling for the omnipresent wig.

Handkerchiefs were of great importance in colonial days and were sometimes willed to descendants. They were large and were made of fine cambric and linen, lace and gauze. Some were edged with gold or had deep mourning bands, and the black gauze handkerchiefs seen at funerals were often a yard square. Today the handkerchief counters are bright with color, stripes, and plaids as well as with linen and lace. Although handkerchiefs have lost much ground in a world that knows Kleenex, they hold their own as gifts and for formal use.

Pins were treasured beyond price in the early days and the Dutch stabbed them into pincushions they wore with their chatelaines. Most of them were made of brass, but there were black pins for mourning. Hairpins, old as the Etruscan civilization, made their appearance in Boston around 1755. They were large enough to be skewered into the hair. Many varieties came and went down the years, from the tortoise-shell and gold-rimmed hairpins of the Victorian age to the bobby pins of today. The era of hairpins, nets, and hair tidies gave way to a world where smart little wig boxes became the newest type of luggage used by women. Yet not so new. Long before the streamlined, lightweight luggage of today, American women learned to carry their hats and wigs in the decorative bandboxes used in the eighteenth century. They were made of cardboard or light wood, and were covered with wallpaper.

The sheltering umbrella and its frivolous twin, the parasol, came into use in America in the middle of the eighteenth century, but it seemed an absurd fashion to the dwellers in a small Connecticut town who in 1740 used broom handles and sieves to mimic a girl who brandished one that she had brought from the West Indies. But within twenty years Boston milliners were advertising green and blue umbrellas with ivory ferules. Actually, the umbrella was a decorative object until used to ward off downpours and symbolize mourning and gloom in the Victorian era, when the furled black umbrella became the hallmark of the Englishman. In the 1880s red umbrellas were favorites in the United States, and the yum-yum umbrellas of plaited China silk were a bright fashion note.

But the earliest use for the umbrella was as a shelter against the sun, and the people of Charleston used them for this purpose, as they did their awnings, or "muschate curtains." In the crinoline days of the Civil War the parasol was a tiny confection, held high above small tilted hats. Although often merely a dome of lacy frills, or of somber taffeta ruching for one in mourning, it seemed as essential as gloves for the well-dressed woman.

As the nineteenth century neared its close parasols grew in circumference, and their ferules of silver, bamboo, or mahogany became longer. They were colored to match the costume, and were more beribboned and flounced than ever, with Dresden china knobs for handles. Since they rose above cartwheel hats the combined effect was overpowering. In addition to protecting the delicately calcimined complexions of the period, they were skillfully used to discourage bores and mashers. Their points could be deadly weapons of attack; Hetty Green, worth millions, poked her lawyer viciously in the stomach by way of reproof in a courtroom where he was representing her in a suit over the handling of her father's inheritance.

Although parasols faded from view after 1910 except for dowagers who clung to tradition, they have reappeared in recent years with slightly different status, for now they are interchangeable with umbrellas. The new version is likely to be colored, flowered, polka-dotted, and made of plastic or vinyl, a parasol in spirit if not in fact.

The Added Touch

The girl who walks in the rain today is a bright and flowery creature, who does not drip and rarely looks dowdy. If she belongs to the moneyed class she can throw Oscar de la Renta's $395 jeweled raincoat over her party dress and set off for the theater. If her budget is small she may splurge on a clear or tinted vinyl raincoat, matched with boots, bag, and sometimes even her dress. With this she knots a simple vinyl triangle in color over her head and sallies forth, a world away from the colonial girl in her calash. Slickers and sou'westers also rest easily on her limber form. Today's raincoats have flourish for the conservative, too. In black or dark colors, they serve for evening as well as for daytime wear, and do not even remotely suggest their real use.

Like the parasol, the fan, steeped in history, has been a significant accessory in the fashion world. Archaic now, it was used to good effect in the eighteenth century by women of wit and taste, who furled it to score a point, whisked it sidewise for implication, held it beneath their eyes in the game of flirtation, flipped it for provocation. It was variously used as a screen for blushes, a defense on the dance floor, a shield while in mourning. Some of the early fans, with their cameos, gem encrustation, and real lace, were as valuable as jewels. Their sticks were often of silver, gold, tortoise shell, mother-of-pearl, or ivory. For a time they had a spread of nearly two feet, and now and again topical interest attached to them, as in the case of Jenny Lind's famous fan. The image of Horace Greeley with fringed beard was silhouetted on a campaign fan when he ran for the Presidency.

Gilbert and Sullivan's *Mikado* touched off a craze for the Japanese variety, and tiny paper fans and parasols were tucked into children's Christmas stockings. The plain parchment fan could be found in nearly every nineteenth-century home and it was a practical aid and comfort in the early days of the republic. It was used to ward off insects, to screen its owners from the open fires, to cool them off. Country dwellers used spreading leaves before the palm-leaf fan took formal shape as indispensable equipment for members of Congress. Before air conditioning fans seemed inseparable from the courtroom, the public platform, and church, where their rustling at times drowned out the voice of the preacher. One early etiquette book warned parishioners to refrain from taking snuff in meeting, and to use their fans gently so as not to interfere with quiet meditation. Excursionists fanned themselves vigorously as they rode in trolleys and ferries, and farmers even took them into the fields. When houses with porches went up, fans were the inevitable accompaniment of leisurely evenings, rocking cradles, and family life as a whole.

All orders for imports in the early days included fans, which were carried quite generally by fashionable women in Europe before

Not until the 1960s were stockings again as decorative as in 1909 when girls stepped out with embroidered, jeweled, and tasseled hose under their petticoat frills. They came in many colors, as in the colonial era and again today. Gold, purple, ruby, and steel were favorite shades for the embroidered patterns that ranged from a daisy motif to strings of jewels. Lord & Taylor advertisement 1909.

The light blue satin brocade slipper patterned in silver was worn no longer ago than 1891. Since then women have danced on stiletto heels and in sandals, but in 1967 styles were back where they began—with the flat, square-toed buckled shoe of colonial days. But with a difference. Now it is fashioned in a vast range of materials and colors with embroideries or glitter of pastel jewels.

Americans adopted the custom. Feathered fans with shaded tips were used with the short sleeves and low necks of the 1880s. But they reached their utmost extravagance when Lillian Russell and other stage stars waved huge feathered fans in the 1890s as they swaggered across the stage, singing their hit songs. With cartwheel hats, leg-of-mutton sleeves, and a maximum of flounces, they reached their crescendo at the turn of the century and played a diminishing role from then on, except on the stage with such ephemeral curiosities as Sally Rand's fan dance. The fan faded away like the chaperone as a social asset, though it remained useful in overheated rooms. But it still turns up in family attics, in museums and historical collections—an echo from the more leisurely past, when it fanned the painted faces of several generations of American women.

It took the Puritan ladies some time to accustom themselves to the cosmetic vanities of the French court. The first painted face publicly observed on Boston Common in 1686 was somberly disapproved. But this early flirtation with a white lead preparation known as ceruse pointed the way ahead. Today the cosmetics industry is one of the most firmly based in the country. In the early days women had lip salves and deerskin powder bags, even if they lacked vanity cases. And they soon learned to dabble in ointments and unguents, stirring up strange concoctions. They washed themselves with lotions made of rosemary and white wine, or charcoal mixed with honey and water. They applied "golden" ointment to their skin and removed it with horseradish steeped in buttermilk. They rubbed sulphur followed by lemon juice on their faces to help fade their freckles, and squeezed lemon juice and soapsuds into their eyes to make them smart and shine.

By the close of the eighteenth century they had access to a variety of professional preparations, like pale pink Portuguese rouge, but it was considered racy to paint oneself. After the Civil War Madame Demorest scolded those who violated the lady's code with the "vulgarity of paint and chalk which belong to the stage, and are best left to the professional beauty there." At the same time her good friend Dr. Henry Ward Beecher was urging his fellow men to wash their faces with Pears soap, just as other social leaders would later be lending their names to paid advertisements for pianos and cold creams, cigarettes, mattresses, and cosmetics. The proceeds always went to charity, but when Mrs. James Brown Potter at an earlier date endorsed Harriet Hubbard Ayer's cold cream from Tuxedo Park, she was branded as a social outcast. And this was before she had decided to decamp with Kyrle Bellew, the actor. The point of view had mellowed by the 1920s, however, when Mrs. Oliver Harriman, Mrs. August Belmont, Mrs. Nicholas Longworth, and a variety of Astors and Vanderbilts allowed their names to be used with advertisements.

American women were spending $62 million a year for cosmetics early in the 1890s, and beauty preparations of all kinds were on the market. Young girls were still protected from the use of paint, however, and mature women who dyed their hair and rouged their cheeks were not considered ladies. The belief that a lady should stay out of the sun for the sake of her complexion was another social principle of the Gay Nineties. A half century later the goal was to toast oneself brown. Hollywood has had much to do with the swing of taste in cosmetics. It opened up dazzling new horizons in the beauty field. Women had picked up the cinema dream that beauty belonged to all, and the stars were showing them how. Preparations aimed to disguise physical flaws reached the market with dynamic impact. Bands for sagging chins, hormones to restore youth, masks to tighten the skin, protective lotions for the beach, creams for night and day, for dry and oily skin, came in handsome vials and jars bearing the classic names of the industry. There was no holding back this tide of radiant promise that gathered force in the twentieth century. By the 1930s the beauty business was steering women away from the pink-and-white complexion, the henna hair, the round doll-like dab of rouge. Makeup gradually became more subtle, and sometimes even dramatic, as in 1966, when a strange new type was created to match the strange new fashions—when *Vogue* pictured a girl with sunken, sooty eyes, turquoise lid shadow, mink lashes, and iridescent lipstick that gave a silvery sheen to her mouth.

The body was carefully tended, too, with dieting, exercise, milk and health farms, and gymnasiums electrically equipped to roll off fat and strengthen muscles. At such spots as Elizabeth Arden's Maine Chance establishments in Maine and Arizona, or at Nieman-Marcus' The Greenhouse, with its Edward Durell Stone architecture and exotic plantings, beauty seekers found their own particular heaven—at a price. Plastic surgery, developed in the course of two world wars, was the added touch in the beauty field. Techniques to reshape the nose, to strip the abdomen of flabby fat, to lift the face, to make a tall girl shorter, and to operate on her toes to fit them comfortably into pointed shoes were variously practiced.

The battle against weight goes back to colonial times, but little was heard about it until the nineteenth century when fashionable women tortured themselves with William Banting's system, which was simply to starve. Tailor-made costumes had fastened attention on their curves. Soon Mrs. Frank Leslie and other enterprising women were in and out of gymnasiums, trying Turkish baths and swinging Indian clubs. At the Berkeley Ladies Athletic Club in New York they had their own gym, bowling alleys, swimming pool, and facilities for tennis, badminton, fencing, whist, and chess. They whacked at the punching bag and were agile on the trapeze. Many took the electric cure, fighting their headaches and nerves with electric massage on the soles of their feet or on their scalps. Russian bath parties, the 1890s version of the Turkish bath, were as popular as beauty parlors are now.

Americans, old and young, are deeply committed to the world of hygiene. Though they lacked the enlightenment and preventive measures of today they strove for a better physical life long before the health benefits of the 1960s or the skillful dentistry now a commonplace in America had come their way. They had a long road to travel on every front. With better diet and regular brushing, American teeth have improved vastly since colonial days, when they were notoriously bad. Cuttlebone, brick dust, and snuff were used to clean teeth in the distant days when frontier children had countless cavities, but by the 1930s more than fifty million toothbrushes and countless pastes and powders were bought by the American public. In 1966 the electric toothbrush became a pastime for the young—an expensive novelty, like the electric shaver, that linked them with the grownup world.

But one luxury to which women have clung down the years is perfume, and the twentieth-century woman moves in a world of fragrance. Perfumes, old as time itself, made slow headway at first in America. The Puritans considered them "worldly and unworthy" and the Quakers thought that the "pungent musks and unctions of early Greece and Rome were not for Spartan America." But the allure of the vanities of the French court, the lingering scents of their own heritage, and the unquenchable feminine instinct overrode the scruples of the founding fathers and brought fragrance into the American home. It was done by simple means at first, with a lavender base imported from England, blended with homemade soaps, ambergris, and camphor, with oil of cloves, orris root, and sweet marjoram.

It was not a sweet-smelling age, yet housewives managed to perfume their linen with musk and civit, and to burn rose leaves and mint at their open hearths. With powders and soils they stirred up an early potpourri with roses plucked from their gardens. Perfume packets—the sachets of today—were tucked into bureau drawers and handkerchief boxes. The light fragrance of jessamine and verbena, heliotrope and lilac, geranium and rose were the favorites, but toward the end of the nineteenth century the air was heavy with Frangipani, Jockey Club, and Night Blooming Cereus. The siren who went in for Turkish Corners dabbed herself with Patchouli and Ylang Ylang.

The scents of hyacinth, tuberose, crab apple, and sweet clover were favorites early in the twentieth century, but when the coal-tar dyes brought synthetic essences to the market, a torrent of exotic perfumes gave fresh stimulus to the world of fashion. Between 1920 and

Of all the fabulous jewels owned by American women
the most unlucky, as well as one of the most valuable, is
the Hope diamond, which first dazzled Washington
in 1912 when Mrs. Evalyn Walsh McLean appeared
with it hanging from a diamond chain around her neck.
It was valued at $176,000, and in spite of its malign
history, she wore it on every possible occasion. When
she died, it was acquired by Harry Winston, the
New York jeweler, but it had been linked with so much
misfortune in Mrs. McLean's history that no one would
buy it. The Smithsonian Institution received it in 1958,
and it now shines in splendor as a museum piece.

Campaign watch, 1888. Grover Cleveland's losing fight for
reelection in 1888 involved many campaign devices, and a
popular novelty was the Waterbury watch, showing the heads
of Cleveland and his running mate, Allen G. Thurman, on
the back of the thick, gold timepiece. Since before the time
of Lincoln, campaign trinkets, buttons, fans, and novelties of
all kinds have been part of the political build-up.

Mrs. John Adams, the famous Abigail, had a large collection
of fans, which she used to good effect. Like her contemporaries,
she matched them when possible with the brocade of her
gown and slippers.

The Tiffany-style jewelry popular early
in the twentieth century was pale and
meager in comparison with the Egyptian
crystal collars and smashing jewel effects
of the 1960s—when women blazed with
massed gems and huge pins, often designed
by the wearer. The Tiffany jewelry ran
to moonstones, sapphires, and platinum,
to small pieces blending softly into
the gowns with which they were worn.

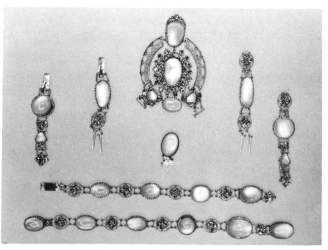

1966 waves of alluring perfumes, from Chanel No. 5 to Joy, sank into the consciousness of the American people. Their names were designed to provoke—Tabu, La Nuit de Noel, and Ecstasy, among others. Paul Poiret introduced Oriental perfumes to match his Turkish costumes. Guerlain's Shalimar rode high, along with the lighter perfumes of Coty and Houbigant. For a time small dram-bottles of the expensive French perfumes lined the perfume counters of department stores, so that the office girl was as exotically scented as the debutante, but this bonanza came to an end. However, the gap was bridged when light colognes suggesting the basic perfume flooded the market. Delicate scents at a price within her means were just what the business girl needed. Soon she was offered matching sets of cosmetics and perfume, and made knowing use of both. She had learned all the vital spots to which to apply perfume, and she knew how much to use at home, in the office, or on the tennis court.

Like perfume, jewelry has winged its way from one generation to another as one of the most ancient and recurrent manifestations of the instinct for personal adornment. At first it was more closely linked to death than to life in Puritan homes, and sometimes as many as two hundred mourning rings were handed out as mementos at funerals. They were made of black enamel and gold, and were frequently imprinted with a family crest, a skeleton, a coffin, or death's head. All the jewelry was simple and inexpensive in the early days of the republic. Its use was frowned on by the zealots, but the instinct for personal adornment was stronger than all the blue laws designed to temper it. Choker necklaces and pendant crosses, jet pins and simple lockets were worn in the late seventeenth century, as well as silver girdles and gold buttons. The Puritans viewed wedding rings as relics of popery, but the founding mothers managed to equip themselves with wedding and betrothal rings. Interlocking hearts or nosegays added a romantic touch to the engagement rings. Boston women in 1755 wore plain gold hoop rings encircled with tiny diamonds, and modest pearl necklaces. Schoolgirls liked to wear three-strand coral necklaces and paste combs along with their love hoods and white cotton stockings. During the Civil War cameos were their mothers' chief adornment, worn so as to hold their fichus in place. Pictures of their children and their men at war were often hidden in their closed lockets. Many had matching sets of bracelets, rings, earrings, and necklaces which were often chain pendants with crystal teardrops, named lavallières after the Duchesse de la Vallière, mistress of Louis XIV.

The jewelry business was firmly established early in the nineteenth century when the Gorham Company began manufacturing gold beads and chains as well as silver spoons. Ball and Frost was founded in New York in 1860, in time to supply Civil War beauties with the ornate jewelry of the period. The war was over when Tiffany and Company opened a shop on Union Square in 1870. Eight years later attention was dramatically focused on diamonds with the discovery in the Kimberly Mine of the Tiffany diamond, weighing 128.51 carats. The fortunes amassed during the gold rush of 1849 fostered the cult for diamonds and other precious stones in America, and men began to adorn their women with costly jewels. But it was not until the 1890s when the great railroad, steel, and oil fortunes were being made, that women literally blazed with stomachers, tiaras, sunbursts, pendants, bracelets, and rings. Mrs. William Astor of New York and Mrs. Potter Palmer of Chicago led this parade with undisputed authority.

When Mrs. Palmer appeared at a charity ball with a seven-strand collar made of 2,268 pearls and seven diamonds, she brought a whiff of the magnificence of European courts to Chicago. This effect was further heightened with a tiara that she often wore, fashioned of diamonds so large that they were likened to Tokay grapes. She had a sunburst ten inches in diameter and a pink pearl as large as a hazelnut. Her star sapphire and canary diamond rings were equally famous, and at the turn of the century her jewel collection was considered one of the choice ones of the world. Mrs. Astor's jewels were valued at $340,000, and she had a dog collar that rivaled Mrs. Palmer's. Mrs. O. H. P. Belmont's pearl necklace had the added touch of glamour of having belonged to Marie Antoinette. Women sparkled as they walked, and diamonds, like yachts, were the last word in luxury. The great balls and masquerades of the era were well exploited in the press and Mrs. Astor's diamonds became even more famous than Mrs. Astor's horse.

The early twentieth century brought a fresh wave of gem-laden dowagers, led by Mrs. Evalyn Walsh McLean, who tempted fate with the Hope diamond and was all too glad to rid herself of this burden when she sold it for $1,500,000 to Harry Winston, the jeweler. But no one sought to buy this ill-starred gem and in the end he gave it to the Smithsonian Institution. Mrs. Merriweather Post continued to wear Marie Antoinette's diamond eardrops, Mrs. Horace Dodge her rope of 389 matched pearls that had once belonged to Catherine the Great, Barbara Hutton her huge pigeon-blood rubies, Mrs. Robert McCormick her black pearls, and Mrs. George Gould her five strings of matched pearls, valued at more than a million dollars. In 1958 a survey showed that thirty-six American women had gem collections worth a million dollars each, and in 1966 Harry Winston harbored a diamond-and-emerald necklace priced at a million dollars and emerald-and-diamond earrings worth another half million.

But jewel robberies had become so frequent, both on the screen and in fact, that women had taken to wearing paste copies of their more fabulous jewels, keeping the originals in bank vaults. With this development costume jewelry reached a new peak of popularity and variety. Deep collar necklaces hung around the necks of stage stars and hostesses alike, with all the distinction of the authentic article. Huge pendant earrings—hoops, balloons, symbols of all kinds, ancient and modern—dangled to the shoulders. The feminine world was ablaze with jewels, genuine or copies, in the 1960s, and the charity balls glittered more resplendently than the fabled parties of the 1890s. A wider range of women had the money to invest in jewelry—the ultimate in accessories, the last word in luxurious personal adornment.

This represented a marked change from the days when the Diamond Horseshoe at the Metropolitan shone with blue fire, and Nob Hill and Lake Forest took note of priceless jewels, but the average American woman contented herself with the same old wedding ring made of gold, and her diamond solitaire. It was not until after World War I that platinum settings came into vogue, and the traditional wide gold band became a rare sight, as wedding and engagement rings, pins, and jewelry of all kinds were set in this new fashion.

The wristwatch came into use at this time, too. The soldiers popularized it for both men and women. The old fashion of carrying a watch on the chatelaine, pinning a small gold or enamel watch to the bodice, suspending one from a black satin ribbon around the neck, or tucking one in the belt died out. The Empress Josephine was the first woman of fashion to order a wristwatch. She gave a jeweled bracelet timepiece as a wedding gift to her son's bride in 1809, nearly a century before a shipment of wristwatches from Switzerland was returned with scorn by an American jeweler. He did not think that he could sell them.

As time went on the feminine variety became tiny, decorative, and frequently jeweled; the masculine wristwatch grew sturdier and more impervious to water and rough usage. But men still clung to their pocket watches, no longer the bulky timepieces wound with a key and hung with a heavy fob, but thin and flat, with delicate chains. Actually, they had first come into general use in the 1690s, when men in America were already wearing seal rings and taking their snuff from gold containers. Hunting watches were still popular in 1915 when the wristwatch took possession in a convincing way. Children and grandmothers became wristwatch wearers, too, and in the thirties Mickey Mouse watches were as popular as the moon calendar type at the turn of the century. Next to wedding and engagement rings the wristwatch is perhaps the most widely used article of jewelry in the United States today.

Until the nineteenth century men outstripped women in the richness and variety of their attire, and today they are experimenting again with color, cut, and form after a century of subdued attire. The Cavalier, with his velvet doublet, lace frills, and plumed hat, fixed an early image of romantic attire on the American scene, but more characteristic was the garb of the early New England settler in Pilgrim cloak and steeple hat. Neither had much relation to the homespun clothes of the men who made their way in the wilderness and established law and order. Most of the colonists wore leather breeches of deer or sheepskin, worsted stockings, and woolen caps in the winter. In summer the farmers and artisans pulled coarse linen smocks over their heads and cinctured them with string.

The more worldly settlers assumed the English fashion of slashed doublets, gold lace, and scarlet hose, encouraged by Governor Winthrop, who ordered scarlet coats and caps for the Bay Colony in 1633. When the lower orders showed signs of aping their masters the Massachusetts General Court announced its detestation of such "gaudy apparel" as gold lace and great boots except for military officers, judges, university men, and those who had more than two hundred pounds sterling. Attire was permitted to define the social status of its wearer, and the favored few were allowed their jeweled hatbands, slashed doublets, and silver-handled rapiers. There was one dispensation for the master, another for his apprentice.

But imported satin, plush, and broadcloth brought the touch of luxury into many homes, and by the middle of the eighteenth century men walked forth in bright blue plush coats with tight trousers, buckled shoes, and wide cravats above their pleated shirt frills. Peter Faneuil was a familiar sight in Boston wearing velvet and lace ruffles. Men ordered their riding clothes from England as well as their half-jack boots, silk stockings, buckskin gloves, and the "falling bands" that preceded the necktie. They imported frieze, kersey, and claret duffel for hard wear.

Before the Revolution coat lapels widened, collars rose so high that necks seemed to vanish, trousers were skintight and the more foppish trimmed their girth with corsets. A long, lean Dick Swiveler look resulted, accentuated by tall and narrow hats. But as the affectations of the early eighteenth century died out after the Revolution, men dressed more simply and their hats became truncated cones with narrow brims, a trend that led eventually to the plug hat.

The new republicanism was typified in the long trousers worn by James Madison. He disliked them heartily but satin breeches and lace ruffles had no place in the new world that had come into being. By the time of the Civil War men's attire was dull and unremarkable. There were slight variations from time to time in the cut of their coats or the width of their trousers; otherwise the picture was static until the 1960s. Like James Madison, another President—James Buchanan—scorned what he called flunkey attire. He was United States Ambassador to Britain and had not yet occupied the White House when he refused to wear knee breeches while having an audience with Queen Victoria. He donned his customary black coat, black pantaloons, dress boots, and waistcoat and cravat, merely adding a black-hilted sword. This was considered a major social error in England, although Queen Victoria merely smiled when she viewed him, simple and unadorned, in the midst of legation glitter. Waistcoats alone retained some of their early character deep into the nineteenth century. From colonial times they were a distinctive part of a man's attire—white, brocaded in gold, striped, made of silk, velvet, plaid, or flowered material. In the 1820s two were worn at times together—white velvet over rose silk, or similar combinations.

James Monroe had just been inaugurated President and New York had a population of 125,000 when Henry Sands Brooks set up shop in downtown New York and treated his seafaring customers to draughts of sherry or Medford rum from under his counter as he sold the first of the famous Brooks suits. The year was 1818. Unconsciously he was creating the American tradition of the Ivy look, to flourish on

Peter Beckford by Benjamin West (1738–1820). Gleaming silks were part of the costume of the man of affairs in the eighteenth century, and when West painted Beckford and his wife, he used the most decorative touches of the era. Puffed shirtsleeves with lace and a loosely folded lace jabot finished off the heavy silk coat with its frogged fastenings. Beckford wore his natural hair in long curls on his shoulders, an early eighteenth-century fashion. He holds in his hand a map of Jamaica, where he owned a plantation. (Left.)

Midshipman Augustus Brine (1770–1840). When Oliver Wendell Holmes cited a portrait by John Singleton Copley as an inheritance essential to family status, a number were already hanging in substantial New England mansions. Among them was this young midshipman. Augustus was only twelve when Copley painted him in 1782, but he looked much older with his proud, bold demeanor, flowing hair, frilled shirt, and the decorative buttons of the Revolutionary era. (Right.)

Henry Clay (1777–1852) by Theodore Sydney Moïse (1806–1883). Not only was Clay the great orator of his day, but he was also known as a dude and a Don Juan. When this picture was painted, the cutaway coat had been fully developed; pantaloons had taken the place of satin breeches; and wide lapels and large buttons were characteristic of the riding coat. Cravats were worn high and loose under stand-up collars. The cane and tall hat were in general use. (Above.)

The tricorne hat and redingote, reaching almost to the ankles, were generally worn by men in the 1780s. This olive-green woolen coat, with double rows of buttons and wide lapels, was high fashion at the time as were striped stockings and buckled shoes. Lace ruffles still appeared at the cuffs and neckline. The tasseled cane was an indispensable accessory. From La Galerie des Modes, Vol. IX. (Left.)

Governor George Clinton (1739–1812) by Saint-Mémin (1770–1852). America's early statesmen were sometimes the Beau Brummells of their day, and Governor George Clinton, who was Vice-President of the United States at the time of his death, was no exception. Here he wears the wide-collared coat and frilled shirt popular at the close of the eighteenth century. The ribboned queue, taking the place of peruke and wig, was his choice of headdress. Saint-Mémin, the French engraver who came to America and left a historical record in his engraved profile portraits of public figures, had just begun his work when he sketched Governor Clinton. (Left.)

the college campus, to be pinpointed in the books of famous writers from Ernest Hemingway to Mary McCarthy. As the years went on the Brooks establishment pushed the sack suit, the four-button suit, the Norfolk jacket, the Tattersall vest, the deerstalker cap, and box-cloth spats, along with other trend-setting fashions.

The matched suit with coat, waistcoat, and trousers was introduced in the 1850s, a significant step. Novel at first, this custom became universal and lasted until waistcoats became less popular in the mid-twentieth century. In 1859 the sack suit reached the market; it has never gone out of fashion. At the same time both frock and tail coats were worn with striped, plaid, or contrasting trousers. Narrow bow ties supplanted the huge cravat, and the turned-down collar the four-in-hand. The double-breasted sack suit still prevailed as trousers got narrower, top hats smaller, and the fedora, the deerstalker cap, and a high-crowned straw hat followed one another in swift succession. The Sherlock Holmes cap never became as popular in the United States as it was in Britain, where it was worn with the Norfolk jacket. The Inverness cape did not penetrate the country as a whole, but was worn with swagger at the opera or by visiting celebrities of one kind or another. Fur-lined topcoats with heavy fur collars became the established style for the man-about-town. Trousers widened again in the 1890s. The center leg-crease was popularized by the Prince of Wales, later King Edward VII. Since English tailoring was closely followed in the United States, the flawless crease became a symbol of careful grooming. Today it is considered Edwardian.

A variety of caps were worn as men became more sports-minded toward the end of the century. Tyrolean shorts and appropriate outfits appeared for mountain climbing, yachting, polo, cricket, and other exotic sports. By the time of World War I men attended church sporting fedora or panama hats. They wore their cutaways instead of the frockcoat at weddings and were no longer afraid of relaxed collars, cummerbunds, and soft-fronted shirts. By degrees they learned to be tweedy and casual, taking to the trenchcoat more readily than to the Chesterfield. In 1938 the Palm Beach suit, an American innovation, added to their comfort and good tailoring in the summer months, to be followed by a variety of light suitings. Writer Damon Runyon helped to lift the seersucker suit from crumpled nonentity to its accepted place among the summer worsteds and synthetics. Other American innovations were moccasin shoes, crêpe soles, the dinner jacket worn in place of the tail coat, and Western fashions, now linked to the mod world.

In the nineteenth century the mature man, like the mature woman, set fashions, but in the twentieth century the swing was to youth, first with college students launching Oxford bags and turtle-neck sweaters, then by the 1960s with the whirlwind march of a great army

The boardinghouse of the 1840s was a showcase for men's fashions of the period. Their cutaways and wide cravats, their lapeled waistcoats and tapering pants showed up in all variations around the parlor fireside. It was customary at that time for families, as well as individuals, to live in hotels and boardinghouses. Rents were high, and both houses and servants were scarce. Catering flourished under this system, and the cuisine often matched that of the best hotels. Men, in particular, enjoyed the good fellowship of the superior boardinghouse, and romances flourished in its carefree atmosphere.

Fashions of 1850. Men at this time often wore corsets and had pinched waists. Trousers were narrow and tapered, as they were again in the 1960s. Coattails fanned out to emphasize the narrow waistline and bulging chest. The frockcoat was as popular as the tailcoat for everyday wear, and it held its ground throughout the nineteenth century, even after the tailcoat had been relegated to formal and evening wear. The topcoat or redingote resembled the frockcoat but reached to mid-calf. Trousers were often striped and in contrasting colors. The spread of a taste for tartans is apparent in the kilted child on the ballroom floor.

Fashions of 1859. The sack suit had come into view with the dawn of the 1860s, a significant decade in American history when uniforms were more generally worn than anything else. But it has held its ground as a perennial in men's fashions down to today. In its earlier form it had a long, loose-fitting, boxy coat with wide sleeves. Tight trousers had given way to an easier cut, and lapels had shrunk to the more familiar measurements of today. The waistcoat had become a matching part of the picture, instead of being a decorative adjunct, but even with the sack suit it still showed up in striped satin, flowered brocade, Paisley prints, or in piqué. From The Gazette of Fashion, 1859.

of teddy boys, hippies, Beatles, beatniks, mods, and Bohemians of various stripes. Men's attire, long immune to change, took on strange aspects with this new development, as Savile Row yielded slightly to the push of Carnaby Street and boutiques catered to this trade in the United States. Regency dandies came next, spurning the old careless ways.

"It's the world of Byron again," said an American ambassador's wife after an evening at a fashionable ball, surveying the shoulder-length hair, the high collars, the languid air of the camp set. But Pierre Cardin, who makes five times as much from his men's fashions as he does from women's clothes, has a different view of things. "I never look backward," he says. "I design for tomorrow. My fashion is elegant and sexy for men." He supplies them with baroque coats, flowered dinner jackets, striped shirts, collars four inches high, and square hats. Meanwhile, the well-established John Weitz, an American designer who puts Roddy McDowell, Cary Grant, and George Hamilton on his list of best-dressed men, fashions contour pants that stay up without belts or suspenders, and polka-dotted shirts that please wives as well as husbands.

The rage for narrow, tapering pants, billowy satin shirts and explosive ties, for Paisley checks, Dutch cabin-boy caps, and frontier floral prints has shaken up the world of men's fashion more drastically than any innovations of the kind since the eighteenth century. Bold-patterned sports shirts and burly weaves abound on the campus, which echoes to some extent the world of the discothèque.

Even before the mod invasion Amy Vanderbilt noticed that American men were no longer afraid to wear yellow wool socks, red ties, or green suits, and of the American man she wrote that "he is no longer a dun-colored bird," proceeding to prove it by pointing out that his undergarments now have patterns rivaling Tahiti's sarong, while his sports clothes, country clothes, and bathing outfits have led to "extravagant emphasis, whipped up by the advertiser, encouraged by growing leisure, and inspired by the copying spirit of his fellow men." Travel has broken down some of the old taboos and given men easy access to London suits, Italian shoes, and French shirts. Air conditioning and electric blankets have modified his summer and winter needs.

And how does he sleep? Mostly in the raw, if a recent estimate that 60 per cent of American men have abandoned pajamas is correct. From ankle-length union suits and tentlike nightgowns with tasseled caps, they have moved through a quiet era of tailored pajamas, striped or plain, silk and monogramed, into the strange bedtime wear of the mod world. This may involve a buttonless wrap with sash, and trousers cut in the floppy judo style; ski pajamas of knitted fabric tailored like ski pants and coralled at the ankles and wrists; a coverall suit in the Winston Churchill tradition; Nehru jackets and short cotton nightshirts with red stripes; two-piece sleeping suits with golf jackets and shorts;

At Princeton's Junior Prom. A postwar generation goes into action on the college front. These young men, in the F. Scott Fitzgerald tradition, set forth for the evening wearing derby hats and Chesterfield coats. Their dinner jackets have notched or peaked lapels. Shirts are stiff, but the turndown collar is present as well as the batwing. There are still a few uniforms in sight, and prohibition is making itself strongly felt. The flapper, with bob, beads, and the mini skirts of the 1920s, is in the ascendant. Drawing by Fell Sharp from Men's Wear, 1927.

The bookstore was as good a place as any for the man about town of 1902 to start a romance with one of Harrison Fisher's seductive girls. The clear-cut jutting profile of the American man, pinpointed in innumerable ways by James Montgomery Flagg, was becoming a familiar image to the magazine-reading public. The high collar, bowler, spats, and cane, with a long Chesterfield coat, were just what the well-dressed men chose to wear at the turn of the century. Drawing by Harrison Fisher, 1902.

Checks and plaids, plus fours, and a return to the striped waistcoat of the nineteenth century are in evidence here. The cardigan or pullover sweater has become standard wear for the golf course. Collars are rounded and worn with pins. Socks are brightly patterned, caps are loudly checked; the snap brim is the style in hats. From Apparel Arts, 1934.

long trousers, short trousers, tops without bottoms, and bottoms without tops. Men's pajamas come in stripes, checks, plaids, or polka dots, and in many materials, synthetic and real, as do their high-rise socks, boxer shorts, and briefs, and the ubiquitous T shirt, with turtle or V neck.

The publicity the mod fashions have received may far outweigh the actual inroads they have made, and the noisy adherents to the strange new styles may add up to less than a major revolution in fashion. The average American male is still inclined to be conservative at heart, wearing the same old fashions in the same old way, except that his trousers may be a little narrower, his ties a trifle wider, his topcoat shortened, his hatbrim infinitesimal if he wears a hat at all, and his shoes of the slip-on variety. No maverick when there is business to be done, he adheres in general to the quiet, groomed look suitable for the board meeting, or the blue-shirted, well-pressed effect for appearing on television. The rising tide of odd styles has caused some of the biggest corporations to lay down certain clothing rules for their employees, both men and women. But when men are in the country, engaged in sports, or at the beach, it's another story. Here the new fashions may rage unchecked and even the conservative dares to be experimental.

Men have been consistently more restrained than women about their beach attire. They moved from barrel stripes to simple combinations of trunks and vests. Topless suits were taboo in the 1920s, and even in 1935 twenty men were arrested at Atlantic City for appearing without tops. In the 1940s they took to splashy Hawaiian prints, and in the 1960s to the longer legs and tighter fit of surf trunks, with corduroys in dull off-colors for deep-sea operations. Surfer swimsuits of woven fabric laced in the black, hip huggers, and tank shorts in navy nylon or silk, all gained ground, and on the mod side arose a flurry of wild stripes and plaids, along with suspendered swimsuits and vinyl vests.

Matching the daring effect in clothes are the hair styles and beards that now flourish in a manner also unparalleled since the nineteenth century. The colonials were clean-shaven and beards did not reach their full estate until the 1870s, although minor sideburns were worn during the War of 1812, and they appeared in their full, bushy glory at the time of the Civil War, when they were named after General Ambrose E. Burnside. Up to this time they had not been popular, even with farmers and men working on the frontier, although Captain John Smith had a full beard at the time of the Jamestown settlement. Later such rugged types as General Custer and Buffalo Bill were bearded men, and the Mormon fathers had patriarchal whiskers.

There was only one bearded man in President Buchanan's Cabinet, but the Civil War led to a heavy rush of whiskers and beards, which were more compatible with the rigors of army life. One variation

The elegance of the 1930s carried over into the first two years of the 1940s, and all during the decade the range of styles was unusually wide. World War II had its effect, however, and the military look, especially the Eisenhower jacket, if not de rigueur, *became extremely popular.*

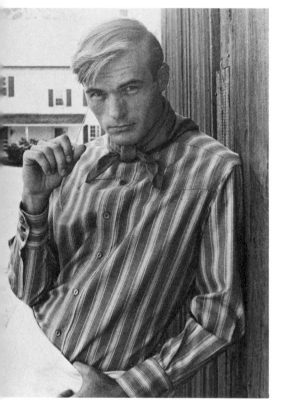

Casual attire for men has the Western look. Bill Miller of *The Village Squire* in New York City designed this trend-setting ensemble. The striped shirt is dacron and cotton in red, blue, and white stripes. The scarf, which is attached to the cadet collar, is red silk. The hipster pants are white dacron and cotton.

This double-breasted camel's-hair suit with purple lining and self-covered buttons has the long coat and flap pockets made popular by Pierre Cardin. Its shaped back has a double boxpleat, and the low-rise trousers have lapped seams at the sides and a wide belt loop.

followed another, including the spade, the imperial, the brush, the fan, the mutton chop, Horace Greeley's moth-eaten fringe, and the drooping Dundreary whiskers inspired by E. A. Sothern in the play *Our American Cousin*. Napoleon III's stylized mustache was reflected in the American imperial, and the trim Vandyke beard became the favorite of doctors and other professional men. Uncle Sam, clean-shaven in his legendary role since the War of 1812, acquired a goatee in 1858, changing his image in the eyes of the world.

American Presidents from General Grant on were bearded, until Grover Cleveland took office. One of the many complaints about Martin Van Buren's sybaritic tastes was that he laved his whiskers in eau de cologne. Rutherford B. Hayes had the longest beard of all the Presidents. James A. Garfield and General Grant both had full whiskers. President McKinley was clean-shaven, but Theodore Roosevelt and William Howard Taft had mustaches. The only man with a beard elected President after Grover Cleveland was Benjamin Harrison.

Abraham Lincoln's gaunt face was clean-shaven when he campaigned for the Presidency and bearded during his strenuous days in office. When a little girl named Grace Bedell, living in Westfield, New York, wrote to him that because his face was so thin he would look a good deal better if he wore whiskers, he answered her in October, 1860: "As to the whiskers, having never worn any, do you not think people would call it a piece of silly affectation if I were to begin now?" He grew whiskers as he was riding into office, and his became the most famous bearded face in American history.

In the 1890s Yale and Harvard students sported a combination of beard and whiskers which gave way in time to the handlebar mustache. The spread of this particular style from tip to tip was sometimes nine inches. Mustaches of one kind or another came and went in the twentieth century. A neat military type was popular during World War I. Charlie Chaplin's tiny dab of brush had some followers, but fewer than Ronald Colman's pencil-thin one. Many outdoor men nurtured mustaches that they kept well trimmed, but the custom was not universal. Now the handlebar is seen again, along with the beards of the 1960s. Another hirsute age has dawned and ancient affectations have been revived in contemporary haircuts. In the days of the Pilgrims men were warned, from the pulpit, against letting their locks flow to their shoulders, and Increase Mather advised the "haughty daughters of Zion" to refrain from "false locks and comet-like effects on their heads" when they chose to wear wigs. The Cavaliers landed with scented forelocks that they finally gave up with reluctance. The college rules at Harvard in 1655 decreed that it was not lawful to wear long hair, locks, or foretops, or to curl, crisp, part, or powder the hair. The Quakers abandoned their long hair early in the eighteenth century in favor of the periwig.

Wigs on males were an inheritance from Louis XIII, who introduced this fashion as his own hair thinned out. As early as 1675 they were legally denounced in Massachusetts and were known as "horrid bushes of vanity." There was great variety in their style and composition. The servants used goat hair, and their masters human hair, silk, mohair, or horsehair. They came in various colors, although flaxen was preferred. Usually they were bound with colored ribbons.

Feathertop wigs were delicate creations made of mallards' wings, but most of the wigs worn by men had sterner names suggestive of the military operations of the period—the campaign wig, the brigadier, the spencer, the albemarle, the Ramillies with its plaited queue. The queue marked a second stage in the use of wigs; it was simple, and better adapted to cocked hats, coats with ruffles of lace, and the buckles that came after rosettes on shoes. When the fashion of powdering the hair was introduced after 1703 wigs diminished in size and the bag wig, with the back hair enclosed in a silk bag, was used for dress wear.

Powder was blown on by bellows and the well-to-do had special wig closets in their houses for this dusty rite. At first the powder was white or gray, but dandies soon experimented with lavender, blue, and other colors. Finally a short-bobbed wig became fashionable. In fact, the "bob" was a term of men's fashion long before it was associated with women. While the guillotine was busy a short bob known as *à la victime* had a brief and grisly history.

When short hair became the Republican fashion after the French Revolution, Jefferson's followers adopted it. Wigs finally faded from sight; even the United States Army changed the fixed regulations to which it had clung and gave them up in 1808.

Recently men have been experimenting with hair styles as well as with beards, in a manner unparalleled since the eighteenth century. After the days of wigs and perukes they wore their hair long, with deep waves, stiffened with pomades and scented with strong lotions in the nineteenth century. During World War I a close military haircut preceded the crew cut that swept the college crowd a little later. Hair was closely and conservatively cut until the duck-tail, the flat-top, the butch cut, and a score of other styles came along. In the wake of the exaggerated effect of the Beatles with their Caesar cut came the dandified waves, billows, and dangling hair of 1966.

From George Washington to President Kennedy, from Valentino to Elvis Presley, hair styles have been affected by men in the public eye, and the moppish, casual effect of the Kennedys has made an impression. But their opposites, the bald-headed men, are wearing hair pieces on an unprecedented scale, and 75 per cent of the sales are to Ivy Leaguers and men under thirty-five. In four years the toupee trade has increased 75 per cent and bald-headed men are no longer ubiquitous

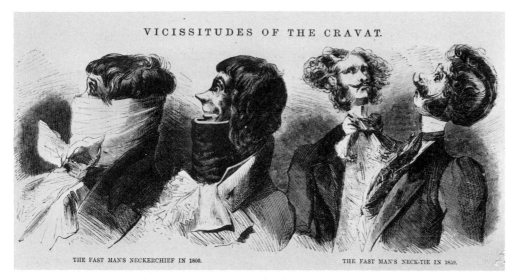

VICISSITUDES OF THE CRAVAT.

THE FAST MAN'S NECKERCHIEF IN 1800.

THE FAST MAN'S NECK-TIE IN 1859.

"Vicissitudes of the Cravat." The cravat ran a dizzy course in the nineteenth century, from the face-enveloping chokers of 1800 to the racy bow and tall, white collar of 1859. The wing collar, with a variety of spreading ties, prevailed in the late nineteenth century, to be followed by the stiff Arrow-type collar that was supplanted by the relaxed neckware of today. From Harper's Weekly, *1859.*

The long, straggling Dundreary whiskers made popular by E. A. Sothern, playing Lord Dundreary in Our American Cousin, *were among the many varieties of beards that flourished in the nineteenth century. Two other popular styles were the sideburns with mustache and the full but neatly trimmed "Ulysses S. Grant look." From* The Graphic, *1870.*

A special drinking cup, with a pronged device to keep their whiskers out of the way, was devised in the 1870s for bearded men and specifically for doctors and other professional men who cultivated the imperial beard. From Scientific American, *1872.*

in urban centers. Moreover, members of the younger set are growing their hair as enthusiastically as girls—an authentic revolution in the bearing of the male, matched to the odd garments of the period.

Although European men have made free use of perfume for years, Americans regarded this custom as effete until the late 1950s when Dana Perfumes' Canoe became popular with college youths. From this point on, cosmetics for men zoomed until the annual volume of men's "grooming aids" reached close to $500 million in 1966, three times what it was in 1963. Their colognes were put up in flasks and cocktail shakers, in heavy crystal decanters and leather bags, with names suggestive of the sporting world—of polo, tigers, golf, and yachting; of leather, tweed, and brandy. Deodorants developed status, and aerosol lathers and sprays took the place of shaving creams and soaps.

Men, too, have matched cosmetic sets now, and the great names that cater to their wives have spread nets around the masculine trade. All is designed not to impair the masculine image, and women have cultivated the idea. The mannish colognes lean on the natural oils of wood, leaves, roots, seed, fruit, and flowers. Sandalwood and rosewood are combined in scents suggestive of the forest. A dash of tobacco is mixed with other essences, and pungent citrus oil is ever present. The advertiser's message is loaded with snob appeal and is addressed to "men who know how to handle women." The Fragrance Foundation, which promotes the perfume industry in America, lists seventy-four varieties of perfume for men, ranging from the traditional Bay Rum to the "urbane, sophisticated Monsieur de Givenchy."

"Keep cologne in the glove compartment of your car, in your desk at the office. It's a quick way to refresh on hot summer days and an excellent pickup for lagging spirits," runs an ad. The Fragrance Foundation sums it all up: "A new kind of man with a new image has emerged in America, the cultured, well-groomed He-Man who has taken the big plunge into an aromatic sea of fragrance—lotions, sprays, colognes, bath oils, scented soaps, even face creams."

But standouts still remain—the strong-willed men who know what they want, and it isn't perfume. They are not susceptible to advertising or suggestion, and are equally immune to slip-on shoes and Paisley ties. But sentiment is against them. All the oracles of etiquette are in on the conspiracy. Amy Vanderbilt points out that the spicy essences used by men today are less penetrating and overpowering than the violet and geranium reek of the old-time shaving and hair lotions. Madison Avenue keeps up an insistent refrain. The farm boy who used to plaster his hair with Bay Rum and his chin with Ed Pinaud's lilac mixture can find something gentler and yet more heady now. He may also have learned that a dab of leathery cologne somewhere in the vicinity of his neck may be subtly attractive to his dancing partner.

II *The Social Image Changes*

Long before John and Abigail Adams held the first New Year's Day reception in the barnlike and unfinished President's House of 1801 there was a well-established social life in the colonies, but it was scattered, regional, and closely linked to fortune and family. With the Adams administration the focus of the social scene shifted to Washington, the seat of government, where it has remained for 166 years.

John and Abigail made no attempt to emulate the stately court of George and Martha Washington; it would not have been in character. Nevertheless, Abigail was in perfect command of the situation when she stood beside the President, who wore black velvet breeches, white waistcoat, and silver buckles. She knew the etiquette of the courts of London and Paris, and she had been close to Martha Washington during the earlier administration. John, with powdered hair and queue, merely bowed to the passersby. The day of hearty handshaking at Presidential receptions had not arrived.

The first great party giver whose reputation has survived was Dolley Madison—the official White House hostess for Jefferson as well as for her husband. Philip Hone called this early First Lady with her feathered turbans and elaborate gowns the "Queen of this new world."

245

But there were hostesses in other cities who had acquired fame in the Revolutionary period. The French alliance had brought Gallic aristocrats into the picture, with resurgent interest in manners, cuisine, and gowns. Mrs. John Jay brought all her prestige and Continental experience to bear on the political scene, and she and Madame de Lafayette set up salons that influenced the social customs of the period. Abigail Adams readily yielded the palm to Mrs. Jay who, she said, had more ease and better manners than anyone she had ever known. Her Dinner List and her Supper List were to that era what Ward McAllister's Four Hundred became to his. And no one discounted Mrs. William Bingham of Philadelphia, one of the wittiest and most worldly hostesses in American history. She could shock, amuse, and dazzle with equal skill.

The Washington parties of the early nineteenth century were not unlike the cocktail crushes of today, as Mrs. Samuel Harrison Smith has pictured them in *The First Forty Years of Washington Society*. Rooms were so crowded that no one could sit down, but manners were much the same as in other parts of the United States, except that women "were taking a station in society which is not known elsewhere." On all public occasions—whether a launching, an oration, an inauguration, in Congress, in court, or in the drawing room—they were treated with "mark'd distinction." One of their favorite gambits was to crowd into the Supreme Court, where Mrs. Smith thought they had no business to be. The rustling of their silks disturbed the justices, and when Dolley Madison showed up with a retinue of ladies the lawyers "used fewer arguments, but scattered more flowers."

When Henry Clay had the floor it was customary to hand up to the ladies in the gallery oranges tied in handkerchiefs and attached to poles. His oratory was so fascinating that none could leave, but all must be refreshed. He usually turned up at parties with a beauty clinging to either arm. Mrs. Smith's own parties, which were typical of the era, were spread over four rooms, with about 120 guests. Dancing was downstairs and supper was served upstairs, with thirty at a time seated at table, and all manner of dishes awaiting them on the sideboard, like the modern buffet.

Mrs. Smith observed that President Monroe was as exacting about form as Thomas Jefferson had been indifferent to it. He continued to wear the cocked hat of the Revolution until his death and he stood stiffly at attention when receiving the legation ministers. Jefferson had dismayed the political hostesses with his disregard for precedence and his pell-mell system of letting his guests find their own partners before settling down at a round table where none was above or below the salt. He gave up all receptions except on New Year's Day and July 4, but in spite of the informality at the President's House during his administration, the finest French cuisine was served all the year round.

Moreover, he established the custom of the President shaking hands with guests instead of bowing, a social gesture that became a scourge when six thousand visitors trooped through the East Room.

Mishaps were common when levees were held, such as the theft in 1860 of General Winfield Scott's pocketbook in a Presidential drawing room. The climactic and unforgettable event, however, was Andrew Jackson's inauguration. After watching the mob that flowed through the White House in 1829, Mrs. Smith later reflected: "The noisy and disorderly rabble in the President's House brought to my mind descriptions I had read of the mobs in the Tuileries and at Versailles." Many of the women wore gowns straight from Paris, but in general the crowd was a tattered army. Once inside, after creating an impenetrable jam outdoors with their carriages, wagons, and carts, they scrambled, fought, and romped. Cut glass and china flew in all directions. Women fainted and men brawled and got bloody noses. Half of the guests climbed out through the windows.

Jackson's second inauguration was notable for its decorum. By that time, Mrs. Smith noted, European habits, hours, and fashions were taking firm hold in America. Gaiety and luxury were on the rise. Sophistication was beginning to touch the world where girls wrote poetry and treasured albums full of paintings; where they played the harp or sang to their own tinkling piano accompaniments. Drawing comparisons between 1846 and 1966 a contemporary Washington society columnist pointed out that today is like yesterday, except that the teas have become cocktail parties; that the British ambassador in 365 days had only five evenings at home; and that the French embassy now needs eighty thousand dollars a year for entertaining. Otherwise things seem to be much the same—the strategy, the cast of characters, the plots and intrigues. There is one colossal difference: instead of being primarily engaged in running the country, Congress is now involved in the problems of the world. Washington is an international city.

Inevitably the capital down the years has reflected the manners and customs of the grass roots, as well as of the historic families of the various states, but after World War I it assumed an identity of its own, irrespective of its social links with New York, Boston, Philadelphia, Baltimore, and Charleston. Since World War II it has had a sophisticated and articulate society of its own, with international links of every degree, in addition to its traditional cliff dwellers.

In colonial times Virginia and Massachusetts laid claim to being the intellectual centers of the nation. Philadelphia, with its sumptuous parties and its *conversaziones*, as its literary evenings were called, combined social and intellectual interests. John Adams, always the advocate of Boston's pre-eminence, said that he looked in vain for a single cultured man in New York City at the time of the Revolution. Although

The arrival of the Great Western Steam Ship at New York
City on April 23, 1838, was the occasion for beating of drums
and rejoicing in the streets, slightly marred by the fact that the
Sirius had arrived the day before. The first ships to cross the
Atlantic under steam, the forerunners of the great passenger
liners of the twentieth century, they heralded a new era in
commerce.

The people of many nations poured into
the United States at the close of the
Civil War. Their first encounter with
the new civilization was at Castle
Garden, the circular building at the
Battery that was the landing station
before Ellis Island came into use.
Farmers came East to enlist the services
of the immigrants. Employers sat on
benches watching for likely maids. This
great groundswell went on for the next
half century, helping to populate the
country and quicken industry. "The
Labor Exchange," from Harper's
Weekly, 1865.

New York Crystal Palace. This glass-
and-iron building with wooden floors
was built for America's first World's
Fair, which opened in 1853 and
illustrated the industrial advance of
the United States. Designed by George
Carstenson and Charles Geldenmeister,
it was modeled after London's Crystal
Palace. It stood close to the reservoir
at Fifth Avenue and Forty-second Street,
and was a glittering wonder until it
burned to the ground in fifteen minutes
in 1858. Lithograph by F. F. Palmer,
published by N. Currier in 1853.

to some it seemed like a jungle filled with savages, impartial observers could find taste, culture, and discrimination among its citizens. Actually, New York by the early nineteenth century had become more worldly and frivolous than Boston. Yet there was nothing pretentious about the Dutch in colonial New York. The Knickerbocker families that had settled along the Hudson lived without show, in substantial comfort, dining at the unfashionable early hours they preferred, and ignoring the social pretensions that were gathering fast around them. With their own manners and customs, they resisted external pressures and kept their heavy accent longer than any of the other colonials. The Dutch were not among those who gadded about town, spending their money on clothes or such "unheard of luxuries as tooth powder and beautifying lotions." Eyebrows went up in the Dutch community when Maria de Peyster Spratt bought a coach and four, the first owned by any woman in New York.

The Civil War stripped Washington of some of its greatest hostesses and beauties from the South, but it left perhaps the most brilliant, politically potent, and ambitious hostess in American history at the troubled court of Mary Lincoln—Kate Chase Sprague, the daughter of Salmon Portland Chase. Her parties made history because of their style and her influence over men of affairs.

When the war ended a period of frantic entertaining began. New York had six hundred balls in the first year and in every northern city relief from the Spartan days of suffering was expressed in entertainment and high living. Fortunes had been made during and after the war and such wealth as the country had never known flowed into the coffers. Banking, land, coal, oil, iron, railroads, cattle, grain, and mining opened up golden vistas, one by one. Business dynasties took shape as railroad tracks were extended across the country; as the gold rush of 1849 made millionaires of miners; as oil gushed for John D. Rockefeller.

The wave of high living had set in before the war. As Lucius Beebe, chronicler of extravagant social gestures, has put it: "After the gold rush grand pianos and diamond brooches, silk hats and frock coats, magnums of champagne, thoroughbred horses with silver-trimmed harnesses, stylish bonnets and gowns from Paris, and an urban style of living complete with grand opera and cotillions suddenly flowered in lonely gulches and desolate deserts where only a year before the sagebrush and rattlesnake held sway."

Slaving housewives, who had cooked for the miners, slung hash, and toiled to prepare meals of beans and sourdough biscuits, suddenly assumed the airs of *grandes dames* in Newport, Beebe pointed out. Horny-handed miners "commanded vintage wines while playing poker with stacks of gold double eagles in sumptuous clubroms." Champagne and caviar had unquestionably reached the mining towns via Wells Fargo & Company, and a moneyed aristocracy was in the making.

The narrow island of Manhattan had become a plot of gold. Land was at the root of much of the wealth amassed in the early days, as it is now. It yielded the lumber, the foods, the oil, the metals needed to build up the country. Great stretches were appropriated and became rich investments for their owners. When the Civil War began the population of New York City was 814,000 and its real estate was valued at more than $398 million. Today 67 per cent of the nation's population is jammed into 9 per cent of its acreage and 130 million people inhabit the 224 communities that are officially classified as metropolitan. But there are still great wide open spaces in the United States.

After the Civil War the nation hummed with factories, mills, and new industries to meet the demands of its prosperous population. Both before and after the war cotton had been a major factor in prosperity. Eli Whitney's cotton gin had raised production from 487,000 pounds a year in 1793 to fantastic levels, and the wheels turned fast in New England to process it. By 1840 there were 1,200 cotton factories in the country and two-thirds of them were in New England, with the farmers' daughters getting their first taste of factory work at Lowell and elsewhere. Power looms were turned out in quantity and 2,250,000 spindles fed an insatiable market at this time.

But the postwar days were blighted by corruption, profiteering, gambling, and fast living, which was halted by the panic of 1873 and the three-year depression that followed. Before the country had recovered economically the Centennial Exposition of 1876 drew attention to the strides America had made in a century. The railroad, the steamship, the telegraph, the sewing machine, illuminating gas, and countless other developments had changed the way of life. The telephone was just coming into use. Typewriters were on the market, although still as curiosities. George M. Pullman was revolutionizing railroad travel.

It was becoming clear that the United States was in the process of emerging as potentially the richest country in the world. Railroads, grain, and metals provided ceaseless excitement on the market. Since the gold scare of the late 1860s the fever of speculation had mounted and messengers crowded the vestibules and aisles surrounding the Gold Room in the Stock Exchange. Wall Street was becoming a symbol abroad. Meanwhile, labor power was gathering force and the half-day holiday law enacted in the late 1880s promised more leisure for workers in all fields.

An unending army of men and women poured through Castle Garden and quickly became part of America's rising economy—130,000 a year in the 1820s, 540,000 in the 1830s, and close to 700,000 in the

1880s. This explosive body was destined to found great fortunes, to enrich the nation's culture, to diffuse their traditions, hopes, ambitions, and hard work. All through the first quarter of the twentieth century the invasion went on and 800,000 passed through Ellis Island in 1921. The influx dwindled after that and, with immigration restrictions, 1931 was the first year in American history when the number of emigrants exceeded arrivals from abroad. The ghettos were changing in character. They were becoming Negro rather than Italian and Jewish. By 1966 the population of New York City exceeded eight million and the nation as a whole had 196,300,000 inhabitants.

With all these forces at work the United States by the 1880s led the rest of the world with men of great wealth. In 1844 fewer than a thousand Americans had fortunes exceeding $100,000, but Cornelius Vanderbilt, Peter Cooper, A. T. Stewart, and Pierre Lorillard had rolled up more than a million each, great wealth for the era. The word "millionaire" was applied first to Lorillard, who had made his fortune on snuff and cigars. Except for the Rothschilds and the Krupps there were few millionaires abroad, while the United States had its Astors, Vanderbilts, Goulds, and Rockefellers, with successive generations running through the nineteenth and twentieth centuries. Such men as Leland Stanford, Russell Sage, Collis P. Huntington, Andrew Carnegie, and Charles M. Schwab made great individual fortunes and were internationally known. By World War I there were fourteen thousand American millionaires. The number shrank to hundreds after the Depression but rose to approximately thirteen thousand in the 1950s and to ninety thousand in the 1960s, with tycoons of a new kind on the horizon.

By the 1880s a good percentage of the nation's wealth had passed into the hands of its women, and by the 1950s they owned 70 per cent of it. Because they lived longer than men they had inherited more than 80 per cent of the life insurance, and owned two-thirds of all privately held government bonds and mutual savings bank accounts, as well as half of the corporate stock. In the 1880s the unmarried women of Massachusetts had $29 million on deposit in savings banks, and the Drexel girls of Philadelphia were the three wealthiest unmarried women in the country. Doris Duke and Barbara Hutton surpassed them a half century later, but Mrs. Hetty Green outplayed them all, with an inherited fortune augmented by her own shrewd operations. With more than $100 million she lived in squalor, a well-known figure on Wall Street, scuttling around in shabby black and outsmarting the best of the financiers.

Hetty lived in the party era, when dowagers gave magnificent balls and dinners with the fortunes that her competitors on Wall Street had amassed. But the only party she was ever known to give was at

The fashionable Gem Saloon of 1854 was as noted for having the largest mirror in New York as the Hoffman House Bar was for having Bouguereau's painting of a nude surrounded by satyrs. The clock under glass has nymphs and cherubs, and the curtained booths to the left suggest the rollicking night life of the period. Next door to the Broadway Theater, the Gem Saloon was popular with stage stars and with politicians fighting a movement to introduce prohibition into New York State. These earnest customers, standing at a slight tilt, seem to be agreeing that what might do in Maine would not do for New York. Lithograph by A. Fay.

The new millionaires of the 1880s watched the market closely. In their clubs, in hotel lobbies, and on the Stock Exchange they followed the ebb and flow of their fortunes. Gold, oil, mining, steel, and railroad stocks kept changing hands, and the grain and meat-packing houses of the Middle West were a new vein of riches. The financiers lounged in their seats, smoking cigars, seemingly casual and at ease, but keen as hawks in their observation. It was part of the game to refrain from showing triumph or dismay. From Harper's Magazine, 1886.

The grain elevator on the Chicago River, 1866, represented the expanding resources of the Middle West as agriculture and commerce boomed after the Civil War. The McCormick reaper paved the way for the quick harvesting of grain, and the new canals, railroads, and highways linked the prairies with metropolitan markets. Fortunes were made as farming was mechanized and stock was bred for meat-packing purposes.

The Easter Parade on Fifth Avenue was a leisurely social rite in
the 1890s, not the crowded spectacle that it is today. Top hats and
bowlers, hansom cabs, flowered hats, and trailing skirts were part
of the street scene outside the Windsor Hotel, later burned to the
ground with great loss of life. First commented on in 1883, the
Easter Parade was an established tradition within a decade.

Women patrons of the Fifth Avenue Bank in the Gay Nineties.
When it became apparent to the nation's bankers that much of the
country's wealth was passing into the hands of widows and daughters,
the Fifth Avenue Bank set the pace by giving them their own
parlor and special tellers to advise them on financial matters. With
such financiers as Hetty Green around, the advice may not have been
greatly needed, but they enjoyed the Gold Room and a friendly
chat while waiting for the grandfather clock to tell them that it
was time for lunch at Sherry's. Some had a second sense about
investments, having listened to much financial talk by their millionaire
fathers. The bankers treated them with all due respect when they
drove down from their homes to attend personally to their banking.

the Plaza Hotel—a gold-plate, ten-course dinner with wine to launch her daughter Sylvia in society. Immediately afterward she returned to her dilapidated roost in Hoboken, costing forty dollars a month, and resumed her life of rags, tatters, and mush. But all Wall Street knew that Hetty could have given the party of the decade, had she cared for ostentation—or for spending money.

Instead, she sat on the cold stone floor of her bank and counted her dollar bills with the claws of a fanatical miser. Hetty felt no need to join the parade of women with trailing skirts and winged hats who were besieging the Fifth Avenue Bank in the 1890s. This bank had wakened to the fact that much of the nation's wealth belonged to women, and was wooing its owners with a practical form of flattery. Special tellers had been assigned to train them in the intricacies of depositing their fortunes and handling them with skill. The grateful dowagers were assigned a special Ladies Parlor until 1910, when they qualified for more luxurious quarters known as the Gold Room. Here they rested on damask chairs, with potted plants around them, and a grandfather clock to remind them that it was time for lunch at Sherry's.

Half a century later, in 1966, the old idea was revived a few doors away on Fifth Avenue, but with a difference, as women with accounts of twenty-five thousand dollars and up banked in a setting of fine eighteenth-century French furniture. The Ladies Salon of La Banque Continentale, a branch of the Franklin National Bank, was luring them in with Louis XVI armchairs, gilt settees in pink-and-gold brocade, tulipwood marquetry, and Sèvres plaques, soothingly arranged against glazed blue walls hung with Fragonards. They had Aubusson rugs and Minton china for good measure, but beyond all that their white-and-gold engraved checks in gold containers were the most chaste and costly ever seen in the banking world.

The formality of the 1880s merged smoothly into the plushy splendor of the 1890s. The great fortunes amassed in the two preceding decades were being spent in princely fashion. Oil wells, mines, railroads were discussed in the Windsor and St. Nicholas hotels, in the Palace and the Palmer House. The millionaires in San Francisco or Chicago not only matched but sometimes outdid the New York breed when it came to worldly possessions. All had their own private ballrooms, and their art collections were being assembled on expert advice. Genealogical research was pursued in a quest for crests and heraldic insignia. To have one's own pew at Grace Church or St. Thomas's was a status symbol of the era, and clubs were sacred retreats. Only a few years earlier, the family of Edwin Augustus Stevens, inventor and engineer, accompanied by liveried servants, had crossed the Hudson from Hoboken in a barge lined with plum velvet, to attend services in

St. Paul's Chapel. Castle Stevens, their family home, was a forty-six-room manor completed in 1856.

Henry Adams found the nineteenth-century American woman much better company than her husband, who seemed to him to be lacking in wit and to be altogether too preoccupied with business matters. Absorbed in the game of making money, intent on acquiring possessions, he lived in a world of opulence that embraced châteaus on Fifth Avenue and villas in Newport, private railroad cars and yachts, great masters on the walls and gold plate on the dinner table, boxes at the Metropolitan Opera and seasonal trips abroad, hunting, racing at Saratoga, and the coaching parades. The Anglophile spirit glowed as the absorbed hedonists haunted Sotheby's and Christie's, followed the Tattersall sales, or were seen in the royal enclosure at Ascot. On July 4 Andrew Carnegie fêted the reluctant Highlanders at Skibo Castle, his shooting lodge on the Dornoch Firth with its 365 windows and thundering pipe organ. In America he helped to popularize the craze for the Scottish shooting box, where Americans shivered in their beds as well as in the heather, but were proud of the grouse they brought down and the salmon they caught in the burns.

The opera was in its heyday and the Diamond Horseshoe blazed with tiaras. Carriage doors were flung open by liveried footmen as the box-holders came out in their velvet cloaks, jewels flashing, aigrettes waving from towering pompadours. The money grubbers responsible for it all looked handsome, staid, and sometimes bored in their top hats, swinging opera capes, and white kid gloves. Ward McAllister had pinpointed the Four Hundred who could fit into Mrs. Astor's drawing room, and had finally given his list to the press in 1892. It was no surprise to anyone, since the nominees were the people who turned up at all the leading parties in any event, but it was a label that lasted for years. The list has lengthened and broadened considerably since then. The Four Hundred outlived the Patriarchs, a group also founded by McAllister. The Patriarchs were twenty-five socially impeccable men who censored guest lists, to the consternation of maneuvering mothers. Theirs was the ultimate test of social acceptance.

At this time social rivalry was at its peak, with Mrs. William Astor in total command. Dark-haired Caroline Schermerhorn Astor, cold and queenly, was death to social climbers. Her town house, her villa at Newport, her country place at Rhinebeck were the inviolable ramparts of social assurance. She yielded only with reluctance to the upstart Vanderbilts from Staten Island when Mrs. William K. Vanderbilt gave a costume party in 1883 in her new château on Fifth Avenue that even Mrs. Astor could not afford to overlook, for the sake of her four daughters—Emily, Helen, Charlotte, and Caroline—if not for her own. It was the great Caroline's custom to receive her guests in front of a life-sized portrait of herself, and in her old age, as the mists closed in on her, she continued to welcome imaginary guests long since dead, like Madame Jumel, living the days of Napoleon all over again in her lonely mansion overlooking the Hudson.

International weddings enlivened the social picture, Jennie Jerome having set the fashion when she married Lord Randolph Churchill in the 1870s. Four thousand uninvited guests stood outside the church in 1895 for the wedding of Anna Gould and the Marquis de Castellane. Victor Herbert's twenty-piece orchestra played at the reception in a forest of flowers. The Marquis soon spent $12 million of his wife's fortune on travel and palaces, race horses, and bibelots. Moreover, he made Anna unhappy, although she smiled on her wedding day, unlike Consuelo Vanderbilt, who was tear-stained during her gorgeous nuptials at St. Thomas's. Although in love with Winthrop Rutherford, her mother had forced her to marry the Duke of Marlborough.

St. Thomas's and St. Patrick's Cathedral had become the focal point of the Easter Parade, one of the sights of the metropolis. Each year it gained in status as women with trailing gowns and enormous hats walked to church with their top-hatted husbands, wearing yellow kid gloves, while the Avenue glowed with flowers and the feeling of springtime. Bustles were waning but leg-of-mutton sleeves billowed out with regal splendor. An occasional covert coat was cutting in on the historic Prince Albert. Not to go to church on Easter morning was to count oneself out of the social swim. A half century later the parade would still draw crowds, but it had lost all standing as a social event.

The parties that were held all through the 1890s left their echoes down the years. Fortunes were spent on these occasions. The public had an outside view of them through the detailed newspaper accounts of the revels, triumphs, and scandals of the glitter set. It did not cheer the slum dwellers to read of the gold favors and diamond necklaces, and explosive forces were beginning to seethe below the surface. Meanwhile, the comfortable middle class continued to enjoy comparative affluence, getting the best they could out of life according to their means and standards. Many were able to afford Irish or German maids, and one good carriage, even if they could not aspire to the staffs of twenty-five who occupied entire floors in some of the Newport villas.

The dinner parties of the rich were interminable, with ten courses, all manner of exotic foods and vintage wines, served on gold or silver plate, with the finest of crystal and china, and smothering waves of blossoms. Earlier in the century Fredrika Bremer, the Swedish author, had reported disgustedly on the dinner parties she had attended

Isabella Stewart Gardner, "Mrs. Jack," as portrayed by John Singer Sargent. Mrs. Gardner was as noted for her parties as she was for her Venetian palace in Boston and the art collection she assembled there with the help of Bernard Berenson. Sargent, Whistler, Henry James, and other art and literary authorities were among her intimate friends. Sargent made eight attempts to paint her and was about to give up when Mrs. Gardner reminded him that nine was Dante's mystic number. He persuaded her to take her pearls with the ruby pendant from her neck and drape them around her waist. She wore a severely plain black gown with deep décolletage that silhouetted her famous figure. The painting was much discussed, and Mrs. Gardner would not permit it to be exhibited until after her death, because her husband disliked the talk it had caused.

Mrs. Potter Palmer, one of America's internationally known hostesses, was noted for her jewels, especially a pink pearl as large as a hazelnut which she often wore as a pendant attached to a seven-strand collar made up of 2,268 pearls. It became almost as famous as the Hope diamond was to be later. She combined tiaras, stomachers, and necklaces after the lavish fashion of the 1890s, and by the turn of the century her jewel collection was rated one of the most distinctive in the world.

Consuelo Vanderbilt (Duchess of Marlborough) with her son, Lord Ivor Spencer-Churchill, as painted by Giovanni Boldini. One of the great beauties and noted hostesses of her era, she was forced into her ducal alliance by an ambitious mother, and her grief was visible on her wedding day. Later she obtained a divorce and married Jacques Balsan. Her long, graceful lines and swanlike neck made her an ideal subject for Boldini, who influenced the course of fashion by veering away from the curvaceous effects of the 1890s and giving length and fluidity to the figure.

on a visit to America. "Is there in this world anything more wearisome, more dismal, more intolerable, more indigestible, more stupefying, more unbearable, anything more calculated to kill both soul and body, than a great dinner in New York?" Fredrika wrote. She complained of the utter silence that prevailed while the guests worked their way through hors d'oeuvres, fish, entrées, roast, birds, salad, and dessert.

The star-spangled parties earlier in the century were the Boz Ball given in 1842 for Charles Dickens, with decorations inspired by *Pickwick Papers*, and *tableaux vivants* from *Oliver Twist* and *Nicholas Nickleby*, and the ball in 1864 for Baron Renfrew, later King Edward VII, held in the Academy of Music in New York on the eve of the Civil War. These historic events were followed by an endless succession of private parties in Delmonico's, Sherry's, and in the mansions of Fifth Avenue, Newport, Lake Forest, and San Francisco.

One of the showiest was arranged in 1873 by Ward McAllister, when drugged swans swam in a thirty-foot artificial lake enclosed in a gold cage for the amusement of seventy guests dining in a bower of violets. But the most daring of all the entertainments was the horse-back dinner given at Sherry's in 1903 by C. K. G. Billings to celebrate the opening of his $200,000 stable. His thirty-six guests from the New York Riding Club rode their horses in to dinner with miniature tables attached to the pommels of their saddles. The horses had been brought up in the freight elevator to a woodland scene, with sodded floor, and bright-plumaged birds in the trees. The diners sipped their champagne from tubes connected with the saddlebags, and ate course after course on their restless mounts. The horses dined afterward from fancy troughs and all the waiters were dressed as grooms. Later Mrs. Astor gave a victory ball—her Gobelin tapestries in the background—that opened with a hobbyhorse quadrille. This time the horses were not live, although covered with genuine hides. The dancers, in riding costume, appeared to be mounted, and once again Mrs. Astor had scored with a much-discussed party.

Mrs. Pierre Lorillard Ronalds, a friend of the Prince of Wales, lit up the scene in New York with a great costume ball where she appeared as "Music." The harp in her hair was lit with tiny gas jets, a prelude to the electrically lit gowns of 1967. But the two great balls of the era—both winding up in a haze of criticism and confusion—were the Bradley Martin ball of 1897 and the James Hazen Hyde ball of 1905. Five thousand orchids with concealed electric bulbs, a band of fifty, and waiters with powdered wigs and knee breeches were features of the Bradley Martin ball, held at the newly opened Waldorf-Astoria. Theodore Roosevelt, then assistant police commissioner, was present and the suckling pig of which he was so fond was served. Mrs. Bradley Martin, costumed as Mary Stuart, wore a priceless ruby necklace that

The Social Image Changes

had belonged to Marie Antoinette. August Belmont turned up in gold-inlaid steel armor from the Metropolitan Museum. Harry Lehr's Louis XV costume was studded with jewels from Tiffany's. Three George Washingtons were on the scene and Mrs. Astor came as a Venetian lady, with $200,000 worth of jewels sparkling on her dark blue velvet gown.

The reverberations were severe, for times were bad and the public was losing its good-humored interest in high-life display. The Hyde ball in Sherry's was the last of the great masquerades of the period. The ballroom represented the court at Versailles and statuary was brought from Paris in the interest of realism. Blankets of roses festooned arches, screens, and trellises, and the floor was carpeted with petals. Réjane gave readings from Racine. Mrs. Clarence Mackay impersonated Adrienne Lecouvreur as Phèdre, wearing silver cloth studded with turquoises. Mrs. Stuyvesant Fish arrived with sixty guests, and immediately became the personality of the evening.

Harry Lehr, who played up to Mrs. Fish as McAllister did to Mrs. Astor, was responsible for the Monkey Dinner, not a particularly popular affair. A pet monkey belonging to Joseph Leiter was introduced as a Corsican prince and was seated at the table to dine with the guests. Animals played a considerable role in these Victorian revels. Dogs, monkeys, birds, horses, swans, frogs—all were used at one time or another. Mrs. W. E. D. Stokes made her guests jump when she unleashed her strange favors, and bullfrogs came hopping out of grass baskets, to the consternation of everyone present. One Newport hostess rode along Bellevue Avenue with a monkey and a pig in her victoria. Mrs. Jack Gardner, who always said that she liked animals better than she did human beings, drove along Beacon Street with two lion cubs beside her. She tied a red ribbon round the neck of one, who was known thereafter as the Society Lion, and she walked around the zoo leading a young lion by the mane. Another daring guest rode into a ballroom in a small cart drawn by a trained seal.

In 1899 Randolph Guggenheimer gave a dinner at the Waldorf at which nightingales sang in a grove of rose trees, and hothouse grapes hung from arbors. The favors were jeweled matchboxes and vinaigrettes. These trifles often added up to small fortunes in themselves—black pearls in the heart of oysters, cigars rolled in hundred dollar bills, shepherdess crooks with golden handles, jeweled cotillion favors from Tiffany's. Men picked up gold cigarette cases at random and girls got Paris hats in decorative bandboxes. When Mrs. George Gould announced the engagement of her daughter Marjorie to Anthony J. Drexel, Jr., the souvenirs were jeweled pins, charms, and rings for the women, jeweled scarfpins for the men.

Another type of party was popular with the sportier characters

259

The Social Image Changes

of the era. For instance, Jim Brady was responsible for a Jack Horner pie dinner that caused much talk. As each guest pulled a satin ribbon attached to a mammoth pie, the sides fell apart and a girl wearing a satin armband, and nothing else, stepped out. It was an era of rowdy floor shows when the traditional gesture was to drink champagne from a girl's slipper and to wallow in bird-and-bottle suppers. Meanwhile, the conservatives held their ground in New York and other cities. The assemblies of New York, Boston, and Philadelphia, the Creole Ball of New Orleans, the Richmond German, the Bachelors Cotillion of Baltimore, and the St. Cecilia of Charleston remained solid links with the statelier past. In 1901 the Junior League was organized by Mrs. Charles Cary Rumsey, who was then Mary Harriman, the daughter of Edward H. Harriman. Her plan was to give focus and useful purpose to the social round of the debutantes. She developed a program of welfare service that was copied in other cities.

In the eighteenth century girls came out at fifteen or sixteen and married early. In the nineteenth century debutante age rose to eighteen. Today, more often than not, the debutante parties are run by specialists but few reach the peak of expenditure they did in the 1920s, when costs ran as high as $100,000. Helen Lee Eames Doherty, daughter of Henry L. Doherty, gave a dozen Ford cabriolets with hunting scenes painted on panels to her most intimate friends when she came out. The debut of Anne Ford, daughter of Henry Ford II, cost $280,000 in 1961.

A swimming pool covered with orchids, a country estate converted to a miniature impression of Versailles were part of the period picture, but the most publicized of all American debutantes, Brenda Diana Duff Frazier, found her $50,000 party at the Ritz-Carlton Hotel in 1938 a bittersweet occasion. She drank Coca-Cola and milk while her 1,240 guests consumed a thousand quarts of champagne. Shivering, with a temperature of 102, she was wrapped in a tablecloth by Douglas Fairbanks, Jr., as the evening ended in illness and disillusionment. "I hated every minute of my debut," she confessed nearly a quarter of a century later, after two marriages, a suicide attempt, and a firm decision to keep her daughter, Victoria Kelly, from having a formal debut.

On the same night that Brenda, a great beauty and heiress to $4 million came out in New York, Mrs. Eleanor Roosevelt's niece and namesake danced the Virginia reel at the White House, with President Roosevelt looking on approvingly. Eleanor later announced: "Coming-out parties are a racket, though a pleasant one." She was the first girl to have her debut at the White House since Helen Taft in 1910.

One of the most unusual of coming-out parties, however, was held in St. Louis in 1950 when Sallie Marie Busch, great-great-grand-daughter of the founder of the Anheuser-Busch brewery, was formally introduced to society in the thirty-room house on the old farm that had belonged to Ulysses S. Grant. The 160-foot terrace was walled and roofed over and Sallie's guests danced to four bands. The Princeton Triangle Club was present and all the guests engaged in a plastic snowball fight. They feasted on roast pig and drank beer from photoelectric dispensers that caught the foamy gush from sensitized spigots.

Such individualistic rites as these faded in the 1950s and 1960s, and debuts tended to follow a conservative pattern. The International Cotillion of recent years has freshened up the picture with an assemblage of the young beauties of many nations in New York, a significant change on the social front expressive of the cosmopolitan spirit of the 1960s.

After World War I a new crop of millionaires sprang up, with fortunes made in chain stores, hotels, insurance, real estate, motor cars, supermarkets, tobacco, oil, shipping, cereals, steel, cosmetics, and a fast-moving range of products fitted to a mercurial age. The old mansions gave way to costly duplex cooperatives. The Tudor villas were augmented by glass and aluminum showcases. The golden children and their elders flitted from Hawaii to Rome, following the seasons, the current sport, the latest fad. Rococo furnishings surrendered to the modern, and then were picked up again for period interest. Parties were free and easy; guest lists were casually prepared, and gate crashers had open hunting. New hostesses emerged, but none with the authority of Mrs. Astor, or the candor or force of Mrs. Fish, whose acerbic wit often startled the two hundred guests assembled in her colonial dining room. She encouraged wit and brains and cared nothing for protocol. Mrs. Fish was, perhaps, the grandmother of the jet set.

It took individualists like Mrs. Fish and Mrs. Evalyn Walsh McLean to imprint their personalities on their generation. Mrs. McLean, a true daughter of the West who had moved from the mines of Colorado to the inner social circle of Washington, spent forty thousand dollars on the dinner party with which she celebrated the acquisition of the Hope diamond. She flew in four thousand yellow lilies from London on this occasion. Another time she had the Ringling Circus stage a special performance for her son. "Friendship," her home outside Washington, was the scene of an endless succession of parties involving Presidents and politicians. The longest continuous party of the 1920s—and there were many—was given at her town house in Washington during the Harding administration. It lasted for three days and three nights, with dancing to Meyer Davis' orchestra.

The Depression brought an end to this sort of high living, and when it was over fortunes had evaporated, fashion houses had died, yachts and private railroad cars were white elephants, servants were a vanishing species, and young brides were more interested in washing

Madame Gabrielle Réjane, star of the James Hazen Hyde ball held at Sherry's in 1905. This was the last major masquerade of the age of opulence as a rising tide of social protest swept the land. It was also the first of the great balls to get the photographic coverage lavished on such events today. Joseph Byron and five assistants took 189 pictures, mirroring the extravagances of the night for posterity. Whitney Warren, the architect, had converted Sherry's ballroom into a facsimile of one wing of the Palace of Versailles. Flowers and statuary had been imported for realism, and smothering masses of roses, with tiny lights winking in their hearts, covered trellises, arbors, and canopies. Madame Réjane, carried in by sedan chair, gave her readings from Racine on a floor lined with rose petals. The entire ballet of the Metropolitan Opera danced in the classical milieu but wound up the night with the can-can. Photograph by Byron.

C. K. G. Billings' Horseback Dinner at Sherry's in 1903 was the most unusual party in the history of New York. Thirty-six members of the New York Riding Club rode their horses into a ballroom converted into a woodland scene with sodded floor. They dined from small tables attached to their saddles and drank their champagne through tubes connected with the saddlebags. The waiters were dressed as grooms, and the horses were fed from troughs after their masters had taken course after course while trying to steady their restless mounts.

Grand Ball at the Academy of Music in honor of the Prince of Wales. The socially elect, drawn from all parts of the country, turned out in their crinolines and finest array in 1860 for the future king, Edward VII of Britain, traveling incognito as Baron Renfrew. Such was the crush that part of the floor collapsed at his feet, and the first dance had to be dropped altogether. This left forever unsolved the much debated question of his first choice of a partner. Carpenters went to work, but between hammering and the crush, little dancing was done; yet it became one of the most famous balls in American history.

machines than in coming-out parties or gowns by Balmain. The common man was coming into his own; the so-called privileged were learning to take their medicine. World War II spun another cycle, and when it was over the social pace became fast, furious, and noticeably offbeat. As the echoes of the parties of the 1890s have reverberated down the years, the twentieth century has reached another pitch with more varied guest lists and a wider spread of interest. No longer is it the Four Hundred. In 1966 it was Truman Capote's 540. Parties had some of the old wham if less of the old formality.

By the 1950s and 1960s animals came back and Elsa Maxwell, most persistent of party impresarios until her death, brought on a baby elephant and a cow. Others followed suit. "A Night in Bombay" on a Long Island estate sported dancing girls with cast marks, British officers in tropical helmets, and a baby elephant munching carrots in a cart. Four hundred guests squatted on cushions on the floor between dances, and 100,000 iridescent lights turned the night to glitter. At another Long Island fiesta, camels greeted the guests in a silk-festooned tent. But all the Arabian Nights' dreams were outdone by New York City's "April in Paris" balls, which soon became known as the biggest and flashiest charity balls in the world.

Thirteen hundred guests wandered through a half dozen rooms in the Waldorf at the 1965 ball. In a Deauville setting white chicken-wire horses, draped with the racing colors of French and American stables, recalled the old hobbyhorse quadrille. It took 170 waiters, 1,000 bottles of wine, 500 pounds of chicken cooked in Calvados, 800 pounds of filet of beef, 300 pounds of cheese, and 600 heads of Boston lettuce to refresh the guests—statistics that might well have dismayed Mrs. Astor. In the same year Boston played it cool and traditionally with its Golden Trumpet Ball at $1,000 a box, celebrating the eighty-fifth birthday of the Boston Symphony Orchestra. Mrs. John F. Kennedy, in a strapless pink gown by Patou, was the evening's star, while waiters in Edwardian costume, mostly Harvard students, served the guests on gold plate.

The tendency to link parties with historical backgrounds was strong in the 1960s, illustrated by the stately Kennedy expedition to Mount Vernon by boat, and the party held with the pillars and statuary of the Metropolitan Museum of Art for a setting. A dinner party may well be the *apéritif* for an art gallery showing, though it is just as likely to be held on a ferryboat circling Manhattan, in pubs or discothèques, on Lake Forest estates, or in San Francisco town houses.

But the party to end all parties was Truman Capote's black-and-white masquerade at the Plaza Hotel in the winter of 1966. The guest of honor was Mrs. Philip Graham, the publisher, and those invited represented the arts and the political world. There were current social celebrities and also many of the Old Guard. Jewels, feathers, lace, fur, and velvet were spun together in masks costing up to six hundred dollars. The author was spending some of the royalties from his best seller, *In Cold Blood*, in staging this fabulous and much-discussed party. It was born out of the mood of the 1960s, and had little relation to the great balls of the McAllister era. Philanthropy and opulence now go hand in hand, and most large parties are given in the name of charity. The cause is the catalyst. Few would dare to arrange a major ball or entertainment today without this saving grace in a troubled world. And few could afford to entertain in the lavish style of the 1890s.

"Any girl who wishes to make her way in society should have a pair of ponies, a pretty trap, with a well-gotten up groom and Worth to dress her," said McAllister in the 1890s. But this was not all life as it was lived during his period, any more than *haute couture* and charity balls represent the intrinsic social pattern of the 1960s. A girl needs some solid assets today, and the social picture calls for new definitions, having moved so far from the tradition of Dolley Madison, Mrs. Bingham, and Mrs. Jay; of Mrs. Harrison Gray Otis, Mrs. Jack Gardner, and Mrs. Potter Palmer; of Mrs. Astor, Mrs. Fish, and a long line of Vanderbilt hostesses.

Mrs. John Fell, a youthful society matron, summed it up neatly in the spring of 1966: "People like to look at those who are prominent in public life. It takes a little politics, a little theater, a little society and a little everything to make an interesting group." The composition of today's most successful parties is a patchwork quilt of society, politics, talent, and eccentricity. The visiting celebrity, the man of the hour, the columnist, the judge or senator, the gambler, the nightclub hit, the best-selling author, the professional beauty, the offbeat professor; the stage, film, or television star; the magic boys and girls of the pop and Beatle world; the wit, the intellectual, and the *arriviste* blend harmoniously with a small core of Social Register names and hostesses par excellence, all in the interest of charity.

It is not a new conception of social success. The unsinkable Mrs. Brown of Denver, snubbed in her own land, won her way to social favor in Europe with her benevolent gestures, and Mrs. John Mackay, grandmother of Mrs. Irving Berlin, whose early days in the western mining region gave her little status at home, became one of the solid hostesses of the Victorian Age in London and Paris. But winning social position has never been practiced so consciously, so systematically as now, in the day of the common man, of integration, strikes, seething politics, and the backwash of war. No longer can any hostess wield the power of a Mrs. Astor on the strength of social prestige alone. Her diamonds must glow in an aura of good works, and the most conservative dowager smiles blandly as she is photographed with the eccentrics of today's world. As Mrs. Robin Butler, publicity director for Dior, puts it: "What do you do? You'd better be doing something, because it's bad form if you're not."

Give it any name—the jet set, the international set, the camp set, the avant-garde, or café society—it reaps a harvest of publicity unparalleled in the social annals of the United States, and ranges freely from the front pages to the society sections and gossip columns. Its flamboyance obscures the more tempered ways of millions of Americans who have not cast off all their ancestral traditions, convictions, or manners. But the Social Register field has narrowed. Only eleven cities now get out the sacred blue book, as against twenty-one in 1925, and there are scoffers who dare to laugh and rejoice at being dropped or left out. Once it was traditional for a woman's name to figure in the news only three times in her lifetime—for her birth, her marriage, and her death. Now the most conservative show little alarm over gossip-column items, and some hire press agents to make sure that they are not overlooked.

James Gordon Bennett, the madcap editor who drove nude through the Bois de Boulogne at night and ripped off restaurant table-cloths when things displeased him, touched off this chronicling of social doings in New York in the *Herald* of 1835: "Our purpose . . . is to give to the highest society of New York a life, a variety, a piquancy, a brilliancy, an originality that will entirely outstrip the worn out races of Europe." He proceeded by gossip, innuendo, and sensation to effect this purpose and succeeded at it beyond his dreams.

Today John B. Fairchild, the youthful and dynamic editor of *Women's Wear Daily*, an irreverent modern version of the elegant Frank W. Crowninshield who influenced and interpreted fashion and society for two decades as the editor of *Vanity Fair*, has given a name to the set that he feels controls society now. He calls them *Les Locomotives* and defines them as the under-forty group who "live the big life and do big things." They are "European-minded, gay, intellectually hungry, outwardly casual but inwardly nervous." As he sees them, they have no desire to live in big castles with many servants, to sit on the beach at Southampton, or to join Le Club. They are keen and active, brittle and travel-minded. Fairchild considers them more influential than the Old Guard, since they have the imagination, the courage, the desire, and also the money to swing. They are daring and set trends. They may be found in Gstaad, or Acapulco; in Sardinia or Antigua; in Rome or back on the old Left Bank; on safari in Africa; in Marrakech or Hawaii. They catch the seasons everywhere, sample the riskiest sports, comport themselves with dash and style. Wherever they chance to be, they are definitely "in" and from the attention they get in the public prints, the naïve might be lulled into thinking the so-called "beautiful people" a happy breed.

265

Americans are the most restless of people, traditionally always on the move. From their early treks west to their encompassment of the globe today their most consistent impulse has been to move, to grow, to seek new horizons. Today the United States has a vast and intricate transportation system, embracing 214,650 miles of railways, 25,260 miles of inland waterways, a mile of paved road for every square mile of its land surface, and 280,696 miles of airline routes. Yet, paradoxically, sixty million Americans have never traveled more than two hundred miles from their homes. But fifteen million went abroad in 1966.

The nation as a whole has played a mighty role in the invention and distribution of moving vehicles—and notably the motorcar. The American's passion for automobiling has had its somber side, too, for the death toll on the nation's streets and highways in 1965 was forty-nine thousand, and nearly two million more were disabled—the grim record of a transportation system that began in a simple way with Indian trails, then widened into bridle paths, cart tracks, carriage roads, post roads, and a variety of highways, multiplying into today's traffic network.

Street accidents and parking problems abounded in colonial days too. Children as well as adults were frequently hurt in collisions and overturnings. The streets were noisy and confusing, with horsemen galloping through them, chaises, carts, and wagons bumping wheel to wheel, and porters' barrows getting in everyone's way. When Charleston first had sidewalks the horses, handcarts, and wheelbarrows were kept off them, a concession to order and the rights of the pedestrian. Porters had a habit of merrily rolling their barrels along a pathway. Pigs and goats ambled about at will until 1762, when scavengers were introduced in Philadelphia, but pigs continued to roam through the streets of New York and were even welcomed by housewives well into the nineteenth century.

Philadelphia, the noisiest of all the cities, suggested a "rattle-gabble" to John Adams. Before there were turnpikes, two-wheeled conveyances were used entirely—sedans, chaises, and sulkies, with sleighs gliding about in winter as early as 1704. But landaus, phaetons, and chariots were soon being imported and carriagemakers in America copied them and built their own. In 1770 New Yorkers had twenty-six pleasure carriages, as well as forty-one post chaises and eighteen phaetons. John Street was so crowded on theater nights that the playbills of 1767 gave directions for getting to the playhouse. Virginia fared best, and early in the eighteenth century most of the residents of Williamsburg had a coach, a chariot, and a sedan chair. Liveried coachmen rode on the post chaise, a name later familiarized to the "one-horse shay."

From the earliest days the carriage was as sure an index to wealth or tradition as the Daimler and the Rolls-Royce a century later. Mrs. Stuyvesant Fish had more than a score of assorted carriages in New York, and John Drexel had twenty-six in Philadelphia. Mrs. Astor's footmen in bottle green were as recognizable on the box seat as Mrs. Vanderbilt's in maroon. The afternoon carriage drive in Central Park was as social as London's Rotten Row in the morning. Phaetons with fringed canopy tops and victorias served for informal calls, but the two-horse victoria with two footmen on the box was used for statelier occasions. The hansom was sporting and romantic; it had a strong appeal for the younger set.

The coaching parties and parades were in the grand tradition and the *grande daumont de visite* was the last word in carriage magnificence, even if this made little difference to the doctors, preachers, and shopkeepers who could afford carriages but not coachmen, and so chose the handy rockaway that they could drive themselves. It was named after Rockaway, Long Island. The high-wheeled gig was popular in rural communities, as well as the buggy and surrey.

But organized carriage travel began in 1765 with the first stage trip from Boston to New York over the highway later known as the Boston Post Road. In the following year a stage wagon described as a "flying-machine" rollicked along from Philadelphia to New York, but until the roads were improved and bridges built the course was precarious. Passengers were expected to sway in sundry directions to balance the coach. Drivers stopped to straighten planks on bridges before crossing them, and even the city streets were pitted with potholes and tree stumps. The mails moved slowly until 1754, but things improved when post riders set out from Philadelphia for New England once a week. They could make a run to New York in thirty-three hours.

Travel speeded up considerably with the turnpikes. Virginia had them first, and soon their picturesque tollhouses showed that the colonists were on the move. As settlers headed west the high-wheeled Conestoga wagons, introduced by the Germans, appeared on the roads in caravan order. With families and produce on board they sometimes traveled two hundred strong, and played a notable role in building up the nation. Even after the railroads were running they plied their sturdy way across the plains. Two-wheeled carts and sleds conveyed freight in winter, and pack trains went into Indian territory to trade. Peddlers journeyed west and south with packs stuffed with everything from pins to axes, and their rafts were used as country stores at river settlements. Milestones came into use when Benjamin Franklin paced the distance of the post road between Boston and Philadelphia with a cyclometer. Gravel served until macadamized roads were introduced in the 1800s.

The waterways were used for transportation from the earliest days, and the colonists made good use of their ketches, shallops, and sloops. As time went on they used schooners and packet vessels for freight and passengers. The opening of the Erie Canal in 1825 affected the country profoundly, particularly its transportation. Distances were cut, and the railroads became the lifestream of the nation.

Travel was becoming every man's dream by the mid-nineteenth century, and the well-off went to Europe for the Grand Tour, a wide sweep that involved interviews with poets and philosophers, endless tramps through galleries and museums, scenic delights, gustatory experiences in different countries, and a general polishing up of crude exteriors and the insular perspective. The summer vacation had become a sacred rite, with hotels going up at Saratoga Springs, Nahant, Newport, Niagara Falls, and along the Jersey coast. In 1855 Nahant, Massachusetts, was the most widely known watering place in the country, and it held its ground with Newport and Narragansett through the 1890s when millionaires as well as poets, painters, and politicians relaxed at the resorts. Writers Henry James and Edith Wharton, artist John Singer Sargent, the witty Oliver Wendell Holmes, and their like gathered in this region. By 1909 Bar Harbor and Newport were rated the two top resorts, followed by the Berkshires, Saratoga, Hot Springs, and Tuxedo Park.

Up to the time of the Civil War it was usual for fifty thousand Southerners to visit the northern resorts, and notably Saratoga Springs, where the recreation possibilities were the most diverse, if not the healthiest, in the country. In 1894, with ten gambling establishments, it was the Las Vegas of its day. Its race track, velvety lawns, garden parties and balls, as well as its mineral springs, brought out the worldly and the well-to-do, with a liberal sprinkling of rogues and gamblers. Piazza-sitting and the afternoon drive, fantastic meals and five changes of costume a day were the accepted pattern at this elm-shaded resort with its great rambling hotels. The Courting Yard was an institution at Saratoga, and White Sulphur Springs had its "Billing, Wooing and Cooing Society." Niagara Falls became known as a honeymoon spot late in the 1800s, when the Erie Railroad ran its luxury cars to the East. Thousands of brides and bridegrooms since then have crossed the bridge to Goat Island, sailed under the Maid of the Mist, and made love to the tune of the roaring falls. Atlantic City became popular in the 1850s but it was not until its plank walk was opened in 1870 that it drew great crowds.

Two world wars changed the travel habits of the American people perhaps more radically than any other development. With more leisure, greater freedom to move around, motels as well as the monster resort hotels, more money to spend and, above all, the airplane to speed the course, worldwide travel came within the scope of men and women of limited means. In place of the leisurely ocean voyage and long stays at rococo hotels, old and young learned to pick up at will for a fast spin abroad. State functionaries whizzed around the world on quick missions. Business girls took brief European vacations. Students went abroad on chartered flights to study, tour, and commune with the young of other nations. By bicycle, scooter, and small motorcar, on foot and by air, they became travelers more interested in human beings than in antiquities, and they ranged across the United States with a new awareness of its people and its history.

All ages travel light nowadays, a total change from the massive cowhide trunks of the seventeenth and eighteenth centuries, the Saratoga trunk with curved top, the huge metal wardrobe trunk that followed it. At the turn of the century train and steamer travel involved a strange medley of curved trunks, portmanteaux, Gladstone bags, hatboxes, morocco cases, jewel boxes, steamer rugs, hold-alls, and other impedimenta. It was not until the age of airplane travel that luggage entered a new phase, with space at a premium and weight a consideration.

A woman's luggage used to be like the insignia on her notepaper, as she traveled with Vuitton or Hermès pieces. Today she is apt to settle for whatever is light, and she can choose from staggered suitcases in subdued or rousing colors. Today both suitcases and bags are made of finely tanned calf, pigskin, pin seal, ostrich, lizard, and cobra. The traveler can pick up a cheap suitcase in the five-and-ten or pay $2,500 for an alligator case at a famous leather store on Fifth Avenue. More simply,

Broadway in 1836, from Canal Street to beyond Niblo's Garden. Stagecoaches and produce carts rumble along this wide avenue of commerce. Street vendors are busy at the corner. The "Emporium of Books, Prints and Stationery" is the corner shop to the right, below the British College of Health, otherwise known as "The General Depot for the sale of Morison's Hygeian Medicines," catering at the time to the passion for patent medicines. Drawn and etched by T. Horner.

The Beekman family coach used in New York City from about 1770. Carriages were still rare, and New York had only twenty-six at this time. But by 1800 a large assortment of landaus, phaetons, and chariots rolled through the street, many imported, some homemade. The more elaborate, like the Beekman coach, usually had a family crest or other insignia. Before long the coachhouses of the well-to-do held several carriages, like the three-car garage of today. The family coach was easily recognized by its liveried attendants.

The Grand Drive, Central Park, in 1869. This was the fashionable parading ground in late afternoon. Coaches, victorias, carriages of all kinds sped past the promenaders and horsemen who shared in this daily outing. Children walked with their parents, and spectators sat on benches under the trees, studying the passing show. Central Park itself was still a novelty to city dwellers and it received as much attention and comment as it does in 1967. Lithograph by Currier & Ives.

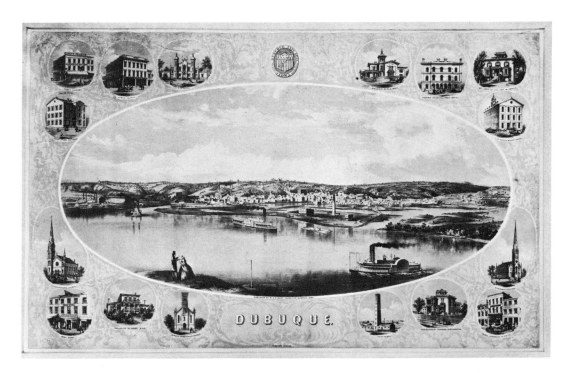

Dubuque, Iowa, 1860. Long before the Lady of Dubuque
became a national symbol of prudery through the New Yorker,
Dubuque was a sturdy pioneering town on the Mississippi
named after Julien Dubuque, the Canadian trader who was
the first white settler there. It had all the tang of the
Mississippi River towns as the paddlewheelers passed through
it, transporting wood, metal, and plumbing materials from its
factories. As a mining and shipbuilding center it figured in
the fast development of the West.

The Postillion, 1876. When turnpikes
were still few and far between, the
postillion could run his narrow coach
along the trails used by farmers and
post riders. He made good speed in a
rough and rollicking way and filled
many functions, from bearing news to
bringing aid to the sick. His carriage
resembled a sedan chair, swung on huge
wheels and drawn by two horses.
Drawing by A. Goubie (1876). Etched
by A. Lalauze.

The new arrivals journeyed across the country, many going by covered wagon with their meager possessions. They forded rivers, cleared the forest, built log cabins, and plowed the land with rough implements. Their children helped with firewood. From The Graphic, *1878*.

Six-horse team and Conestoga wagon. As one of the chief freight carriers of the East from about 1750 until the railroads were built, the Conestoga wagon was vital to the growth of the country. It was named for the Pennsylvania region where it was first built. Its boat-shaped body was devised to shift weight more readily on the hills. Painted red, with a blue underbody and white canvas hood, it enlivened its main routes—the National Road and the Philadelphia-Pittsburgh pike.

she can eke out her weight allowance with plaid canvas and plastic garment bags. The young like duffel or tote bags, while their elders succumb to the new antique-velvet bags in rich Italian colors. Gaily printed attaché cases are turned out for the traveling businesswoman, and men are offered sober-looking models fitted with all the equipment of their office desks. The traveler may now roll her jewelry in a leather wallet in place of the morocco jewel case that once proclaimed to the world where her diamonds were.

With service declining, porters a vanishing species, and travel greatly extended, both men and women seek to travel light, and designers see to it that they also do it with style. It is part of the new fluidity of motion, of being on the go. All this activity was preceded by the slow development of comfort and safety on the railroads. When the Civil War ended there were thirty-five thousand miles of track across the country and people went journeying without sleeping cars or diners, and making light of the recurrent and serious accidents along the way. They slept in bunks, using candlelight; and Clara Barton, on one of her trips, was astounded to find a man gazing down at her. Food was hawked in the boxlike cars; bars were sometimes set up in the baggage cars, but the prevailing custom for passengers was to get out at the canary-yellow depots and fight their way to quick lunches. Meanwhile, the railroad builders—Cornelius Vanderbilt, Leland Stanford, Henry Villard, and Collis P. Huntington—grew into giants in the world of finance.

One mogul of railroad travel came along in 1858 when a cabinet maker named George Mortimer Pullman began to experiment with sleeping and eating arrangements on the train. A decade later he introduced the "Delmonico," the first dining car. From this point on the railroad companies competed for priority in their cuisine, using regional delicacies, expert chefs, and exacting standards in service. The trains might be moving through Indian territory, with some of the tribes still on the warpath, but inside the Pullman coaches all would be crystal, soft lights, and excellent food. By the 1890s wine cabinets and iceboxes were in use to protect their wines and delicacies. The trains still competed with the steamboats, and the Creole touch was maintained. Organ music flowed through the dining car as it traveled at a mile a minute, without spilling the champagne. This luxurious trend reached its height with the New York Central's Twentieth Century, which became as legendary as the Orient Express or the Blue Train. Celebrities of the day boarded it from a crimson carpet spread between rows of potted palms, and millionaires relaxed over a modestly priced dinner that included terrapin Maryland or Lobster Newburg, as well as sirloin steak, game, and butter from Vermont.

Swivel-style chairs with movable footrests were the first type of parlor-car chair, giving each passenger ample room and a deep wide seat.

The sleeping car never came up to the standard of the dining car, and visitors from abroad complained bitterly about their curtained cubicles, and the cramped drawing rooms that followed. But Presidents and board members of the railroad companies traveled in their own private cars, which matched their yachts in fittings. Some had gold dinner services, jewel safes, and wine chests. Adelina Patti had a sunken marble bathtub in a private car named for her. In later years extra-fare trains running between New York and Los Angeles became lounging grounds for the screen stars before there were jets to whisk them across the country.

Elevated railroads quickened transportation for a time in the larger cities and in 1883 more than ninety million fares were bought on the New York elevated, which had proved to be so successful that Chicago, St. Louis, Philadelphia, and Cincinnati all tried this rackety form of transportation. Horsecars in the same year carried 116,065,223 New Yorkers to their destinations. But when the subway opened in 1904 the horse was on his way to retirement. He could no longer compete with the trolleys and the underground railway, and the happy days when horse-drawn cars careened through the streets strung with colored lights and gay with music for neighborhood outings were at an end. By this time the theatrical center of town was well established at Longacre Square and the lights of the Gay White Way blazed over Broadway. Hansoms were still gliding about like ebony shadows, but the social nucleus formed by Ward McAllister was beginning to lose its unity as the population grew larger and more cosmopolitan. The formal call and the social note, usually delivered by carriage, were yielding to the telephone and telegraph. The rising skyline proclaimed a new age, but brownstone fronts with striped awnings stood pat for a time in face of an irresistible tide of destruction.

By this time the man in the street, like the millionaire, had found his favorite, speediest, and most practical conveyance in the automobile. Road travel received its first great push when the motorcar eased into the picture by slow stages between 1886 and 1900. Charles Edgar Duryea was credited with being the father of the automobile when he showed his model in 1892 in Springfield, Massachusetts. But the genius in this field was Henry Ford, who wheeled his auto out of a barn in 1897 for its first road test, and ended up by changing the face of the world. It looked like a box with a seat on top and wheels suggestive of a bicycle. But it soon fascinated the public, if not for its looks, at least for its promise, and experiments proceeded with chassis resembling carriages until the automobile took shape in a primitive form.

Half a million of Henry Ford's Model T, or Tin Lizzie, were sold before World War I. By 1965 there were more than seventy-nine million cars and trucks on the American highways, and the Ford Company alone made a profit of $703 million in a single year. The automobile had become one of the nation's dominant industries and the most prized recreation of its people. Its proliferation was unprecedented. There were no more than three hundred of the horseless carriages—gasoline buggies, electric broughams, and steam cars—when the first moving picture was shown on a screen in 1895. Both industries took wings early in the century and they grew up together. These bubbles, as the cars were called, had names like "Blue Butterfly" and "Red Devil," and the first transcontinental auto trip in 1903 caused national excitement. It took ten weeks, with pauses, but was considered a miracle of speed and endurance.

This new pastime called for special costuming that in its way came up to contemporary mod standards. Women looked distinctly odd as they set forth swathed in linen dusters, with goggles, and foolproof veils clamping down their cartwheel hats, but by 1915 they had taken to silk caps with visors. Men wore jaunty single-breasted dusters with Eton collars and patch pockets. They wore huge adjustable goggles, visored caps, and leggings for the dirty work beneath the tonneau. The sport was vigorous, for blowouts were common and service stations had not yet become wayside shrines. Cars lay open to the rain, the dust, and the wind, though leather flaps were supposed to keep out the storm and high wheels were expected to protect the motorist from flying mud. Only the acetylene lamps, bright and brassy, did their work, and sometimes they guttered out.

The American way of life had changed with the coming of the automobile. Churchgoing and porch-sitting suffered, but there were bright new horizons. Town and country were more closely linked; people were drawn from dim Victorian parlors onto the open road; the young fled from their elders and romance flourished in the automobile; visiting, dining, and recreation away from home became a new preoccupation. It was easier to shop, to golf, to picnic, to attend meetings, to go to business or the bathing beach, to hunt and fish, to take the children to school and pursue the social life, to see distant friends and visit other parts of the country. It also contributed greatly to the rise of crime and a defiant attitude in the young.

The jokes and gibes about the early automobiles were legion. The Tin Lizzie usually invoked good-natured laughter. The legend of keeping up with the Joneses flourished, as comparisons were drawn between the owners of Model T's and the proud possessors of Cadillacs, Packards, and Pierce Arrows. Old ladies emerged from sylvan cottages to join in the fun. But it took the horse some time to face up to these rude invaders, and early in the century a thoughtful motorist would brandish a red flag in front of his car to warn the approaching carriage of its danger.

The automobile brought another benefit to the public, as highways were built from coast to coast. By 1930 there were 750,000 miles

The Overland Pony Express. In April 1860 the first pony express carried mail between St. Joseph, Missouri, and San Francisco. Hardy little ponies galloped at top speed, with their skillful riders changing mounts at 190 stations along the 2,000-mile route. The trip took eight or ten days, and riders were often shot down from their saddles by Indians. The pony express created its own frontier tradition of speed and valor. The promise of a faster means of communication lies in the telegraph poles being put up as the pony express rides by. Photographed by Savage, Salt Lake City, from a painting by George M. Ottinger.

Henry Ford and David Gray in the Model N car, 1907, forerunner of the famous Model T. There is nothing in the demeanor of these two gentlemen to suggest that a new world is in the making and that Henry Ford is its creator. But he had started something in the field of transportation that would change the life and customs of people around the world. From the beginning the public seemed to be fascinated by this primitive object that was just one step ahead of the bicycle.

The nation was literally on wheels by the end of 1945. Great metropolises like Los Angeles must now depend on intricate systems of freeways to unsnarl the ever-growing problems of traffic.

The first railway train in New York State begins its initial formal run. Crowds
gathered for this historic event, and even the cows lined up at the pasture fence.
The date was September 9, 1831, and it followed the furore a year earlier over Peter
Cooper's Tom Thumb engine. But it took another thirty-eight years before the
Golden Spike Ceremony in Utah marked the joining of the Central Pacific Railway
and the Union Pacific in the first transcontinental railroad. This had been a dream of
Abraham Lincoln for preserving the Union. The settlement of the West leaped ahead
from this point on, and the simple train of 1831 in time developed into the sophisticated
Twentieth Century Limited. From the painting by Edward Lamson Henry in the
Albany Institute of History and Art, Albany, New York.

"A Limited Express." "Five Seconds for Refreshments!" This was a
familiar sight in the early days of the railroad, and these passengers
of 1884 are scrambling madly to reach the lunch counter. Their
wives and children look on with a mixture of indignation and
frustration. When traveling any distance it was wise to take a
well-packed lunch, for refreshment stands were few and far between
and there was scant time for service when the hordes broke in.
Currier & Ives.

of hard-surfaced roads for the twenty-five million automobiles then in use. The trailer, thought up by Glenn Curtiss, appeared late in the 1920s and touring became commonplace, with two-thirds of all American families owning automobiles in the 1930s. The look of the highways changed as billboards, gas stations, hot-dog stands, motels, and tourist camps ran for mile after mile along the way. The first rotary grade intersection was introduced in 1920 and the first cloverleaf a decade later. The Holland Tunnel in 1927 set a precedent; now automobiles could travel beneath a river. All manner of improvements were made in the highways between the two world wars. Bus lines became as ubiquitous as the stagecoaches of old, and concrete highways, then parkways and freeways, speeded the traveler on his way.

The nation was literally on wheels by the end of World War II, as old and young drove about in their cars, and high school students learned to drive as routinely as they studied algebra. The automobile industry became fiercely competitive, with each company striving to outdo the other at the annual automobile shows, changing their designs, streamlining, lengthening, shortening, adding more accessories and, in 1966, preaching safety through seat belts and foam-padded seats with shoulder harness for children. Each year there were a few more luxury touches, like reading lights over the rear seat, perfume pockets, shaving kits for men, tape recorders, and small television sets. Robin's-egg blue, scarlet, and gold automobiles flourished in Hollywood; the all-purpose station wagons grew ever more imposing; the tiny imported cars darted like gnats through city traffic. The American auto population has nearly tripled in twenty years, and is growing eight times faster than the human population.

But as the automobile reached the peak of its popularity, men turned to flight and became airborne by choice. Both interests were developing at about the same time early in the century, but although the Wright brothers flew at Kitty Hawk in 1903 it took longer for aeronautics to move ahead. The great age of the airplane began in the 1920s and crystallized in the flight of Charles A. Lindbergh across the Atlantic in 1927. From then on it was one historic milestone after another, as aviators flew around the world, over the North Pole and the South Pole, made speed records and height records, creating a line of heroes and heroines in storybook fashion. In 1932 the early Boeings and DC's introduced the age of the modern airliner by carrying twelve passengers at 150 miles an hour. They were compact, metal planes, rising from the ground like birds. By 1962 more than eighty thousand Americans owned private planes, helicopters flew over New York, or landed on the White House lawn, and a large part of the population was being wooed away from ocean liners and railroads by sky travel—one of the major revolutions of the twentieth century.

13   *The Great Awakening*

AFTER showing their strength and independence in the eighteenth century, American women seemed to retire for a time from life's battles, except for the feminists and reformers whose frenzy at the election platforms drove mild men to drink and induced their softer sisters to sink back against their antimacassars and reach for *sal volatile*. While one bold woman ran for the Presidency, another became a doctor, a third smashed saloons, a fourth went to the battlefields, and a number wore bloomers, the majority lived in a state of domesticity that was part bliss and part sheer anemia. They were married at sixteen and old at forty. Pale as their favorite anemones and drooping like willows they bore innumerable children and then lay down and died. The gadfly Mrs. Trollope commented on their "lamentable insignificance," always separated from their husbands, powdering themselves immoderately, using false hair and too much soap.

Margaret and Basil Hall, an English couple touring America in the 1820s, were amazed to find the "great separation between the ladies and gentlemen in society," the lack of a flirtatious spirit, and the general absence of feminine influence—an opinion that they might have had reason to revise a century later. They noticed that few women attended the New York theater. They were missing from the race track at

Charleston, and the Halls could find only nine of the cowed creatures among several thousand men at a country fair in Massachusetts. Other visitors early in the century thought them spiritless, leading dull lives and knowing little of the larger issues of the day.

Until the 1880s the morbid spirit prevailed. The constant preoccupation with death was not unrelated to the number of babies and mothers who faded from the scene. The women of the seventeenth and eighteenth centuries were hardy, with the strength of pioneers. Bright, vigorous, and independent, they helped to populate and build up the land for future generations. With primitive tools and few comforts they ran their simple homes, fed their families direct from the earth, the sea, or the garden, and trained their children along sturdy lines. They committed themselves heartily to farm festivals, husking bees, and country frolics, while wealthier families went in for great balls and masquerades, racing, hunting, and the sporting life.

But the generation of drooping violets that lounged against the antimacassars in the nineteenth century were a sickly lot, perhaps because of ill health induced by tight lacing, anemia from poor nutrition, and a general lack of fresh air and exercise, a state from which even Lydia Pinkham's pills could not rescue them. They went into limbo for months before being confined, donning hideous and distorting garments. Today, in contrast, a sunny, open-air philosophy surrounds childbirth. Pregnant women dress like their sisters and glory in their state. With cunningly contrived shifts, subtly cut bathing suits, flat heels, and an air of insouciance they no longer hide their condition but stay in the open until the last possible moment, seeking no favors as they move in and out of the supermarkets and hold down their jobs.

Visitors often commented on the prudish tone of American life, in spite of its highly publicized night life, political corruption, and raffish concerns. On the family side the worldliness of the eighteenth century had been followed by the restraints and taboos of the Victorian Age, which ran to such oddities as a solemn warning by one etiquette writer in 1863 to the perfect hostess to separate the works of male and female authors on her bookshelves, since their proximity "unless they happen to be married should not be tolerated." More to the point was novelist Captain Frederick Marryat's merry jest, which has been dubbed apocryphal, that even the piano legs in America seemed to be wrapped in little pantaloons with frills. But there was no doubt about the uproar when Hiram Powers' statue "The Greek Slave" was exhibited in the 1840s. Flannel drawers and a calico blouse were first proposed as camouflage before exposing the statue to the ladies of Cincinnati. New York took it more calmly, and crowds turned out to view the naked slave.

Sex had a way of edging itself into the public eye with each successive generation. The open dormitory doors of today are not such a jump from the ancient art of bundling. Courting habits in the United States, as elsewhere in the world, have been more instinctive than devised, but the most discussed in a Puritan age was the well-established custom of bundling, practiced in rural districts during cold weather, and particularly by the discreet and modest Dutch, who called it "questing." It was not indigenous, but was a well-known courting practice in Scotland, Ireland, and the Scandinavian countries as well as in Holland. Theoretically, bundling was an innocent rite, with the mother sometimes tucking her daughter into the feather bed, fully clad except for her shoes. The young man, equally well covered up, would then slip in beside her. Occasionally a dividing board separated them, but this barrier was not a requisite, and the young pair, heading toward marriage or already engaged, were expected to bundle in a tentative way.

The spirit of dalliance was not the accepted approach to the bundling bed. The youth was supposed to be definitely committed to the girl involved. However, visiting strangers occasionally found their way into a girl's bed, perhaps even in the room occupied by her parents, when there was no other place to give them lodging. Thomas Anburey, an officer in Burgoyne's captive army, was astonished to encounter this form of hospitality in 1777 at Williamstown, Massachusetts. The girl's mother took him in tow and announced: "Jonathan and I will sleep in this and our Jemima and you shall sleep in that." And next day the girl acknowledged cheerfully that she had bundled with a "'Britainer."

In spite of all the ridicule and disapproval accorded bundling it persisted until 1800 and was practiced in Pennsylvania, New York, New Jersey, New England, and in some of the southern states. Cape Cod was the last area to abandon it. Harvard students debated whether it was "fornication to lye with one's Sweetheart." Even John Adams conceded that he could not wholly disapprove of bundling, and Abigail commented casually on it in her letters. A Connecticut girl, writing blithely to her sister in 1775, told of bundling "till sun about three hours high." Washington Irving took it all quite seriously and although defining bundling as a singular custom he considered it an "indispensable preliminary to matrimony, their courtships commencing where ours usually finish . . . ." There was as much comment on this courting custom as on "going steady" today, and one young man's verse on the subject was freely quoted:

Night is the time, and it's no crime
To bundle in our clothes . . .
Since in a bed, a man, a maid
May bundle and be chaste;
It doth no good to burn up wood;
It is a needless waste.

Fathers sometimes brought suit when their daughters became pregnant, but the courts ruled that any parent who would permit the practice was not entitled to redress. The justification usually advanced was that it saved firewood, gave visitors lodging when space was limited, and speeded up the courting process. In truth, there were few places for the young to go on cold nights.

Another makeshift was the "courting stick," a hollow tube six feet long, into which the lovers could whisper through mouth and ear pieces, while the other members of the family milled around the fireplace, hearing nothing. This was an early form of the "telephonitis" that besets the young today. Bundling in itself had some of the matchmaking possibilities of the buggy, the sleigh, the porch, the hammock, the picnic and, finally, the automobile. Proposals were numerous on buggy rides. Even tongue-tied Ulysses S. Grant summoned up courage to propose to Julia Dent of St. Louis while crossing a rocky plank bridge in a buggy. She landed precipitately in his arms as they went over a loose plank, and this overwhelmed the shy West Pointer.

But difficult as it was for the young to find privacy in the days when family life centered in one large room, there were always those who lingered at the pump, hung around the country store, held hands surreptitiously in stagecoaches, frolicked at country dances, embraced in rose-embowered summerhouses, or went boating on the river. These were early variations of automobiles and drive-in movies, of motels, discothèques, swimming pools, and beaches. Sex was as provocative a topic in the pioneer days as now, if without Freudian-Kinsey interpretations and scientific lore amassed by applying clinical techniques to studying the natural instincts of men and women.

In bringing the subject into the daylight the feminists had circumvented one of the most rigid Victorian taboos, now long lost in the dustbin and alien to a world where the young no longer worry about being oversexed but fear, rather, that they may not meet the prevailing tests of virility and total fulfillment. Freud gave sex scientific interpretation; a world war gave it free expression; and the flashing life of the 1920s shattered ancient restraints. It was old hat by the time the beatnik generation came along, but the parental and academic sanctions were not. Perhaps no change in civilized taste is more clearly defined today than this one, and the Victorian girl, sometimes less naïve than she seemed, would be laughed to scorn in a tougher world where sex is flaunted on billboards, in books and pictures; where panel shows explore it from every angle; where the magazines that once pussyfooted on the subject now treat it with clinical precision. What was considered bad taste a half century ago is just realism today, and the gravest error is to be childishly innocent and uninformed. The schools and colleges accept these conditions and lower the barriers with the knowledge that they cannot stem the tide. However, even the young themselves are wearying of all the fuss and clatter about life's fundamentals. "Sex is passé," quipped a bored Vassar girl in 1966.

A students' manual of 1835 devoted a chapter to rebellion on the campus, warning the leaders that their futures were in jeopardy. Another chapter proclaimed the evils of smoking and drinking in terms that fit today's picture. The same spirit flashed into view after World War I, with the spread of agnosticism, the defiant spirit of the 1920s, and the impact of the Freudian searchlight directed at parents and home. The Depression years and World War II led by degrees to the full-blown rebellion of the 1960s, the assault on authority, the strikes and parades, the fight for civil rights, the attack on the Vietnam war.

But with more causes to back, and a spectacular showcase in television, they have pushed harder and further than any youthful generation in American history. The campus has become a testing ground for the changed social outlook. With marijuana, LSD, the contraceptive pill, and the relaxation of moral standards as immediate issues, there has been plenty to jazz up the picture. To appraise their professors, to rebel against their parents, to run the world their way—an old student tradition—has become the dominant philosophy with some. The rise of the hippies has brought another element into view, with love, love, love the constant refrain. The psychedelic world is the new paradise, only one step from limbo.

In many respects courtship had become a precise science by the 1960s, documented with books and surveys, timetables, techniques, and medical advice. For the most part this clinical approach has left the spirit untouched, to soar in the old romantic way. Long before Kinsey, however, a few feminine voices were raised on behalf of sex education, the most scientific being that of Elizabeth Blackwell, the first woman doctor, who lectured on sex hygiene and advocated a free life in the open air, the abandonment of confining garments, and a clear view of the world by the growing girl. In general, however, the relationship of the sexes was viewed from the moral and theological standpoint in the early days. Without benefit of the contraceptive devices of today the average family ran to eight and often reached twenty, although three wives might have been involved in mothering so large a brood. Women died young and often in childbirth, and their infants petered out as frequently as they lived, but the social goal was to have large families to populate a new nation, to cultivate the soil and develop its resources. By 1966 a different philosophy prevailed, as the Planned Parenthood Federation worked around the world to check explosive birth rates, and new contraceptive devices became more available to the public. In 1965 the births in the United States dropped to 3,767,000, their lowest point in more than a decade. Marriages were down, too, but divorces were on the increase—three to every ten marriages.

283

The Great Awakening

The New York Decorative Art Society in the
1880s. This was the decade in which there
was a great surge toward the arts as women
dared to venture out of their homes and even
to attend college, although few were ready
yet for the vote. The foundation for today's
interest in the fine arts was being laid across
the country during this transition period, and
girls with artistic instincts at last had
somewhere specific to go. Chicago, Boston,
and New York lighted the way. The
Metropolitan Museum had technical schools.
Cooper Union had opened a Women's Art
School. The Art Students League dared to
hold an evening life class for women. The
Society of Decorative Arts drew women of
all ages to classes in china painting, pottery,
embroidery, screen-making, and other
home-building graces. Sunflowers, hollyhocks,
buttercups, and daisies soon bloomed on any
object that lent itself to this handiwork.
Jenny June, a stern critic of the spirit of
dilettantism and founder of the Sorosis Club,
wrote that the "daubing, hammering, sewing
and painting done in the name of decorative
art was a childish waste of time." She
demanded professionalism. It came, in time.
Frank Leslie's Illustrated Newspaper, 1884.

Thomson's Skirt Manufactory in 1859. The sewing machine had taken the feminine world by storm when it reached the market shortly before the Civil War. Five hundred girls are gathered here, working on the hoops of the crinoline age. They had found a new way to earn a living, without the endless tedium of hand sewing, and they left their homes in droves to work for a mere pittance in this type of factory. The sewing machine had revolutionized the world of fashion and tailoring. From Harper's Weekly, 1859.

"Age of Iron." Women's rights had become a major issue by the end of the 1860s, and the caricaturists had a fresh theme in the fate of the neglected husband. These two are sourly doing the washing, rocking the cradle, and putting in a stitch or two, while their bewigged wives serve as coachman and footman for the lady in bustle and stripes about to enter the carriage. All are committed to the cause of women's rights, and the coachman looks ready to settle the matter with her whip. Currier & Ives, 1869.

Men hoot and jeer in the galleries of Mozart Hall in 1857 at what was currently described as an "Amazonian Convention." Since holding their first convention in Seneca Falls in 1848 the suffragettes had become obstreperous, and on this occasion one of them was boldly challenging the scoffers in the balconies. Another had her opera glasses turned on the scoundrels. The suffragettes had some men on their side—good fellows all, who sat among them and gave them moral support. Few believed that they needed it. Drawing by J. M. Nevin in 1857. This wood engraving of the caricature appeared in Harper's Weekly in 1859.

The bundling of two hundred years ago has its counterpart today in the much discussed premarital relationship. With a quarter of a million illegitimate births now recorded in the nation each year, the question "Why Wait for Marriage?" is baldly stated in magazine headlines, and church and state give separate and united attention to the issue. The constant fraternizing of the sexes has tended to break down the old myth that sex and sin must be synonymous, as they were considered to be at the turn of the century and still more so in the 1850s when Mrs. Sarah Josepha Hale preached meekness as the most beautiful virtue, modesty as the most commendable, and self-denial as the exercise of the civilized. But education, she added, was the sure road to breeding. With the Bloomer costume in mind Mrs. Hale made some observations that might be repeated today. "Are not those nations most morally refined in civilization and Christianity where the costume of men and women differs most essentially?" she asked. Mrs. Hale expressed her approval of married women controlling society but deplored the "present practice of abandoning it to young girls as lowering in its tone, and pernicious in its effects." She was scathing about overdone gentility, and sometimes let salt winds blow through *Godey's Lady's Book*.

Concern for manners, as for morals, was an old American tradition. By Mrs. Hale's time a number of homes had family silver, a showing of claw-footed chairs and bevel-edged mirrors; some even had family portraits by Copley, all of which were required to establish the social status of a man of family, in the opinion of Oliver Wendell Holmes. Nevertheless, all but a few of the assorted settlers who came to these shores had to forge their way with less than this kind of inheritance. From the earliest days they made self-conscious efforts at social improvement, except for the frontiersmen who gloried in the rugged tradition and lived by their own robust standards. Women at the end of the seventeenth century were poring over imported manuals on manners, a taste that has persisted down to the days of Emily Post and Amy Vanderbilt. In 1673 they were drawing sustenance from Richard Allestree's *The Ladies Calling*, moving eagerly from subjects such as piety and morality to modes of dress and social interchange.

These early books of advice were heavily tinctured with the importance of catching a man, and treating him with good nature once he was captive. This was a problem that did not arise on the frontier, since women there were rare jewels, hard to find and essential to keep. But in general the weak sisters were reminded not to show wit (a dangerous gift that flourished in the eighteenth century), or too much good sense, or to indicate in any way that they were well educated if, by some miracle, they had been educated at all in the new land. John Gregory advanced the base thought in *A Father's Legacy to His Daugh-*

ters that men looked with a jealous and malignant eye on a "woman of great parts, and a cultivated understanding." Equally emphatic was the Rev. John Bennett, who reminded them that metaphysics, philosophy, and politics were not their province. Paradoxically he warned them against powder, perfume, and cosmetics, urging them to dress in a neat and simple way, to show timidity and diffidence, to maintain a "countenance always modest and undesigning; a tongue often silent, and ears always attentive," and not to marry against their parents' wishes. Above all, he reminded them that they should avoid the daring décolletage of the era: "Young ladies should not be too liberal in the display of their charms. Too much exposure does not enhance their value. The bosom should throb unseen."

But the good clergyman had a few words for men, too. They should refrain from smoking, spitting, or wearing their outdoor garb in the presence of ladies. They should not sleep in their daytime clothes, laugh uproariously, or rest their feet on the andirons. Spitting seemed to be a national characteristic that caught the eye of all visitors to America, as cigar chewing drew attention at a later date. "The gentlemen spit, talk of elections, and the price of produce, and spit again," said Mrs. Frances Trollope scornfully, noting also that the "ladies look at each other's dress till they know every pin by heart." Another visiting Briton observed that "Americans ate with their knives, picked their teeth with their forks and virtually tubbed in their finger-bowls." Dickens, Bernard Shaw, Kipling—all were relentless critics of American manners. Lord Bryce, Winston Churchill, and Harriet Martineau were among the few visitors who had anything good to say about the United States.

Forty printings of Lord Chesterfield's *Letters to His Son* were circulated across the country during the eighteenth century, but this sophisticated masterpiece was received with mixed feelings. It had little effect one way or another on the social mores of the country, and Abigail Adams denounced Chesterfield for putting "immoral, pernicious and libertine principles into the mind of a youth." She remarked that etiquette was not to be found in the nation's capital, but neither did she think it lay in the principles set forth by Chesterfield. However, there was much else from which to choose. Cotton Mather, George Washington, and Benjamin Franklin pushed the subject with authority. Perhaps the ablest shepherd along the way was Franklin, who brought out *The Friendly Instructor: or, a Companion for Young Ladies and Young Gentlemen*, a best seller in its day.

For table manners the young consulted *A Pretty Little Pocket Book*, which bore small relation to the book written on teen-age table manners by Walter Hoving, chairman of Tiffany's, a popular guide widely distributed in the 1960s. The earlier work informed them that they should never ask for anything at the table, never speak unless spoken to, never take salt with a clean knife or throw bones under the table. Children of that era often stood as they ate, or sat on long, narrow benches on each side of the table. Sometimes they occupied side tables and took their trenchers to the great table for second helpings.

As time went on the children in comfortable homes became more familiar with genuine silver at table than many of the boys and girls today. Governor Winthrop was the first person in America to use a fork. It was brought to him in 1633 in a leather case with a knife and bodkin. Some two-tined iron and silver forks showed up in New England and Virginia by the end of the century but it was a long time before they were in common use, and they were the basis of repeated flurries in the world of manners. Around 1890 the absurdity of lapping up ice cream with a fork was under discussion. It took several years to settle this issue; the ultimate decision was that puddings, ices, sauces, and berries should be eaten with spoons. In another decade the unwary were warned against using a spoon for anything that could possibly be taken with a fork. And all well-brought-up children were reminded not to fiddle with the salt and pepper, and not to be restless at table or to make bread pellets—a weakness of General Grant's that his devoted wife, Julia, could not curb. He fired them like toy cannon at Mrs. Stuyvesant Fish's table, but this did not bother her; she was, after all, an individualist in her own right who had cut the three-hour-dinner routine to fifty minutes and telescoped the courses from twelve to four. She was one hostess who did not worry about the uses of the knife or fork—British or American style. Some traveling Americans had picked up the custom of keeping the fork firmly in the left hand instead of transferring it to the right in the American way before conveying food to the mouth. Stay-at-homes observing these barbarians thought that they knew no better.

But in the twentieth century Amy Vanderbilt finally settled the knife-and-fork issue to everyone's satisfaction. She found a combination of the two methods acceptable. "Even when one uses the American zigzag method, it is sensible to convey food one has just cut to the mouth with the fork in the left hand, if one wishes," she decreed. Emily Post would have no two ways about it. She held firm to the Continental manner. The diner continued to do as he liked.

The introduction of service à la Russe in sophisticated circles in the late nineteenth century did much to break up the chummier ways of early Americans. No longer did father carve the roast and pass it around. The meat was carved in kitchen or pantry. Vegetables were served and were then taken away. All extras disappeared from the table, except salt and pepper, nuts and ashtrays. Breakfast was served from the sideboard, with spirit lamps and heaters. But service à la

Russe was limited in its application and it required servants. Life on the farms continued much as before, with cruets, ketchup and pickles, sugar and cream, vegetables and sauces, relishes and bread cluttering up the table. The Lazy Susan went wheeling around to ease the serving pressure in many homes. Regardless of innovations and Continental tricks picked up by the traveler, the average American continued at his own steady gait, eating at regular hours and usually preferring his dinner in the middle of the day. He never accepted the Continental breakfast or dinner served extremely late at night.

The customary form of entertaining included formal and informal receptions, breakfasts, state dinners, high teas, and luncheons. Dinners were usually limited to twelve persons in the average home. High teas on Sunday evenings were considered worldly, with oysters, cold meats, charlotte russe, gelatin molds, sardines, and ice cream invariably served. The gourmet feasts at Delmonico's, the hotels and men's clubs that made lively newspaper reading a half century later, were reflected only in a moderate way in the everyday life of the American. Single women and bachelors favored breakfast involving hot chocolate and coffee, cold game pie, partridge, waffles, and other oddments. Bachelors were among the most favored of individuals at the close of the century and they were invited to the best parties. They found good spots in the clubs. It was their custom to give midnight feasts in their quarters, and they were popular with the artistic, advanced women as well as with the more raffish element. Margaret E. Sangster, taking note in *Collier's Weekly* of the lolling about on scattered cushions with soft lights, and suppers of partridge and quail, wrote that "we are sometimes afraid that the bachelor apartment is a foe to domesticity."

However, there was always marriage, and plenty of children to spur wives to look for suitable homes. This was especially true in New York, where houses were scarce. They rented at from two hundred to a thousand dollars a year, and substantial ones sold for ten thousand dollars and up. Good servants, coming in through Ellis Island, could be had for fifteen dollars a month with board. A prosperous wife put in as busy a day as the tenement wife, though along somewhat different lines. In the morning she saw her children, dressed carefully, and consulted the cook. In the afternoon she went driving, shopped, and paid calls, scattering cards. This involved a ritual of its own—a snowstorm of cards with appropriate touches for each occasion—the turned-down corners, the correct form for condolence, the happy note of congratulation. Only in Washington does the calling card carry any conviction today. After a whirlwind tour by carriage there was always the theater, the opera, a dinner, a ball, or a quiet evening at home with games and music. Fans, smelling salts, and flowers bolstered her at the theater, but the early custom of passing around boxes of bonbons between the acts died out in the United States long before it did in Britain.

The woman of this era liked to write her notes on rough parchment with deckle edges. Whenever possible she used a crest, or a tiny sketch of gates, lodges, or doorways if her family owned a country estate. She topped all this with generous blobs of colored wax to seal the envelope, a custom revived from colonial days. White was for weddings, purple for mourning, lavender for condolences, and chocolate for dinner invitations.

Wedding gifts were a recurrent concern and here there was a wide choice, from Tiffany diamonds and Steinway pianos to lace parasols, or crewel-worked hand screens. Silver baskets and epergnes were standard gifts, and so were silver eggstands, Dresden candelabra, Venetian mirrors, bonbon dishes, and etchings or chromos in arabesque frames. But old silver and limp leather books were infallibly right, and silver toastracks were as popular as the electric toasters of today. While marriage flourished, divorce was a subject mentioned with bated breath, if at all.

Theatrical stars were not the social favorites they are today, partly because they were prone to seek divorce. They were a group apart, who thrilled their audiences but were received at the kitchen entrance. Fanny Kemble and Mrs. Trollope both fought this intolerance. Sarah Bernhardt was coolly received in Chicago until Mrs. Potter Palmer insisted that she have the best suite in the Palmer House and sent in her own linen and silver for the actress' use. Mrs. Jack Gardner of Boston went still further, breaking down all barriers where artists were concerned and inviting them to stay at her home. In course of time they were made welcome at the White House, too, until by 1966 they dined in droves with the Johnsons and a cinema star was the approved beau of a White House daughter.

Earlier in the century it was another White House daughter—Alice Roosevelt—who created a scandal by smoking in the East Room, and William Howard Taft was the President who had to light her cigarette. He already knew that Theodore Roosevelt's dashing daughter was a smoker, for on their trip with congressmen to the Orient in 1905 he had watched her drawing cigarettes from her gold hairpin case. When Baroness Rosen, wife of the Russian ambassador, lit a cigarette, the President, who did not smoke, felt obliged to provide a flame for the eager Alice. Washington seethed with gossip next day, although she was not doing anything that some of the most distinguished ladies of the Revolution had not tried. Some had puffed on clay pipes and had even chewed tobacco and inhaled snuff. Moreover, Mrs. Zachary Taylor's history in this respect had once clouded the

"The Greek Slave," on view at New York's Dusseldorf Gallery in 1858. This statue was the work of Hiram Powers, first American sculptor to win fame. The beauteous slave was alternately the scandal and the delight of the moment, having roused such a storm in Cincinnati that local clergymen had been called on to view her and give her clearance. Some of the local ladies had demanded draperies for her appearance in the Queen City. Their New York sisters look more interested than scandalized. They even brought along their children for the viewing. Engraving by E. Thew.

Chaperonage was tight in the 1870s, and parents were usually at hand to guard their darling daughters, except in the country where young men found many ways of catching up with them in the garden or arbor, of lingering by the well, or stealing kisses at picnics and on boating parties. The buggy served just as well as the automobile, and bundling was still in style, but this modest maiden seems to be coyly resisting such forward behavior.

Ladies' luncheon at Delmonico's, 1902. By the turn of the century American women were firmly committed to the luncheon habit so well established today. The organization of the Sorosis Club on its premises had linked the worldly Delmonico's with the women's cause, and the dowdier women of earnest purpose were as welcome in this gourmet's paradise as their flashier sisters, who invariably arrived escorted by men. This group seems to have taken note of fashion, although an occasional Victorian bonnet is in view.

White House. Even the fastidious Mrs. Taft had tried cigarettes as a girl in Cincinnati, and had smoked them on the beach at Narragansett. However, her fellow Ohioan William McKinley thought as late as 1891 that no girl should even be seen with a man who smoked in public. And an etiquette writer in 1887 said that the prospects of future happiness were slight for a girl who would let herself stumble into this trap.

Adah Isaacs Menken, the actress who also pioneered with bobbed hair, caused excitement in New Orleans before the Civil War by smoking cigars in resturants. The *New Orleans Picayune* accused her of "destroying the delicate fabric of feminity," and Adah retorted that she did not question the editor's right to use "segars," a fashion that had been brought into the country by soldiers returning from the Crimean War. By the end of the nineteenth century Amy Lowell was puffing at stogies in conservative Boston, and in 1966 elegant little pipes and miniature cigars were showing up at the smartest haunts.

But early in the twentieth century the whole subject was bathed in scandal, and only the boldest individualists dared assert themselves in this respect. In 1904 a woman was arrested for smoking on Fifth Avenue and soon afterward Mrs. Frederick Lewisohn was forced to abandon her cigarette at Sherry's. Mrs. Patrick Campbell had the same experience at the Plaza. But it was becoming clear by this time that women not only liked to smoke in private, but many were willing to admit a fondness for the combination of tweed and tobacco in their men. World War I encouraged this taste, as women drove ambulances abroad and lived in a man's world.

The cigarette manufacturers were quickly attuned to the new mood and the famous Chesterfield advertisement "Blow Some My Way" and Murad's "Be Nonchalant, Light a Murad" helped to break the ice. Soon women were smoking almost as freely as men, except that they favored Egyptian and Turkish brands, a suitable accompaniment for their Turkish trousers, piles of cushions, and incense-burning evenings in Bohemian apartments. The 1920s was the natural setting for this sort of thing, and soon the public accepted the sight of slouching girls, waving long cigarette holders with bracelet-laden arms and disappearing behind clouds of smoke.

Filters came next, and by 1957 Emily Post decreed that no hostess could afford not to offer her guests cigarettes after dinner. Smoking was accepted at country clubs, at the races, in drawing rooms and restaurants, but temperance advocates and many clubwomen turned chilly glances at the puffing sisterhood. Amy Vanderbilt had some reservations, finding it impossible to imagine a "lady walking along a city street either chewing gum or smoking." But she conceded that it might pass muster in the country, where a "man's pipe, like his dog, is classically his inseparable companion" and the woman's cigarette might go along with the man, his pipe and his dog. However, the habit was not confined to country lanes, and soon women were seen on the street, in the supermarket, in theater lobbies, and in a good many other places puffing contentedly at their cigarettes. The cancer-prevention campaign made some slight difference, but did not slow up the more confirmed smokers. The death rate of men who smoked was found to be five times higher than in the case of women, allowing for the fact that men smoke more and inhale more consistently than women.

Chaperonage—which was dying out as smoking came to the fore—became a fixed social convention in the 1880s, but it existed in one form or another from the days of the Pilgrims, and the "matronizing" of the Civil War era was a well-established custom. As Americans traveled more they picked up European conventions, but in rural places the two sexes continued to mingle with freedom and to go buggy riding in the moonlight without an attendant. In urban centers the vigil was tight and parents were warned by etiquette writers not to let their daughters sit in the parlor with young men late at night. They might go to church services, picture galleries, or make afternoon calls by themselves, but they should never go to the theater with a young man unless a chaperone was at hand. They might drive in the country and attend picnics but they were forbidden to stop at "saloons" for ice cream while on their way.

To ride alone in an omnibus in the middle of the nineteenth century was considered racy and no nice girl went without a chaperone to a skating rink, a ball, or the races. Even after she was engaged she could not ride with her fiancé in a closed carriage. It took time to break down these taboos but chaperones melted away in the twentieth century, except for the most formal events. Mrs. Emily Post decreed in 1957 that the only chaperone worth having was a "young girl's efficiency in chaperoning herself." Training, she added, had taken the place of protection. Two world wars had helped to break down the barriers. College degrees, an abundance of jobs, sex education, more relaxed social views, sports, and the vigorous outdoor life had helped to sever the chain that had held the young girl in tow.

The tradition began with *Daisy Miller*, Henry James's much-discussed creation. His book, published in 1879 and dramatized in 1883, drew attention to the American girl's ways abroad and made her a conversation piece. Out of it all sprang the vogue for chaperoned "excursion parties." Soon carefully nurtured girls were traveling under the sheltering wing of a matriarchal type who could steer them away from professional mashers and was equally at home in the Garden of the Gods or St. Mark's Square. Although admired abroad for her spirit and style the American girl came under fire on many counts.

While conceding that she was "stylish to the backbone, independent, but very pure, devoted to dress, pleasure, spending money," a French commentator added: "Parisian women detest her; provincial women despise her; men of all countries adore her, but will not marry her unless she has an immense fortune. She is a wild plant put in a hothouse; feels cramped in Europe and pushes her branches through the panes without the least heed of the fragile plants and vegetables on all sides of her."

But once out in the business world the American girl found new horizons and cultivated her own set of rules. The few who had college degrees, apartments of their own, bank accounts, and an enterprising spirit used all of them to good effect. "Catlike, she may do a little stalking," said Emily Post. "But run? Not a step. The freedom of today allows her to go to meet him halfway, but the girl who runs, runs after a man who runs faster."

It was not really until the 1880s that women pulled themselves wholly out of the Victorian fog, took up sports and exercise, went about town in fine attire, traveled, lunched at Delmonico's, founded clubs, and showed the dash and spirit that traditionally belong to the American woman. Marriage at first was their sole career and a good one it seemed, too. Most of them liked it and thought that they were fulfilling their destinies until the message reached them that they were spiritless creatures who could not help their children if they did not help themselves. As the ferment of unrest got to work they learned about property rights, voting rights, conjugal rights, and a dozen other varieties pointed out to them by the campaigning feminists. Yet at heart the majority were with Queen Victoria when she urged women on both sides of the Atlantic "to join in checking this mad, wicked folly of Woman's Rights on which my poor sex is bent, forgetting every sense of womanly feeling and propriety." The more wary types, well pleased with their man-made world, still preferred the devious approach and the kind of silent influence Abigail Adams exercised through her husband.

Actually, the pace was set for all time by Abigail when she wrote to John, urging him to remember the ladies in drawing up the Constitution. Playfully she reminded him not to put "such unlimited power into the hands of the Husbands" and suggested that she might foment a rebellion among the ladies against a government in which they had no representation. She considered herself "destitute in every part of education" and wrote: "I most sincerely wish that some more liberal plan might be laid and executed for the benefit of the rising generation and that our new Constitution may be distinguished for encouraging learning and virtue. If we mean to have heroes, statesmen, and philosophers, we should have learned women."

That was the core of the matter. Bear them. Train them. Breed men who could do things. John Adams replied that he thought women should be barred from politics because of their physical delicacy and preoccupation with home life. But he conceded that women and children had minds at least as good, and judgment as independent, as men lacking in property. And if such men were given the ballot, why not women, too?

Some of the women who tried to answer this question in the nineteenth century were learned, like Lucy Stone, and others were merely rabid in their cause. Between them all they moved heaven and earth, beginning with the day in 1848 when they gathered at Seneca Falls by carriage and cart to hold the first Women's Rights Convention, and ending with their victory parade in 1920, when the vote at last had been won. Some brilliant and courageous figures traveled the long hard road in between—the noble, like Mrs. Lucretia Mott and Susan Anthony; the warm, human and informed, like Mrs. Elizabeth Cady Stanton; the thoughtful and pragmatic, like Lucy Stone; the eloquent and reckless, like Victoria Woodhull. Circling all around them were fervent doers backing other, allied causes—Harriet Beecher Stowe, who shook up a nation and helped to start a war; Elizabeth Blackwell, who opened the medical world to women; Antoinette Blackwell, who breached the pulpit; Dorothea L. Dix, who affected prison and asylum reform; Clara Barton, who founded the Red Cross in America; Sarah and Angelina Grimké, the southern sisters who were ardent abolitionists, the cause on which all these women were agreed; Scottish-born Frances Wright, who preached free love as well as abolition and woman suffrage; and the shining star, impressively successful in her field, Frances Willard, who organized the Women's Christian Temperance Union in 1874 and became known around the world for her spectacular crusade.

Right on her heels came Carry Nation of Kansas, who wielded a hatchet in her one-woman campaign and wrecked saloons from California to Nova Scotia. Carry was one of the lunatic members of this nineteenth-century procession, but the thousands who followed her thought her a martyr when she was jailed on scores of occasions. She had some of her most effective moments in Ohio, where women sang hymns outside saloon doors and knelt before the bar to pray. Not until the 1960s brought a new brand of agitator had so troublesome a group crossed the national scene as Carry's hatcheteers. Like Frances Willard, Mrs. Nation hypnotized large sections of the public and paved the way for temperance legislation that resulted in the prohibition amendment of the 1920s. Carry's attacks were not confined to drink. With equal fluency she ranted against tobacco, Masonry, sex, and everything else she regarded as sin. She even insisted on

The Great Awakening

"Blow Some My Way," the Chesterfield cigarette advertisement that roped in countless women smokers in the 1920s, was symbolic of their new emancipation. They had stormed the business world. They had won the vote. Soon they were smoking almost as freely as men, although up to the time of World War I they had been subject to heavy censure and ostracism if seen puffing cigarettes. There were many exceptions, but Alice Roosevelt Longworth raised a storm when she smoked openly in the East Room in 1907.

The bundling tradition, an early form of courtship, received national attention in 1933 when The Pursuit of Happiness, a Theater Guild production dealing with this custom, was a Broadway hit. A notched bundling board separated the two stars, Peggy Conklin and Toni Selwart, after the fashion of the early bundling bed. For the time being this quaint and ancient form of courtship, known in Scandinavia, Holland, Scotland, and Ireland before it reached America, became a conversation piece across the country. Any bed would do, but the dividing board was considered mandatory in the best-run households. The custom was more innocuous than it sounds, and it was often supervised by the girl's parents.

bartenders draping their wax nudes when she went smashing their saloons with her hatchet.

Whatever their tactics these individualists roused women from their apathy, but even more potent forces had drawn them out into the working world. The typewriter and the sewing machine, which freed many from the endless drudgery of their needlework and fitted them for jobs, had much to do with the feminine emergence from the Victorian chrysalis. Each was a mechanical marvel in its day; each in its own way freed women for the larger life. The sewing machine came first and was a combination of at least a dozen American inventions, but Isaac M. Singer's model, with a foot-powered treadle leaving both hands free to handle cloth, swept the field. The distribution of paper patterns by Madame Demorest and the Buttericks in the 1870s dovetailed neatly with the sewing machine, and home dressmaking lost its negligible quality and became more professional. The tailoring and dressmaking world was profoundly affected by this innovation, and the United States started on its long drive toward primacy in garmentmaking. Soon sewing machines were being exported in greater numbers than any other American commodity, and they turned up in darkest Africa as well as in Buckingham Palace.

In 1868 a typewriter patent was taken out by Christopher Latham Sholes of Milwaukee, who five years later sold out to the Remington Arms Company. The Remington typewriter was later perfected from the Sholes model and it sold well as soon as it reached the market. The first typewriters, some of which had wooden keys, used only capital letters. In 1878 the keyshift encompassed upper and lower shift. The touch system, which has simplified life for millions of office girls, was introduced in the 1890s, and now only authors and other backward people boast that they use the two-finger method. Typewriters came smaller, lighter, portable, and in colors. Like attaché cases they became the symbol of the traveling American around the world. Girls swarmed into offices, with Gregg or Pitman training and, in more recent times, Speedwriting. Business speeded up, jobs abounded, and it soon became good form to use the typewriter for social correspondence. Emily Post finally conceded that a "typewritten letter is not only proper but to be preferred in all letter writing of length."

A golden door had opened for American girls. They found independence such as they had never known before and they were brought in touch with a man's world of vivid action. Although a million and a half women had moved out of the home by 1870 they worked mostly as teachers, governesses, seamstresses, or domestics. Only seven had been bold enough that year to take jobs as secretaries. By 1905 five million were at work, and one million were in factories. But with their new skill on the typewriter they could walk down many avenues, and with every decade the horizons have widened. In 1963 there were 2,570,000 secretaries, stenographers, and typists across the country, and 23,479,000 women employed in all. Moreover, since 1955 the number of working women aged thirty-five to sixty-four has risen from 11.4 million to 15 million. It has been noted that some of the old prejudice against hiring younger women lest they marry, become pregnant, or precipitately leave their jobs has eased to some extent with the more general use of the birth-control pill.

Though women have cracked practically all barriers on the job level only 1 per cent earn $10,000 or more and 3 per cent have incomes over $7,000. In general they earn only about half as much as men do for equal work and their median income has been set at $3,145, compared with $5,308 for men. But a limited number have reached the top echelons and thousands have found glamour and satisfaction in their work. Today the executive secretary flies around the world on important missions with her employer. Her professional capacity has opened the door to executive jobs, to power and travel, to a front seat at conferences of worldwide interest. Women have moved much faster than men in the last century—perhaps because they had further to go. They are now installed at the seat of government, svelte and respected, if not politically potent. Each President remembers the women voters and President Johnson has outdone all others in the number of women he has appointed to office. Though only 15 per cent of the nation's executives are women, they have come a long way from the Victorian parlors where all the fuss began. At the time there were dire predictions about the fate of the home. Emancipation was a way of life that radically altered both the home and the business picture; in fact, it was the biggest revolution in family life. It fattened the family purse and fed the feminine ego, but it also created new problems with children and husbands. It made women more efficient, fast-moving, and better groomed, but critics also viewed them as being "hard and brilliant, their glitter the glitter of ice." In any event, women's freedom had come to stay, and there was nothing anyone could do about it. Some men delighted in it; others hated it, where their own wives were concerned. It sent grandmothers back to college, when they could break away from baby sitting with their grandchildren.

When Mary Lyon founded Mount Holyoke in 1837 and Lucy Stone was accepted at Oberlin, college doors began to open to women. In 1882 at least twenty-five were receptive if doubtful. Would studies ruin the girls' health and make them unfit as wives and mothers? Many thought so. Though the question found a variety of answers, the doubters need not have worried. Few had gone truly blue stocking. In odd moments the more frivolous ones still trapped young men on the croquet lawn as easily as they netted butterflies in their flower gardens.

A study made of 1,400 college graduates in the 1880s showed that they stood up to life better than those who had never earned a diploma. The death rate of their children was uncommonly low for the era, and 78 per cent of the girls themselves were in robust health.

Beginning with the 1920s the career drive was stronger than the marriage impulse in the college set, although many managed both. In the next thirty years careers were played to the limit, but in the 1950s a study made at Vassar showed that "strong commitment to an activity or career other than that of housewife is rare." On the other hand, in the summer of 1966 Professor H. Lee Hornbake, of the University of Maryland, said that the "career drive in girls today exceeds the mating drive." But regardless of the limitations of such surveys, evidence abounds that the drive is all in favor of love and marriage, and that home and large families have not loomed so clearly on the horizon in the last hundred years. More than 60 per cent of the nation's girl students leave college before graduation, and mostly to get married.

While one faction upholds Betty Friedan's contention in *The Feminine Mystique* that the college woman is bored to death with kitchen and nursery, the other exalts the all-feminine role of the wife who devotes herself wholeheartedly to her family and would never consider working away from home. The fact is that a great many do it. In the last fifteen years 58 per cent of the older women holding jobs have college degrees; in many instances their children are grown up.

In spite of the long hard drive for academic equality the zest for advanced degrees is on the wane. In 1930 women held 40 per cent of the masters' degrees and 15 per cent of the doctorates. By 1964 the percentages had fallen to 32 per cent for the one and 11 per cent for the other. The percentage of American women in technical or professional jobs has slipped in the last twenty years, but the number holding down unusual jobs or running businesses of their own has gone up. Even in the nineteenth century the individualists found a foothold. While women were scrabbling their way into colleges, uninvited and unwelcome, some of their sex were operating successfully as cattle dealers, ranch owners, dairy farmers, and fruit growers. Cattle herds roamed the plains and the biggest ranch in the world was run by Mrs. Henrietta King in Texas. As in the colonial days women sometimes took hold of the empires their husbands had founded, like women dominant in the newspaper field today. But these were the exceptions.

In general New York was still distinctly a man's town in the 1880s, and the nation as a whole was dead to its feminine potential, except as the breeders of men. Ladies, as they were still inevitably known, were just beginning to get involved in the public ferment. Some had time to themselves, since many families lived in hotels and boardinghouses, and catering was a well-established custom. During the nineteenth century more than 70 per cent of the American population lived in boardinghouses at one time or another. Installment buying flourished as World War I broke out. The American home was being furbished up with all the new conveniences, and garages were being built to house the new cars. The millionaire was in disrepute as the so-called muckrakers exposed the way in which some had made their fortunes. They had become the arch villains, no matter how fast they tied their kites to the philanthropic standard.

But things in general livened up in the twentieth century. Americans had been pretty well persuaded through their own travels and their visiting critics that they were in need of social polish. The image of the blustering, noisy American, boasting and chewing gum, and of pert, ill-mannered children was pervasive, however unjust. With typical energy they immersed themselves all over again in a series of self-improvement books, and Dale Carnegie helped to restore self-confidence after Sinclair Lewis had done his worst to his fellow countrymen of the Middle West. Emily Post kept up her barrage in books and syndicated columns against the pretentious word, loud talk, the "twang and slur and shout and burr," the use of the unspeakable "pardon me" and such words as "brunch" and "dandy." But so swift is the flow of social change that "brunch" had become high style, in fact and in name, by the 1960s, with the smartest hotels and restaurants giving it the accolade. While not against slang, Mrs. Post felt that it should be fresh and applicable. She discouraged hand kissing in a nation not attuned to it, and she thought it unfair for children to call their parents by their first names.

But other powerful forces were at work: the fashion, home, and town and country magazines, *Vanity Fair*, the *Smart Set*, and *The New Yorker*, which flashed into view in 1925 with plush advertising, wry wit, and snob appeal; the expatriates; and the gradual birth of café society. *Vogue* boasted that 42 per cent of its readers had their homes done by decorators, that 80 per cent used wine in their cooking, that 95 per cent had one or more cars and 86 per cent traveled on the grand scale, not to speak of all those who had period furniture, were dressed by Mainbocher, had dazzling country places, and knew how and where to be seen. But no longer, as in the 1890s, did they stand apart as fabulous privileged women. The ease with which girls with good jobs zoomed around the world in jets, the clever clothes they bought at bargain counters, the sophisticated meals they whipped up (and cooked with wine), their dancing in the discothèques and their interest in public causes, had been a leveling force with the traditional smart set. It was still all right to be chic, original, dashing, and different, but not to be a snob, though it took two world wars to establish this.

Once World War I had been won and the prosperity of the

1920s enfolded the land, the productivity of the average American increased by 43 per cent. Motorcars by the thousands rolled along the highways. Skyscrapers rose almost overnight. Prohibition cast its blight on the social life of a high-paced decade. Radio swept the country and farmers listened to sermons by the kitchen fire or heard an inaugural address before their newspapers reached them. Their daughters went off to Hollywood to become movie stars, beauty queens or, sometimes, carhops.

In the 1930s the country reeled under the effects of the Depression. This changed the face of the world, and the spirit of revolt and protest burned high among writers and artists. The farmers talked of the Dust Bowl and the sharecroppers, of soil conservation, irrigation, flood control, rural electrification, and the new technology in which they found themselves entangled by government control. Their wives enjoyed electrified kitchens and their children drove in public buses to consolidated schools instead of wandering along country lanes to the one-room schoolhouse, as they had done before. They became used to the newsreel, the loudspeaker, the tabloid newspaper, and the whining instruments of the Jazz Age.

Then came the 1940s with war and the atomic bomb. With this cataclysmic event the social pattern changed forever and the Space Age was born, leading to the fantastic journeys of the satellites and the landing on the moon. Life grew faster-paced, more filled with threat and promise. America moved deeper into the international picture and faced new domestic crises. At no time in American history had more been heard about the underprivileged and their woes. Although the gross national product rose from $104 billion in 1929 to more than $700 billion in 1966, between forty and fifty million persons were still rated poor, with only 48 per cent making six thousand dollars a year. With this went a restless moving about, from job to job, from home to home. One American in five changes his place of residence each year.

Both men and women live in a different world and cope with new realities. The scientific, political, and human developments of the twentieth century have altered not only the thinking but also the customs and manners of the American people. As John Gunther has pointed out, the last century has seen greater changes than all the preceding years in American history—"dynamic, desperate, picturesque and revolutionary in spirit as well as in substance." The spectrum has moved from the lonely prairie to the horse and buggy, and then to outer space; from the Indian arrow to the nuclear bomb; and from the wilderness to the luxury and plenty of today. Its power, its glory, and its horror have been graphically caught on the television screen, where both young and old have seen a President assassinated, an atom bomb exploding, and men walking in space.

The Great Awakening

Sources of Illustrations

KEY: T = *Top*, C = *Center*, B = *Bottom*, TR = *Top Right*, TL = *Top Left*, TC = *Top Center*, CR = *Center Right*, CL = *Center Left*, BR = *Bottom Right*, BL = *Bottom Left*, BC = *Bottom Center*.

Sources not acknowledged in this list may be found within the caption accompanying the illustration.

Page 4: T Courtesy of New-York Historical Society; B Courtesy of New York Public Library, Stokes Collection

Page 11: T Courtesy of Metropolitan Museum of Art; c Courtesy of Library of Congress, Historic American Buildings Survey; BR Courtesy of Virginia State Chamber of Commerce, *photograph by P. I. Flournoy*; BL Courtesy of Essex Institute, Salem, Massachusetts

Page 12: T Courtesy of Essex Institute, Salem, Massachusetts; c Courtesy of Chicago Historical Society; B Courtesy of Los Angeles State and County Arboretum, Arcadia, California

Page 18: T Courtesy of Essex Institute, Salem, Massachusetts; c Courtesy of Library of Congress; B Courtesy of New York Public Library, Stokes Collection

Page 20: T Courtesy of New York Public Library, Picture Collection; c Photograph courtesy of Museum of the City of New York, Edward W. C. Arnold Collection, lent by Metropolitan Museum of Art; B Courtesy of New York Public Library, Picture Collection

Page 27: R Courtesy of Library of Congress, Historic American Buildings Survey; L Courtesy of Library of Congress, Historic American Buildings Survey

Page 28: T Courtesy of Museum of the City of New York, J. Clarence Davies Collection; c Courtesy of Mission San Gabriel Arcangel, San Gabriel, California; B Courtesy of St. John's Abbey, Collegeville, Minnesota

Page 37: T Courtesy of J. B. Lippincott and Co.; c Courtesy of Metropolitan Museum of Art, gift of Samuel P. Avery, 1897; B Courtesy of Smith College, Northampton, Massachusetts

Page 42: T Courtesy of William L. Clements Library, University of Michigan; B *Photograph by Bosshart*

Page 44: T Courtesy of Brentano's Bookstore, New York; B Courtesy of Museum of the City of New York

Page 48: T Courtesy of New-York Historical Society; B Courtesy of Lincoln Center for the Performing Arts, *photograph by Martha Swope*

Page 49: T Courtesy of New-York Historical Society; c Courtesy of Vermont Development Department; B Courtesy of Museum of Modern Art, *photograph by Alexandre Georges*

Page 57: T Courtesy of New-York Historical Society; CR Courtesy of New-York Historical Society, Bella C. Landauer Collection; CL Courtesy of Museum of the City of New York; B Courtesy of Museum of the City of New York

Page 66: T Courtesy of New-York Historical Society, Bella C. Laudauer Collection; C Courtesy of Shelburne Museum, Inc., *photograph by Einars J. Mengis*; B Courtesy of New-York Historical Society

Page 75: T Courtesy of Library of Congress, William Howard Taft Family Papers; B Courtesy of Chicago Historical Society

Page 85: T Courtesy of Shelburne Museum, Inc., *photograph by Einars J. Mengis*; B Courtesy of Metropolitan Museum of Art, gift of Mrs. Vincent Lockwood, 1923

Page 86: T Courtesy of New-York Historical Society; C Courtesy of New-York Historical Society; B Courtesy of Library of Congress

Page 87: T Photograph courtesy of Museum of the City of New York, the Edward W. C. Arnold Collection, lent by Metropolitan Museum of Art; B Courtesy of New-York Historical Society

Page 93: T Courtesy of Museum of the City of New York

Page 94: T Courtesy of New-York Historical Society, George Bagoe Collection; B Courtesy of Historical Society of Pennsylvania

Page 100: T Courtesy of Old Sturbridge Village, Sturbridge, Massachusetts; B Courtesy of National Gallery of Art, Index of American Design

Page 101: T Courtesy of Metropolitan Museum of Art, Rogers Fund, 1940; CL Courtesy of Old Sturbridge Village, Sturbridge, Massachusetts; CR Courtesy of Shelburne Museum, Inc., *photograph by Einars J. Mengis*; B Courtesy of Metropolitan Museum of Art, gift of Mrs. Russell Sage, 1909

Page 102: T Courtesy of Metropolitan Museum of Art, Rogers Fund, 1945; B Courtesy of Metropolitan Museum of Art, Rogers Fund, 1923

Page 104: T Courtesy of Metropolitan Museum of Art, gift of Mrs. Russell Sage, 1909; C Courtesy of Metropolitan Museum of Art, purchase 1940, Joseph Pulitzer bequest; B Courtesy of Henry Francis du Pont Winterthur Museum, Winterthur, Delaware, *photograph by Gilbert Ask*

Page 109: T Courtesy of Metropolitan Museum of Art, gift of Mrs. Russell Sage, 1909; C Courtesy of Metropolitan Museum of Art, gift of Mr. and Mrs. Paul Moore, 1946; BL Courtesy of Metropolitan Museum of Art, gift of Mrs. Samuel Auchmuty Tucker (née Anne Derby), 1947; BC Courtesy of Metropolitan Museum of Art, Rogers Fund, 1954; BR Courtesy of Metropolitan Museum of Art

Page 111: T Courtesy of Metropolitan Museum of Art, gift of Mr. and Mrs. William A. Moore, 1923; B Photograph courtesy of New-York Historical Society

Page 113: T Courtesy of Herman Miller Inc., photograph courtesy of Ruff, Kiek and McAuliffe, Inc.; B Courtesy of Knoll Associates, Inc.

Page 115: T Courtesy of Shelburne Museum, Inc., *photograph by Einars J. Mengis*; C Courtesy of Henry Francis du Pont Winterthur Museum, Winterthur, Delaware, *photograph by Gilbert Ask*; B Courtesy of Los Angeles County and State Arboretum, Arcadia, California

Page 116: T Courtesy of Henry Francis du Pont Winterthur Museum, Winterthur, Delaware, *photograph by Gilbert Ask*; CL Courtesy of Metropolitan Museum of Art, gift of the Members of the Committee of the Bertha King Benkard Memorial Fund, 1946; CR Courtesy of Metropolitan Museum of Art, gift of Mrs. Bayard Verplanck, 1940; B Courtesy of Old Salem, Inc., Winston-Salem, North Carolina

Page 117: T Courtesy of Henry Francis du Pont Winterthur Museum, Winterthur, Delaware, *photograph by Gilbert Ask*; B Courtesy of *House Beautiful*, *photograph by Ezra Stoller Associates*

Page 119: T Courtesy of Old Salem, Inc., Winston-Salem, North Carolina; C Courtesy of Metropolitan Museum of Art; B Courtesy of Villa Boscobel, Garrison-on-Hudson, New York, *photograph by Danny Wann*

Page 124: T Courtesy of Vermont Development Department; B Courtesy of The Tile Council of America, Inc.

Page 128: T Courtesy of New York Public Library, Picture Collection; B Courtesy of The Tile Council of America, Inc.

Page 136: TR Courtesy of Museum of the City of New York, Byron Collection, *photograph by Byron*; TL Courtesy of New York Public Library, Picture Collection; BL Courtesy of Shelburne Museum, Inc., *photograph by Einars J. Mengis*; BR Courtesy of Wide World Photos

Page 141: T Courtesy of Brooklyn Museum; C Courtesy of Museum of the City of New York, Byron Collection, *photograph by Byron*; B Courtesy of Melanie Kahane Associates, *photograph by Fred Winchell*

Page 149: T Courtesy of Museum of the City of New York; C Courtesy of New-York Historical Society, Bella C. Landauer Collection; B Courtesy of Museum of the City of New York, "Changing New York," *photograph by Berenice Abbott*

Page 152: T Courtesy of Otis Elevator Company; B Courtesy of Museum of the City of New York

Page 153: T Courtesy of Library of Congress; B Courtesy of New-York Historical Society, Bella C. Landauer Collection

Page 158: T Courtesy of Rockefeller Center, Inc.; C Courtesy of Skidmore, Owings & Merrill, *photograph by Ezra Stoller Associates*; B Courtesy of TWA, *photograph by Ezra Stoller Associates*

Page 162: B Courtesy of Chicago Historical Society, *photograph by D. Ward*

Page 163: T Courtesy of Isabella Stewart Gardner Museum, Boston, Massachusetts; CR Courtesy of Wallace Neff, F.A.I.A., *photograph by Maynard Parker*; BL *Photograph for Reston by William A. Graham*

Page 168: T Courtesy of Metropolitan Museum of Art, bequest of Susan Ludlow Parish, 1950; C Courtesy of Metropolitan Museum of Art, bequest of John R. Morron, 1950; B Courtesy of Metropolitan Museum of Art, gift of Dr. Hanson K. Corning, 1944

Page 169: T Courtesy of Metropolitan Museum of Art, Rogers Fund, 1920; C Courtesy of Metropolitan Museum of Art, gift of Courtlandt Palmer, 1950; B Courtesy of Metropolitan Museum of Art, gift of Dabney William Diggs, 1924

Page 176: TL Courtesy of Museum of the City of New York; C Courtesy of Museum of the City of New York; B Courtesy of New-York Historical Society

Page 177: Courtesy of Library of Congress

Page 181: B Courtesy of New-York Historical Society, George Bagoe Collection

Page 192: T Courtesy of *Harper's Bazaar*; C Courtesy of *Vogue*, copyright © 1925, 1953, The Condé Nast Publications, Inc.; B Courtesy of *Harper's Bazaar*

Page 195: TR Courtesy of *Vogue*, copyright © 1935,

1953, The Condé Nast Publications, Inc.; TL Courtesy of *Vogue*, copyright © 1928, 1953, The Condé Nast Publications, Inc.; B Courtesy of *Vogue*, copyright © 1944, 1953, The Condé Nast Publications, Inc.

Page 197: T Courtesy of Chanel, *portrait by Christian Bérard*; B Courtesy of Chanel

Page 199: TL Courtesy of Christian Dior, *photograph by Maywald*; TC Courtesy of Alexander's, New York; C Courtesy of Mollie Parnis, New York; BL Courtesy of United Press International, Inc.; BR Courtesy of Ohrbach's, New York

Page 200: T Courtesy of Metropolitan Museum of Art, gift of Mrs. H. Lyman Hooker, 1936; R Courtesy of Brooklyn Museum; BL Courtesy of Priscilla of Boston

Page 208: TR Courtesy of Shelburne Museum, Inc., *photograph by Einars J. Mengis*; BR Courtesy of the Kenneth Beauty Salon & Products, Inc., New York

Page 210: TL Courtesy of Metropolitan Museum of Art, bequest of Mrs. Maria P. James, 1911; CR Courtesy of Metropolitan Museum of Art, bequest of Mrs. Maria P. James, 1911; BL Courtesy of Connecticut Historical Society

Page 213: T Courtesy of New-York Historical Society, *photograph by Pach Brothers, New York*; B Courtesy of New-York Historical Society, Bella C. Landauer Collection

Page 219: TL Courtesy of New-York Historical Society, Bella C. Landauer Collection; BL Courtesy of Franklin Simon & Company, New York; BR Courtesy of United Press International, Inc.

Page 224: CR Courtesy of Metropolitan Museum of Art, gift of Finley J. Shepard, 1939; BL Courtesy of Ohrbach's, New York

Page 228: TR Courtesy of Harry Winston, Inc., New York; CL Courtesy of Essex Institute, Salem, Massachusetts; CR Courtesy of New-York Historical Society, Bella C. Landauer Collection, scrapbook; BR Courtesy of Metropolitan Museum of Art, anonymous gift, 1953

Page 234: TL Courtesy of Metropolitan Museum of Art, bequest of John R. Morron, 1950; TR Courtesy of Metropolitan Museum of Art, gift of Grace H. Dodge, 1909; C Courtesy of Metropolitan Museum of Art, bequest of Richard DeWolfe Brixey, 1943; BC Courtesy of Metropolitan Museum of Art, purchase 1940, anonymous gift

Page 236: TL Courtesy of Museum of the City of New York, J. Clarence Davies Collection; C Courtesy of Museum of the City of New York, J. Clarence Davies Collection

Page 238: TL Courtesy of New York Public Library, Picture Collection; CR Reprinted by permission of *Men's Wear* Magazine, June 25, 1965, issue, copyright 1965, Fairchild Publications, Inc.

Page 240: T Reprinted by permission of *Men's Wear* Magazine, June 25, 1965, issue, copyright 1965, Fairchild Publications, Inc.; C Courtesy of Village Square, New York; B Courtesy of Ohrbach's, New York

Page 248: T Courtesy of New York Public Library, Stokes Collection; B Courtesy of Museum of the City of New York, J. Clarence Davies Collection

Page 252: T Courtesy of Museum of the City of New York, Byron Collection, *photograph by Byron*; B Courtesy of Library of Congress

Page 253: T Courtesy of New-York Historical Society, George Bagoe Collection; B Courtesy of The Bank of New York

Page 257: TL Courtesy of Isabella Stewart Gardner Museum, Boston, Massachusetts; CR Courtesy of Chicago Historical Society; B Courtesy of Metropolitan Museum of Art, gift of Consuelo Vanderbilt Balsan, 1946

Page 262: TL Courtesy of Museum of the City of New York, Byron Collection, *photograph by Byron*; CR Courtesy of Museum of the City of New York, Byron Collection, *photograph by Byron*; B Courtesy of Museum of the City of New York.

Page 270: TR Courtesy of New York Public Library, Prints Division; CR Courtesy of New-York Historical Society; BL Courtesy of Museum of the City of New York, J. Clarence Davies Collection

Page 271: T Courtesy of New York Public Library, Stokes Collection; B Courtesy of New-York Historical Society

Page 272: B Courtesy of New-York Historical Society

Page 276: C Courtesy of Ford Motor Company Archives; B Photograph courtesy of California Division of Highways

Page 277: T Courtesy of New-York Historical Society; B Courtesy of New-York Historical Society

Page 286: T Courtesy of New-York Historical Society

Page 292: TL Courtesy of New York Public Library, Prints Division; CL Courtesy of Museum of the City of New York, Byron Collection, *photograph by Byron*; BR Courtesy of New York Public Library, Picture Collection

Page 297: T Courtesy of Liggett & Myers Tobacco Company; B Courtesy of New York Public Library, Theater Collection

Notes

General References (excluding encyclopedias)

Adventures of America: 1857–1900, a Pictorial Record from Harper's Weekly, edited by John A. Kouwenhoven. New York: Harper & Brothers, 1938.

Album of American History, editor in chief, James Truslow Adams. 6 vols. New York: Charles Scribner's Sons, 1944–1960.

American Historical Prints, I. N. Phelps and Daniel C. Haskell. New York: New York Public Library, 1933.

The Columbia Historical Portrait of New York, edited by John A. Kouwenhoven. Garden City: Doubleday & Co., 1953.

A History of American Magazines, Frank Luther Mott. 4 vols. Cambridge, Mass.: Harvard University Press, 1938.

History of the City of New York: Its Origin, Rise and Progress, Martha J. Lamb. 5 vols. New York: A. S. Barnes & Company, 1877.

History of the United States from the Compromise of 1850, James Ford Rhodes. 9 vols. New York: The Macmillan Company, 1892–1922.

Life in America, Marshall B. Davidson. 2 vols. Boston: Houghton Mifflin Company, 1951.

Our Times: The United States, 1900—1925, Mark Sullivan. 6 vols. New York: Charles Scribner's Sons, 1926–1935.

The Pageant of America: A Pictorial History of the United States, edited by Ralph H. Gabriel. 15 vols. New Haven: Yale University Press, 1925–1929.

Picturesque America, 1794–1878, edited by William Cullen Bryant. 2 vols. New York: D. Appleton & Company, 1894.

The World in Vogue, compiled by the Editors of The Viking Press and *Vogue*. Editors for *Vogue*, Jessica Daves and Alexander Liberman. Editors for Viking, Bryan Holme and Katharine Tweed. New York: The Viking Press, 1963.

Magazines

Antiques; Architectural Review; Demorest's Family Magazine and Young America; Frank Leslie's Illustrated Newspaper; Frank Leslie's Illustrated Weekly; Frank Leslie's Ladies Gazette of Paris, London, and New York Fashion; Gazette of Fashion; Gentlemen's Quarterly; Godey's Lady's Book; Good Housekeeping; Graham's American Monthly Magazine; Harper's Bazar and Harper's Bazaar; Harper's Magazine; Harper's New Monthly Magazine; Harper's Weekly; House Beautiful; Ladies' Home Journal; Life; Look; McCall's; Madame Demorest's Mirror of Fashions; Men's Wear; Metropolitan; The New Yorker; Peterson's Magazine; Pictorial Review; Reader's Digest; Smart Set; Vanity Fair; Vogue; Woman's Home Companion; The Woman's Journal; Women's Wear Daily.

Chapter 1   *A New Land*

Wayne Andrews, *Architecture, Ambition and Americans* and *Architecture in America*; Carl Bridenbaugh, *Peter Harrison, First American Architect* and *Cities in Revolt* and *Cities in the Wilderness* and *The Colonial Craftsman*; Henry Collins Brown, *In the Golden Nineties*; Mark H. Brown and W. R. Felton, *The Frontier Years*; John Burchard and Albert Bush-Brown, *The Architecture of America*; Henry Steele Commager and Allan Nevins, *The Emergence of Modern America*; Ralph Adams Cram, *My Life in Architecture* and *The Gothic Quest*; Marshall B. Davidson, *Life in America*; Emmett Dedmon, *Fabulous Chicago*; Andrew Jackson Downing, *The Architecture of Country Houses and Cottage Residences*; Antoinette F. Downing and Vincent J. Scully, Jr., *The Architectural Heritage of Newport, Rhode Island, 1640–1915*; William Dunlap, *History of the Rise and Progress of the Arts of Design in the United States*; Alice Morse Earle, *Customs and Fashions in Old New England* and *Home Life in Colonial Days*; Charles L. Eastlake, *A History of the Gothic Revival*; William Fleming, *Art and Ideas*; O. S. Fowler, *A Home for All*; Sigfried Giedion, *Space, Time and Architecture*; Talbot Hamlin, *Greek Revival Architecture in America* and *The American Spirit in Architecture*; H. Hudson Holly, *Modern Dwellings in Town and Country*; Philip Hone, *The Diary of Philip Hone, 1828–1851*; Washington Irving, *Knickerbocker's History of New York*; Sidney Fiske Kimball, *American Architecture*; Helen M. Knowlton, *Art-Life of William Morris Hunt*; Minard Lafever, *The Complete Architectural Instructor*; Oliver W. Larkin, *Art and Life in America*; Benjamin Henry Latrobe, *The Journal of Latrobe*; Editors of *Life*, *America's Arts and Skills*; Russell Lynes, *The Domesticated Americans* and *The Tastemakers*; Charles Moore, *Daniel H. Burnham, Architect, Planner of Cities*; Samuel Eliot Morison, *The Oxford History of the American People*; Lloyd R. Morris, *Not So Long Ago* and *Incredible New York*; Lewis Mumford, *Roots of Contemporary American Architecture* and *Sticks and Stones* and *The Brown Decades* and *Technics and Civilization*; Alexander F. Oakey, *Building a Home*; Frederic L. Paxson, *History of the American Frontier*; C. A. Place, *Charles Bulfinch, Architect and Citizen*; Richard Pratt, *Houses, History and People*; Alfred Coxe Prime, *The Arts and*

Crafts in Philadelphia, Maryland and South Carolina; Julian Ralph, *Harper's Chicago and the World's Fair*; Arthur M. Schlesinger, *The Rise of the City 1878–1898* and *The Rise of Modern America 1865–1951*; Montgomery Schuyler, *American Architecture*; Mary Newton Stanard, *Colonial Virginia, Its People and Customs*; Russell Sturgis, *A Dictionary of Architecture and Building, Biographical, Historical and Descriptive* and *A History of Architecture* and *Homes in City and Country*; Thomas C. Tallmadge, *The Story of Architecture in America*; Elizabeth Tower and R. T. H. Halsey, *The Homes of Our Ancestors*; Richard M. Upjohn, *Colonial Architecture of New York and the New England States*; Mrs. Schuyler Van Rensselaer, *Henry Hobson Richardson and His Works*; Calvert Vaux, *Villas and Cottages*; Frank Edwin Wallis, *American Architecture, Decoration and Furniture of the Eighteenth Century*; Gervase Wheeler, *Homes for the People in Suburb and Country*. *Proceedings* of the Third Annual Convention of the American Institute of Architects, November 17, 1869; *Saturday Review*, architectural issue, March 12, 1966; data on Redwood Library, Newport, from Donald T. Gibbs; on St. Michael's Chapel, Burlington, Vermont, from T. D. Seymour Bassett, Curator, Wilbur Collection, University of Vermont; on organs from E. H. Swavely, Moravian Historical Society, Nazareth, Pennsylvania; on lich gates from the Rev. R. E. Joseph, of the Church of St. James the Less, Philadelphia, the Rev. George C. Stierwald, St. Clement's Church, St. Paul, Minnesota, the Rev. W. E. Hogg, Church of St. Mary the Virgin, Falmouth, Maine, and the Rev. James Greene, St. Mary's Episcopal Church, Burlington, New Jersey.

Chapter 2   *Civilizing Forces*

Charles Francis Adams (ed.), *Familiar Letters of John Adams and His Wife Abigail Adams, during the Revolution*; James Truslow Adams, *Provincial Society, 1690–1763*, and *Revolutionary New England 1691–1776*; Charles M. Andrews, *Colonial Folkways*; Charles A. Beard and Mary R. Beard, *The Rise of American Civilization*; Carl Bridenbaugh, *Cities in Revolt* and *Rebels and Gentlemen*; Van Wyck Brooks, *The World of Washington Irving*; Arthur W. Calhoun, *A Social History of the American Family, from Colonial Times to the Present*; Henry Steele Commager, *The American Mind*; Jane C. Croly (Jenny June), *The History of the Woman's Club Movement in America*; Frederic H. Curtiss and John Heard, *The Country Club*; Alexis de Tocqueville, *Democracy in America*; J. R. Dolan, *The Yankee Peddlers of Early America*; George F. Dow, *Every Day Life in the Massachusetts Bay Colony and Domestic Life in New England in the Seventeenth Century*; Fairfax D. Downey, *Our Lusty Forefathers*; Alice Morse Earle, *Customs and Fashions in Old New England* and *Home Life in Colonial Days*; Edward Eggleston, *A History of the United States and Its People*; Benjamin Franklin, *Benjamin Franklin's Autobiographical Writings* and *Satires and Bagatelles*; Oscar Handlin (ed.), *This Was America*; Carl Holliday, *Woman's Life in Colonial Days*; Washington Irving, *Knickerbocker's History of New York*; John A. Kouwenhoven, *Adventures of America, 1857–1900*; Oliver W. Larkin, *Art and Life in America*; Irving Lowens, *Music and Musicians in Early America*; Harriet Martineau, *Society in America*; Perry Miller, *The Life of the Mind in America: From the Revolution to the Civil War*; Samuel Eliot Morison, *The Oxford History of the American People*; Lewis Mumford, *The Conduct of Life* and *The Culture of Cities*; Allan Nevins, *American Social History—as Recorded by British Travelers*; Vernon L. Parrington, *Main Currents in American*

Thought, 3 vols.; Frederic L. Paxson, *History of the American Frontier*; Clinton Rossiter, *Seedtime of the Republic*; William Sidney Rossiter, *Days and Ways in Old Boston*; Arthur M. Schlesinger, *The Rise of Modern America, 1865–1951*; Arthur M. Schlesinger, Jr., *Paths of American Thought*; William Buell Sprague, *Annals of the American Pulpit, 1857–69*; Mary Newton Stanard, *Colonial Virginia, Its People and Customs*; Elizabeth Tower and R. T. H. Halsey, *The Homes of Our Ancestors*; Thomas Jefferson Wertenbaker, *The First Americans, 1607–1690*; John Winthrop, *The History of New England from 1630–49*; Louis B. Wright, *The Cultural Life of the American Colonies*. F. S. Arnett, "American Country Clubs," *Munsey's*, July, 1902; C. W. Whitney, "Evolution of the Country Club," *Harper's Magazine*, XC, 1894; K. E. Meyer, "Clubs: Selective and Otherwise," *Holiday*, April, 1962; Grover Cleveland, "Woman's Mission and Woman's Clubs," *Ladies' Home Journal*, May, 1905; James Huneker, "The Passing of the Piano," *Harper's Bazaar*, May 12, 1900; James Parton, "The Piano in the United States," *Atlantic Monthly*, July, 1867; Samuel Eliot Morison, "Precedence at Harvard College in the Seventeenth Century," *Proceedings* of the American Antiquarian Society, October, 1932; *Publishers' Weekly*, March 14, 1966; *Saturday Review*, August 21, 1965; *Newsweek*, July 25, 1966; *Time*, September 3, 1965 and October 4, 1966; *New York Times*, August 22, 1965 and April 9, 1967; Louis Kronenberger, "The Boom in Art Books," *Atlantic Monthly*, May, 1966; Russell Lynes, "Who Wants Art?" *Harper's Magazine*, July, 1965; data from New York Telephone Company.

Chapter 3 *World of Plenty*

Charles Francis Adams (ed.), *Familiar Letters of John Adams and His Wife Abigail Adams, during the Revolution*; Editors of American Heritage Publishing Company, *American Heritage Cookbook and Illustrated History of American Eating and Drinking*; Cleveland Amory, *The Last Resorts* and *The Proper Bostonians*; Charles M. Andrews, *Colonial Folkways*; Richard W. Armour, *Drug Store Days*; Lucius Beebe, *The Big Spenders* and *Mansions on Rails*; Mary Sumner Benson, *Women in Eighteenth Century America*; Fredrika Bremer, *America of the Fifties* and *The Homes of the New World*; Carl Bridenbaugh, *Cities in Revolt* and *Cities in the Wilderness*; Mark H. Brown and W. R. Felton, *The Frontier Years*; Andrew Burnaby, *Travels through the Middle Settlements in North America*; Arthur W. Calhoun, *A Social History of the American Family, from Colonial Times to the Present*; Gerald Carson, *The Polite Americans*; David L. Cohn, *The Good Old Days*; Caroline Crawford, *Social Life in Old New England* and *Romantic Days in Old Boston*; Richard Osborn Cummings, *The American and His Food*; Marshall B. Davidson, *Life in America*; J. R. Dolan, *The Yankee Peddlers of Early America*; Leslie Dorsey and Janice Devine, *Fare Thee Well*; George F. Dow, *Domestic Life in New England in the Seventeenth Century*; Foster Rhea Dulles, *America Learns to Play*; Alice Morse Earle, *Customs and Fashions in Old New England* and *Home Life in Colonial Days*; Edward Field, *The Colonial Tavern*; Christine Frederick, *The New Housekeeping: Efficiency Studies in Home Management*; Bess Furman, *White House Profile*; Francis J. Grund, *The Americans in their Moral, Social and Political Relations*; Lady Duffus Hardy, *Through Cities and Prairie Land*; Constance (Cary) Harrison, *Recollections Grave and Gay*; Stewart H. Holbrook, *The Age of the Moguls* and *The Old Post Road* and *The Story of American Railroads*; Philip Hone, *The Diary of Philip Hone, 1828–1851*; Paul Lewis, *Queen of* the *Plaza*; Editors of *Life*, *America's Arts and Skills*; Marjorie Longley, Louis Silverstein and Samuel A. Tower (eds.), *America's Taste: The Cultural Events of a Century Reported by Contemporary Observers in the Pages of The New York Times*; Robert B. Ludy, *Historic Hotels of the World, Past and Present*; Russell Lynes, *The Domesticated Americans* and *The Tastemakers*; Ward McAllister, *Society as I Have Known It*; Charles Merz, *The Great American Band Wagon*; Meade Minnegerode, *The Fabulous Forties*; Samuel Eliot Morison, *The Oxford History of the American People*; Lloyd R. Morris, *Incredible New York* and *Not So Long Ago*; Allan Nevins, *American Social History—as Recorded by British Travelers*; Emily Post, *Emily Post's Etiquette, the Blue Book of Social Usage*; Ishbel Ross, *Silhouette in Diamonds* and *Crusades and Crinolines*; Arthur M. Schlesinger, *The Rise of the City 1878–1898*; Karl Schriftgiesser, *Oscar of the Waldorf*; Margaret Bayard Smith, *The First Forty Years of Washington Society*; Mary Newton Stanard, *Colonial Virginia, Its People and Customs*; Pauline Dakin Taft, *The Happy Valley, the Elegant Eighties in Upstate New York*; Amy Vanderbilt, *Amy Vanderbilt's Complete Book of Etiquette*; Dixon Wecter, *The Saga of American Society*; Jefferson Williamson, *The American Hotel*; William E. Woodward, *The Way Our People Lived*; Louis B. Wright, *The Cultural Life of the American Colonies*; Gerald Carson, "Rum and Reform in Old New England," *New England Galaxy*, Winter, 1965; Henry Hall, "The Ice Industry of the United States," *Fourth Census of the United States*, 1880; Ellwood Kendrick, "Vitamines: New Light on the Mysteries of Nutrition," *Harper's Magazine*, March, 1921; Charles F. Langworthy, "Food Customs and Diet in the American Home," United States Experiment Stations Office, 1911; G. W. Pierson, "The Moving American," *Yale Review*, September, 1954; Richard Harrison Shryock, "Sylvester Graham and the Popular Health Movement," *Mississippi Valley Historical Review*, September, 1931; William Taylor, "Influence of Refrigerator on the Fruit Industry," *United States Department of Agriculture Yearbook*, 1900; Don Wharton, "Look What's Happened to Ice Cream," *Reader's Digest*, June, 1966; *Harper's Weekly*, December 8, 1877; *New York Herald Tribune*, March 13, 1966; *Philadelphia Inquirer*, September 26, 1965; *Publishers' Weekly*, September 13, 1965; *Newsweek*, September 13, 1965 and March 14, 1966; *Time*, August 13, 1965, February 18, 1966, and June 3, 1966; *New York Journal-American*, May 21, 1965; Sears, Roebuck and Montgomery Ward catalogues.

Chapter 4   *A Sporting Nation*

Grace K. Adams, *The Mad Forties*; Frederick Lewis Allen, *Only Yesterday*; Cleveland Amory, *Who Killed Society?* and *The Last Resorts*; Charles M. Andrews, *Colonial Folkways* and *Pilgrims and Puritans*; Richard W. Armour, *Drug Store Days*; Richmond B. Barrett, *Good Old Summer Days*; Lucius Beebe, *The Big Spenders*; Thomas Beer, *The Mauve Decade*; Daniel J. Boorstin, *The Americans: The National Experience*; Claude G. Bowers, *The Tragic Era*; Carl Bridenbaugh, *Cities in Revolt*; Henry Collins Brown, *In the Golden Nineties*; Gerald Carson, *The Polite Americans*; David L. Cohn, *The Good Old Days*; Cecil K. Drinker, *Not So Long Ago*; Foster Rhea Dulles, *America Learns to Play* and *The United States Since 1865*; Alice Morse Earle, *Customs and Fashions in Old New England* and *Home Life in Colonial Days*; John Fairchild, *The Fashionable Savages*; Catherine E. Havens, *Diary of a Little Girl in Old New York*; Washington Irving, *Knickerbocker's History of New York*; Oliver Jensen, *The Revolt of American Women*; Harnett T. Kane, *The Southern Christmas Book*; Sarah

Kemble Knight, *The Private Journal of a Journey from Boston to New York in the Year 1704*; John A. Kouwenhoven, *Adventures of America, 1857–1900*; Oliver W. Larkin, *Art and Life in America*; Russell Lynes, *The Domesticated Americans* and *The Tastemakers*; Ward McAllister, *Society as I Have Known It*; Grace M. Mayer (ed.), *Once Upon a City*; Charles Merz, *The Great American Band Wagon*; Samuel Eliot Morison, *The Oxford History of the American People*; Allan Nevins, *American Social History—as Recorded by British Travelers*; Mary Newton Stanard, *Colonial Virginia, Its People and Customs*; Alvin Toffler, *The Culture Consumers*; Editors of The Viking Press and *Vogue, The World in Vogue*; Dixon Wecter, *The Saga of American Society*; William E. Woodward, *The Way Our People Lived*. Frederick Lewis Allen, "When America Learned to Dance," *Scribner's*, September, 1937; James Gordon Bennett, *New York Herald*, August 17, 1836; Joseph Bennette, *Proceedings of the Massachusetts Historical Society*, 1861; Larry Clinton, "Swing Grows Up," *Good Housekeeping*, October, 1938; John Kieran, "The Ski's the Limit," *American Magazine*, February, 1937; Clark Kinnaird, *New York Journal-American*, January 24, March 4, and April 22, 1966; Nita Reed, "Country Dance Forty Years Ago," Vermont Historical Society, XXIII, April, 1955; Arthur B. Reeves, "What America Spends for Sports," *Outing*, LVII, 1910; Grantland Rice, "The National Rash," *Collier's*, October 20, 1928; John R. Tunis, "The Great God Football," *Harper's Magazine*, November, 1928, and "Olympic Games," *Harper's Magazine*, August, 1928; *New York Times*, August 14, 1966; *Time*, August 3 and October 1, 1965, and February 11, March 4, April 22, 1966; *Newsweek*, February 14 and 21, May 2, and June 6, 1966.

Chapter 5   *Fashioning the Home*

Catharine Beecher and Harriet Elizabeth Stowe, *The American Woman's Home*; Mary Sumner Benson, *Women in Eighteenth Century America*; Carl Bridenbaugh, *Cities in Revolt* and *Cities in the Wilderness*; Nathaniel Burt, *The Perennial Philadelphians*; Arthur W. Calhoun, *A Social History of the American Family, from Colonial Times to the Present*, 3 vols.; Lydia Maria Child, *The Frugal Housewife*; David L. Cohn, *The Good Old Days*; Mary Caroline Crawford, *Romantic Days in the Early Republic*; Marshall B. Davidson, *Life in America*, 2 vols.; J. R. Dolan, *The Yankee Peddlers of Early America*; Leslie Dorsey and Janice Devine, *Fare Thee Well*; George F. Dow, *Domestic Life in New England in the Seventeenth Century*; Walter A. Dyer and Esther S. Fraser, *The Rocking Chair, an American Institution*; Alice Morse Earle, *Customs and Fashions in Old New England* and *Home Life in Colonial Days*; Charles L. Eastlake, *Hints on Household Taste in Furniture, Upholstery and Other Details*; Christine Frederick, *The New Housekeeping: Efficiency Studies in Home Management*; Sigfried Giedion, *Mechanization Takes Command*; Sarah Josepha Hale, *Manners: or Happy Homes and Good Society All the Year Round*; Oscar Handlin (ed.), *This Was America*; Carl Holliday, *Woman's Life in Colonial Days*; H. Hudson Holly, *Modern Dwellings in Town and Country*; Julia Ward Howe, *Reminiscences 1819–1899*; Gaillard Hunt, *Life in America One Hundred Years Ago*; Marion Day Iverson, *The American Chair*; Oliver Jensen, *The Revolt of American Women*; Oliver W. Larkin, *Art and Life in America*; Editors of *Life, America's Arts and Skills*; Sarah M. Lockwood, *Antiques*; Russell Lynes, *The Domesticated Americans* and *The Tastemakers*; Samuel Eliot Morison, *The Oxford History of the American People*; Lewis Mumford, *The Brown Decades*;

Thomas Hamilton Ormsbee, *Early American Furniture Makers*; Richard Pratt, *Houses, History and People*; Alfred Coxe Prime, *The Arts and Crafts in Philadelphia, Maryland and South Carolina*; John Pudney, *The Smallest Room*; Laura E. Richards, *Abigail Adams and Her Times*; Jacob Riis, *How the Other Half Lives*; William Sidney Rossiter, *Days and Ways in Old Boston*; Jonathan Routh, *The Better John Guide*; Charles (Chic) Sale, *The Specialist*; Arthur M. Schlesinger, *The Rise of the City 1878–1898*; Esther Singleton, *The Furniture of Our Forefathers* and *Dutch New York*; Margaret Bayard Smith, *The First Forty Years of Washington Society*; Mary Newton Stanard, *Colonial Virginia, Its People and Customs*; Russell Sturgis, *Homes in City and Country*; George Fisher Sydney, *Men, Women and Manners in Colonial Times*, vol. 1; Pauline Dakin Taft, *The Happy Valley, the Elegant Eighties in Upstate New York*; Elizabeth Tower and R. T. H. Halsey, *The Homes of Our Ancestors*; Andrew Tully, *Era of Elegance*; Carl Van Doren, *Benjamin Franklin*; Mrs. Schuyler Van Rensselaer, *History of the City of New York in the Seventeenth Century*; Calvert Vaux, *Villas and Cottages*; Frank Edwin Wallis, *American Architecture, Decoration and Furniture of the Eighteenth Century*; Dixon Wecter, *The Saga of American Society*; Gervase Wheeler, *Homes for the People in Suburb and Country*; William E. Woodward, *The Way Our People Lived*; Lawrence Wright, *Clean and Decent*; Louis B. Wright, *The Cultural Life of the American Colonies, 1607–1763*. Clark Kinnaird, "Stationary and Portable Beds," *New York Journal-American*, March 30, 1966, and "Clocks," *New York Journal-American*, April 8, 1966; Alexander Kira, *The Bathroom*, Research Report No. 7, Center for Housing and Environmental Studies, Cornell University, 1966; Helen Papashvily, "Holiday Handbook of American Spas," *Holiday*, May, 1965; *Newsweek*, January 18 and December 13, 1965, and February 20, 1967; *Time*, October 1, 1965; data from General Electric and Westinghouse Electric Corporations, and from Sears, Roebuck, Montgomery Ward, and Twyford's catalogues.

Chapter 6 *Plush and Pomp*

Cleveland Amory, *The Proper Bostonians* and *The Last Resorts*; C. C. Baldwin, *Stanford White*; Richmond B. Barrett, *Good Old Summer Days*; Cecil Beaton, *The Glass of Fashion*; Lucius Beebe, *The Big Spenders* and *Mansions on Rails*; Thomas Beer, *The Mauve Decade*; Therese M. Bonney, *Remember When*; Claude G. Bowers, *The Tragic Era*; Fredrika Bremer, *The Homes of the New World*; Carl Bridenbaugh, *Cities in Revolt*; Henry Collins Brown, *Brownstone Fronts and Saratoga Trunks* and *In the Golden Nineties*; Nathaniel Burt, *The Perennial Philadelphians*; Gerald Carson, *The Polite Americans*; David L. Cohn, *The Good Old Days*; Russel Crouse, *It Seems Like Yesterday*; Marshall B. Davidson, *Life in America*, 2 vols.; Elsie de Wolfe, *The House in Good Taste*; William H. Dixon, *New America*; J. R. Dolan, *The Yankee Peddlers of Early America*; Leslie Dorsey and Janice Devine, *Fare Thee Well*; Andrew Jackson Downing, *The Architecture of Country Homes and Cottage Residences*; Cecil K. Drinker, *Not So Long Ago*; Foster Rhea Dulles, *The United States since 1865*; William Dunlap, *History of the Rise and Progress of the Arts of Design in the United States*; Charles L. Eastlake, *Hints on Household Taste in Furniture, Upholstery and Other Details*; Emily Faithfull, *Three Visits to America*; Ruth E. Finley, *The Lady of Godey's: Sarah Josepha Hale*; O. S. Fowler, *A Home for All*; Jessie Benton Frémont, *Souvenir of My Time*; Bess Furman, *White House Profile*; Sigfried Giedion, *Mechanization Takes Command*; Marian (Campbell)

Gouverneur, *As I Remember: Recollections of American Society during the Nineteenth Century*; Stewart H. Holbrook, *The Age of the Moguls*; M. Hudson Holly, *Modern Dwellings in Town and Country*; Philip Hone, *The Diary of Philip Hone, 1828–1851*; Charles Hurd, *The White House Story*; Henry James, *The American Scene*; Matthew Josephson, *The Robber Barons*; Robert Koch, *Louis C. Tiffany*; John A. Kouwenhoven, *Adventures of America, 1857–1900* and *Made in America*; Oliver A. Larkin, *Art and Life in America*; Editors of *Life*, *America's Art and Skills*; Robert B. Ludy, *Historic Hotels of the World, Past and Present*; Russell Lynes, *The Domesticated Americans* and *The Tastemakers*; Grace M. Mayer (ed.), *Once Upon a City*; Charles Merz, *The Great American Band Wagon*; Samuel Eliot Morison, *The Oxford History of the American People*; Lloyd R. Morris, *Incredible New York* and *Not So long Ago* and *Postscript to Yesterday*; Edward Sylvester Morse, *Japanese Homes and Their Surroundings*; Lewis Mumford, *The Brown Decades*; Richard Pratt, *Houses, History and People*; Agnes Rogers, *The American Procession*; Kate Ellen Rogers, *The Modern House*; Arthur M. Schlesinger, *The Rise of Modern America 1865–1951*; Gilbert Seldes, *The Stammering Century*; Matthew Hale Smith, *Successful Folks: How They Live* and *Sunlight and Shadow in New York*; Russell Sturgis, *Homes in City and Country*; Alvin Toffler, *The Culture Consumers*; Elizabeth Tower and R. T. H. Halsey, *The Homes of Our Ancestors*; Andrew Tully, *Era of Elegance*; Editors of The Viking Press and *Vogue*, *The World in Vogue*; Dixon Wecter, *The Saga of American Society*; William E. Woodward, *The Way Our People Lived*. *The New York Times*, February 11, April 3, and May 30, 1966.

Chapter 7 *Sky High*

Frederick Lewis Allen, *Only Yesterday*; Wayne Andrews, *Architecture, Ambition and Americans* and *Architecture in America*; Lucius Beebe, *The Big Spenders*; Francis R. Bellamy (ed.), *The Architect at Mid-Century*; *Conversations across the Nation*; Albert Bemis and John Burchard, *The Evolving House*; Alfred C. Bossom, *Building to the Skies*; Royal Cortissoz, *John La Farge*; Marshall B. Davidson, *Life in America*, 2 vols.; Emmett Dedmon, *Fabulous Chicago*; George H. Edgell, *The American Architecture of Today*; James Fergusson, *History of the Modern Style of Architecture*; Hugh Ferriss, *The Metropolis of Tomorrow*; James Marston Fitch, *American Building*; William Fleming, *Art and Ideas*; Sigfried Giedion, *Space, Time and Architecture*; Constance McLaughlin Green, *The Rise of Urban America*; Henry Russell Hitchcock, *The International Style*; *Architecture Since 1922* and *Modern Architecture, Romanticism and Reintegration* and *Architecture, Nineteenth and Twentieth Centuries*; Raymond M. Hood, *Raymond M. Hood*; Jane Jacobs, *The Death and Life of Great American Cities*; Ely Jacques Kahn, *Design in Art* and *Industry and Contemporary American Architects*; Sidney Fiske Kimball, *American Architecture*; Robert Koch, *Louis C. Tiffany*; John A. Kouwenhoven, *Made in America*; Minard Lafever, *The Beauties of Modern Architecture*; Oliver W. Larkin, *Art and Life in America*; Editors of *Life*, *America's Arts and Skills*; Russell Lynes, *The Domesticated Americans* and *The Tastemakers*; Charles Moore, *Daniel H. Burnham, Architect, Planner of Cities*, 2 vols.; Lloyd R. Morris, *Incredible New York*; George E. Mowry, *The Urban Nation: 1920–1960*; Lewis Mumford, *Roots of Contemporary American Architecture* and *The Culture of Cities*; George Nelson, *Industrial Architecture of Albert Kahn*; Richard J. Neutra, *Survival through Design*;

Kate Ellen Rogers, *The Modern House*; Tyler Stewart Rogers, *Plan Your House to Suit Yourself*; Eliel Saarinen, *The City, Its Growth, Its Decay, Its Future*; Vincent Scully, Jr., *Modern Architecture* and *The Shingle Style*; Gustav Stickley, *Craftsman Homes*; Russell Sturgis, *A Dictionary of Architecture and Building, Biographical, Historical and Descriptive*; Thomas C. Tallmadge, *The Story of Architecture in America*; C. H. Whitaker (ed.), *Bertram Grosvenor Goodhue, Architect and Master of Many Arts*; Frank Lloyd Wright, *An American Architecture* and *An Autobiography* and *Architecture and Modern Life* and *The Future of Architecture* and *The Living City*. Richard M. Upjohn, "Colonial Architecture of New York and the New England States," *Proceedings* of the Third Annual Convention of the American Institute of Architects, November 17, 1869; Frank Lloyd Wright, "In the Cause of Architecture," *Architectural Review*, May–June, 1927, August–October, 1927, and April–August, 1928; *Sweet's Architectural Catalogue*, 1934; *Look*, November 30, 1965; "Reston—A Billion Dollar Bet on a New Way to Live," *New York Times*, July 24, 1966; *Newsweek*, September 13 and November 1, 1965, and May 9, 1966; *Time*, May 21, September 3, and December 10, 1965, and February 24, 1967; Lillian Hart Tryon, "Reflections of a Housewife," *House Beautiful*, May–November, 1915, and January, 1916; data from Irene Hayes, Wadley & Smythe, Inc., and Robert E. Simon, Jr.

Chapter 8 *Eve's Daughters*

Katharine Anthony, *Dolly Madison, Her Life and Times*; Gertrude Aretz, *The Elegant Woman*; Bettina Ballard, *In My Fashion*; Cecil Beaton, *The Glass of Fashion*; Lucius Beebe, *The Big Spenders*; Mary Sumner Benson, *Women in Eighteenth Century America*; Eliza S. Bowne, *A Girl's Life Eighty Years Ago*; Carl Bridenbaugh, *Cities in Revolt*; David L. Cohn, *The Good Old Days*; Mila Contini, *Fashion from Ancient Egypt to the Present Time*; Mary Caroline Crawford, *Romantic Days in Old Boston*; J. R. Dolan, *The Yankee Peddlers of Early America*; George F. Dow, *Every Day Life in the Massachusetts Bay Colony*; Cecil K. Drinker, *Not So Long Ago*; Foster Rhea Dulles, *America Learns to Play*; Alice Morse Earle, *Two Centuries of Costume in America*, 2 vols. and *Customs and Fashions in Old New England* and *Home Life in Colonial Days*; Elizabeth F. Ellet, *Queens of American Society*; John Fairchild, *The Fashionable Savages*; Ruth E. Finley, *The Lady of Godey's, Sarah Josepha Hale*; Bess Furman, *White House Profile*; Carl Holliday, *Woman's Life in Colonial Days*; Oliver Jensen, *The Revolt of American Women*; Oliver W. Larkin, *Art and Life in America*; James Laver, *Costume of the Western World* and *Edwardian Promenade* and *Panic among the Puritans* and *Style in Costume* and *Taste and Fashion from the French Revolution until Today*; Phyllis Lee Levin, *The Wheels of Fashion*; Elisabeth McClellan, *History of American Costume, 1607–1870*; Paul McPharlin, *Life and Fashion in America*; Samuel Eliot Morison, *The Life and Letters of Harrison Gray Otis* and *The Oxford History of the American People*; Lloyd R. Morris, *Incredible New York*; Blanche Payne, *History of Costume*; Agnes Rogers, *Women Are Here to Stay*; Carmel Snow, *The World of Carmel Snow*; Mary Newton Stanard, *Colonial Virginia, Its People and Customs*; Andrew Tully, *Era of Elegance*; Mrs. Schuyler Van Rensselaer, *History of the City of New York in the Seventeenth Century*; Editors of The Viking Press and *Vogue*, *The World in Vogue*; Edward Warwick, Henry C. Pitz, and Alexander Wyckoff, *Early American Dress*; Dixon Wecter, *The*

Saga of American Society; Ruth Turner Wilcox, *Five Centuries of American Costume*; Anne Green Winslow, *Diary of a Boston School Girl of 1771*; Helen Woodward, *Through Many Windows*; Louis B. Wright, *The Cultural Life of the American Colonies, 1607–1762*. *Vogue; Harper's Bazaar; Godey's Lady's Book; New Yorker; The New York Times*, March 28, 1865, and February 28, March 23, April 16, and August 26, 1966; *New York Herald*, April 8, 1900; *New York World Telegram and Sun*, March 22, 1966; *New York Herald Tribune*, 1950–1967; *New York Post*, January 11, 1967; *Newsweek*, August 16, October 4, and October 25, 1965, and March 14 and October 4 and 31, 1966; *Time*, January 29, 1965, and August 6, 1965, and March 18, June 24, and October 22, 1966 and February 24, 1967.

Chapter 9 *The Added Touch*

Charles M. Andrews, *Pilgrims and Puritans*; Katharine Anthony, *Dolly Madison, Her Life and Times*; Gertrude Aretz, *The Elegant Woman*; Bettina Ballard, *In My Fashion*; Cecil Beaton, *The Glass of Fashion*; Mary Sumner Benson, *Women in Eighteenth Century America*; David L. Cohn, *The Good Old Days*; Mila Contini, *Fashion from Ancient Egypt to the Present Time*; Richard Corson, *Fashions in Hair, the First Five Thousand Years*; M. D. C. Crawford and Elizabeth A. Guernsey, *The History of Corsets in Pictures*; Foster Rhea Dulles, *America Learns to Play*; Alice Morse Earle, *Customs and Fashions in Old New England* and *Two Centuries of Costume in America*; John Fairchild, *The Fashionable Savages*; Ruth E. Finley, *The Lady of Godey's, Sarah Josepha Hale*; Clifton J. Furness, *The Genteel Female*; Constance (Cary) Harrison, *Recollections Grave and Gay* and *History of Feminine Fashion*; Alice Hoge, *Cissie Patterson*; Stewart H. Holbrook, *The Age of the Moguls*; Carl Holliday, *Woman's Life in Colonial Days*; Oliver Jensen, *The Revolt of American Women*; Robert Koch, *Louis C. Tiffany*; James Laver, *Taste and Fashion from the French Revolution until Today* and *Panic among the Puritans* and *Edwardian Promenade*; Phyllis Lee Levin, *The Wheels of Fashion*; Russell Lynes, *The Domesticated Americans* and *The Tastemakers*; Elisabeth McClellan, *History of American Costume, 1607–1870*; Paul McPharlin, *Life and Fashion in America*; Blanche Payne, *History of Costume*; Ishbel Ross, *Crusades and Crinolines* and *Silhouette in Diamonds*; Carmel Snow, *The World of Carmel Snow*; Editors of The Viking Press and *Vogue*, *The World in Vogue*; Dixon Wecter, *The Saga of American Society*; Thomas Jefferson Wertenbaker, *The First Americans, 1607–1690*; Ruth Turner Wilcox, *Five Centuries of American Costume*; Jean Philippe Worth, *A Century of Fashion*. Dr. John Cook, "Receipt for Changing Yellow Hair," *The Lady's Magazine*, June, 1775; Louise Hall Tharp, "Bonnet Girls," *New England Galaxy*, vol. 1, no. 3; R. Riegel, "Women's Clothes and Women's Rights," *American Quarterly*, Autumn, 1963; *Godey's Lady's Book; Vogue; Vanity Fair; Harper's Bazaar; New Yorker; Ladies' Home Journal, McCall's, Good Housekeeping, Life, Look, Time*, and *Newsweek*; data from Peck & Peck, Harry Winston, Inc., Christian Dior, Chanel, Berkshire International, and Kenneth.

Chapter 10 *Male Plumage*

Cleveland Amory, *The Last Resorts* and *Who Killed Society?*; Charles M. Andrews, *Pilgrims and Puritans*; Cecil Beaton, *The Glass of Fashion*; Lucius Beebe, *The Big Spenders*; Gerald Carson, *The Polite Americans*; David L. Cohn, *The*

Good Old Days; Richard Corson, *Fashions in Hair, the First Five Thousand Years*; Millia Davenport, *The Book of Costume*; Fairfax Downey, *Our Lusty Forefathers*; Foster Rhea Dulles, *America Learns to Play*; Alice Morse Earle, *Customs and Fashions in Old New England* and *Two Centuries of Costume in America; Esquire Fashions for Men*, by the editors of *Esquire*; Thomas Hamilton, *Men and Manners in America*; Stewart H. Holbrook, *The Age of the Moguls*; James Laver, *Costume of the Western World* and *Edwardian Promenade*; Russell Lynes, *The Domesticated Americans* and *The Tastemakers*; Ward McAllister, *Society as I Have Known It*; Elisabeth McClellan, *History of American Costume, 1607–1870*; Samuel Eliot Morison, *The Oxford History of the American People*; Blanche Payne, *History of Costume*; Mary Newton Stanard, *Colonial Virginia, Its People and Customs*; Benjamin Stolberg, *Tailor's Progress*; Editors of The Viking Press and *Vogue, The World in Vogue*; George Waller, *Saratoga*; Edward Warwick, Henry C. Pitz, and Alexander Wyckoff, *Early American Dress*; Dixon Wecter, *The Saga of American Society*; Thomas Jefferson Wertenbaker, *The First Americans, 1607–1690*; Ruth Turner Wilcox, *Five Centuries of American Costume*; John Winthrop, *The History of New England from 1630–1649*; Louis B. Wright, *The Cultural Life of the American Colonies, 1607–1763*; Ernest Boyd, "Beards in America," *New Statesman and Nation*, August, 1931; G. A. Dondero, "Why Lincoln Wore a Beard," *Journal of the Illinois State Historical Society*, July, 1931; *Men's Wear*; *Gentlemen's Quarterly*; scrapbooks on hair and beards, Rare Book Room, New York Public Library; data from Dana Perfumes Corporation and Fabergé.

Chapter 11   *Americans on the Move*

Frederick Lewis Allen, *Only Yesterday*; Editors of American Heritage Publishing Company, *American Heritage Cookbook* and *Illustrated History of American Eating and Drinking*; Lucius Beebe, *Mansions on Rails* and *The Big Spenders*; Carl Bridenbaugh, *Cities in the Wilderness*; Mark H. Brown and W. R. Felton, *The Frontier Years*; David L. Cohn, *The Good Old Days*; Marshall B. Davidson, *Life in America*; J. R. Dolan, *The Yankee Peddlers of Early America*; Foster Rhea Dulles, *America Learns to Play*; Alice Morse Earle, *Customs and Fashions in Old New England*; Sigfried Giedion, *Mechanization Takes Command*; Stewart H. Holbrook, *The Old Post Road* and *The Story of American Railroads*; Edward Hungerford, *The Story of Wells Fargo*; Editors of *Life, America's Arts and Skills*; Charles Merz, *The Great American Band Wagon*; Samuel Eliot Morison, *The Oxford History of the American People*; Frederic L. Paxson, *History of the American Frontier*; Mary Newton Stanard, *Colonial Virginia, Its People and Customs*; Mark Sullivan, *Our Times: The United States, 1900–1925*; George Waller, *Saratoga*; Louis B. Wright, *The Cultural Life of the American Colonies, 1607–1763*; *New York Times*, January 29, 1967, and February 16, 1967; *Time*, February 18 and March 25, 1966; *Newsweek*, March 14, 1966; Clark Kinnaird, *New York Journal-American*, May 21, 1965; data from Ford Motor Company and the American Can Company.

Chapter 12   *The Social Image Changes*

Charles Francis Adams (ed.), *Familiar Letters of John Adams and His Wife Abigail Adams, during the Revolution*; James Truslow Adams, *Provincial Society, 1690–1763*; Cleveland Amory, *The Proper Bostonians* and *The Last Resorts* and *Who Killed Society?*; Katharine Anthony, *Dolly Madison, Her Life and Times*; Louis Auchincloss, *Portrait in Brownstone*; Consuelo Balsan, *The Glitter and the Gold*; Lucius Beebe, *The Big Spenders*; Fredrika Bremer, *America of the Fifties*; Eve Brown, *Champagne Cholly*; Henry Collins Brown, *In the Golden Nineties*; Nathaniel Burt, *The Perennial Philadelphians*; Arthur W. Calhoun, *A Social History of the American Family from Colonial Times to the Present*; Michel Chevalier, *Society, Manners and Politics in the United States*; Mary Caroline Crawford, *Social Life in Old New England*; Ethel Nathalie Dana, *Young in New York*; Foster Rhea Dulles, *America Learns to Play*; Alice Morse Earle, *Customs and Fashions in Old New England*; John Fairchild, *The Fashionable Savages*; Constance (Cary) Harrison, *Recollections Grave and Gay*; Catherine E. Havens, *Diary of a Little Girl in Old New York*; Alice Hoge, *Cissie Patterson*; Philip Hone, *The Diary of Philip Hone, 1828–1851*; Julia Ward Howe, *Reminiscences, 1819–1899*; Matthew Josephson, *The Robber Barons*; Lucy Kavaler, *The Private World of High Society*; Arthur H. Lewis, *The Day They Shook the Plum Tree*; Ward McAllister, *Society as I Have Known It*; Elsa Maxwell, *The Celebrity Circus*; Grace M. Mayer, *Once Upon a City*; Lloyd R. Morris, *Not So Long Ago*; Ben Perley Poore, *Reminiscences of Sixty Years in the National Metropolis*; Lanfranco Rasponi, *The International Nomads*; Agnes Rogers, *The American Procession*; Madeleine Stern, *Purple Passage*; Louise Hall Tharp, *Mrs. Jack*; Mrs. John King Van Rensselaer, *Newport our Social Capital*; Editors of The Viking Press and *Vogue, The World in Vogue*; Stanley Walker, *Mrs. Astor's Horse*; Dixon Wecter, *The Saga of American Society*; Anne H. Wharton, *Social Life in the Early Republic*; Edith Wharton, *The Age of Innocence*. "A New Day of Elegance for Sherry's," *New York Times*, July 24, 1966; Charlotte Curtis, "April in Paris Ball," *New York Times*, October 30, 1965; Eugenia Sheppard, "The Capote Caper," *New York Herald Tribune*, November 29, 1966; Nancy Randolph, "Newport Goes to a Party," *New York Daily News*, June 25, 1966; *Life*, January 6 and November 24, 1947, and January 23, 1950, and December 6, 1966; *New York Herald*, July 19, 1853; *Frank Leslie's Illustrated Newspaper*, August 22, 1837; data from La Banque Internationale and Fifth Avenue Bank of New York.

Chapter 13 *A Great Awakening*

Richard Allestree, *The Gentleman's Calling* and *The Ladies Calling*; Cleveland Amory, *Who Killed Society?*; Thomas Anburey, *Travels through the Interior Parts of America*; Charles M. Andrews, *Colonial Folkways*; Katharine Anthony, *First Lady of the Revolution*; Charles A. Beard and Mary R. Beard, *The Rise of American Civilization*; Rev. John Bennett, *Letters to a Young Lady, on a Variety of Useful and Interesting Subjects*; Eliza S. Bowne, *A Girl's Life Eighty Years Ago*; Carl Bridenbaugh, *Cities in Revolt*; Gerald Carson, *The Polite Americans*; Gilbert K. Chesterton, *What I Saw in America*; David L. Cohn, *The Good Old Days*; Henry Steele Commager, *A Short History of the United States* and *The American Mind*; Mary Caroline Crawford, *Social Life in Old New England*; Herbert D. Croly, *The Promise of American Life*; Jane C. Croly (Jenny June), *The History of the Woman's Club Movement in America*; Frances Wright D'Arusmont, *View of Society and Manners in America*; Marshall B. Davidson, *Life in America*; Cecil K. Drinker, *Not So Long Ago*; Alice Morse Earle, *Customs and Fashions in Old New England*; Elizabeth F. Ellet, *Queens of American Society*; Mrs. John Farrar, *The Young Lady's Friend*; Millicent Fenwick, *Vogue*

Book of Etiquette; Ruth E. Finley, *The Lady of Godey's, Sarah Josepha Hale*; George Sydney Fisher, *Men, Women and Manners in Colonial Times*; Benjamin Franklin, *Poor Richard's Almanack*; Betty Friedan, *The Feminine Mystique*; Clifton Furness, *The Genteel Female*; Sigfried Giedion, *Mechanization Takes Command*; Marian (Campbell) Gouverneur, *As I Remember*; Sarah Josepha Hale, *Manners: or Happy Homes and Good Society All the Year Round*; Basil Hall, *Travels in North America in the Years 1827 and 1828*; Margaret Hunter Hall, *The Aristocratic Journey*; Thomas Hamilton, *Men and Manners in America*; Oscar Handlin, *This Was America*; Lady Duffus Hardy, *Through Cities and Prairie Lands*; Constance (Cary) Harrison, *The Well-Bred Girl in Society*; Oliver Wendell Holmes, *Autocrat of the Breakfast-Table*; Henry James, *The American Scene*; Oliver Jensen, *The Revolt of American Women*; Louis Kronenberger, *Company Manners; Lady Gough's Etiquette*; Editors of *Life*, *America's Arts and Skills*; Marjorie Longley, Louis Silverstein and Samuel A. Tower (eds.), *America's Taste: The Cultural Events of a Century Reported by Contemporary Observers in the Pages of The New York Times*; Abby B. Longstreet, *Social Etiquette of New York*; Alice Longworth, *Crowded Hours*; Russell Lynes, *The Domesticated Americans* and *The Tastemakers*; Ward McAllister, *Society as I Have Known It*; Harriet Martineau, *Society in America*; Grace M. Mayer, *Once Upon a City*; Perry Miller, *The Life of the Mind in America*; Samuel Eliot Morison, *The Life and Letters of Harrison Gray Otis, Federalist* and *The Oxford History of the American People*; Emily Post, *Emily Post's Etiquette, The Blue Book of Social Usage*; Arthur M. Schlesinger, *Learning How to Behave*; Mrs. John Sherwood, *Manners and Social Usages*; Lydia H. Sigourney, *Letters to Young Ladies*; Andrew Sinclair, *The Better Half*; Ellen Maury Slayden, *Washington Wife*; Mrs. Frances Trollope, *Domestic Manners of the Americans*; Amy Vanderbilt, *Amy Vanderbilt's Complete Book of Etiquette*; Margaret Wade, *Social Usage in America*; Dixon Wecter, *The Saga of American Society*; Anne H. Wharton, *Social Life in the Early Republic*; John Winthrop, *The History of New England from 1630–1649*. James L. Ford, "Luxurious Bachelordom," *Munsey's Magazine*, January, 1899; Edmund Wilson, "Books of Etiquette and Emily Post," *New Yorker*, July 19, 1947; "Etiquette Hints," *Designer*, November, 1902; Margaret Sangster, "Shall Wives Earn Money?" *Woman's Home Companion*, April, 1905; Mary Bull, "Woman's Rights and Other Reforms in Seneca Falls," *Good Company*, 1870; W. P. Garrison, "The Isms of Forty Years Ago," *Harper's New Monthly Magazine*, January, 1880; *The Report of the President's Commission on the Status of Women and Other Publications of the Commission*, edited by Margaret Mead and Frances Balgley Kaplan; W. E. Bridges, "Family Patterns and Social Values in America, 1827–1875," *American Quarterly*, XVII, no. 1; Ellen and Kenneth Kenniston, "An American Anachronism, The Image of Women and Work," *American Scholar*, Summer, 1964; John Gunther, "Inside the Twentieth Century," *Look*, January 12, 1965; Mary G. Humphreys, "Women Bachelors in New York," *Scribner's*, 1896; "The Old Maid," *Harper's Bazar*, XII, 1879; "The Marriage Rate of College Women," *Century*, 1895; *New York Times*, April 25 and May 9, 1966; *Time*, August 27, 1965, and May 6, 1966; *New York Herald*, December 4, 1889; *New Orleans Picayune*, March 10, 1859.

Bibliography

Adams, Charles Francis (ed.), *Familiar Letters of John Adams and his wife Abigail Adams, during the Revolution: with a Memoir of Mrs. Adams.* Cambridge, Mass.: The Riverside Press, 1876.

Adams, Grace K., *The Mad Forties.* New York: Harper & Brothers, 1942.

Adams, Henry, *The Education of Henry Adams.* Boston: Houghton Mifflin Company, 1918.

Adams, James Truslow, *Provincial Society: 1690–1763.* New York: The Macmillan Company, 1927.

———, *Revolutionary New England: 1691–1776.* Boston: The Atlantic Monthly Press, 1923.

——— (editor in chief), *Album of American History.* 6 vols. New York: Charles Scribner's Sons, 1944–1960.

Allen, Frederick Lewis, *The Great Pierpont Morgan.* New York: Harper & Brothers, 1949.

———, *Only Yesterday.* New York: Harper & Brothers, 1932.

Allestree, Richard, *The Gentleman's Calling.* London: E. Pawlet, 1717.

———, *The Ladies Calling.* Edinburgh: G. Swintoun, 1675.

American Heritage Publishing Company, Editors of, *American Heritage Cookbook* and *Illustrated History of American Eating and Drinking.* New York: Simon and Schuster, 1964.

Amory, Cleveland, *The Last Resorts*. New York: Harper & Brothers, 1952.

———, *The Proper Bostonians*. New York: Harper & Brothers, 1947.

———, *Who Killed Society?* New York: Harper & Brothers, 1960.

Anburey, Thomas, *Travels Through the Interior Parts of America*. Boston: Houghton Mifflin Company, 1923.

Andrews, Charles M., *Colonial Folkways*. New Haven: Yale University Press, 1920.

———, *Pilgrims and Puritans*. New Haven: Yale University Press, 1919.

Andrews, Wayne, *Architecture, Ambition and Americans*. New York: Harper & Brothers, 1947.

———, *Architecture in America*. New York: Atheneum Publishers, 1960.

Anthony, Katharine, *Dolly Madison, Her Life and Times*. Boston: Houghton Mifflin Company, 1949.

———, *First Lady of the Revolution*. Garden City: Doubleday & Company, 1958.

Aretz, Gertrude, *The Elegant Woman*. New York: Harcourt, Brace & Company, 1932.

Armour, Richard W., *Drug Store Days*. New York: McGraw-Hill Book Company, 1959.

Asbury, Herbert, *A Methodist Saint: The Life of Bishop Asbury*. New York: Alfred A. Knopf, 1927.

Auchincloss, Louis, *Portrait in Brownstone*. Boston: Houghton Mifflin Company, 1962.

Baldwin, C. C., *Stanford White*. New York: Dodd, Mead & Company, 1931.

Ballard, Bettina, *In My Fashion*. New York: David McKay Company, 1960.

Barr, Alfred (ed.), *Art in Our Time*. New York: Museum of Modern Art, 1939.

Barrett, Richmond B., *Good Old Summer Days*. Boston: Houghton Mifflin Company, 1952.

Beard, Charles A. and Mary R., *The Rise of American Civilization*. 2 vols. New York: The Macmillan Company, 1927.

Beaton, Cecil, *The Glass of Fashion*. Garden City, N.Y.: Doubleday & Company, 1954.

Beebe, Lucius, *Mansions on Rails*. Berkeley, Calif.: Howell-North, 1959.

———, *The Big Spenders*. Garden City, N.Y.: Doubleday & Company, 1966.

Beecher, Catharine, and Harriet Elizabeth Stowe, *The American Woman's Home*. Boston: H. A. Brown & Company, 1869.

Beer, Thomas, *The Mauve Decade*. New York: Alfred A. Knopf, 1926.

Bellamy, Francis R. (ed.), *The Architect at Mid-Century: Conversations Across the Nation*. New York: Reinhold Publishing Corp., 1954.

Bemis, Albert, and John Burchard, *The Evolving House*. New York: Technology Press, 1953.

Bennett, Rev. John, *Letters to a Young Lady, on a Variety of Useful and Interesting Subjects*. New York: John Buel for E. Duyckinck & Company, 1716.

Benson, Mary Sumner, *Women in Eighteenth Century America*. New York: Columbia University Press, 1935.

Bonney, M. Therese, *Remember When*. New York: Coward-McCann, 1933.

Boorstin, Daniel J., *The Americans: The National Experience*. New York: Random House, 1965.

Bossom, Alfred C., *Building to the Skies*. London: Studio, 1934.

Bowers, Claude G., *The Tragic Era*. Boston: Houghton Mifflin Company, 1929.

Bowne, Eliza S., *A Girl's Life Eighty Years Ago*. New York: Charles Scribner's Sons, 1887.

Bremer, Fredrika, *America of the Fifties: Letters of Fredrika Bremer*. New York: The American-Scandinavian Foundation, 1924.

———, *The Homes of the New World*. New York: Harper & Brothers, 1853.

Bridenbaugh, Carl, *Cities in Revolt*. New York: Alfred A. Knopf, 1955.

———, *Cities in the Wilderness*. New York: The Ronald Press Company, 1938.

———, *The Colonial Craftsman*. New York: New York University Press, 1950.

———, *Peter Harrison, First American Architect*. Chapel Hill: University of North Carolina Press, 1949.

———, *Rebels and Gentlemen*. New York: Reynal & Hitchcock, 1942.

Bromfield, Louis, *The Farm*. New York: Harper & Brothers, 1935.

Brooks, Van Wyck, *The World of Washington Irving*. New York: E. P. Dutton & Company, 1944.

Brown, Eve, *Champagne Cholly*. New York: E. P. Dutton & Company, 1947.

Brown, Henry Collins, *Brownstone Fronts and Saratoga Trunks*. New York: E. P. Dutton & Company, 1935.

———, *In the Golden Nineties*. Hastings-on-Hudson: Valentine's Manual, 1928.

Brown, Mark H., and W. R. Felton, *The Frontier Years*. New York: Henry Holt, 1955.

Bryant, William Cullen (ed.), *Picturesque America, 1794–1878*. 2 vols. New York: D. Appleton & Company, 1894.

Burchard, John, and Albert Bush-Brown, *The Architecture of America*. Boston: Little, Brown & Company, 1961.

Burman, Ben Lucien, *It's a Big Country: America Off the Highways*. New York: Reynal & Co., 1956.

Burnaby, Andrew, *Travels Through the Middle Settlements in North America*. London: T. Payne, 1775.

Burrow & Company Ltd., Ed J. (printed by), *History of Feminine Fashion*. London: 1928.

Burt, Nathaniel, *The Perennial Philadelphians*. Boston: Little, Brown & Company, 1963.

Calhoun, Arthur W., *A Social History of the American Family, from Colonial Times to the Present*. 3 vols. New York: Barnes & Noble, 1945.

Canby, Henry Seidel, *The Age of Confidence*. New York: Farrar & Rinehart, 1934.

Carson, Gerald, *The Polite Americans*. New York: William Morrow & Company, 1966.

Chase, Stuart, *The Tragedy of Waste*. New York: The Macmillan Company, 1925.

Chesterton, Gilbert K., *What I Saw in America*. New York: Dodd, Mead & Company, 1922.

Chevalier, Michel, *Society, Manners and Politics in the United States*. Boston: Weeks, Jordan & Company, 1839.

Child, Lydia Maria, *The Frugal Housewife*. London: T. T. & J. Tegg, 1832.

Cohn, David L., *The Good Old Days*. New York: Simon and Schuster, 1940.

Cole, A. C., *The Irrepressible Conflict*. New York: The Macmillan Company, 1934.

Commager, Henry Steele, *The American Mind*. New Haven: Yale University Press, 1950.

———, *A Short History of the United States*. New York: Modern Library, 1945.

———, and Allan Nevins (eds.), *The Emergence of Modern America*. New York: The Macmillan Company, 1927.

Contini, Mila, *Fashion from Ancient Egypt to the Present Time*. New York: The Odyssey Press, 1966.

Conway, Moncure D., *George Washington's Rules of Civility*. New York: United States Book Company, 1890.

Corson, Richard, *Fashions in Hair: The First Five Thousand Years*. London: Peter Owen, 1965.

Cortissoz, Royal, *John La Farge: A Memoir and a Study*. Boston: Houghton Mifflin Company, 1911.

Cram, Ralph Adams, *The Gothic Quest*. New York: Baker & Taylor, 1907.

———, *My Life in Architecture*. Boston: Little, Brown & Company, 1936.

Crawford, Mary Caroline, *Romantic Days in the Early Republic*. Boston: Little, Brown & Company, 1912.

———, *Romantic Days in Old Boston*. Boston: Little, Brown & Company, 1910.

———, *Social Life in Old New England*. Boston: Little, Brown & Company, 1912.

Crawford, M. D. C., and Elizabeth A. Guernsey, *The History of Corsets in Pictures*. New York: Fairchild Publications, 1951.

Croly, Herbert D., *The Promise of American Life*. New York: The Macmillan Company, 1911.

Croly, Jane C. (Jenny June), *The History of the Woman's Club Movement in America*. New York: Henry G. Allen & Co., 1898.

Crouse, Russel, *It Seems Like Yesterday*. Garden City, N.Y.: Doubleday, Doran & Company, 1931.

Cummings, Richard Osborn, *The American and His Food*. Chicago: University of Chicago Press, 1941.

Curtiss, Frederic H., and John Heard, *The Country Club, 1882–1932*. Brookline, Mass.: Privately printed, 1932.

Dana, Ethel Nathalie, *Young in New York*. Garden City, N.Y.: Doubleday & Company, 1963.

D'Arusmont, Frances Wright, *View of Society and Manners in America*, edited by Paul R. Baker. Cambridge, Mass.: Belknap Press, 1963.

Davenport, Millia, *The Book of Costume*. 2 vols. New York: Crown Publishers, 1948.

Davidson, Marshall B., *Life in America*. 2 vols. Boston: Houghton Mifflin Company, 1951.

Day, Charles W., *Etiquette; Or, a Guide to the Usage of Society, with a Glance at Bad Habits*. New York: Nelson & Company, 1846.

Dedmon, Emmett, *Fabulous Chicago*. New York: Random House, 1953.

De Tocqueville, Alexis, *Democracy in America*, edited by P. Bradley. Vol. 2. New York: Alfred A. Knopf, 1945.

De Voto, Bernard, *The Course of Empire*. Boston: Houghton Mifflin Company, 1951.

De Wolfe, Elsie, *The House in Good Taste*. New York: The Century Company, 1913.

Dexter, Mrs. Elisabeth Williams (Anthony), *Colonial Women of Affairs*. Boston: Houghton Mifflin Company, 1924.

Dixon, William H., *New America*. Philadelphia: J. B. Lippincott Company, 1867.

Dolan, J. R., *The Yankee Peddlers of Early America*. New York: Clarkson N. Potter, 1964.

Dorsey, Leslie, and Janice Devine, *Fare Thee Well*. New York: Crown Publishers, 1964.

Dow, George F., *Domestic Life in New England in the Seventeenth Century*. Topsfield, Mass.: Perkins Press, 1925.

———, *Every Day Life in the Massachusetts Bay Colony*. Boston: The Society for the Preservation of New England Antiquities, 1935.

Downey, Fairfax D., *Our Lusty Forefathers*. New York: Charles Scribner's Sons, 1947.

Downing, Andrew Jackson, *The Architecture of Country Houses and Cottage Residences*. New York: D. Appleton & Company, 1850.

Downing, Antoinette F., and Vincent J. Scully, Jr., *The Architectural Heritage of Newport, Rhode Island, 1640–1915*. Cambridge, Mass.: Harvard University Press, 1952.

Drinker, Cecil K., *Not So Long Ago*. New York: Oxford University Press, 1937.

Dulles, Foster Rhea, *America Learns to Play*. New York: D. Appleton-Century Company, 1940.

———, *The United States since 1865*. Ann Arbor: University of Michigan Press, 1959.

Dunlap, William, *History of the Rise and Progress of the Arts of Design in the United States*. 2 vols. New York: G. P. Scott & Company, 1834.

Dyer, Walter A., and Esther S. Fraser, *The Rocking Chair, an American Institution*. New York: The Century Company, 1928.

Earle, Alice Morse, *Customs and Fashions in Old New England*. New York: Charles Scribner's Sons, 1896.

———, *Home Life in Colonial Days*. New York: The Macmillan Company, 1962.

Eastlake, Charles L., *Hints on Household Taste in Furniture, Upholstery, and Other Details*. London: Longmans, Green, 1868.

———, *A History of the Gothic Revival*. London: Longmans, Green, 1872.

Edgell, George H., *The American Architecture of Today*. New York: Charles Scribner's Sons, 1928.

Eggleston, Edward, *A History of the United States and Its People*. New York: American Book Company, 1888.

Ellet, Elizabeth F., *Queens of American Society*. New York: C. Scribner & Company, 1867.

———, *The Women of the American Revolution*. 3 vols. New York: Baker & Scribners, 1850.

Esquire Magazine, Editors of, *Esquire Fashions for Men*. New York: Harper & Row, 1966.

Fairchild, John, *The Fashionable Savages*. New York: Doubleday & Company, 1965.

Faithfull, Emily, *Three Visits to America*. New York: Fowler & Wells Company, 1884.

Fenwick, Millicent, *Vogue Book of Etiquette*. New York: Simon and Schuster, 1948.

Fergusson, James, *History of the Modern Styles of Architecture*. London: John Murray, 1862.

Ferriss, Hugh, *The Metropolis of Tommorrow*. New York: Ives Washburn, 1929.

Field, Edward, *The Colonial Tavern*. Providence, R.I.: Preston & Rounds, 1897.

Finley, Ruth E., *The Lady of Godey's, Sarah Josepha Hale*. Philadelphia: J. B. Lippincott Company, 1931.

Fisher, George Sydney, *Men, Women and Manners in Colonial Times*. Vol. 1. Philadelphia: J. B. Lippincott Company, 1898.

Fitch, James Marston, *American Building*. Boston: Houghton Mifflin Company, 1948.

Fleming, William, *Art and Ideas*. New York: Holt, Rinehart and Winston, 1963.

Flexner, Eleanor, *Century of Struggle*. Cambridge, Mass.: Harvard University Press, 1959.

Fowler, O. S., *A Home for All*. New York: Fowler & Wells, 1854.

Franklin, Benjamin, *Autobiography of Benjamin Franklin*, edited by John Bigelow. Philadelphia: J. B. Lippincott Company, 1868.

———, *Benjamin Franklin's Autobiographical Writings*, selected and edited by Carl C. Van Doren. New York: The Viking Press, 1945.

———, *Poor Richard's Almanack*. New York: The Century Company, 1898.

———, *Satires and Bagatelles*. Detroit: Fine Book Circle, 1937.

Frederick, Christine, *The New Housekeeping: Efficiency Studies in Home Management*. Garden City, N.Y.: Doubleday, Page & Company, 1913.

Frémont, Jessie Benton, *Souvenir of My Time*. Boston: D. Lothrop & Company, 1887.

Funk, Wilfred J., *So You Think It's New*. New York: Funk & Wagnalls, 1937.

Furman, Bess, *White House Profile*. Indianapolis: Bobbs-Merrill, 1951.

Furness, Clifton J., *The Genteel Female*. New York: Alfred A. Knopf, 1931.

Gabriel, Ralph H. (ed.), *The Pageant of America: A Pictorial History of the United States*. 15 vols. New Haven: Yale University Press, 1925–1929.

Geddes, Norman Bel, *Horizons*. Boston: Little, Brown & Company, 1932.

Giedion, Sigfried, *Mechanization Takes Command*. New York: Oxford University Press, 1948.

———, *Space, Time and Architecture*. Cambridge, Mass.: Harvard University Press, 1941.

Gouverneur, Marian (Campbell), *As I Remember: Recollections of American Society during the Nineteenth Century*. New York: D. Appleton & Company, 1911.

Green, Constance McLaughlin, *The Rise of Urban America*. New York: Harper & Row, 1965.

Greenough, Horatio, *Letters of Horatio Greenough to his brother, Henry G. Greenough*, edited by Frances Boott Greenough. Boston: Ticknor & Company, 1887.

Grund, Francis J., *The Americans in their Moral, Social and Political Relations*. London: Longman, Rees, Orme, Brown, Green and Longman, 1837.

Hahn, Emily, *Diamond: The Spectacular Story of Earth's Rarest Treasure and Man's Greatest Greed*. Garden City, N.Y.: Doubleday & Company, 1956.

Hale, Sarah Josepha (Buell), *Manners: or Happy Homes and Good Society All the Year Round*. Boston: J. E. Tilton & Company, 1868.

———, *Woman's Record; or Sketches of all Distinguished Women from the Creation to A.D. 1854*. New York: Harper & Brothers, 1855.

Hall, Basil, *Travels in North America in the Years 1827 and 1828*. Philadelphia: Carey, Lea & Carey, 1829.

Hall, Margaret Hunter (Mrs. Basil Hall), *The Aristocratic Journey*. New York: G. P. Putnam's Sons, 1931.

Halsey, R. T. H., *The Homes of Our Ancestors*. Garden City, N.Y.: Doubleday, Doran & Company, 1925.

Hamilton, Thomas, *Men and Manners in America*. Edinburgh: W. Blackwood, 1833.

Hamlin, Talbot F., *The American Spirit in Architecture*. New Haven: Yale University Press, 1926.

———, *Architecture Through the Ages*. New York: G. P. Putnam's Sons, 1940.

———, *Greek Revival Architecture in America*. New York: Oxford University Press, 1944.

Handlin, Oscar (ed.), *This Was America*. Cambridge, Mass.: Harvard University Press, 1949.

———, *The Uprooted*. Boston: Little, Brown & Company, 1951.

Hardy, Lady Duffus (Mary McDowell), *Through Cities and Prairie Lands*. New York: R. Worthington, 1881.

Harrison, Constance (Cary), *Recollections Grave and Gay*. New York: Charles Scribner's Sons, 1911.

———, *The Well-Bred Girl in Society*. New York: Doubleday & McClure Company, 1898.

Hartley, Cecil B., *The Gentlemen's Book of Etiquette*. Boston: G. W. Cottrell, 1860.

Hartley, Florence, *The Ladies Book of Etiquette, and Manual of Politeness*. Boston: Lee & Shepard, 1872.

Havens, Catherine E., *Diary of a Little Girl in Old New York*. New York: Henry Collins Brown, 1919.

Hitchcock, Henry Russell, *The Architecture of H. H. Richardson and His Times*. New York: Museum of Modern Art, 1936.

———, *Architecture, Nineteenth and Twentieth Centuries*. Baltimore: Penguin Books, 1958.

———, *The International Style: Architecture Since 1922*. New York: W. W. Norton & Company, 1932.

———, *Modern Architecture, Romanticism and Reintegration*. New York: Harcourt, Brace, 1929.

———, *Painting toward Architecture*. New York: Duell, Sloan and Pearce, 1948.

Hoge, Alice, *Cissie Patterson*. New York: Random House, 1966.

Holbrook, Stewart H., *The Age of the Moguls*. Garden City, N.Y.: Doubleday & Company, 1953.

———, *The Golden Age of Quackery*. New York: The Macmillan Company, 1959.

———, *The Old Post Road*. New York: McGraw-Hill Book Company, 1962.

———, *The Story of American Railroads*. New York: Crown Publishing Company, 1947.

Holliday, Carl, *Woman's Life in Colonial Days*. Boston: The Cornhill Publishing Company, 1922.

Holly, H. Hudson, *Modern Dwellings in Town and Country*. New York: Harper & Brothers, 1878.

Holmes, Oliver Wendell, *Autocrat of the Breakfast-Table*. Boston: Houghton Mifflin Company, 1858.

Hone, Philip, *The Diary of Philip Hone, 1828–1851*. New York: Dodd, Mead & Company, 1889.

Hood, Raymond M., *Raymond M. Hood*. New York: McGraw-Hill Book Company, 1931.

Hoving, Walter, *Tiffany's Table Manners for Teen-agers*. New York: I. Washburn, 1961.

Howe, Julia Ward, *Reminiscences 1819–1899*. Boston: Houghton Mifflin Company, 1899.

Howe, M. A. De Wolfe, *A Venture in Remembrance*. Boston: Little, Brown & Company, 1941.

Hunt, Gaillard, *Life in America One Hundred Years Ago*. New York: Harper & Brothers, 1914.

Irving, Washington, *Knickerbocker's History of New York*. New York: G. P. Putnam's Sons, 1894.

Jacobs, Jane, *The Death and Life of Great American Cities*. New York: Random House, 1961.

James, Henry, *The American Scene*. New York: Harper & Brothers, 1907.

Jeffries, Ona Griffin, *In and Out of the White House*. New York: Wilfred Funk, Inc., 1960.

Jensen, Amy (La Follette), *The White House and Its Thirty-two Families*. New York: McGraw-Hill Book Company, 1958.

Jensen, Oliver, *The Revolt of American Women*. New York: Harcourt, Brace & Company, 1952.

Josephson, Matthew, *The Robber Barons*. New York: Harcourt, Brace & Company, 1934.

Kahn, Ely Jacques, *Contemporary American Architects*. New York: Whittlesey House, 1931.

———, *Design in Art and Industry*. New York: Charles Scribner's Sons, 1935.

Kalm, Peter, *Travels in North America*. Warrington: Printed by William Eyres, 1770.

Kane, Harnett T., *The Southern Christmas Book*. New York: David McKay Company, 1958.

Kavaler, Lucy, *The Private World of High Society*. New York: David McKay Company, 1960.

Kenrick, William, *The Whole Duty of a Woman*. London: Dean & Munday, 17– .

Kimball, Sidney Fiske, *American Architecture*. Indianapolis: Bobbs-Merrill, 1928.

Kluckhohn, Florence Rockwood, *The American Family and the Feminine Role in Human Relations*, edited by Hugh Cabot and Joseph A. Kahl. Cambridge, Mass.: Harvard University Press, 1953.

Knight, Sarah Kemble, *The Private Journal of a Journey from Boston to New York in the Year 1704*. Albany: F. H. Little, 1865.

Knowlton, Helen M., *Art-Life of William Morris Hunt*. Boston: Little, Brown & Company, 1899.

Koch, Robert, *Louis C. Tiffany*. New York: Crown Publishing Company, 1964.

Kouwenhoven, John A., *Adventures of America, 1857–1900*. New York: Harper & Brothers, 1938.

———, *Made in America: The Arts in Modern Civilization*. Garden City, N.Y.: Doubleday & Company, 1948.

——— (ed.), *The Columbia Historical Portrait of New York*. Garden City, N.Y.: Doubleday & Company, 1953.

Kronenberger, Louis, *Company Manners*. Indianapolis: Bobbs-Merrill, 1954.

Lafever, Minard, *The Beauties of Modern Architecture*. New York: D. Appleton & Company, 1935.

———, *The Complete Architectural Instructor*. New York: G. P. Putnam's Sons, 1857.

Lamb, Martha J., *History of the City of New York: Its Origin, Rise and Progress.* 5 vols. New York: A. S. Barnes & Company, 1877.

Langdon, W. C., *Everyday Things in American Life.* New York: Charles Scribner's Sons, 1937–1941.

Larkin, Oliver W., *Art and Life in America.* New York: Rinehart & Company, 1949.

Latrobe, Benjamin Henry, *The Journal of Latrobe.* New York: D. Appleton & Company, 1905.

Laver, James, *Costume of the Western World.* New York: Harper & Brothers, 1951.

———, *Edwardian Promenade.* London: Edward Hulton, 1958.

———, *Panic Among the Puritans.* New York: Farrar & Rinehart, 1936.

———, *Style in Costume.* London: Oxford University Press, 1949.

———, *Taste and Fashion from the French Revolution until Today.* London: George G. Harrap & Company, 1937.

Levin, Phyllis Lee, *The Wheels of Fashion.* Garden City, N.Y.: Doubleday & Company, 1965.

Lewis, Paul, *Queen of the Plaza.* New York: Funk & Wagnalls Company, 1964.

Life, Editors of, *America's Arts and Skills.* New York: E. P. Dutton & Company, 1957.

Lockwood, Sarah M., *Antiques.* Garden City, N.Y.: Doubleday, Doran & Company, 1930.

Longley, Marjorie, Louis Silverstein and Samuel A. Tower (eds.), *America's Taste: The Cultural Events of a Century Reported by Contemporary Observers in the Pages of The New York Times.* New York: Simon and Schuster, 1960.

Longstreet, Abby B., *Social Etiquette of New York.* New York: D. Appleton & Company, 1879.

Longworth, Alice, *Crowded Hours.* New York: Charles Scribner's Sons, 1933.

Lowens, Irving, *Music and Musicians in Early America.* New York: W. W. Norton & Company, 1964.

Ludy, Robert B., *Historic Hotels of the World, Past and Present.* Philadelphia: David McKay Company, 1927.

Lutes, Della T., *Home Grown.* Boston: Little, Brown & Company, 1937.

Lutz, Alma, *Susan B. Anthony.* Boston: Beacon Press, 1959.

Lynd, Robert S., and Helen Merrell Lynd, *Middletown, a Study in Contemporary American Culture.* New York: Harcourt, Brace & Company, 1929.

Lynes, Russell, *The Domesticated Americans.* New York: Harper & Row, 1963.

———, *The Tastemakers.* New York: Harper & Brothers, 1949.

McAdoo, Eleanor Wilson, and M. J. Gaffey, *The Woodrow Wilsons.* New York: The Macmillan Company, 1937.

McAllister, Ward, *Society as I Have Known It.* New York: Cassell & Company, 1890.

McClellan, Elisabeth, *History of American Costume, 1607–1870.* New York: Tudor Publishing Company, 1937.

McHale, John, *R. Buckminster Fuller.* New York: George Braziller, 1962.

McPharlin, Paul, *Life and Fashion in America.* New York: Hastings House, 1946.

Martineau, Harriet, *Retrospect of Western Travel.* 3 vols. New York: Harper & Brothers, 1838.

———, *Society in America.* 3 vols. New York: Harper & Brothers, 1942.

Maxwell, Elsa, *The Celebrity Circus.* New York: Appleton-Century, 1963.

Mayer, Grace M. (ed.), *Once Upon a City.* New York: The Macmillan Company, 1958.

Merz, Charles, *The Great American Band Wagon.* New York: The John Day Company, 1928.

Miller, Perry, *The Life of the Mind in America: from the Revolution to the Civil War.* New York: Harcourt, Brace & World, 1966.

Minnegerode, Meade, *Certain Rich Men.* New York: G. P. Putnam's Sons, 1927.

———, *The Fabulous Forties.* New York: G. P. Putnam's Sons, 1924.

Moore, Charles, *Daniel H. Burnham: Architect, Planner of Cities.* 2 vols. Boston: Houghton Mifflin Company, 1921.

Morison, Samuel Eliot, *The Life and Letters of Harrison Gray Otis, Federalist, 1765–1848.* 2 vols. Boston: Houghton Mifflin Company, 1913.

———, *The Oxford History of the American People.* New York: Oxford University Press, 1965.

Morris, Lloyd R., *Incredible New York.* New York: Random House, 1951.

———, *Not So Long Ago.* New York: Random House, 1949.

———, *Postscript to Yesterday.* New York: Random House, 1947.

Morrison, Hugh, *Early American Architecture.* New York: Oxford University Press, 1952.

———, *Louis Sullivan, Prophet of Functionalism.* New York: W. W. Norton, 1935.

Morse, Edward Sylvester, *Japanese Homes and Their Surroundings.* Boston: Ticknor & Company, 1885.

Mott, Frank Luther, *A History of American Magazines.* 4 vols. Cambridge, Mass.: Harvard University Press, 1938.

Mowry, George E., *The Urban Nation: 1920–1960.* New York: Hill & Wang, 1965.

Mumford, Lewis, *The Brown Decades.* New York: Harcourt, Brace, 1931.

———, *The Conduct of Life.* New York: Harcourt, Brace, 1951.

———, *The Culture of Cities.* New York: Harcourt, Brace, 1938.

———, *Roots of Contemporary American Architecture.* New York: Reinhold Publishing Company, 1952.

———, *Sticks and Stones.* New York: Boni & Liveright, 1924.

———, *Technics and Civilization.* New York: Harcourt, Brace, 1934.

Nelson, George, *Industrial Architecture of Albert Kahn.* New York: Architectural Book Publishing Company, 1939.

Neutra, Richard J., *Survival Through Design.* New York: Oxford University Press, 1954.

Nevins, Allan, *American Social History—as Recorded by British Travelers.* New York: H. Holt & Company, 1923.

———, *The Emergence of Modern America, 1865–1878.* New York: The Macmillan Company, 1935.

Oakey, Alexander F., *Building a Home.* New York: D. Appleton & Company, 1881.

Owen, Wilfred, *Cities in the Motor Age.* New York: The Viking Press, 1959.

Parrington, Vernon L., *Main Currents in American Thought.* 3 vols. New York: Harcourt, Brace & Company, 1927–1930.

Paxson, Frederic L., *History of the American Frontier, 1763–1893.* Boston: Houghton Mifflin Company, 1924.

Payne, Blanche, *History of Costume.* New York: Harper & Row, 1965.

Place, C. A., *Charles Bulfinch, Architect and Citizen.* Boston: Houghton Mifflin Company, 1925.

Poore, Ben Perley, *Reminiscences of Sixty Years in the National Metropolis.* 2 vols. Philadelphia: Hubbard Brothers, 1886.

Post, Emily, *Etiquette in Society, in Business, in Politics and at Home.* New York: Funk & Wagnalls Company, 1923.

———, *Emily Post's Etiquette: The Blue Book of Social Usage.* New York: Funk & Wagnalls Company, 1957.

Pratt, Richard, *Houses, History and People.* New York: M. Evans & Company, 1965.

Prime, Alfred Coxe, *The Arts and Crafts in Philadelphia, Maryland and South Carolina.* Topsfield, Mass.: The Walpole Society, 1929.

Pudney, John, *The Smallest Room.* London: Michael Joseph, 1954.

Ralph, Julian, *Harper's Chicago and the World's Fair.* New York: Harper & Company, 1893.

Rasponi, Lanfranco, *The International Nomads.* New York: G. P. Putnam's Sons, 1966.

Rhodes, Harrison G., *American Towns and People.* New York: R. M. McBride & Company, 1920.

Rhodes, James Ford, *History of the United States from the Compromise of 1850.* 9 vols. New York: The Macmillan Company, 1892–1922.

Richards, Laura E., *Abigail Adams and Her Times.* New York: D. Appleton & Company, 1917.

Richardson, E. P., *Painting in America: The Story of 450 Years.* New York: Thomas Y. Crowell Company, 1956.

Riis, Jacob, *How the Other Half Lives.* New York: Charles Scribner's Sons, 1890.

Rogers, Agnes, *The American Procession.* New York: Harper & Brothers, 1933.

———, *Women Are Here to Stay.* New York: Harper & Brothers, 1949.

Rogers, Kate Ellen, *The Modern House*. New York: Harper & Row, 1962.

Rogers, Tyler Stewart, *Plan Your House to Suit Yourself*. New York: Charles Scribner's Sons, 1942.

Rossiter, Clinton, *Seedtime of the Republic*. New York: Harcourt, Brace & Company, 1953.

Rossiter, William Sidney, *Days and Ways in Old Boston*. Boston: R. H. Stearns & Company, 1915.

Routh, Jonathan, *The Better John Guide*. New York: G. P. Putnam's Sons, 1966.

Saarinen, Eliel, *The City: Its Growth, Its Decay, Its Future*. New York: Reinhold, 1934.

Sale, Charles (Chic), *The Specialist*. St. Louis: Specialist Publishing Company, 1929.

Schlesinger, Arthur M., *Learning How to Behave*. New York: The Macmillan Company, 1946.

———, *The Rise of the City 1878–1898*. New York: The Macmillan Company, 1933.

———, *The Rise of Modern America: 1865–1951*. New York: The Macmillan Company, 1951.

Schlesinger, Arthur M., Jr., *Paths of American Thought*, edited by Arthur M. Schlesinger, Jr., and Morton White. Boston: Houghton Mifflin Company, 1963.

Schriftgiesser, Karl, *Oscar of the Waldorf*. New York: E. P. Dutton & Company, 1943.

Schuyler, Montgomery, *American Architecture*. New York: Harper & Brothers, 1892.

Scully, Vincent, Jr., *Modern Architecture*. New York: George Braziller, 1961.

———, *The Shingle Style*. New Haven: Yale University Press, 1955.

Seitz, Don C., *The Dreadful Decade, 1869–1879*. Indianapolis: Bobbs-Merrill, 1926.

Seldes, Gilbert, *The Seven Lively Arts*. New York: Harper & Brothers, 1924.

———, *The Stammering Century*. New York: John Day Company, 1928.

Sherwood, Mary Elizabeth Wilson (Mrs. John Sherwood), *Manners and Social Usages*. New York: Harper & Brothers, 1884.

Sigourney, Lydia H., *Letters to Young Ladies*. New York: Harper & Brothers, 1857.

Sinclair, Andrew, *The Better Half*. New York: Harper & Row, 1965.

Singleton, Esther, *Dutch New York*. New York: Dodd, Mead & Company, 1909.

———, *The Furniture of Our Forefathers*. New York: Doubleday, Page & Company, 1901.

Slayden, Ellen Maury, *Washington Wife*. New York: Harper & Row, 1963.

Smith, Margaret Bayard (Mrs. Samuel Harrison Smith), *The First Forty Years of Washington Society*, edited by Gaillard Hunt. New York: Charles Scribner's Sons, 1906.

Smith, Matthew Hale, *Successful Folks: How They Live*. Hartford: American Publishing Company, 1878.

Snow, Carmel, with Mary Louise Aswell, *The World of Carmel Snow*. New York: McGraw-Hill Book Company, 1962.

Sprague, William Buell, *Annals of the American Pulpit, 1857–69*. New York: R. Carter & Brothers, 1857–1869.

Stanard, Mary Newton, *Colonial Virginia, Its People and Customs*. Philadelphia: J. B. Lippincott Company, 1917.

Starbuck, March, *My House and I*. Boston: Houghton Mifflin Company, 1929.

Stern, Madeleine, *Purple Passage*. Norman: University of Oklahoma Press, 1953.

Stickley, Gustav, *Craftsman Homes*. The Craftsman Publishing Company, 1909.

Stokes, I. N. Phelps, and Daniel C. Haskell, *American Historical Prints*. New York: New York Public Library, 1933.

Stolberg, Benjamin, *Tailor's Progress*. New York: Doubleday & Company, 1944.

Sturgis, Russell, *A Dictionary of Architecture and Building, Biographical, Historical and Descriptive*. New York: The Macmillan Company, 1901–1902.

———, *A History of Architecture*. 4 vols. New York: The Baker & Taylor Company, 1906–1915.

———, *Homes in City and Country*. New York: Charles Scribner's Sons, 1893.

Sullivan, Louis H., *Kindergarten Chats*. Washington: Scarab Fraternity Press, 1934.

Sullivan, Mark, *Our Times: The United States, 1900–1925*. 6 vols. New York: Charles Scribner's Sons, 1926–1935.

Taft, Pauline Dakin, *The Happy Valley, the Elegant Eighties in Upstate New York*. Syracuse: Syracuse University Press, 1965.

Tallmadge, Thomas C., *The Story of Architecture in America*. New York: W. W. Norton & Company, 1927.

Thane, Elswyth, *Washington's Lady*. New York: Dodd, Mead & Company, 1960.

Tiffany & Company, *Tiffany Table Settings*. New York: Thomas Y. Crowell Company, 1960.

Toffler, Alvin, *The Culture Consumers*. New York: St. Martin's Press, 1964.

Tower, Elizabeth, and R. T. H. Halsey, *The Homes of Our Ancestors*. New York: Doubleday, Doran & Company, 1925.

Trollope, Anthony, *North America*. New York: Harper & Brothers, 1863.

Trollope, Mrs. Frances (Milton), *Domestic Manners of the Americans*, edited by Donald Smalley, with a history of Mrs. Trollope's adventures in America. New York: Alfred A. Knopf, 1949.

Tully, Andrew, *Era of Elegance*. New York: Funk & Wagnalls Company, 1947.

Vanderbilt, Amy, *Amy Vanderbilt's Complete Book of Etiquette*. Garden City, N.Y.: Doubleday & Company, 1957.

Van Doren, Carl, *Benjamin Franklin*. New York: The Viking Press, 1952.

Van Rensselaer, Mrs. John King, *Newport Our Social Capital*. Philadelphia: J. B. Lippincott Company, 1905.

Van Rensselaer, Mrs. Schuyler, *Henry Hobson Richardson and His Works*. Boston: Houghton Mifflin Company, 1888.

———, *History of the City of New York in the Seventeenth Century*. New York: The Macmillan Company, 1909.

Vaux, Calvert, *Villas and Cottages*. New York: Harper & Brothers, 1857.

Viking Press and *Vogue*, Editors of, *The World in Vogue*. Editors for *Vogue*, Jessica Daves and Alexander Liberman; editors for Viking, Bryan Holme and Katharine Tweed. New York: The Viking Press, 1963.

Wade, Margaret, *Social Usage in America*. New York: Thomas Y. Crowell Company, 1924.

Walker, Stanley, *Mrs. Astor's Horse*. New York: Stokes, 1935.

Wallis, Frank Edwin, *American Architecture, Decoration and Furniture of the Eighteenth Century*. New York: P. Wenzel, 1896.

Warwick, Edward, and Henry C. Pitz, *Early American Dress*. New York: The Century Company, 1929.

Webb, Walter Prescott, *The Texas Rangers*. Boston: Houghton Mifflin Company, 1935.

Wecter, Dixon, *The Age of the Great Depression, 1929–1941*. New York: The Macmillan Company, 1948.

———, *The Saga of American Society*. New York: Charles Scribner's Sons, 1937.

Wertenbaker, Thomas Jefferson, *Father Knickerbocker's Rebels; New York City During the Revolution*. New York: Charles Scribner's Sons, 1948.

———, *The First Americans, 1607–1690*. New York: The Macmillan Company, 1927.

Wharton, Anne H., *Social Life in the Early Republic*. Philadelphia: J. B. Lippincott, 1902.

Wharton, Edith, *The Age of Innocence*. New York: D. Appleton & Company, 1920.

Wheeler, Gervase, *Homes for the People in Suburb and Country*. New York: Charles Scribner's Sons, 1855.

Whitaker, C. H. (ed.), *Bertram Grosvenor Goodhue, Architect and Master of Many Arts*. New York: American Institute of Architects, 1925.

Wilcox, Ruth Turner, *Five Centuries of American Costume*. New York: Charles Scribner's Sons, 1963.

Williamson, Jefferson, *The American Hotel*. New York: Alfred A. Knopf, 1930.

Winchester, Alice, and staff of *Antiques*, *The Antique Treasury*. New York: E. P. Dutton & Company, 1959.

Winslow, Anne Green, *Diary of a Boston School Girl of 1771*, edited by Alice Morse Earle. Boston: Houghton Mifflin Company, 1894.

Winthrop, John, *The History of New England from 1630–1649*. Boston: Phelps & Farnham, 1825–1826.

Woodward, Helen, *Through Many Windows*. New York: Harper & Brothers, 1926.

Woodward, William E., *The Way Our People Lived*. New York: E. P. Dutton & Company, 1944.

Worth, Jean Philippe, *A Century of Fashion*. Boston: Little, Brown & Company, 1928.

Wright, Frank Lloyd, *An American Architecture*, edited by Edgar Kaufmann. New York: Horizon Press, 1955.

———, *An Autobiography*. New York: Duell, Sloan and Pearce, 1943.

———, *The Future of Architecture*. New York: Horizon Press, 1953.

———, *The Living City*. New York: Horizon Press, 1958.

———, and Baker Brownell, *Architecture and Modern Life*. New York: Harper & Brothers, 1937.

Wright, Lawrence, *Clean and Decent*. London: Routledge & Kegan, 1960.

Wright, Louis B., *The Cultural Life of the American Colonies, 1607–1763*. New York: Harper & Brothers, 1857.

Adam brothers, 10, 15
Adams, Henry, 255
Adams, John, 7, 55, 107, 122, 245, 247, 267, 281, 295, 296
Adams, Mrs. John (Abigail), 7, 68, 74, 191, 228, 245, 246, 281, 288, 295
Adams, John Quincy, 15, 79, 185
Adolfo (designer), 183
advertising (*see also* catalogues), 36, 65, 106, 131, 166, 188, 191, 212, 222, 225, 244, 301
agnosticism, 38, 40
agricultural equipment, 62, 252
air conditioning, 63, 97, 123, 125, 145
airplanes, 269, 274, 278, 301
alcohol, 35
Alcoholics Anonymous, 65
Alcott, Bronson, 60
Alexandra, Queen, 191
Alexandre (glovemaker), 216
Allen, Fred, 45
Allestree, Richard, 287
American Ballet Theater, 47
American Radiator Building (New York), 156
amusements, 78–97
Anburey, Thomas, 281
Angelus Temple (Los Angeles), 38
animals, wild, 79
Anne, Queen (England), 22
Anthony, Susan B., 174
aprons, 220–221
archery, 97

architecture, 3–29, 39, 68–69, 89, 118, 134, 135, 144, 145, 147, 150, 151, 152, 154–165, 171, 226
Arden, Elizabeth, 226
Argenson, Marquis d', 131
art, 41, 45, 46, 49, 137–138, 140, 161, 164, 165, 257, 284, 292
art movies, 46
Astor, Mrs. John Jacob, 126, 164, 215–216
Astor, Vincent, 92
Astor, William, 96
Astor, Mrs. William, 230, 255, 258, 259, 261, 263, 264, 267
Astor family, 225, 251, 255–256
Astor Hotel (New York), 14
Astor House (New York), 69, 126–127
Atlantic & Pacific Tea Company, (A & P), 61
atomic bomb, 302
Austen, James, 17
automobiles, 92, 95, 110, 144, 146, 165, 266, 274–275, 276, 278, 282, 301
Avedon, Richard, 202
Ayer, Harriet Hubbard, 225

baby foods, 63
Bacall, Lauren, 205
badminton, 97
Baker, Alfred E., 87
Baker, Mrs. Obed, 207
Ball and Frost, 229
ballet, 47
balloons, 89

balls, 82
Balsan, Jacques, 257
Bank of Pennsylvania, 13, 17
banks, 253
Banting, William, 226
Bardot, Brigitte, 205
Barnum, P. T., 86, 174
Barton, Clara, 273, 296
baseball, 95
bathing (*see also* swimming), 90, 125–126, 189
bathing beauty contests, 189
bathing suits, 180, 181, 185–186, 188–189, 199, 239
bathrooms, 125–132
Bay Psalm Book, 34, 35, 41
bay windows, 147
beaches, 146, 185–186, 188–189
beards, 239, 241, 242, 243
Beatles, 236, 242
beatniks, 217, 282
Beaton, Cecil, 139
Becket, Walton, 159
Beckford, Peter, 234
Beckford, Mrs. Peter, 168
Bedell, Grace, 241
bedrooms, 119
beds, 105–106, 107, 108, 119, 121, 133, 135
Beebe, Lucius, 249
Beecher, Catharine, E., 123
Beecher, Henry Ward, 225
Beekman, James, 8
Beekman family, 270
beer, 59

Belcher, Colonel, 16
Bell, Alexander Graham, 52
Bellew, Kyrle, 225
Belmont, August, 259
Belmont, Mrs. August, 225
Belmont, Mrs. O. H. P., 23, 230
Belmont family, 188
Benjamin, Asher, 14, 15
Bennett, James Gordon, 50, 83, 265
Bennett, John, 288
Bennette, Joseph, 80–81
Benny, Jack, 45
Berenson, Bernard, 257
Berlin, Irving, 83
Berlin, Mrs. Irving, 264
Bernhardt, Sarah, 69, 72, 216, 291
Bernstein, Leonard, 91
Berry Hill, 11
Bible, 34, 36
bicycles, 89, 92, 93, 166, 179
Biddle church, *see* St. James the Less Church
bidets, 131
billiards, 79
Billings, C. K. G., 258, 262
Billings, William, 42
Bingham, Mrs. William, 246, 264
Birdseye, Clarence, 63
birth-control pills, 299
Blackwell, Antoinette, 296
Blackwell, Elizabeth, 283, 296
Bloomer, Amelia, 60, 174, 175, 177
boating, 96–97
Bogardus, James, 152, 154
Boldini, Giovanni, 179, 257
bookcases, 107
books, 34–35, 107, 139, 301
boots, 215, 217–218, 220
Booz, E., 138
Borotra, Jean, 95
Boston Latin School, 33
Boucicault, Dion, 50
Bourdelle, Emile, 138
Bowery Theater (New York), 14
bowling, 95, 97
Bowling Green (New York), 148
Boylston, Nick, 107
Brady, Diamond Jim, 73, 260
"Brandon," 8
bras, 212
brass, 114
Brattle Street Church (Boston), 25
bread, 60
Bremer, Fredrika, 256, 258
Brentano, August, 44
Breuer, Marcel, 28, 110, 157
Brevoort, Henry, 14
bridal attire, 194, 196, 198, 200
bridges, covered, 16
Brine, Augustus, 234
Bromfield family, 7
Brooklyn Bridge, 154–155
Brooks, Henry Sands, 233
Brooks Brothers, 216, 233, 235
Browning, Elizabeth Barrett, 169, 204
Bruce, James Cole, 11
Bryn Mawr College, 26
Buchanan, James, 74, 131, 191, 233, 239

Bucklin, J. C., 16
Buffalo Bill, 239
Buffington, L. S., 155
building materials, 6, 99, 154, 160
buildings (*see also* architecture; houses; mansions; plantations; skyscrapers):
  commercial, 6, 13, 14, 20, 154, 161, 165, 166
  public, 6, 10, 13, 14, 16, 17, 154, 159, 165
Bulfinch, Charles, 10, 15, 17, 18
bullfights, 79
bundling, 281–282, 292, 297
Bunshaft, Gordon, 157, 158, 159
Burgis, William, 4
burials, 40
Burnham, Daniel H., 155, 160, 161
Burnside, Ambrose E., 239
Busch, Sallie Marie, 260–261
Bush Terminal Tower Building (New York), 156
bust building, 212
Butler, Mrs. Robin, 265
Butterick, Ebenezer, 171, 298
Byrd, William, 8, 35
Byron, Joseph, 262

California, University of, 35
calling cards, 184, 290
Calyo, Nicolino V., 57
Campbell, Mrs. Patrick, 293
camp meetings, 36, 38, 49
Canal Street Greek Doric church (New York), 14
candles, 118
canning, 63
Capen, Joseph, 6, 11
Capitol, U. S., 10
Capote, Truman, 262, 263–264
Cardin, Pierre, 237, 240
cards, playing, 79
Carmer, Carl, 23
Carnegie, Andrew, 43, 164, 251, 255
Carnegie, Dale, 301
Carnegie, Margaret, 164
carpets, 115, 116, 117, 119, 128, 134, 139, 140
cars, *see* automobiles
Carstenson, George, 248
Carter, Elias, 16
cartoons, 36, 51, 175, 176, 185
Cartwright, Alexander J., 95
Cartwright, Peter, 38
Cary, Alice, 51
Cassatt, Mary, 138, 161
Castellane, Marquis de, 256
Castle, Irene, 83, 194
Castle, Vernon, 83
Castle Garden (New York), 248
catalogues, mail-order, 61, 129, 188
catering, 67, 73, 236, 300
Catherine the Great, 230
Cavaliers, 32
Central Park (New York), 21, 23, 92, 148, 150, 176, 267, 270
Century Association of New York, 47
Chagall, Marc, 45, 46

chairs, 105, 107–108, 109, 110, 111, 113, 115, 116, 117, 135, 137, 141, 142, 146, 162
chamber pots, 130, 132
chandeliers, 104, 117, 118, 136, 139, 142
Chanel, Gabrielle (Coco), 182, 197, 199
Chapbooks, 34
chaperones, 292, 294
Chaplin, Charlie, 241
Charles I, King (England), 32
Charles II, King (England), 107
Chase, Salmon Portland, 249
Chautauqua, 38
Chesterfield, Lord, 288
chests, 102, 103, 134, 137
Childs', 59
chinaware, 103, 104, 112, 114, 130, 143
Chippendale, Thomas, 23, 99, 107, 108, 112
Christ Church (Boston), 25, 132
Christian Science Church (Berkeley, Cal.), 29
Christmas, 81
Christmas trees, 81
Chrysler Building (New York), 156
churches, 14, 15, 16, 17, 20, 21, 24–26, 27, 28, 29, 39–40, 138, 139, 154, 165, 202, 254, 255, 256, 275, 287
Churchill, Randolph, 256
Churchill, Winston, 237, 288
Church of Saint Mary the Virgin (Falmouth, Me.), 29
Church of the Ascension (New York), 139
Church of the Transfiguration (New York), 26
cider, 59, 68, 80
cigarettes, 297
circus, 89
Claflin, Tennessee, 64, 173
Clagge, William, 118
class distinctions, 31–33
Clay, Henry, 234, 246
Cleveland, Grover, 51, 228, 241
Clinton, George, 234
clocks, 114, 116, 118
clothing:
  children's, 201, 236
  men's, 167, 170, 183, 186, 189, 232–239, 240, 243, 275
  teenager's and, 201
  women's, 14, 88, 92, 93, 103, 167–202, 206–207, 209–210, 212, 214, 275
clubs, 47, 50–51, 84, 88, 92, 95, 96, 97, 138, 139, 146, 151, 189, 254, 265, 295
Coca-Cola, 59
Cochrane, Alexander Smith, 134
cockfighting, 78, 79
cocktails, 59, 68
Coe, Adam S., 104
coffee, 59–60, 61
coffeehouses, 66, 68, 82
Cole (designer), 189
Coleman, Ronald, 241

college commencements, 82
Colony Club (New York), 140
Columbian Exposition (Chicago), 160–161
Columbus, Christopher, 147, 161
coming-out parties, 260–261
commodes, 106, 130
Conestoga wagons, 272
Coney Island, 153, 181, 188
Conklin, Peggy, 297
Constitution, U.S., 295
cookbooks, 76–77
Coolidge, Calvin, 76, 96, 124, 191
Coolidge, Mrs. Thomas Brewster, 169
Cooper, Peter, 251, 277
Copley, John Singleton, 6, 103, 168, 234, 287
Corcoran Gallery of Art (Washington, D.C.), 26
cordials, 59
Cornell, Kate Lyon, 169
Cornell University, 35, 132
corsets, 210, 212, 219, 236
cosmetics, 189, 206, 212, 225–226, 244
Cosmos Club (Washington, D.C.), 50
costume jewelry, 139, 199, 231
cotton, 250
Cotton, John, 170
country clubs, 47, 50, 146
country stores, 66
Courrèges (designer), 215
courtship, 281–283, 297
Coventry, William H., 20
covered bridges, 16
covered wagons, 272
Cram, Ralph Adams, 26
Cranbrook Academy, 159
credit cards, 65
crewel work, 101
cricket, 95
crime, 120, 275
Crocker, Charles, 164
croquet, 92, 94, 179
Crosby, Bing, 45
Crowninshield, Frank W., 265
Crystal Palace (New York), 248
cuisine, see food
cupboards, 103, 104, 166
Curtiss, Glenn, 278
Custer, General, 239

Dagmar, 212
Dakin, Charles, 16
Dakin, James, 16
Damrosch, Walter, 41
dancing, 78, 79, 80, 81, 82–84, 86, 88, 96, 146, 150, 182, 261, 301
Danforth, Thomas, III, 101
Davis, Alexander Jackson, 21, 117
Davis, Meyer, 261
debates, 36, 47, 78
debutantes, 260–261
Decatur, Stephen, 68
Dechaux, Edward, 87
Deering, James, 165
Delaware, Lord, 107
delftware, 114
Delmonico brothers, 72, 73

democracy, 154
Demorest, Madame, 51, 171, 178, 185, 212, 225, 298
Dent, Julia, see Grant, Mrs. Ulysses S.
dentistry, 64, 227
De Pouilly, Jacques, 16
Depression, 165, 302
Derby, Elias Hasket, 11, 104
Derby House (Mass.), 11, 15
Devonshire, Duchess of, 191
dice, 79
Dickens, Charles, 7, 36, 44, 51, 69, 120, 258, 288
Dietrich, Marlene, 194
Diggs, Mrs. Dabney William, see Cornell, Kate Lyon
Dior, Christian, 182, 199
discrimination, 50
dishwashers, 123
divorce, 283, 291
Dix, Dorothea L., 296
doctors, 64–65
Doherty, Helen Lee Eames, 260
Doherty, Henry L., 260
Doolittle, Amos, 18
Doubleday, Abner, 95
Downing, Andrew Jackson, 17, 20, 21, 22, 135, 145, 150
drama, 46, 48, 82, 97, 150
Drexel, Anthony J., Jr., 259
Drexel, John, 267
Drexel girls, 251
drinks, 57, 59, 79
drugs, 65
Drummond, I. W., 149
Dubuque, Iowa, 17, 271
Dubuque, Julien, 271
Duke, Doris, 251
Duncan, Isadora, 193
dune-buggying, 97
duPont, Eugene, 164
Durant, Charles F., 89
Duryea, Charles Edgar, 274
Dutch, in America, 31, 33, 54, 59, 81, 95, 99, 103, 105, 107–108, 114, 145, 151, 170, 214, 220, 249, 281
Dwight, Timothy, 80

Eames, Charles, 110, 113
Easter Parade, 253, 256
Eastlake, Charles L., 134, 135, 137, 140
eating habits, see food
Edison, Thomas A., 120–121
education, 32–34, 37, 42, 89
    sex, 283, 294
Edward VII, King (England), 193, 235, 258
Edwards, Jonathan, 25, 38, 39, 42
Eisenhower, Dwight D., 76, 96
Eisenhower, Mrs. Dwight D., 191
Election Day, 82
electrical appliances, 122–123
electric lights, 120–121
elevators, 152, 166
Emerson, Ralph Waldo, 36, 44
Empire State Building (New York), 155, 156
Englishmen, in America, 31

entertainment, 78–97, 146
escalators, 166
etiquette, 287–290, 293, 294, 301
Eugénie, Empress, 191
evangelism, 38–39

Fairbanks, Douglas, Jr., 260
Fairchild, John B., 265
fairs, 87, 97, 160–161
falsies, 212
Faneuil, Peter, 233
Faneuil family, 7
Faneuil Hall (Boston), 100
fans, 223, 225, 228
farming, 252
Farrow, Mia, 205
fashions, see clothing
Fay, A., 252
Fell, Mrs. John, 264
feminist movement, 33, 51–52, 286, 295–296, 298
Fillmore, Millard, 21, 126
fireplaces, 98, 103, 115, 117, 121–122, 135, 141, 166
fires, 4, 120
fireworks, 89
Fish, Mrs. Stuyvesant, 259, 261, 264, 267, 289
Fisher, Harrison, 238
fishing, 79, 80, 97
Fitzgerald, F. Scott, 238
Flagg, James Montgomery, 238
Flagler, Henry M., 188
flappers, 195, 238
Flatiron Building (New York), 155
flowers, 142–143, 145, 147, 148, 149, 150, 151
flower shows, 151
food, 31, 54–67, 72–77, 78, 79, 81–82
football, 89, 96
Ford, Henry, 274, 276
Ford Company, 274
Forrest, Edwin, 14, 149
Forsyth, John, 28
Fortuny (designer), 193
Foster, Stephen, 43
Four Hundred, the, 255, 263
Four Square Gospel, 38
Fowler, O. S., 12, 23, 24, 146
fox hunting, see hunting
Franklin, Benjamin, 7, 32, 36, 59, 107, 108, 111, 121–122, 129, 130, 171, 268, 288
Franklin, Deborah, 171
fraternities, 34, 47
Frazier, Brenda Diana Duff, 260
Freemasons, 47
French, in America, 31
Freret, James, 16
Freud, Sigmund, 282
Frick, Henry C., 43, 164
Friedan, Betty, 300
Fry, Henry L., 137
Fry, William, 137
Fuller, Loie, 193
Fuller, R. Buckminster, 165
Fundamentalism, 39
funerals, 40

furnishings, *see* interior decoration
furniture, 99, 101, 102, 103, 104, 105–108, 109, 110, 111, 112, 113, 115, 116, 119, 128, 130, 133, 135, 137, 139, 140, 141, 160
furs, 173, 182

Gainsborough, Thomas, 179, 191, 207, 209
Galitzine, Princess, 214
Galliers, James, 16
Galliers, James, Jr., 16
gambling, 78, 79, 80, 129, 250, 269
games, 78, 79, 81, 82, 87, 88, 89, 92, 95, 96, 97, 137, 145
gander pulling, 78
Garbo, Greta, 194, 205
gardens, 150–151
Gardiner, Julia, *see* Tyler, Mrs. John
Gardner, Mrs. Jack, 147, 163, 164, 257, 259, 264, 291
garters, 210
gaslight, 121
Gauguin, Paul, 46
Geldenmeister, Charles, 248
Gem Saloon (New York), 252
General Federation of Women's Clubs, 51
George, Henry, 148
George IV, King (England), 126
Georges, Alexander, 49
Germans, in America, 31, 41, 59, 121
Gernreich, Rudi, 183, 189, 212, 217
Gershwin, George, 43
Gibbs, James, 5, 14, 25, 27
Gibson, Charles Dana, 179, 187
Gibson girl, 173, 179, 187, 210
Gilbert, Cass, 29, 155
girdles, 210, 212
glass, 101, 136, 138, 139, 157, 159, 160
gloves (*see also* mittens), 180, 216–217, 220
Goelet, Robert, 164
Gogh, Vincent van, 46
golf, 89, 95–96, 146
Goodhue, Bertram, 26
Good Humor man, 58
Goodman, Charles M., 163
Gorham Company, 229
Goubie, A., 271
Gould, Anna, 256
Gould, Mrs. George, 230, 259
Gould, Jay, 117
Gould, Mrs. Jay, 216
Gould family, 225, 251, 259
Grace, Princess, 53
Grace Church (New York), 26
Graham, Billy, 39
Graham, Mrs. Philip (Kay), 262, 263
Graham, Sylvester, 60
Graham, William A., 163
Grand Central Station (New York), 156–157
Grant, Cary, 237
Grant, Nellie, *see* Sartoris, Mrs. Algernon
Grant, Ulysses S., 44, 74, 76, 173, 194, 241, 261, 282, 289

Grant, Mrs. Ulysses S., 74, 76, 194, 282, 289
Gray, David, 276
Great American Tea Company, 60
Great Awakening, 25, 38, 39
Greeley, Horace, 60, 173, 174, 177, 223, 241
Green, Edward H., 130
Green, Hetty, 130, 222, 251, 253, 254
Green, Sylvia, 254
Greene, J. H., 16
Gregory, John, 287
Grimké, Angelina, 296
Grimké, Sarah, 296
Gropius, Walter, 157
Gross, William, 57
Gruen, Victor, 159
Grund, Francis J., 61–62
Guaranty Building (Buffalo, N.Y.), 155
Guggenheimer, Randolph, 259
Guggenheim Museum (New York), 45, 160
Gunther, John, 302
Guy, Francis, 66
Gwyn, Nell, 205
gymnasiums, 94
gyrocopting, 97

hairpins, 221–222
hair styles:
men's, 203, 234, 239, 241, 242, 244
women's, 14, 167, 169, 170, 171, 195, 200, 203–206, 208, 241, 293
Hale, Mrs. Sarah Josepha, 287
Halfpenny, William, 5, 23
Hall, Basil, 279
Hall, Margaret, 279
Hamilton, George, 237
Hamilton, Thomas, 7
Hamlin, Talbot, 13
hammocks, 146–147, 149
Hancock, Thomas, 147
Hancock family, 7
handball, 97
handkerchiefs, 221
Harding, Chester, 129
Hardy, Lady Duffus, 69
Harlow, Jean, 194
Harper, James, 149
Harriman, Mrs. Oliver, 225
Harriman family, 260
Harrison, Benjamin, 8, 241
Harrison, Peter, 14–15
Harrison, Wallace K., 159
Harrison, William Henry, 74, 138
Hart, Charles, 153
Hartford, George Huntington, 60
Harvard University, 33, 35, 43, 47, 82, 89, 157, 241, 263, 281
hats:
men's, 206, 233, 234
women's, 176, 180, 184, 187, 190, 206–207, 209, 210, 213
Haughwout, E. V., & Co., 166
Havemeyer family, 134
Haviland, John, 16
Hayes, Irene, 143

Hayes, Rutherford B., 76, 241
Hayes, Mrs. Rutherford B. (Lucy), 76
health, 61–62, 64–65, 146, 227
Hearst, William Randolph, 164
Held, John, Jr., 195
Henry, Edward Lamson, 277
Henry, O., 26
Henry, Patrick, 76
Hepplewhite, George, 99, 107, 108, 130
Herbert, Victor, 41, 256
highways, *see* roads
Hirshhorn, Joseph H., 46
Hitchcock, Lambert, 108
Hoban, James, 10
Hobbs, Isaac H., 20
hockey, 97
Hogarth, William, 175
Holabird and Roche (architects), 155
holidays, 81, 82, 85
Holland Tunnel, 278
Holly, Henry Hudson, 22
Holmes, Oliver Wendell, 62, 234, 268, 287
home furnishings, *see* interior decoration
Home Insurance Building (Chicago), 155
Homer, Winslow, 90
Hone, Philip, 20, 26, 245
Hood, Raymond, 156
Hoover, Herbert, 76
Hope, Bob, 45
Hope diamond, 46, 228, 230, 261
Hopkins, Mark, 164
Horn & Hardart's, 59
Hornbake, H. Lee, 300
Horner, T., 270
horse racing, *see* racing
horseshoe pitching, 97
hosiery, 212, 214–216, 224
hotels, 67–74, 75, 126–127, 132, 140, 146, 154, 166, 186, 202, 236, 254, 268, 269, 300, 302
hourglasses, 114
House of Representatives, U. S., 10
houses, 3–10, 13–17, 20–24, 32, 99, 103
housing developments, 165
Hoving, Walter, 288
Hubbard, Elbert, 137
Hunt, Richard Morris, 23, 150, 161, 162, 164
hunting, 78, 79, 84, 96
Huntington, Collis P., 251, 273
husking bees, 87
Hutton, Barbara, 230, 251
Hyde, James Hazen, 258, 259, 262
hygiene, 227, 283
hymns, 42

ice cream, 56–58, 74
ice skating, 84, 88, 93, 150
immigration, 248, 250–251, 272
Indians, 5, 41, 43, 54, 79, 81, 99, 127, 276
infant mortality, 63
Ingalls, David S., 159

Ingham, Charles Cromwell, 169
interior decoration, 9, 14, 15, 20, 25, 69, 98–143, 301
Irish, in America, 31
Irving, Washington, 20, 80, 141, 281
Italians, in America, 31

Jackson, Andrew, 247
Jackson, Rachel, 291
Jaeger, Dr., 212
James, Henry, 257, 268, 294
Jay, Mrs. John, 246, 264
jazz, 43, 84
"Jazz Age," 84, 210, 302
Jefferson, Thomas, 13, 23, 72, 74, 75, 76, 79, 110, 242, 245, 246
Jefferson, Mrs. Thomas, 64
Jenney, William Le Baron, 155
Jerome, Jennie, 256
jewelry, 206, 228, 229–231, 257, 273
  costume, 139, 199, 231
Jews, in America, 31
Johnson, Howard, 58
Johnson, Lyndon B., 69, 76, 96, 138, 262, 291, 299
Johnson, Mrs. Lyndon B., 76, 96, 147, 193, 291
Johnson, Luci Baines, see Nugent, Mrs. Patrick
Johnson, Nancy, 56
Johnson, Philip, 142, 156, 157, 159
Jones, Inigo, 22, 27
Jones, Sam, 38
Josephine, Empress, 191, 231
journalism, 36
juleps, 68
Jumel, Madame, 256
June, Jennie, 51, 186, 284
Junior League, 260

Kahane, Melanie, 141
Kahn, Albert, 165
Kalm, Peter, 7
Kaufmann, Edgar J., 160
Keeley cure, 65
Keene, Foxhall, 73
Keene, James, 73
Keim, Henry, 57
Kellerman, Annette, 188, 189
Kelly, Victoria, 260
Kemble, Fanny, 174, 198, 291
Kennedy, John F., 69, 74, 76, 96, 108, 242
Kennedy, Mrs. John F., 76, 96, 143, 193, 263
kerosene, 122
King, Mrs. Henrietta, 300
King's Chapel (Boston), 25
King's College (New York), 6
Kipling, Rudyard, 23, 72, 288
Kira, Alexander, 132
kitchens, 121–125
Knickerbocker Club, 50
Knight, Sarah Kemble, 84
Komyo, Emperor, 191
Kosygin, Premier, 138

Lacour, Peter, 18
La Farge, John, 23, 26, 50, 138, 139, 164
Lafayette, Madame de, 246
La Guardia, Fiorello, 45
Lake, Veronica, 205
Lalauze, A., 271
Lalique, René, 138
lamps, 100, 118, 120, 121, 128, 134, 136, 139, 140
landscaping, 8, 21, 142, 147, 150
Lane, Harriet, 191
Lane Theological Seminary (Cincinnati), 17
Langtry, Lily, 193
Lannuier, Charles Honoré, 117
lanterns, 118
Larkin Building (Buffalo), 160
Latrobe, Benjamin Henry, 10, 13, 16, 17, 18, 21, 126
Leadville, Colorado, 86
League of American Wheelmen, 92
Le Corbusier, 157
lectures, 36, 44, 47, 60, 82
Lehr, Harry, 259
Leiter, Joseph, 259
Lelong (designer), 192
L'Enfant, Pierre Charles, 10, 18
Lenglen, Suzanne, 95
Leslie, Frank, 91
Leslie, Mrs. Frank, 210, 226
Lever House (New York), 156, 157, 158
Levitt, William J., 165
Lewis, Sinclair, 301
Lewisohn, Mrs. Frederick, 293
Liberace, 130
libraries, 35, 36, 46, 139, 147, 159, 164
lighting, 100, 118–121
Lincoln, Abraham, 69, 74, 106, 111, 241, 277
Lincoln, Mary, 216
Lincoln Center for the Performing Arts (New York), 45, 48, 50, 156, 159
Lind, Jenny, 86
Lindbergh, Charles A., 278
linen, 106, 140
lingerie, 212, 214, 219
Lipton, Sir Thomas, 96–97
Little Church Around the Corner, see Church of the Transfiguration
Little Egypt, 161
living rooms, 137
Livingston family, 8
log cabins, 9, 115
Longfellow, Henry Wadsworth, 153
Longworth, Alice Roosevelt, 96, 191, 198, 225, 291, 297
Longworth, Nicholas, 137
Lord & Taylor's, 152, 166
Loren, Sophia, 212
Lorillard, Pierre, 251
lotteries, 80
Loudon, Samuel, 35
Louis XIII, King (France), 241
Lowell, Amy, 293

Ludlow, Mary Duncan, 168
luggage, 269, 273
lyceums, 36, 44
Lyndhurst, 117
Lynes, Russell, 46
Lyon, Mary, 33, 299

McAllister, Ward, 246, 255, 258, 259, 264, 274
McCormick, Harold F., 164
McCormick, Mrs. Robert, 230
McDonald, Mack, 58
McDonald, Richard, 58
McDowell, Roddy, 237
McIntire, Samuel, 15
Mackay, Mrs. Clarence, 259
Mackay, Mrs. John, 264
McKim, Charles F., 161, 164
McKinley, William, 146, 241, 293
McLean, Mrs. Evalyn Walsh, 228, 230, 261
McPherson, Aimee Semple, 38–39
Madison, Dolley, 12, 56, 74, 191, 206, 213, 245, 246, 264
Madison, James, 12, 233, 245
magazines, 301
maids, 67, 148, 256
Mainbocher (designer), 301
makeup, see cosmetics
Mallory, Molla, 95
Mancini (designer), 215
Manhattan Club, 50
Mann, Horace, 207
manners, 287–290
mansions, 11, 12, 13, 15, 16, 17, 22, 43, 46, 117, 134, 137, 138, 140, 145, 147, 154, 161, 162, 164, 165, 256, 258, 261
maple sugar, 57
Marie Antoinette, 17, 140, 168, 171, 191, 204, 230, 259
markets, street, 56
Marlborough, Duke of, 196, 256
Marryat, Frederick, 280
Martin, Bradley, 258–259
Martin, Mrs. Bradley, 259
Martin, Darwin, 160
Martineau, Harriet, 288
Mary, Queen (England), 191
Masonic Temple (Chicago), 155
Massachusetts General Hospital, 15
matches, 120
Mather, Cotton, 30–31, 35, 81, 288
Mather, Increase, 203, 241
mattresses, 105
Maurier, George du, 193
Maxwell, Elsa, 263
Maybeck, Bernard, 29, 165
Mead, William, 161
medicine, 42, 63–65, 270
meetinghouses, 39
Menches, Charles E., 58
Menken, Adah Isaacs, 293
Menken, H. L., 138
Metcalf, Betsey, see Baker, Mrs. Obed
Metropolitan Museum of Art (New York), 45, 46, 119, 159, 263

Metropolitan Opera Club, 50
Metropolitan Opera House (New York), 41, 45, 48, 50, 255
Metternich, Princess, 175
Mies van der Rohe, Ludwig, 110, 113, 142, 157
milk, 60
milkmen, 57
Miller, Bill, 240
Miller, Elizabeth Smith, 174
Miller, Ludwig, 42
millinery (see also hats), 206–207, 209
millionaires, 251, 252, 254, 261, 268, 301
Mimée, E. W., 28
miniskirts, 212, 215, 238
minstrel shows, 41
missions, 10, 28, 165
mittens (see also gloves), 217
Mizner, Addison, 164
Modernism, 39
Moholy-Nagy, Lazlo, 157
Moïse, Theodore Sydney, 234
molasses, 55, 61
Monroe, James, 136, 143, 233, 246
Monroe, Marilyn, 194
Monticello, 13, 145
Moody, Dwight L., 38
Morgan, J. P., 72, 96, 121, 126, 164
Mormons, 239
Morris, John, 42
Morris, Roger, 8
Morris, William, 20, 134, 135, 137, 140, 157
Morse, Samuel F. B., 17
Moses, Robert, 150
Mosley, C. C., 163
motels, 269
motion pictures, 46, 97, 146, 275
Mott, Mrs. Lucretia, 296
"Mount Airy," 8, 24
Mount Holyoke College, 33, 299
movies, see art movies; motion pictures
muffs, 217
Muhlenberg, Adeline Trapp, 188
Mumford, Lewis, 22, 161
Murray, Charles Augustus, 186
Murray, Robert, 8
Museum of Modern Art (New York), 45, 49
museums, 45, 46
music, 31, 41, 43, 45, 46, 80, 83–84, 88, 89, 92, 150, 247
  church, 42
musical instruments, 43, 45
mustaches, 241, 243

Nation, Carry, 296, 298
Neal, David, 103
Neff, Wallace, 163
Neutra, Richard J., 165
Nevin, J. M., 286
New Deal, 165
newspapers, 36, 65
New Year's Day, 81

New York City Ballet, 47
New York Philharmonic Orchestra, 41
New York Press Club, 51
New York Yacht Club, 47, 96
Nieuw Amsterdam, 3, 4, 5, 54
night clubs, 84, 88
nightgowns, 214
Norell (designer), 214
Norton, Charles Eliot, 161
Nugent, Patrick, 198
Nugent, Mrs. Patrick (Luci), 96, 193, 198
nutrition, 60

Oberlin College, 299
obesity, 62
octagon houses, 12, 23–24
Old Farmer's Almanack, 34
Olmsted, Frederick Law, 148, 150
Olympic Games, 89
Oneida Colony, 174
opera, 41, 45, 46, 48, 97, 148, 255
organs, 43, 45, 255
oriels, see bay windows
Otis, Charles, 166
Otis, Elisha Graves, 166
Otis, Harrison Gray, 15
Otis, Mrs. Harrison Gray, 264
Otis, Norton, 166
Ottinger, George M., 276
Oud, J. H. P., 157
outhouses, 131

Pain, William, 14, 15
pajamas:
  men's, 237, 239
  women's, 214, 219
Palace Hotel (San Francisco), 69, 72, 254
Palladio, Andrea, 13, 15
Palmer, Amelia, 169
Palmer, F. F., 248
Palmer, Potter, 12
Palmer, Mrs. Potter, 12, 126, 134–135, 161, 230, 257, 264, 291
Pan-American Building (New York), 157
Paolozzi, Christina, 183
parasols, 184, 222, 223
Parker, Harvey D., 73
Parker, Timothy, 16
parks, public, 78, 80, 147, 148, 150
Parks, William, 76
Park Theater (New York), 48
parlors, 104, 115, 117, 136, 137, 147
Parnis, Mollie, 199
Parris, Alexander, 16
Parton, James, 60
patios, 151
Patou (designer), 263
Patriarchs, 255
Patti, Adelina, 274
Paulding, Philip, 117
Paulding, William, 20, 117
Peale, Rembrandt, 168
Peck, Mrs. Carleton, 173
Peck, Wells, 173

Peck & Peck, 215, 216
peddlers, 85
Penn, William, 7, 13, 129, 214
Pennsylvania Gazette, 36
Pennsylvania Station (New York), 156, 164
Penguins, 50
perfume, 182, 197, 227, 229, 244
petticoats, 214, 219
pewter, 99, 101, 102, 103, 114, 118
Phi Beta Kappa, 34
Phipps, J. S., 64
Phyfe, Duncan, 105, 109, 110, 116
Picasso, Pablo, 45
Pickford, Mary, 193
Picturephone, 53
Pilgrims, 41, 54, 81, 127, 148, 151, 170, 201, 232, 241
Pine, Theodore E., 169
Pinkham, Lydia, 64, 280
pins, 221
Planned Parenthood Federation, 283
plantations, 9, 17, 32
plays, see drama
playthings, see toys
Plaza Hotel (New York), 72, 198, 254, 262, 263, 293
Poe, Edgar Allan, 25, 135
Poiret, Paul, 182, 190
Pompadour, Madame de, 131, 171, 204
pony express, 276
Poor Richard's Almanack, 34
porches, 144–147, 149, 151, 166, 223, 275
Post, Emily, 287, 289, 293, 294, 295, 298, 301
Post, Mrs. Merriweather, 230
postillions, 271
Potter, Mrs. James Brown, 225
pottery, 99, 103, 112, 114
Powers, Hiram, 280, 292
Prang, Louis, 134
Pratt, Matthew, 37
Presley, Elvis, 242
Price, William, 24–25
Priessnitz, Vincenz, 60, 127
Princeton University, 26, 33, 82, 89, 238
Priscilla (designer), 200
prizefights, 97
prohibition, 302
Protestants, 38, 39
public buildings, see buildings
public opinion, 36
Pucci (designer), 214, 219
Pullman, George Mortimer, 250, 273
pumps, 129, 130
punches, 59
Puritans, 30, 39, 40, 41, 78, 82, 125, 167, 170, 171, 178, 182, 218, 225, 227, 229

Quakers (Society of Friends), 31, 36, 39, 82, 170, 227, 241
Quincy, Josiah, 7

Rachel (actress), 193
racing, 79, 82, 84, 89, 96–97, 129, 188

rackets, 97
radio, 45, 84, 97, 302
ragtime, 43, 83
railroads, 273–274, 277
railroad stations, 156–157
raincoats, 223
Rainier, Prince, 53
ranch houses, 10, 165
Rand, Sally, 225
Rand McNally building (Chicago), 155
Randolph, John, 169
reading habits, 34–35, 41
recreation, 78–97
Redfern & Company, 179
reducing, 226
refrigerated cars, 63
refrigerators, 123, 124
regattas, 91, 96, 97
Reid, Hugo, 12
Reid, Victoria, 12
Réjane, Gabrielle, 259, 262
religion, 38–40
Rembrandt, 45
remedies, medical, 63–64
Remington Arms Company, 298
Renta, Oscar de la, 223
Renwick, James, Jr., 26
resorts, 153
restaurants, 72–74
Revere, Paul, 42
revivalism, 38, 49
Reynolds, Sir Joshua, 37, 168
Rhinelander family, 8
Rice, Grantland, 96
Richards, A. C., 20
Richardson, Henry Hobson, 22, 25, 161
"Ridgeview," 20
riding the rapids, 96, 97
Rikli, Arnold, 127
Rittenhouse, David, 114
roads, 268, 275, 276, 278
Roberts, Gideon, 118
Robie, Frederic C., 160, 162
Rockefeller, John D., 64, 141, 249
Rockefeller, William A., 64
Rockefeller Center (New York), 156, 158, 159
Rockefeller family, 134, 251
rocking chairs, 108, 110, 111
Rodin, Auguste, 138
Roebling, John A., 154
Roebling, Washington, 154
Rogers, Isaiah, 14, 16, 68, 69
roller skating, 88
Ronalds, Mrs. Pierre Lorillard, 258
roof gardens, 151
Roosevelt, Alice see Longworth, Alice Roosevelt
Roosevelt, Eleanor, 74, 260
Roosevelt, Franklin D., 76, 96, 260
Roosevelt, Theodore, 75, 76, 96, 241, 259, 262, 291
Root, John W., 155, 161
Rosen, Baroness, 291
Rosenstein, Nettie R., 195
Rothschilds, 251

rounders, 79, 95
Rouse, F., 153
Rousseau, Jean-Jacques, 17
Row, Savile, 237
rowing, 89
Royall, Anne, 56, 185
rugby, 89
rugs, see carpets
rum, 59, 68
Rumsey, Mrs. Charles Cary, 260
Runyon, Damon, 235
Rush, Benjamin, 65
Ruskin, John, 135, 157
Russell, Lillian, 44, 193, 210, 213, 216, 225
Rutherford, Winthrop, 256

Saarinen, Eero, 158, 159
Saarinen, Eliel, 159
Sage, Russell, 251
sailing, 96
St. Bartholomew's Church (New York), 26
St. Cecilia Society, 41
St. Clement's Church (St. Paul, Minn.), 29
Saint Gaudens, Augustus, 138, 160, 161, 164
St. James the Less Church (Philadelphia), 29
St. Laurent (designer), 175, 183, 191, 198, 199, 202
St. Mark's-in-the-Bouwerie (New York), 14
St. Mary's Church (Chicago), 24
St. Mary's Episcopal Church (Burlington, N. J.), 26, 29
Saint-Mémin, 234
St. Michael's Chapel (Burlington, Vt.), 29
St. Michael's Church (Charleston, S. C.), 25, 27
St. Patrick's Cathedral (New York), 26, 158
St. Paul's Church (New York), 25
St. Philip's Church (North Carolina), 25
St. Thomas's Church (New York), 26, 139
Sale, Charles (Chic), 131
"Samurai Formula," 212
Sand, George, 204
Sangster, Margaret E., 290
Sankey, Ira D., 38
Sargent, John Singer, 179, 257, 268
Sartain, John, 213
Sartoris, Algernon, 198
Sartoris, Mrs. Algernon (Nellie), 198
Sassoon, Vidal, 205
Schermerhorn family, 8
Schiaparelli, Elsa, 182
Schlesinger, Arthur M., 33, 262
schools, see education
Schuyler, Peter, 8
Schwab, Charles M., 43, 251
Scott, Sir Walter, 17
Scott, Winfield, 247

Seagram Building (New York), 156, 157
"Sedgeley," 21
self-help idea, 34
Selwart, Toni, 297
Serra, Junipero, 28
servants, 67, 81, 236, 290
settees, 109, 116
sewing machines, 171–172, 285, 298
sex, 280–283, 287, 296
Shakers, 38
Sharp, Fell, 238
Shaw, Bernard, 288
Shaw, Edward, 21
Shaw, Richard Norman, 22
shawls, 221
Sheraton, Thomas, 99, 107, 108, 130
Sheraton Palace (San Francisco), 72
Sherman, Watts, 22, 161
shoes, 217–218, 220, 224, 235
Sholes, Christopher Latham, 298
shopping centers, 61
Shryock, Gideon, 16
Shryock, Matthias, 16
sideburns, 66, 239, 243
silverware, 112, 114, 135
Simitière, Pierre du, 148
Singer, Isaac M., 130, 298
skating (see also ice skating; roller skating), 79, 179
Skidmore, Owings & Merrill (architects), 156, 158
skiing, 88, 96
sky diving, 97
skyscrapers, 3, 24, 147, 148, 151, 154–156, 158, 160, 166, 302
sleighing, 84, 86
Sloane, William, 134
Smith, B. J., Jr., 153
Smith, Gypsy, 38
Smith, John, 39, 239
Smith, Mrs. Samuel Harrison, 246, 247
Smith College, 21, 37
Smithsonian Institution, 26, 46, 228, 230
smoking, 297
social class, 31–33
social life, 245–265
Society of American Artists, 139
Society of Friends, see Quakers
sofas, 105, 108, 116, 130, 133, 140, 147
soft drinks, 59
Sorosis Club, 51, 284, 292
Sousa, John Philip, 41, 43, 83
Sothern, E. A., 241, 243
space age, 302
spas, 70–71, 94, 127, 129, 146
Spencer-Churchill, Lord Ivor, 257
spirituals, 43
sports, 78–80, 84, 88, 89, 95, 96, 137, 189
Sprague, Kate Chase, 249
Spratt, Maria de Peyster, 249
Spry, Constance, 143
squash, 97
stained glass, 139
Stanford, Leland, 164, 251, 273

Stanford University, 35, 43
Stanton, Mrs. Elizabeth Cady, 174, 296
Statler, Ellsworth M., 127
Statue of Liberty, 164
stays, 209, 210
steamships, 248
Stevens, Edwin Augustus, 254
Stevens, Paran, 72
Stevenson, Robert Louis, 23
Stewart, A. T., 210, 251
Stickley, Gustav, 137
Still, John, 203
stockings, *see* hosiery
Stokes, Mrs. W. E. D., 259
Stokowski, Leopold, 41
Stone, Edward Durell, 128, 159, 226
Stone, Lucy, 296, 299
stores (*see also* country stores; supermarkets), 61, 120
Stotesbury, E. T., 164
stoves, 121–122, 125
Stowe, Harriet Beecher, 296
Strickland, William, 16
Sturgis, Russell, 21
styles, *see* clothing; hair styles
suicide, 65
Sullivan, Louis, 154, 155, 159, 164
sunbathing, 189
Sunday, Billy, 38
sundials, 114
supermarkets, 55, 60–61, 67, 77
Swanson, Gloria, 194
sweaters, 216, 235
swimming, 90, 96, 185–186, 188–189
swimming suits, *see* bathing suits

tables, 106, 107, 116, 117, 128, 132, 133, 134, 135, 136, 137, 140, 141, 142, 143
Tacoma Building (Chicago), 155
Taft, Alphonso, 137
Taft, Mrs. Charles Phelps, 126
Taft, Helen, 260
Taft, William Howard, 75, 76, 96, 126, 146, 241, 291
Taft, Mrs. William Howard, 291
Tavern Club (Boston), 47
taverns, 66, 67–68, 74, 79, 83
Tayloe, John, II, 8
Tayloe, John, III, 24
tea, 59–60, 80
telephones, 52–53, 132, 250
television, 89, 97, 123, 125, 302
temperance movement, 296
tennis, 92, 95, 96, 146, 179
Terry, Eli, 118
Thackeray, William Makepeace, 20
Thanksgiving, 81, 85
theater, *see* drama
Thew, E., 292
Thomas, Seth, 118
Thomas, Theodore, 41
Thompson, Benjamin (Count Rumford), 122
Thonet (designer), 113
Thornton, William, 10, 12, 24
Thurman, Allen G., 228

Tiffany, Louis Comfort, 50, 136, 138–139, 140
Tiffany and Company, 230, 259
Tilden, William T., 95
tinware, 114, 118
toasts, 68
tobacco, 35, 61, 79
toleware, 114
tombstones, 40
Tontine Coffee House (New York), 66
Toscanini, Arturo, 43
Toulouse-Lautrec, Henri, 138
Town, Ithiel, 16
town-ball, *see* rounders
toys, 81, 85, 115
track and field events, 89
Transcendentalists, 36
transportation, 248, 266–278
travel, 266–278, 301
"treenware," 101
Tremont House (Boston), 68–69, 126
trestles, 106
Triangle Shirtwaist Company, fire at, 179
Trinity Church (Boston), 25, 139
Trinity Church (Newport), 26
Trinity Church (New York), 4, 25–26, 28
Trollope, Mrs. Frances, 80, 279, 288, 291
Truman, Harry S., 76, 96, 126, 146, 262
Truman, Margaret, 96, 262
Tryon, Mrs. Lillian H., 146
Tschirky, Oscar, 72
turbans, 206, 213
Turner, A. A., 22
turnpikes, *see* roads
Twain, Mark, 201
Twelve, Robert, 25
Tyler, John, 176, 191
Tyler, Mrs. John (Julia), 176, 191
typewriters, 298

umbrellas, 222
Underwood, Clarence F., 187
Union Club, 50
Union Square (New York), 148
United Nations Secretariat building, 159
Unity Temple (Oak Park, Ill.), 29
Upjohn, Richard, 21, 25, 28

vacuum cleaners, 123
Valentina (designer), 194
Valentino, 242
Van Buren, Martin, 74, 76, 241
Van Cortlandt family, 8
Vanderbilt, Amy, 237, 244, 287, 289, 293
Vanderbilt, Consuelo, 196, 256, 257
Vanderbilt, Cornelius, 50, 173, 251, 273
Vanderbilt, Mrs. Cornelius, 216, 267
Vanderbilt, George, 126, 128
Vanderbilt, William H., 157
Vanderbilt, William K., 162, 164

Vanderbilt, Mrs. William K., 255
Vanderbilt family, 136, 188, 225, 255, 264
Vassar College, 210, 299
Vaux, Calvert, 21, 145–146, 150
verandas, *see* porches
Victoria, Queen (England), 83, 86, 131, 184, 191, 218, 233, 236, 295
Victorian Age, 280
village stores, 61
Villard, Henry, 164, 273
Vionnet, Madeleine, 182, 192, 199
Virginia, University of, 13
Virginia Almanack, 34
visiting, 80
volley ball, 97

Waddell, W. H. Coventry, 17, 21
Waddell, Mrs. W. H. Coventry, 20
Wainwright Building (St. Louis), 155
waist lines, 209–210
Waldorf-Astoria Hotel (New York), 72
wallpaper, 104, 110, 112, 116, 119, 128, 132, 135, 139, 140
Walpole, Horace, 17, 21
Ware, Isaac, 5
Warren, Russell, 16
Warren, Whitney, 262
washing machines, 122, 123
Washington, George, 18, 56, 68, 74, 79, 82, 114, 127, 144, 168, 171, 242, 245, 288
Washington, Martha, 74, 76, 168, 171, 191, 194, 245
watches, 228
water supply, 129, 153
Watterson, Henry, 50
weather vanes, 3, 99, 100
Webster, Daniel, 153, 169
Webster, Noah, 34
wedding gifts, 291
weddings, 40, 194, 196, 198, 256
Weems, Parson, 34
Weitz, John, 183, 237
Welles, Mrs. Gordon (Sophia Woodhouse), 207, 210
Wellesley College, 26
Welsbach, Carl, 121
Wenberg, Ben, 73
Wesley, John, 42
West, Benjamin, 37, 168, 234
"Westover," 8, 11, 35
West Point, 26
Wetmore, George, 164
Wharton, Edith, 268
Wheeler, Gervase, 22
whiskers, 239, 241, 243
Whistler, James, 138, 257
White, Stanford, 138, 156, 161, 164
White House, 10, 12, 18, 52, 62, 74, 82, 96, 106, 111, 124, 126, 136, 143, 146, 150, 155, 166, 191, 193, 198
Whiteman, Paul, 43
Whitney, Eli, 250
wigs, 203, 204, 205, 208, 221, 241–242
Wildenstein's art gallery, 46
Willard, Frances, 296

342

Index

Willard, Simon, 118
Willard, Solomon, 16
Willetts, Ward H., 160
William and Mary College, 34, 82
Williams, Roger, 170
Wills, Helen, 95
Wilson, Woodrow, 76, 155
windows, bay, 147
wine, 59, 68, 76, 301
Winston, Harry, 228, 230
Winthrop, John, 64, 118, 170, 232, 289
Wise, John, 89
Wolfe, Elsie de, 139–140, 141, 142, 143

women, 279–302
Women's Christian Temperance
    Union, 296
Woodhouse, Sophia, *see* Welles, Mrs.
    Gordon
Woodhull, Victoria, 64, 173–174, 296
Woollcott, Alexander, 92
Woolworth Building (New York),
    155, 156
Worth, Charles Frederick, 178, 191
Worth, Madame, 191
Wren, Sir Christopher, 13, 22, 24–25,
    27

Wright, Frances, 296
Wright, Frank Lloyd, 20, 23, 29, 154,
    157, 159–160, 161, 162, 164
Wright, Job, 115
Wright brothers, 46, 278
wristwatches, 231

yachting, 96–97, 188, 189
Yale University, 21, 33, 35, 47, 55, 80,
    82, 89, 112, 159, 241

Zanuck, Darryl, 92
Zenger, Peter, 36